MOON   HANDBOOKS

COASTAL
OREGON

W. C. McRAE & JUDY JEWELL

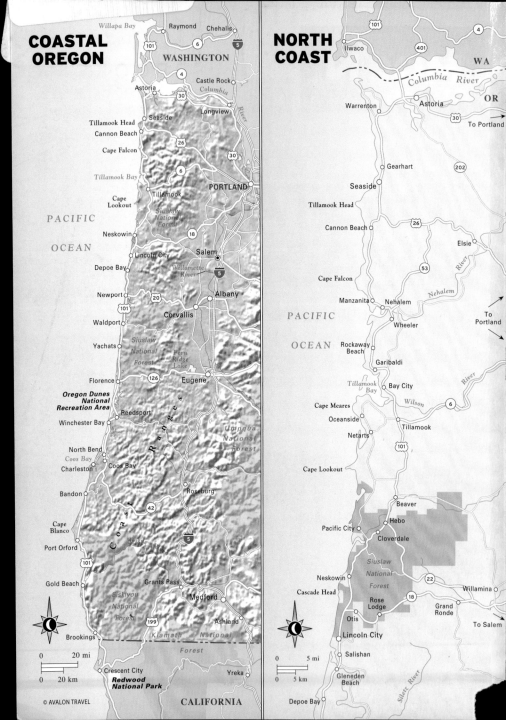

COASTAL OREGON

NORTH COAST

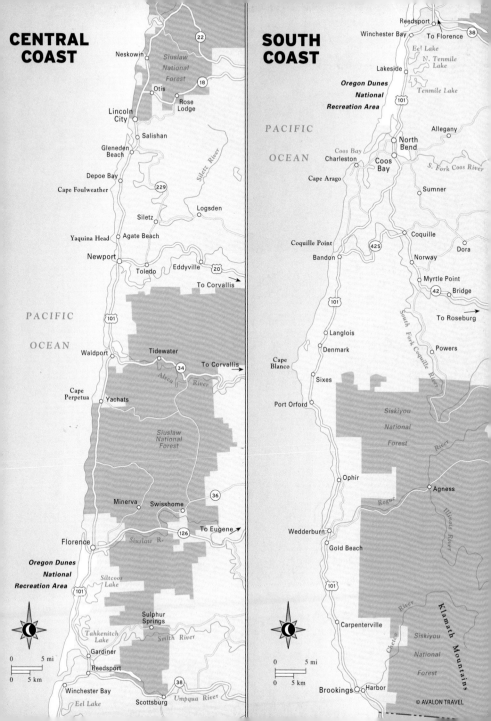

Contents

DISCOVER
Coastal Oregon

I n few other places on earth is the meeting of land and sea as dramatic and beautiful as along Oregon's 360 miles of Pacific coastline, from the mouth of the Columbia River to the redwood forests at the California border. Here, at the far western skirt of the continent, nature has found an expansive stage on which to act out the full range of its varied and ceaseless dramas, from the microcosm of a tidepool to the ferocious storms that make first landfall here. Rocky headlands rise high above the ocean, dropping away to the pounding waves in cliffs hundreds of feet high. Lone fingers of rock poke through sandy beaches and march out far into the surging waves. Seals, sea lions, puffins, and innumerable shorebirds make their home in this marine wilderness.

Here you can find intense solitude, in the company of only the calling seabirds, and experience firsthand why residents refer to this coast as "The Edge." The comforts of civilization and human company are also close by in an inviting string of towns and villages, each with its own character and charms.

Don't neglect the opportunity to get outdoors and experience the full range of recreation available here. Cycling the Oregon Coast Bike Route is a rite of passage for many bicyclists from around the world. The Oregon

Coast Trail provides hikers many opportunities to explore the coastline. The bays and estuaries are tempting destinations for kayakers, as they provide a watery backdrop for excellent marine bird and wildlife viewing. Diminished wild salmon runs have limited some coastal sportfishing expeditions, but the catch is still good for halibut, tuna, and bottom fish. And when fishing boats from Newport, Depoe Bay, Garibaldi, and Astoria aren't seeking the catch of the day, many offer whale-watching trips. Surfing the chill waters of the north Pacific demands a particular brand of hardiness, but many find that, with the right wetsuit, they're able to catch some waves.

Considering the scenic splendor of the Oregon coast, it may seem odd that it remains largely unblemished by upscale tourist infrastructure. In part, this is due to a farsighted state government, which in the 1910s set aside as public land the entire length of Oregon's Pacific coastline. The Oregon coast belongs to the people. It's a place where human visitors can encounter the creatures of the sea and forest, and observe the mighty forces of nature.

Planning Your Trip

▶ WHERE TO GO

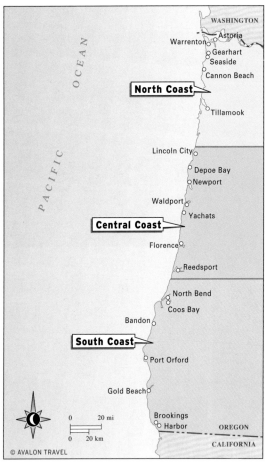

Although part of a seamless whole, sharing a common shoreline and linked by an unbroken scenic highway, each part of the coast possesses a distinct regional flavor and allure that have attracted visitors for centuries.

North Coast

In the north—journey's end for Lewis and Clark—steep headlands break up wide sandy beaches. The northern Oregon coast—just 1.5 hours from Portland—is the most developed and heavily populated part of the coast. Historic Astoria, fun-loving Seaside, and artsy Cannon Beach are all within a short drive of one another, but are remarkably different in character. But don't think it's just one town after another—huge areas of the coast are set aside as state parks, and there are ample opportunities to hike, camp, and explore tidepools.

Central Coast

The central coast is anchored at its northern end by sprawling Lincoln City and its family-friendly wide beaches and is centered around Newport, the largest city in the area, with

Historic Astoria Column

harbor in Newport

charming older neighborhoods, very good restaurants, an active fishing port, and the Oregon Coast Aquarium. Farther south, Florence and Reedsport border the astounding Oregon Dunes, an otherworldly sandscape with massive sand dunes, lakes, and broad lazy estuaries.

IF YOU HAVE . . .

- **A WEEKEND:** Visit Astoria, Seaside, and Cannon Beach on the north coast.
- **ONE WEEK:** Explore the central coast and add Lincoln City, Newport, and an excursion to the Oregon Dunes.
- **TWO WEEKS:** Explore the south coast and add Bandon, Port Orford, and Gold Beach. If you have any extra time, the coastal estuaries south of Coos Bay are worth the trip.

South Coast

The south coast feels far from everything: a landscape of ocean-fronting mountains cloaked by dense evergreen forest, wild rivers, and black sand beaches punctuated with dramatic rock formations. Postindustrial Coos Bay need't delay you, but just to the west are wild and beautiful natural areas, including Cape Arago and the fascinating estuarine area at South Slough. Bandon is small, cozy, and full of tourists, many there for the world-class golf courses at Bandon Dunes. The southernmost part of Oregon's coastline may well be its most scenic, especially the stretch between Port Orford and Brookings.

Astoria-Megler Bridge

▶ WHEN TO GO

Unless you're a dyed-in-the-wool rain-loving Pacific Northwesterner, you'll most likely want to visit the Oregon coast during the summer and early fall (July-September), when there's a far better chance of sunshine. Even then, coastal fogs can put a chill on things, so it's nearly essential to bring a fleece jacket, as well as a windbreaker for the gale-force gusts that locals call "the breeze." It's also best to bring rain gear—we somewhat superstitiously consider it to be insurance against a summertime storm. But it's not always cold here: Don't be surprised if a mid- to late-summer trip sees you wearing little more than shorts, a T-shirt, flip-flops, and sunscreen.

From late fall through spring, storm watchers come to the coast to feel the blustery bite of rain pelting their faces as they walk the beaches. It can be really thrilling to stay in a beachfront motel or cottage (paying a fraction of the summertime rates) and to watch the storm clouds roll in. And the big secret is that there can be absolutely beautiful weather in between storms when the sun breaks through and temperatures are generally much milder than in other parts of the state.

Another reason to visit in December or late March (roughly Christmastime or spring break) is to see whales migrating between their winter homes off Baja California and their summertime grounds near Alaska. Look for "Whale Watching Spoken Here" signs to find good vantage points.

Coastal Road Trip

For many travelers, following the coastal highway U.S. 101 along the rugged Oregon coast is the trip of a lifetime. Although the coast route counts just 360 miles, don't try to rush this trip or squeeze it into anything less than three days. Twisting roads, slow-moving traffic, and jaw-dropping vistas are sure to slow you down, so start out by planning flexibility into your schedule.

If you're not lucky enough to have time for a trip spanning the entire coast and need to sample just a section of the coast, it's easy to use the I-5 freeway corridor (roughly 60-80 miles inland) as a quick north or south arterial, cutting over to the coast near your destination.

So feel free to tinker with this strict north-south itinerary. If you are flying in and out of Portland, it may make sense to leapfrog your way down the coast, catching the intervening towns on your way back north.

Day 1

From Portland, drive northwest to Astoria, a city full of history and spunky do-it-yourself charm. Visit the Columbia River Maritime Museum to learn about the area's maritime past, and check out the city's many art galleries to sense its more contemporary currents. Walk the hilly streets behind downtown to view resplendent Victorian homes. Spend the night at the Cannery Pier Hotel beneath the more than four-mile-long Astoria-Megler Bridge, which spans the mighty Columbia.

Day 2

Drive south, stopping at Fort Clatsop National Memorial, which features a replica of the winter home Lewis and Clark used in 1805 and 1806. If the day is fair, drive to Fort Stevens State Park to stroll along the shore and watch the Columbia River roll into the Pacific, or simply continue to Cannon Beach, with its

Crescent Beach

dramatic shoreline dominated by sea stacks. Stroll through the town's attractive and maze-like downtown shopping district, and spend the night at the Stephanie Inn.

Day 3

From Cannon Beach, drop through the lush temperate rainforest in Oswald West State Park, stopping on the flanks of Neahkahnie Mountain, atop 700-foot cliffs, to admire the views of the Pacific and the Nehalem River Bay. Stop for lunch in the commercial fishing village of Garibaldi, with some of the freshest and tastiest fish-and-chips you're likely to eat. In Tillamook, it's almost mandatory for visitors to stop at the Tillamook Cheese Factory, both for the cheese (now made off site) and the tasty ice cream cones. Continue south to Lincoln City via U.S. 101, staying at the Starfish Manor Hotel.

Day 4

From Lincoln City continue south to Depoe Bay, worth a stop to admire the pocket harbor and scan for spouting whales, then take the Otter Crest scenic loop, cresting at the Cape Foulweather vista. You'll reach Newport before lunch, which is lucky because you'll want to have two meals' worth of eating to explore the good food here. Spend the afternoon at the Oregon Coast Aquarium and the night at the Elizabeth Street Inn.

Day 5

This is a short day of driving, because you'll want to save time to hike. Proceed south to Yachats, one of the coast's most charming towns and gateway to Cape Perpetua, a wonderful natural area where mountains meet the sea and acres of tidepools rise above the surf. Check in at the very comfortable Overleaf Lodge, and reward yourself for hiking along Cape Perpetua with dinner at one of Yachats's excellent restaurants.

Day 6

Florence is set alongside the Siuslaw River, and its riverside Old Town will briefly steal your attention away from the ocean. It's a good base for exploring the Oregon Dunes, which start just south of town and rise up to 500 feet tall. Hike through this striking

view from an overlook in the Oswald West area

Bandon Beach

habitat, or go for the thrills of sandboarding or a dune buggy ride. Spend the night in Florence.

Day 7

Although Coos Bay doesn't beckon the average traveler, it is the gateway to some astoundingly beautiful headlands and beaches just west. Don't miss blustery Cape Arago and the gardens of Shore Acres State Park. Head south along Seven Devils Road and spend the night in Bandon. With its Old Town, beaches, and golfing at the internationally acclaimed Bandon Dunes Golf Resort, this town demands attention. Bandon is laid-back and easy to explore on foot, with more good restaurants than you'd expect.

Day 8

It's tempting to shrug off Gold Beach's jet-boat tours up the mighty Rogue River as hokey tourist schlock, but these rides are actually pretty great, with good commentary and the chance to see bald eagles and other wildlife.

Day 9

Between Gold Beach and Brookings, the coastline is at its finest, with many pull-outs offering paths down to secluded rocky beaches. Come prepared with a sweatshirt and a windbreaker and spend an afternoon exploring this stretch. In Brookings, it's important to stop for a walk and some bird-watching at Harris Beach State Park, but it's also worthwhile to get off the coastal strip and explore the Chetco River. Alfred A. Loeb State Park has good river access and a path through myrtle and redwood trees.

Day 10

If you're heading back to the I-5 corridor after your tour of the coast, consider dropping down to Crescent City in California, and heading inland on U.S. 199. This highway, which you pick up 22 miles south of the state border, passes through the northern edge of the California redwoods on its way to I-5 at Grants Pass, Oregon.

Coastal Camping

NORTH COAST

- **Saddle Mountain:** One of Oregon's best wildflower hikes is the late spring or early summer climb of Saddle Mountain, about 10 miles inland from the beach. Most hikers just come for a day trip, but the primitive campsites at the trailhead are a good base camp for the hike to the summit.

- **Nehalem Bay State Park:** This campground has beach access to the Pacific on one side and sandy Nehalem Bay on the other; bike and hiking trails make it easy to get around.

- **Cape Lookout State Park:** At the base of a secluded sand spit, with easy access to hiking on Cape Lookout, one of the coast's top hiking trails, this campground has popular yurts and cabins.

CENTRAL COAST

- **South Beach State Park:** Just south of Newport, this large campground has easy access to the beach. Lucky folks who sign up early and pay a few bucks extra can join a guided paddle trip up the nearby Beaver Creek estuary.

- **Carl G. Washburne State Park:** On the central coast between Florence and Yachats, camp on the inland side of the highway in a thicket of huge salal bushes. Pile your gear into a wheelbarrow (provided) and trundle it to one of the great walk-in campsites, then hike along the Hobbit Trail. There are also plenty of standard spots for car and RV camping.

- **Jesse M. Honeyman State Park:** A few miles south of Florence, this large campground is a playground for sandboarders and dune riders. Two miles of sand dunes separate the park from the ocean. The two freshwater lakes within the park's boundaries are popular places to boat and swim.

SOUTH COAST

- **Sunset Bay State Park:** Not only is this bay-fronting campground a lovely and quiet haven, it's adjacent to several of the southern Oregon coast's top sights: Shore Acres State Park, Cape Arago, and South Slough National Estuarian Research Reserve.

- **Cape Blanco State Park:** A beautiful and often-blustery campground at the state's westernmost point, just north of Port Orford and Humbug Mountain. Campground trails lead down to the beach and to the nearby lighthouse.

- **Harris Beach State Park:** Just north of Brookings, this magical campground sits in a grove of spruce and firs, and just off the beach are menhir-like sea stacks busy with seabirds.

- **Alfred A. Loeb State Park:** On the north bank of the Chetco River, find aromatic old-growth myrtlewood and the nation's northernmost naturally occurring redwood trees at Loeb State Park. The 1.2-mile nature trail winds through the redwoods, passing one tree with a 33-foot girth. When the south coast is foggy and cold on summer mornings, it's often warm and dry here.

camping at Nehalem Bay State Park

Trails and Tidepools

Visitors to coastal Oregon are often astounded at the large number and high quality of the state parks here. Indeed, there are nearly 80 state parks—19 with campgrounds—easily accessible from U.S. 101 in Oregon. Parks are located at all of the coast's most beautiful places, making access easy and affordable.

North Coast

A dramatic start to a tour of the coast's parks begins at the point where the Columbia River enters the Pacific, at the northern edge of the huge Fort Stevens State Park. Miles of bike and hiking trails lead past abandoned gunneries (this was originally a Civil War military station); along the beach, the skeletal remains of the *Peter Iredale* shipwreck are a focal point. The campground here is the state's largest—stay here if you want showers and a kid-friendly atmosphere; for more solitude and almost no amenities except for those provided by nature, head

south and inland a bit to camp at Saddle Mountain State Park at the base of a fantastic hiking trail.

Get up early and drive south past Cannon Beach to Oswald West State Park, where trails through an old-growth forest lead to Short Sands Beach, Cape Falcon, and Neahkahnie Mountain. Although there are the remains of a campground here at Oz West, it's now closed because the ancient trees have become unstable; plan to spend the night at Nehalem Bay State Park, a short beach walk from the lovely little town of Manzanita.

Head south to Tillamook and pick up the Three Capes Scenic Loop. Take time to explore the parks at Cape Meares (bring the binoculars and look for puffins on the rocks here) and Oceanside. The 2.5-mile Cape Lookout Trail takes you out onto a narrow, steep-sided finger of land jutting into the sea. It's one of the coast's most dramatic hikes and particularly popular during the

the *Peter Iredale* shipwreck in Fort Stevens State Park

Nehalem Bay State Park

late-March whale-watching season. South of Cape Lookout, visit Cape Kiwanda to climb up on the bluff and run down the sand dunes.

Central Coast

As you pass through the more developed areas of Lincoln City, Depoe Bay, and Newport, be sure to stop at some of the day-use parks along the way. Boiler Bay, a mile north of Depoe Bay, is a great place to explore tidepools and ponder the power of the surf, and Yaquina Head, at the north end of Newport, is a good place to spend a few hours exploring. Beachside, a Siuslaw National Forest campground, is between the towns of Waldport and Yachats.

After hiking the trails and exploring the tidepools at Cape Perpetua, continue south to the Oregon Dunes. Hikes in the dunes can be either random (even disorienting) explorations or can follow more defined routes. The blue-topped posts marking the John Dellenback Trail, about 10 miles south of Reedsport, guide you through a narrow band of coastal evergreen forest and 2.5 miles of 300- to 400-foot-high dunes to the beach.

Here you'll have your choice between a number of Forest Service campgrounds between Florence and Reedsport, including those at the Waxmyrtle, Carter, and Taylor Dunes Trails, and a couple of state park spots (Tugman and Umpqua Lighthouse) south of Reedsport.

South Coast

Head to the western edge of the continental United States and pitch your tent at Cape Blanco State Park. Along with the trails around the cape and down to the beach, be sure to visit the historic lighthouse.

Take your time on the trip south from Cape Blanco. The 1,756-foot-high Humbug Mountain, six miles south of Port Orford, is one of the highest mountains rising directly off the Oregon shoreline. A 3-mile trail to its top yields both great views of the coastline and a chance to see wild rhododendrons 20-25 feet high. Rising above the rhodies and giant ferns are bigleaf maple, Port Orford cedar, and Douglas and grand firs.

In the far-south stretch between Gold

Bird-watching is a popular pastime on the coast.

When the tide pulls back, tidepools appear along Oregon's rocky coast.

Beach and Brookings are the many road-side pullouts along the 12 miles of Samuel H. Boardman State Park. Drop in for a walk along the beach, or hike the Oregon Coast Trail between a couple of coves. At the north end of Brookings, Harris Beach State Park is a bustling campground near another lovely beach.

Foraging the Coast

Fishing, crabbing, clamming, and mussel-gathering isn't just fun, it will fill your dinner plate, too. There's plenty for foragers to eat along the Oregon coast, if you know where to look for it.

All crabbers and clam diggers need a shellfish license, available at pretty much anyplace that rents crab traps ($7 resident, $20.50 out of state, $11.50 for a three-day nonresident license).

Clamming is best during a "minus" tide, when more beach is exposed. Equipment consists of a shovel, a bucket, and—ideally—rubber boots. It's also helpful to have a dowel or stick to use as a probe and clam-marker. Look for the clam holes, and dig toward the ocean side.

Pay attention to the signs at the entrance to the beach—they may be telling you about health precautions. Occasionally shellfish toxins mandate the closure of certain areas. These higher levels of bacteria and toxins are most likely to occur during the summer, and they are carefully monitored by the Oregon Department of Agriculture (check www.oregon.gov for details).

Astoria

The mother of all salmon rivers is the Columbia. While Astoria was once one of the world's top fishing ports, precipitous declines in salmon runs have spelled doom for its abundant salmon packaging plants. However, there is seasonal sportfishing for most salmon runs, and tuna, halibut, and bottom fish harvesting is strong; plenty of

Cape Perpetua

charter fishing operations are ready to take you out to where the big ones are biting.

Garibaldi

Garibaldi is a scrappy little fishing village on Tillamook Bay, where you'll have no trouble joining a charter boat heading out for whatever's in season. Crabbing is also a high point, as are local oysters, found at the Pacific Oyster processing plant at nearby Bay City, where you can forgo foraging and just buy and eat your seafood while watching shuckers tackle a mountain of bivalves.

Newport

Oregon's second-largest fishing fleet departs from Newport, and the bay front here is a wonderful spot to plan a fishing or whale-watching trip. Down at the bay, right in the midst of barking seals and salt spray, you can buy fish directly off the boat. If you're not up for cooking, the fish is equally fresh at most of the of harborside restaurants.

Cape Perpetua

The black-shelled bivalves that coat the rocks and tidepools here are particularly good eating. Harvesting wild mussels along the rugged Cape Perpetua shores is easy. Bring a pot, a bottle of white wine, and some garlic. Light a campfire, and you've got a meal. As you harvest, be sure to watch for signs, particularly in hot summer weather, of toxic algae blooms and dangerous levels of bacteria.

Winchester Bay

Just south of Reedsport, the tiny town of Winchester Bay is almost entirely given over to fishing. Along with a busy commercial fishing port, there are many charter operators here who will take you out to the ocean for salmon, halibut, tuna, or bottom fish. Even if you aren't fishing, a meal at one of the dockside restaurants will allow you to eat close to the source.

Charleston

Charleston is so thoroughly pervaded with seafood that even an angler's grudging spouse will get caught up in the excitement. Don't like fishing charters, or want to forage on the cheap? No problem: Get to crabbing and clamming instead. Local shops here rent gear; you can crab right off the pier and clam on the beaches at Charleston or on Coos Bay's North Spit.

Bandon

In Bandon, stop at the bait store at the Old Town docks to pick up some crab traps, then go toss them over the side of the dock. Hang around and check the traps every so often— if you bring in a haul and don't want to fuss with the cooking and cleaning, ask the bait store to prepare them.

Rogue River

Anglers will want to stay a couple of days in Gold Beach, either in town or up the Rogue River. Spring chinook salmon, fall king salmon, silver salmon, summer and winter steelhead—all these runs are of legendary proportion. It's best to go with a guide in a boat, and just about every local you'll meet is a guide.

Chetco River

Although it's not as well known as the Rogue, the Chetco River upstream from Brookings is also good for late fall and winter salmon and steelhead fishing. Mostly, though, Brookings is a good place to take a charter out into the ocean to fish for salmon and bottom fish.

Top 10 Photo Ops

The Oregon coast is so photogenic that both professional and amateur photographers vie for the best shots, which, given coastal conditions, can be challenging. Greg Vaughn, professional landscape photographer and author of the helpful guide *Photographing Oregon,* notes that during the long light-drenched summer days, photographers must get up really early and stay out late to capture the "golden hours." He also notes that cloudy or foggy days are ideal for photographing the forests and waterfalls in the Coast Range mountains, and winter storms make for the most dramatic seascapes.

While there are stunning vistas around nearly every corner along the Oregon coast, here are some don't-miss photo opportunities.

Sunset: Astoria-Megler Bridge

This soaring, four-plus-mile bridge across the vast Columbia River is photographic eye candy. Alameda Avenue, carved into Astoria's steep hillsides, is an excellent perch for snapping photos of the bridge, oceangoing vessels, and the distant hills of Washington State.

Sunrise: Ecola State Park and Haystack Rock

Cannon Beach offers postcard-perfect views of sea stacks and craggy offshore islands. Haystack Rock serves as a looming backdrop to nearly every beach photo taken here, while the scattered rocks of Ecola State Park are more like chess pieces tossed out to sea—perfect as a foreground for sunrise photos.

Midday: Oswald West State Park

It's not always easy to get up close and personal with giant trees in coastal old-growth forests, but at Oswald West, it's as easy as a stroll to Short Sands Beach: The trail winds through a grove of centuries-old Sitka spruce whose massive size will clog your viewfinder.

Late Afternoon: Kites at Lincoln City

Nothing says fun at the beach like colorful kites diving and dancing in the air, and the long breezy expanses of sand at Lincoln City make it a center for kite-flying. Even when there's not a kite festival on, this is one kite-loving town. Climb the steep bluffs behind

Save It for a Rainy Day

Sometimes the coastal weather is a little daunting. And although we strongly encourage you to layer up, get out there, and enjoy yourself in the pelting rain, we know that these wet outings need to be brief and interspersed with some inside time. Fortunately, there are plenty of indoor places to enjoy along Oregon's coast without feeling like you could be just anywhere.

ASTORIA

- **Columbia River Maritime Museum:** We'll gladly visit this museum in any kind of weather, but when storms rage outside, it gives visitors special insight into the dangerous jobs of those who guide ships across the Columbia River's bar and up its braided channel.
- **Fort Clatsop:** Lewis and Clark wrote of being "cold, wet, and miserable" here. Here's your chance to relive history. (Remember, they were here all winter.)

SEASIDE

- **Arcades:** It's the tackiest sort of beach fun, but sometimes the whole family needs to pile into bumper cars.

LINCOLN CITY

- **Jennifer Sears Art Studio:** Blow your own glass float or paperweight at this Taft-neighborhood studio. Other galleries in the area feature glass and other art.

NEWPORT

- **Oregon Coast Aquarium:** Trance out watching jellyfish or walk through the Passages of the Deep, a 200-foot-long acrylic tunnel offering 360-degree underwater views in three diverse habitats, from Orford Reef to Halibut Flats to Open Sea, where you're surrounded by free-swimming sharks. It's easy to spend several hours here.

FLORENCE

- **Sea Lion Caves:** Join about 200 Steller sea lions in this cliff-side cave north of Florence.

These sea lions occupy the cave during the fall and winter; in spring and summer, they breed and raise their young on the rock ledges just outside the cave.

BANDON

- **Face Rock Creamery:** After several cheeseless years, Bandon once again is home to a cheese factory. Stop in for some Grand Opening Cheddar or Black Jack; Umpqua ice cream is another extremely popular option.

BROOKINGS

- **Bars:** Back when we first started coming to this part of the coast, the Pine Cone Tavern was the logger's bar, and the Sporthaven was for the folks working on fishing boats. Now, they're both considerably less seedy—the Pine Cone's almost hip and the Sporthaven has pretty good food—but they're still good places to soak up the local atmosphere.

Oregon Coast Aquarium

the beach for a rare bird's-eye view of kiting activity.

Sunset: Yaquina Bay Bridge
Of the many handsome bridges designed by 1930s bridge-design master Conde McCullough, this high-flying structure, which spans Newport's harbor, is the most striking. With the busy boat basin in the foreground, it's one of the top photo subjects in the state, particularly from viewpoints east along Bay Avenue.

Morning: Cape Perpetua
Drive up to the top of the cape and take the short Whispering Spruce Trail to a fabulous overlook. Then head back down to the beach, and during low tide, explore this area's tidepools.

Sunset: Heceta Head Lighthouse
Rumored to be the most photographed vista in Oregon, this stark white lighthouse wedged into the flanks of a 1,000-foot rocky outcrop is impossible to miss.

You'll run through millions of megapixels trying to capture the crashing waves, deep forests, and offshore crags from a cannily placed highway turnout just west of the Cape Creek Bridge.

Morning Low Tide: Tidepools at Cape Arago State Park
Rocky tidepools filled with neon-hued starfish, spiky sea urchins, and shell-appropriating hermit crabs make fascinating photo subjects: Some of the best tidepooling along the coast is at this state park. From the parking area, the north beach trail also offers views of seals and sea lions basking on offshore rock ledges, although this trail is closed in summer when these sea mammals are rearing their young (the south beach trail remains open year-round).

Mid-Morning: Bandon
Bandon's beautiful beach is studded with rocky fingers and promontories, but the most arresting vista is of Face Rock, a basalt monolith pounded by waves that from certain

Cannon Beach at sunset

Heceta Head Lighthouse beams across the sea.

Samuel H. Boardman State Scenic Corridor

angles takes on a human profile. Indian legend claims it's the visage of a young maiden frozen into rock. It's a postcard-ready image that bespeaks the beauty and mystery of the Oregon coast.

Sunset: Samuel H. Boardman State Scenic Corridor

It's often referred to as the most scenic 12 miles along the Oregon coast, but photographers don't find it easy to capture the drama of this stunning seascape: It's hard to encapsulate the vastness of the scene. Of the 11 named stops along this stretch of U.S. 101, Whaleshead Island is perhaps the most photogenic viewpoint, with tripod-ready vistas of a tiny beach flanked by rocky crags and wave-pounded islands.

Cozy Seaside Inns

Oregon has only a few big resorts along the coast—instead, it features many smaller inns and bed-and-breakfasts that are top spots for a cozy and comfortable stay at smaller and typically Oregon-style lodgings.

ASTORIA
Astoria's **Hotel Elliott** isn't really an inn—in fact, when it was built in the 1920s, it was the classiest place to stay in Astoria. And with its lovingly restored rooms and rooftop sitting area, it still is. This historic hotel situated in Astoria's vibrant downtown will get a coast trip off to a great start.

NEHALEM BAY
After nosing in and out of coastal harbors, you may wish that you had brought your boat along. Why bother—at Nehalem's **Ripple Run Resort,** you can settle in for the night on one of many floating but moored boats, including a tugboat and a choice of barges, in a quiet spot along the Nehalem River.

DEPOE BAY
The **Channel House** in Depoe Bay offers that perfect contrast of luxury and rustic charm. Watch the surging tides collide with the rocky shore and fishing boats negotiate the narrow harbor from the comfort of your outdoor whirlpool tub.

NEWPORT
History and literature intersect at the **Sylvia Beach Hotel** in Newport, a one-of-a-kind historic hotel-turned-B&B where all the rooms are decorated in literary themes. The Edgar Allan Poe room, anyone?

BANDON
Bandon's **Sea Star Guesthouse** is right in Old Town, just across from the waterfront. Although there are more elegant places to stay in Bandon (for instance, any of the accommodations at the Bandon Dunes Golf Resort), this is the place that'll make you feel like you're part of the heartbeat of this charming town.

PORT ORFORD
Drop into a meditative calm at **Wildspring Guest Habitat,** perched above the Pacific Ocean in Port Orford. Everything here is designed to lead you to a state of serenity, whether it's the labyrinth walk, the exquisite hot tub, the meditation alcoves, or the hammock outside your cabin.

GOLD BEACH
Upriver from Gold Beach, **Tu Tu Tun Resort** is the only full-on resort on the south coast, and it's a wonderful place to feel pampered in a thoroughly Oregonian kind of way. But another good bet along the lower Rogue is the **Morrison's Rogue River Lodge,** an erstwhile budget motel that's been totally remodeled into comfy riverside suites.

BROOKINGS
Down in Brookings, there are a couple of fine B&Bs. If you want to be near the ocean, stay at the **South Coast Inn B&B,** an elegant Bernard Maybeck-designed house.

Sylvia Beach Hotel in Newport

The beaches along Oregon's coast offer varied views.

Life's a Beach

With 360 miles of coastline, Oregon has lots of sandy waterfront. However, not all beaches are created equal. Here are some of our favorite, lesser-known beaches.

Hug Point State Recreation Site

When nearby Cannon Beach is just too busy, head to Hug Point. You can see Haystack Rock in the distance, but not the crowds. Check out the two caves in the headlands and the old wagon trails carved into the stone—stagecoaches used to travel along the beach before roads were cut into the forests.

Short Sands Beach

This small beach, part of Oswald West State Park, is wedged between the rocky cliffs of Neahkahnie Mountain and Cape Falcon, making it feel cut off from the rest of the world.

You'll need to follow a half-mile trail through old-growth rainforest to reach the beach, which is nearly always active with surfers.

Rockaway Beach

Sure, the town of Rockaway may lack upscale charm, but the seven-mile-long beach itself is lovely. Just offshore are the Twin Rocks, two massive promontories, one carved through with an arch. This is a magic spot to watch the sunset.

Seal Rock State Recreation Site

Stop at this quiet beach to find a bit of the best of everything: broad sandy strands, tidepools, curious rock formations in the surf, and shady picnic tables. The park is named for a large seal-like rock, and in fact you can often spot real seals on the islands. Whales pass by here on their twice-yearly migration.

Neptune State Park

At this magical spot, tongues of lava form mazelike walls in the sand to the delight of children of all ages. It's a great place to play hide-and-seek or to spread a blanket and picnic. Immediately to the south (and also part of the state park) is Strawberry Hill, a wayside that gives access to acres of tidepools, where a broad expanse of ancient lava meets the Pacific.

Scenic Beach Loop

South of Bandon, drive the Scenic Beach Loop and witness some of the most evocative offshore rock formations in the state. With names like Cat and Kittens Rocks, Face Rock, and the Garden of the Gods, you'll likely search for something magical in the various monoliths and islands. As you walk along the beach, watch for seabirds—Elephant Rock is a rookery for puffins, murres, and auklets.

Battle Rock Park

Just below the town of Port Orford, a craggy, steep-sided headland rises from the sands. In 1851 this promontory was the site of conflict between local Native Americans and would-be white settlers, earning it the name Battle Rock. You can climb the trail to the rock's crest, where the settlers took shelter during a 14-day siege. Scattered along the beach are other dramatic sea stacks; this is also a good spot to beachcomb for agates.

Myers Creek Beach

The southern Oregon coastline is chock-a-block with dramatic vistas. Out of the many choices, a personal favorite is the sea-stack-studded beach at Myers Creek, part of Pistol River State Park south of Gold Beach. The cove is brimming with wave-battered monoliths, and the mile-long beach is just big enoug h for a good saunter but small enough to feel private.

Seal Rock State Recreation Site

Riding the Pacific Waves

Surfing is increasingly popular in Oregon, but it can be a little confusing to know where to go, especially if you're a novice. Spend a week dropping in on the following spots, selected with a special nod to places where a beginner can show up without feeling too out of place.

Before setting out on this surf vacation, invest in or rent a good **wetsuit;** that, along with strong swimming skills, will go a long way toward making this a fun trip rather than an ordeal. Don't skimp on the wetsuit accessories—a hood and booties are often the key to staying comfortable. Surf shops in Seaside, Cannon Beach, Pacific City, Lincoln City, and Newport can supply **rental gear.** Surf with a buddy, and be aware that sharks do occasionally show up at surf spots. A good website, www.oregon-surf.com, has some tips and links to forecasting sites and webcams.

CANNON BEACH AREA

Start off with a class. Oregon Surf Adventures (run out of the Seaside Surf Shop) and Northwest Women's Surf Camps both offer friendly, supportive instructors and fun programs.

Set up camp at Nehalem Bay State Park, then head a few miles north and spend the day practicing at Oswald West State Park's **Short Sands Beach.** More advanced surfers may want to check out the cove at **Indian Beach,** at the foot of Ecola State Park; this beach is also popular with surf kayakers. Seaside can be fiercely locals-only and is not the best choice for unaccompanied beginners.

LINCOLN CITY TO NEWPORT

Another spot for surfers who know what they're doing is the **Road's End State Recreation Area** beach at the very north end of Lincoln City. Stop here for a while or continue south to the somewhat protected beach at **Otter Rock,** a few miles south of Depoe Bay. Otter Rock is quite popular, and it's a good place for beginners, although you'll need to be strong enough to schlep your board down (and back up) a long flight of steps to the beach.

In Newport, you can try **Agate Beach** (the parking is right next to the tall Best Western hotel) or head south of town to **South Beach State Park.**

FLORENCE TO CHARLESTON

Pack up and head south, perhaps with a stop at Florence's South Jetty, to Charleston, where you can check out the waves at **Bastendorff Beach County Park.** There's also a nice campground at Bastendorff, as well as the large Sunset Beach State Park campground a few miles away. (Sunset Beach itself is mostly a swimming beach.)

FLORAS LAKE

Head south of Bandon to the little town of **Langlois,** and turn in toward the ocean and Floras Lake, where you can take a break with a day of windsurfing or kiteboarding at Floras Lake. Lessons and equipment rentals are easy to come by here, and the wind is almost always ripping.

PORT ORFORD TO BROOKINGS

It may be time to head back north, dropping in on your new favorite surf spots. But if you're headed all the way down the coast, pull off the highway at Port Orford to see if the surf is up at **Battle Rock Beach.** Otherwise, aim for **Sporthaven Beach** on the Brookings jetty south of the Chetco River, a popular all-levels surf beach.

Surfers need wetsuits here, even in the summer.

NORTH COAST

The north coast, from the mouth of the Columbia River south to Lincoln City, is little more than an hour's drive from the Portland metro area, and the region is the most popular part of Oregon's Pacific shoreline. Still, apart from the weekend crush at Cannon Beach and Seaside, there's more than enough elbow room for everyone along this enchanting and varied coast.

Overlooking the Columbia River as it flows into the Pacific, the former shipping and fishing center of Astoria is fast rediscovering its own potential, with a lively arts scene, adventurous cuisine, and fine hotels and B&Bs hosting overnighters. Its long-idle waterfront is growing busy again with tourist attractions—most notably the Columbia River Maritime Museum, one of the best museums in Oregon.

West of Astoria, at Oregon's far northwestern tip, where the mighty Columbia River meets the Pacific, visitors to Fort Stevens State Park can inspect the skeleton of a century-old shipwreck and a military fort active from the Civil War to World War II—as well as revel in miles of sandy beaches. Fort Clatsop National Memorial, part of Lewis and Clark National Historical Park, includes a re-creation of the Corps of Discovery's winter 1805-1806 quarters—a must-stop for Lewis and Clark buffs.

Cannon Beach and Seaside are two extremely popular resort towns that are polar opposites of one another. Cannon Beach, an enclave of tastefully weathered cedar-shingled architecture, is chockablock with art galleries, boutiques, and upscale lodgings and restaurants. A few miles north, Seaside is Oregon's

HIGHLIGHTS

◖ Columbia River Maritime Museum: One of Oregon's top museums tells the story of seafaring on the Columbia River (page 36).

◖ Fort Clatsop National Memorial: This replica of Lewis and Clark's 1805-1806 winter camp offers a fascinating glimpse into frontier life (page 39).

◖ Haystack Rock: This soaring sea stack on Cannon Beach is home to thousands of seabirds (page 64).

◖ Saddle Mountain State Natural Area: This knobby mountain rises high above the northern coast, with a hiking trail leading through unusual plantlife on the way to an eye-popping vista (page 66).

◖ Cape Lookout Hikes: Go for the great views of rocks and surf, the chance of seeing a whale, or to totally immerse yourself in the foggy coastal atmosphere (page 91).

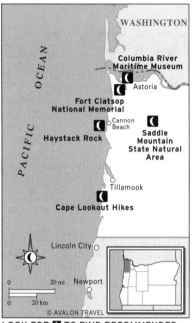

LOOK FOR ◖ TO FIND RECOMMENDED SIGHTS, ACTIVITIES, DINING, AND LODGING.

quintessential family-friendly beach resort, with a long boardwalk, candy and gift shops, and noisy game arcades.

Just south of Cannon Beach, Oswald West State Park is a gem protecting old-growth forest and handsome little pocket beaches, as well as, some believe, a Spanish pirate treasure buried on Neahkahnie Mountain. Beyond Neahkahnie's cliff-top viewpoints along U.S. 101, the Nehalem Bay area attracts anglers, crabbers, and kayakers, as well as discriminating diners who come from far and wide to enjoy surprisingly sophisticated cuisine.

Tillamook County is home to more cows than people and is synonymous with delicious dairy products—cheese and ice cream

in particular. It's no surprise that Tillamook's biggest visitor attraction is cheese-related. More than a million people a year come to the Tillamook Cheese Factory to view the cheese-making operations and sample the excellent results. The Tillamook Air Museum is another popular diversion, housing an outstanding collection of vintage and modern aircraft in gargantuan Hangar B, the largest wooden structure in the world. Tillamook Bay, fed by five rivers, yields oysters and crabs, while the active Garibaldi charter fleet targets salmon, halibut, and tuna in the offshore waters.

South of Tillamook, the Coast Highway wends inland through lush pastureland to

NORTH
COAST

Ilwaco

WA

Columbia River

Fort Stevens
State Park
Warrenton

Astoria

COLUMBIA RIVER
MARITIME MUSEUM

PACIFIC

OCEAN

FORT CLATSOP
NATIONAL MEMORIAL

To
Portland

OR

Gearhart

SADDLE MOUNTAIN
STATE NATURAL AREA

Seaside

Tillamook Head

HAYSTACK ROCK

Cannon
Beach

Elsie

Cape Falcon
Oswald West
State Park
Manzanita
Nehalem

Nehalem

To
Portland

Nehalem Bay
State Park
Wheeler

Rockaway
Beach

To
Portland

Garibaldi

Bay City

Tillamook Bay
Cape Meares

Wilson

Oceanside

Netarts

Tillamook

CAPE LOOKOUT HIKES

Cape Lookout

Beaver

Hebo

Pacific City

Cloverdale

Siuslaw

To
Portland

Neskowin

National

Cascade Head

Forest

Otis

Willamina

Grand
Ronde

To
Salem

Lincoln City

Rose
Lodge

Salishan

Gleneden Beach

Depoe Bay

Siletz River

Logsden

Siletz

© AVALON TRAVEL

0   10 mi

0   10 km

Neskowin. It's a pleasant enough stretch, but the Three Capes Scenic Loop, a 35-mile scenic coastal detour, is a more attractive, if time-consuming, option. The spectacular views and bird-watching from Capes Meares and Lookout are the highlights of this beautiful drive. At Pacific City, at the southern end of the Three Capes Loop, commercial anglers launch their dories right off the sandy beach and through the surf in the lee of Cape Kiwanda and mammoth Haystack Rock—a sight not seen anywhere else on the West Coast. Just north of Lincoln City, Cascade Head beckons hikers to explore its rare prairie headlands ecosystem.

PLANNING YOUR TIME

Although most Oregonians have a favorite beach town that they'll visit for weekends and summer vacations, if this is your grand tour of the Oregon coast, plan to spend a few days exploring the northern coast's beaches and towns. If you're interested in history, architecture, or ship-watching, be sure to spend a night in **Astoria**—it's one of our favorite coastal cities, even though it's several miles from the Pacific Ocean; if you can't wait to walk on Pacific beaches, head to **Cannon Beach** (for a more upscale stay) or **Seaside** (which the kids will love) and begin your trip there. By driving from north to south, you'll be able to pull off the highway more easily into beach access areas. Campers might want to reserve a space at Nehalem Bay State Park, near the small laid-back town of **Manzanita,** a few miles south of Cannon Beach; Manzanita is also a good place to rent a beach house for a weekend. Aside from the near-mandatory stop at the Tillamook Cheese Factory, you'll probably want to skip the town of Tillamook and head to the **Three Capes Loop,** where a night in Pacific City offers easy access to Cape Kiwanda as well as comfy lodgings and a good brewpub. On your way south to the central coast or to the Highway 18 route back through the Willamette Valley wine country to Portland, do stop for a hike at **Cascade Head.**

Astoria and Vicinity

The mouth of the mighty Columbia River, with its abundance of natural resources, was long a home for Native Americans; artifacts found in the area suggest that people have been living along the river for at least 8,000 years. Early European explorers and settlers also found the river and its bays to be propitious as a trading and fishing center. Astoria's dramatic location and deep history continue to attract new settlers and travelers drawn to the area's potent allure.

Astoria (pop. about 10,000) is the oldest permanent U.S. settlement west of the Rockies, and its glory days are preserved by museums, historical exhibits, and pastel-colored Victorian homes weathered by the sea air. Hollywood has chosen Astoria's picturesque neighborhoods to simulate an idealized all-American town, most notably in the cult classic *The Goonies.*

However, Astoria is a real city, warts and all. The preserved pioneer past and attractive Victorian homes may soften the rough edges of a once-bustling port that has seen better days, but not enough for anyone to mistake blue-collar Astoria for a cute tourist town. The decommissioning of the U.S. Naval station after World War II, the decline in the logging and fishing industries, and the closure of several dozen canneries on the waterfront have had lasting effects. Empty storefronts tell the story of a resource-based economy bruised by progress, but there's plenty of pluck left in this old dowager, and her best years may be yet to come.

Astoria has many charms: Historic buildings downtown are undergoing restoration, cruise ships are calling, fine restaurants are multiplying, a lively arts scene is thriving, and there's new life along the waterfront, anchored by the excellent Columbia River Maritime Museum.

History

The Clatsop Indians, a Chinook-speaking group, lived in this area for thousands of years before Astoria's written history began. When Lewis and Clark arrived in 1805, the Clatsops numbered about 400 people, living in three villages on the south side of the Columbia River, but began a steady decline soon after contact with whites.

The region was first chronicled by Don Bruno de Heceta, a Spanish explorer who sailed near the Columbia's mouth in August 1775. He named it the Bay of the Assumption of Our Lady, but the strong current prevented his ship from entering. American presence on the Columbia began with Captain Robert Gray's discovery of the river in May 1792, which he christened after his fur-trading ship, *Columbia Rediviva.*

Thereafter, Lewis and Clark's famous expedition of 1803-1806, with its winter encampment at Fort Clatsop, south of present-day Astoria, helped incorporate the Pacific Northwest as part of a new nation. In 1811,

Astoria-Megler Bridge

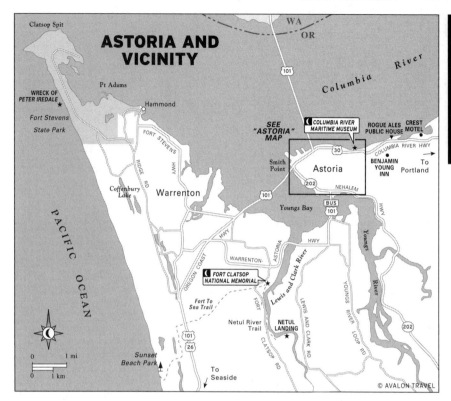

John Jacob Astor's agents built Fort Astoria on a hillside in what would eventually grow into Astoria—the first American settlement west of the Rockies. The trading post was occupied by the British between 1813 and 1818, and the settlement was renamed Fort George. Real development began in the 1840s as settlers begin pouring in from the Oregon Trail. During the Civil War, Fort Stevens was built at the mouth of the Columbia to guard against a Confederate naval incursion.

Commerce grew with the export of lumber and foodstuffs to gold rush-era San Francisco and Asia. Salmon canneries became the mainstay of Astoria's economy during the 1870s, helping it grow into Oregon's second-largest city—and a notorious shanghaiing port. From that time through the early 1900s, the dominant immigrants to the Astoria area were

Scandinavian, and with the addition of these seafaring folk, logging, fishing, and shipbuilding coaxed the population up to 20,000 by World War II.

Some believe that the port city at the mouth of the Columbia might have grown to rival San Francisco or Seattle had it not been for the setback of a devastating fire in 1922. In the early morning hours of December 8, a pool hall on Commercial Street caught fire, and the flames spread rapidly among the wooden buildings, many supported on wooden pilings, in Astoria's business district. By daybreak more than 200 businesses in a 32-block area had been reduced to ashes. The downtown was rebuilt in the ensuing years, largely in brick and stone, but the devastation changed the fate of Astoria.

Near the end of World War II, a Japanese submarine's shelling of Fort Stevens made it the only fortification on U.S. soil to have sustained an attack in a world war. After the war, the region's fortunes ebbed and flowed with its resource-based economy. In an attempt to supplement that economy with tourism, the State Highway Division began constructing the Astoria-Megler Bridge in 1962 to connect Oregon and Washington. When it opened in 1966, the bridge provided the final link in the 1,625-mile-long U.S. 101 along the Pacific Coast.

Unfortunately, preserving Astoria's glory days could not make up for the closing of the canneries and the decline of logging and fishing. The modern era has been characterized by a steady cultivation of tourism dollars, resulting in the thoughtful development of the waterfront, including the four-mile River Walk. Astoria is becoming an increasingly popular port of call for cruise ships, with more than 50 visiting per year. Whether or not Astoria's metaphoric ship ever comes in, let's hope the unpretentious charm of this hillside city where the river meets the ocean will not be lost in the process.

Orientation

The waters surrounding Astoria define the town as much as the steep hills it's built on. Along its northern side, the mighty Columbia, four miles wide, is a mega aquatic highway carrying a steady flow of traffic, from small pleasure boats to massive cargo ships a quarter mile long. Soaring high over the river is an engineering marvel that's impossible to miss from most locations in town. At just over four miles long, the Astoria-Megler Bridge, completed in 1966, is the longest bridge in Oregon and the longest bridge of its type (cantilever through-truss) in the world. On Astoria's south side, Young's River, flowing down from the Coast Range, broadens into Young's Bay, separating Astoria from its neighbor Warrenton to the west.

A few miles to the northwest, the Columbia River finally meets the Pacific, 1,243 miles from its headwaters in British Columbia. Where the tremendous outflow (averaging 118 million gallons per minute) of the River of the

sea lions basking on the Astoria waterfront

West encounters the ocean tides, conditions can be treacherous, and the sometimes-monstrous waves around the bar have claimed more than 2,000 vessels over the years. This rivermouth could well be the biggest widow-maker on the high seas, earning it the title "Graveyard of the Pacific." Lewis and Clark referred to it as "that seven-shouldered horror" in a journal entry from the winter of 1805-1806.

Any visitor to Astoria should consider crossing the Astoria-Megler Bridge to visit the extreme southwest corner of Washington State. Here the sands and soil carried by the Columbia create a 20-mile-long sand spit called the Long Beach Peninsula. Some of the West Coast's most succulent oysters grow in Willapa Bay, the body of water created by this finger of sand. Historic beach communities plus numerous Lewis and Clark sites also reward visitors to this charming enclave.

SIGHTS

After getting a bird's-eye view from Coxcomb Hill, you might want to take a closer look at

Astoria on foot. The town is home to dozens of beautifully restored 19th-century and early-20th-century houses. Here's a suggested route: From the Flavel House Museum at 8th Street and Duane Street, start walking south on 8th Street and turn left on Franklin Avenue. Continue east to 11th Street, then detour south one block on 11th Street to Grand Avenue; head east on Grand, north on 12th Street, and back to Franklin, continuing your eastward trek. Walk to 17th Street, then south again to Grand, double back on Grand two blocks to 15th Street, then walk north on 15th to Exchange Street and east on Exchange to 17th, where you'll be just two blocks from the Columbia River Maritime Museum. The route takes you past 74 historical buildings and sites.

Download free two-hour audio tours and accompanying maps from the **Chamber of Commerce** (www.oldoregon.com); one focuses on history and the other on movie sites.

Astoria Column

The best introduction to Astoria and environs is undoubtedly the 360-degree panorama from atop the 125-foot-tall **Astoria Column** (2199 Coxcomb Dr., 503/325-2963, www.astoria-column.org, dawn-dusk daily, $1 requested for parking) on Coxcomb Hill, the highest point in town. Patterned after the Trajan Column in Rome, the reinforced-concrete tower was built in 1926 as a joint project of the Great Northern Railway and the descendants of John Jacob Astor to commemorate the westward sweep of discovery and migration. The graffito frieze spiraling up the exterior illustrates Robert Gray's 1792 discovery of the Columbia River, the establishment of American claims to the Northwest Territory, the arrival of the Great Northern Railway, and other scenes of the history of the Pacific Northwest. The vista from the surrounding hilltop park is impressive enough, but for the ultimate experience, the climb up 164 steps to the tower's top is worth the effort.

Before ascending, get oriented with the annotated bronze relief map in front of the column, which notes the distances and directions

to landmarks near and far. From this vantage point you can see across the rooftops of the town, the Astoria-Megler Bridge, giant freighters gliding up and down the Columbia, and a long sweep of the Washington shore. To the northwest are the Columbia Bar and Cape Disappointment. On clear days, look northeast to Mount St. Helens and to Mount Hood on the far eastern horizon. Looking over Young's Bay south and west of Astoria, the Clatsop Plains extend to Tillamook Head and Saddle Mountain.

If you have kids in tow, be sure to stop by the tiny gift shop to buy a balsa wood glider. Lofting a wooden airplane from the top of the tower is an Astoria tradition.

Get to the Astoria Column from downtown by following 16th Street south (uphill) to Jerome Avenue. Turn west (right) one block and continue up 15th Street to the park entrance on Coxcomb Drive.

The Waterfront

While most of Astoria's waterfront is lined with warehouses and docks, the **River Walk** will get you front-row views of the river. The River Walk provides paved riverside passage for pedestrians and cyclists along a four-mile stretch between the Port of Astoria and the community of Alderbrook. The path continues unpaved another two miles eastward to Tongue Point.

An excellent way to cover some of the same ground, accompanied by color commentary on sights and local history, is by taking a 40-minute ride on Old Number 300, the **Astoria Riverfront Trolley** (503/325-6311, www.old300.org, noon-7pm daily Memorial Day-Labor Day weather permitting, noon-6pm Sat.-Sun. fall and spring, $1 per ride or $2 all day), which runs on Astoria's original train tracks alongside the River Walk as far east as the East Mooring Basin. Trolley shelters are at several locations along the route; you can also flag it down by waving a dollar bill. The lovingly restored 1913 trolley originally served San Antonio and later ran between Portland and Lake Oswego in the 1980s.

Toward the eastern end of the River Walk, at

Pier 39, the **Hanthorn Cannery** (100 39th St., 503/325-2502, www.canneryworker.org, 9am-6pm daily, free) is a rather informal but fascinating museum housed in an old Bumble Bee tuna cannery. Exhibits include some lovely old wooden boats, eye-catching photos, and canning equipment. There's also a coffee shop and a brewpub at this location, so it's a good place to take a break.

Columbia River Maritime Museum

On the waterfront a few blocks east of downtown Astoria, the **Columbia River Maritime Museum** (1792 Marine Dr., 503/325-2323, www.crmm.org, 9:30am-5pm daily, closed Thanksgiving and Christmas, $12 adults, $10 seniors, $5 children ages 6-17, under 6 free) is hard to miss. The roof of the 44,000-square-foot museum simulates the curvature of cresting waves, and the gigantic 25,000-pound anchor out front is also impossible to ignore. What's inside surpasses this eye-catching facade. The introductory film is excellent and intense, giving a good glimpse of the jobs of bar pilots, who climb aboard huge ships to navigate them through tricky passages. Floor-to-ceiling windows in the Great Hall allow visitors to watch the river traffic in comfort.

Times when tribal canoes plied the Columbia, Lewis and Clark camped on the Columbia's shores, and dramatic shipwrecks occurred on its bar are recounted with scale models, exquisitely detailed miniatures of ships, paintings, and artifacts. The most dramatic exhibit is of a 44-foot U.S. Coast Guard motor lifeboat, poised precariously on a wave in a life-size re-creation of a rescue on the Columbia River Bar. The chance to walk the bridge of a World War II destroyer, steer a tugboat, or tie a cleat hitch and other useful knots adds a hands-on aspect to the experience. Local lighthouses, the evolution of boat design, and harpoons are the focus of other exhibits here. There are also some artifacts from the *Peter Iredale* and other ships that have met their ends on the Oregon coast. Still other items of interest include

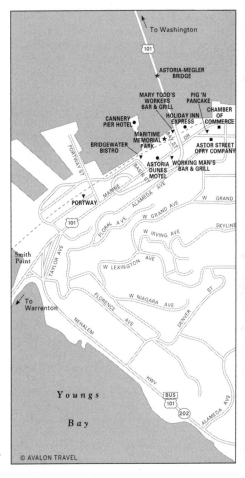

scrimshaw, fishing and cannery memorabilia, a small watercolor of the harbor by a crew member on Robert Gray's 1792 voyage of discovery, and sea charts dating as far back as 1587.

Museum admission lets you board the 128-foot lightship *Columbia,* now permanently berthed alongside the museum building. This vessel served as a floating lighthouse, marking the entrance to the mouth of the river and helping many ships navigate the dangerous waters. After almost three decades of service it was replaced in 1979 by an unstaffed 42-foot-high

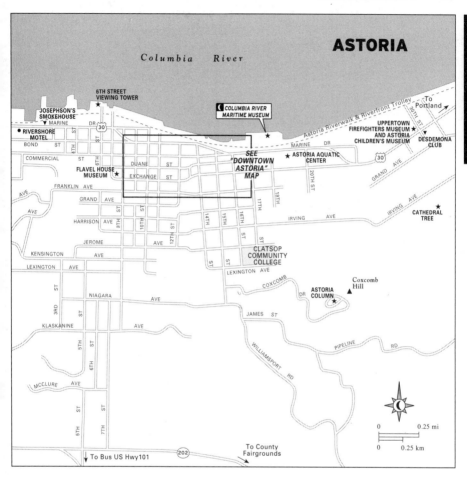

navigational buoy. The gift shop has a great collection of books on Astoria's history and other maritime topics.

Also berthed at the museum is the pilot boat *Peacock,* which crossed the Columbia bar more than 35,000 times during her 30-plus year career.

Heritage Museum and Research Library

The Clatsop County Historical Society operates the **Heritage Museum** (1618 Exchange St., 503/325-2203, www.cumtux.org, 10am-5pm daily May-Sept., 11am-4pm Tues.-Sat. Oct.-Apr., $4 adults, $2 children ages 6-12). Housed in the handsome neoclassical building that was originally Astoria's city hall, it has several galleries filled with antiquities, tools, vintage photographs, and archives chronicling various aspects of life in Clatsop County. The museum's centerpiece exhibit concentrates on the culture of the local Clatsop and Chinook people, from before European contact up to the present day. Other exhibits highlight natural history, geology, early immigrants and settlers in the region, and the development of

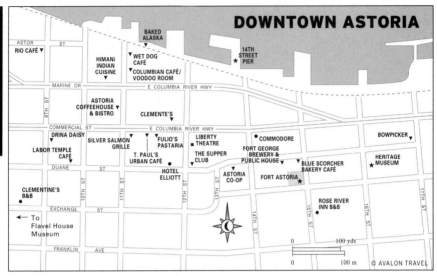

DOWNTOWN ASTORIA

commerce in such fields as fishing, fish packing, logging, and lumber. The **research library** is open to the public.

The historical society also operates the **Uppertown Firefighters Museum** (30th St. and Marine Dr., 503/325-2203, noon-3pm Sat. or by appointment, free), which displays an extensive collection of firefighting equipment dating from 1873 to 1963. Featured are hand-pulled, horse-drawn, and motorized fire engines, including a 1912 American LaFrance fire truck, a Stutz fire engine, and a 1946 Mack fire truck. The photos and information about the devastating fires of 1893 and 1922 are fascinating.

Fort Astoria

In a tiny park at the corner of 15th and Exchange Streets, a reproduction of a rough-hewn log blockhouse and a mural commemorate the spot where Astoria began, when John Jacob Astor's fur traders originally constructed a small fort in 1811. It's worth a quick stop for buffs of early Pacific Northwest history.

Flavel House Museum

Captain George Flavel, Astoria's first millionaire, amassed a fortune in the mid-19th century through his Columbia Bar piloting monopoly and later expanded his empire through shipping, banking, and real estate. Between 1884 and 1886 he had a home built in the center of Astoria, now the **Flavel House Museum** (441 8th St., 503/325-2203, 10am-5pm daily May-Sept., 11am-4pm Tues.-Sat. Oct.-Apr., $5 adults, $4 seniors and students, $2 children ages 6-17, 5 and younger free) overlooking the Columbia River, where he retired with his wife and two daughters. From its fourth-story cupola, Flavel could watch the comings and goings of his sailing fleet. Although the captain died in 1893, members of the family lived in the house until 1933. The amazing story of the Flavel family was depicted in colorful detail by Calvin Trillin in the February 8, 1993, issue of the *New Yorker*.

When the Clatsop County Historical Society assumed stewardship in 1951, the mansion was slated for demolition, to be paved over as a parking lot for the adjacent courthouse. Fortunately, thanks to the efforts of the historical society and many volunteers, the house still stands today, at the corner of 8th and Duane Streets. The splendidly extravagant Queen Anne mansion reflects the rich style and

© BILL MCRAE

While in Astoria, be sure to visit the Columbia River Maritime Museum, which includes tours of historic boats.

elegance of the late Victorian era and the lives of Astoria's most prominent family.

The property encompasses a full city block. With its intricate woodwork inside and out, period furnishings, and art, along with its extravagantly rendered gables, cornices, and porches, the Flavel House ranks with the Carson Mansion in Eureka, California, as a Victorian showplace. The 14-foot ceilings, Persian rugs, and an array of imported tiles are upstaged only by the fireplaces framed in exotic hardwoods in every room. The Carriage House, on the southwest corner of the property, serves as an orientation center for visitors, with exhibits, an interpretive video, and a museum store.

Lewis and Clark National Wildlife Refuge

Six miles east of Astoria in the Burnside area is the **Twilight Creek Eagle Sanctuary.** To get there, drive seven miles east of town on U.S. 30 and turn left at Burnside. A viewing platform on the left 0.5 mile later overlooks the 35,000 acres of mudflats, tidal marshes, and islands (which Lewis and Clark called "Seal Islands") of the **Lewis and Clark National Wildlife Refuge.** Bald eagles live here year-round, and the area provides wintering and resting habitat for waterfowl, shorebirds, and songbirds. Beavers, raccoons, weasels, mink, muskrats, and river otters live on the islands; harbor seals and California sea lions feed in the rich estuary waters and use the sandbars and mudflats as haul-out sites at low tide.

Fort Clatsop National Memorial

On November 7, 1805, after a journey of nearly 19 months and 4,000 miles, the Lewis and Clark expedition thought they had at last reached their destination, the Pacific Ocean. "Ocian in View! O! the joy," wrote William Clark in his journal. Alas, they were close, but from the Washington side of the Columbia River they had mistaken its broad mouth for the sea itself. Hindered by waves and foul

ASTORIA GOES TO THE MOVIES

In recent decades, the Victorian homes and ocean view in Astoria's hillside neighborhoods and the surrounding maritime settings have provided the backdrop for such fanciful modern sagas as *Free Willy I* and *II*, *Kindergarten Cop*, *Teenage Mutant Ninja Turtles III*, *Short Circuit*, *Come See the Paradise*, and *The Goonies*. The last movie, a cult favorite shot in 1985, concerns a gang of local kids hunting for pirate's treasure; happy memories of the movie continue to attract a steady stream of visitors looking for the locations used in the film. More recently, films shot in Astoria have gravitated toward horror, including *The Ring Two* and *Cthulhu*, a film based on the horror novels of H. P. Lovecraft. Download an audio tour and map to movie sites at www.oldoregon. com (click on Visitor Information). A guide to movie locations is available at the Oregon Welcome Center in Astoria, the Heritage Museum, Flavel House Museum, and the Warrenton Visitors Center. If you're really into it, stop by the **Oregon Film Museum** (732 Duane St., 503/325-2203, www.oregonfilmmuseum.org, 10am-5pm daily, $5 adults, $2 children ages 6-17), which ostensibly celebrates the various films shot in Oregon, but is mostly a paean to all things Goonie. The museum is housed in the old Clatsop County Jail (from 1914), which famously starred in *The Goonies* jailbreak scene.

weather, it would take nearly another week before they actually beheld the Pacific. They explored farther west, to Cape Disappointment, and spent 10 uncomfortable days exposed to the elements on the north shore of the Columbia, then decided to move south for a more suitable location to pass the coming winter.

They chose a thickly forested rise alongside the Netul River (now the Lewis and Clark River), a few miles south of present-day Astoria, for their campsite. There, the Corps of Discovery quickly set about felling trees and building two parallel rows of cabins, joined by a gated palisade. The finished compound measured about 50 feet on each side. The party of 33 people, including one African American and a Native American woman and her baby, moved into the seven small rooms on Christmas Eve and named their stockade Fort Clatsop for the nearby Indian people.

The winter of 1805-1806 was cold, wet, rainy, and generally miserable. Of the 106 days spent at the site, it rained on all but 12. The January 18, 1806, journal entry of expedition member Private Joseph Whitehouse was typical of the comments recorded during the stay: "It rained hard all last night, & still continued the same this morning. It continued Raining during the whole of this day."

While at Fort Clatsop, the men stored up meat and other supplies, sewed moccasins and new garments, and traded with local tribes, all the while coping with the constant damp conditions, illness and injuries, and merciless plagues of fleas. As soon as the weather permitted, on March 23, 1806, they finally departed on their homeward journey to St. Louis.

Within a few years the elements had erased all traces of Fort Clatsop, and its exact location was lost. In 1955, local history buffs took their best guess and built a replica of the fort, based on the notes and sketches of Captain Clark. In 1999 an anthropologist discovered a 148-year-old map identifying the location of Lewis and Clark's winter encampment, and as it turns out the reproduction is sited very close to the original. In 2005, this replica of Fort Clatsop burned, and a new replica, built mostly by volunteers using period tools, was reopened in 2006. Compared to the previous one, this new Fort Clatsop is a more authentic replica of the actual fort that housed the intrepid Corps of Discovery.

Today, in addition to the log replica of the fort, a well-equipped visitors center, a museum, and other attractions make **Fort Clatsop National Memorial** (92343 Fort Clatsop Rd., 503/861-2471, www.nps.gov/lewi, 9am-6pm

THE LONG BEACH PENINSULA

If you've come as far as Astoria, at the edge of the continent and at the mouth of the Columbia River, you should consider crossing the soaring Astoria-Megler Bridge to explore sights on the Columbia's northern shore. There are both scenic and historical reasons to visit this remote corner of Washington State. The Lewis and Clark National and State Historical Parks aggregation includes a number of sites just across from Astoria in Washington, notably **Cape Disappointment State Park,** with a newly expanded Lewis and Clark Interpretive Center.

The **Long Beach Peninsula,** the thin sand spit just north of the mouth of the Columbia River, claims to have the world's longest beach. And with 28 unbroken miles of it, the boast has to be taken seriously. Like Seaside in Oregon, beach resorts at Seaview and Long Beach have a long pedigree, dating from the 1880s, when Portland families journeyed down the Columbia River by steamboat to summer at the coast. The bay side of the Long Beach sand spit creates **Willapa Bay,** known to oyster-lovers around the country for the excellent bivalves that grow in this shallow inlet, which is fed by six rivers. Most of Willapa Bay is protected as a national wildlife refuge, and it's an excellent bird-watching site. **Oysterville,** a tiny village along the bay, stands largely unchanged since the 1880s, and the entire town has been placed on the National Register of Historic Places. The very tip of the peninsula is preserved as 807-acre **Leadbetter Point State Park,** with informal hiking trails along both sandy beaches and the reedy bay.

Another good reason to cross the bridge is to dine at the area's top restaurant: **Pelican Restaurant** (177 Howerton Way SE, Ilwaco, 360/642-4034, http://pelicanorestaurant. com, 5pm-9pm Wed.-Sun. $19-26), right above the harbor in the fishing village of Ilwaco. The food is beautifully prepared Mediterranean via Pacific Northwest cuisine, with the freshest of local fish, seafood, produce, beef, and lamb given an expert French and Italian twist by chef/owner Jeff McMahon.

daily mid-June-Labor Day, 9am-5pm daily Labor Day-mid-June, $3 adults, children under 16 free) a must-stop for anyone interested in this pivotal chapter of American history. The expedition's story is nicely narrated here with displays, artifacts, slides, and films, but the summertime "living history" reenactments are the main reason to come. Paths lead through the grove of old-growth Sitka spruce, with interpretive placards identifying native plants. A short walk from the fort leads to the riverside, where dugout canoes are modeled on those used by the corps while in this area. In addition, the 6.5-mile **Fort to Sea Trail** follows the general route blazed by Captain Clark from the fort through dunes and forests to the Pacific at Sunset Beach.

The winter of 1805-1806 put a premium on wilderness survival skills, some of which are exhibited here by rangers in costume. You may see the tanning of hides, making of buckskin clothing and moccasins, and the molding of tallow candles and lead bullets. In addition, visitors may occasionally participate in the construction of a dugout canoe or try their luck at starting a fire by striking flint on steel. Rangers also lead guided hikes and canoe trips.

This 1,500-acre park sits six miles southwest of Astoria and three miles east of U.S. 101 on the Lewis and Clark River. To get there from Astoria, take Marine Drive and head west across Young's Bay to Warrenton. On the other side of the bay look for signs for the Fort Clatsop turnoff; turn left off the Coast Highway about a mile after the bridge and follow the signs to Fort Clatsop.

Fort Stevens State Park
Ten miles west of Astoria, in the far northwest corner of the state, the Civil War-era outpost of **Fort Stevens** (100 Peter Iredale Rd., Hammond, 503/861-1671 or 800/551-6949,

NORTH COAST

© BILL MCRAE

The *Peter Iredale* wrecked on the Oregon coast in 1906.

www.oregonstateparks.org, $5 day use for historic military area and Coffenbury Lake, $21 tent camping, $27 RV camping, $41 yurt, $85 cabin) was one of three military installations (the others were Forts Canby and Columbia in Washington) built to safeguard the mouth of the Columbia River. Established shortly before the Confederates surrendered on April 9, 1865, Fort Stevens served for 84 years, until just after the end of World War II. Today, the remaining fortifications and other buildings are preserved along with 3,700 acres of woodland, lakes, wetlands, miles of sand beaches, and three miles of Columbia River frontage.

The fort's creation was not the only outgrowth of the Civil War on the West Coast. The year before, President Abraham Lincoln had founded the city of Port Angeles, Washington, for "lighthouse purposes." Given the creation of Fort Stevens shortly thereafter, it's a logical assumption that "lighthouse purposes" also meant watching out for Confederate ships and the British, whom the Union feared would ally with the South. The remote northwest Oregon

coast may seem a world away from the bloody battles of the Civil War, until you consider that the last shots of the conflict were fired even farther away, in the Bering Strait. On June 5, 1865, the *Shenandoah* attacked a fleet of Yankee whalers because the Confederate skipper was unaware of the Appomattox Treaty, which had ended the war two months before.

Although Fort Stevens did not see action in the Civil War, it sustained an attack in a later conflict. On June 21, 1942, a Japanese submarine fired 17 shells on the gun emplacements at Battery Russell, making it the only U.S. fortification in the 48 states to be bombed by a foreign power since the War of 1812. No damage was incurred, and the Army didn't return fire. Shortly after World War II, the fort was deactivated and the armaments were removed.

Today, the site features a **Military Museum** (503/861-1470 or 503/861-2000, 10am-6pm daily June-Sept., 10am-4pm daily Oct.-May) with old photos, weapons exhibits, and maps, as well as seven different batteries (fortifications) and other structures left over from almost a century of service. Climbing to the commander's station for a scenic view of the Columbia River and South Jetty are popular visitor activities. The massive gun batteries, built of weathered gray concrete and rusting iron, eerily silent amid the thick woodlands, also invite exploration; small children should be closely supervised, as there are steep stairways, high ledges, and other hazards.

During the summer months, guided tours of the underground **Battery Mishler** (12:30 and 2:30pm daily, $4) and a narrated tour of the fort's 37 acres on a two-ton U.S. Army truck (12:30 and 2:30pm Mon.-Thurs., 11am, 12:30, 2:30, and 4pm Fri.-Sat., May 1-Sept. 30, $4) are also available. Summer programs include Civil War reenactments and archaeological digs.

Nine miles of bike trails and five miles of hiking trails link the historic area to the rest of the park and provide access to Battery Russell and the 1906 wreck of the British

schooner *Peter Iredale*. You can also bike to the campground one mile south of the Military Museum.

Parking is available at four lots about a mile from one another at the foot of the dunes. The beach runs north to the Columbia River, where excellent surf fishing, bird-watching, and a view of the mouth of the river await. South of the campground (east of the *Peter Iredale*) is a self-guided nature trail around part of the two-mile shoreline of **Coffenbury Lake.** The lake also has two swimming beaches with bathhouses and fishing for trout and perch.

To get to Fort Stevens State Park from U.S. 101, drive west on Harbor Street through Warrenton on Highway 104 (Ft. Stevens Hwy.) to the suburb of Hammond, and follow the signs to Fort Stevens Historic Area and Military Museum.

SPORTS AND RECREATION
Bicycling
You don't need a fancy bike to pedal the River Walk; rent a hefty cruiser from **Bikes and Beyond** (1089 Marine Dr., 503/325-2961, www.bikesandbeyond.com). This friendly little shop also caters to bicycle tourists.

Diving and Kayaking
Astoria Scuba (on Pier 39, 503/325-2502, www.astoriascuba.com) offers diving lessons and kayak rentals for $25 for half a day.

Fishing Charters
More than any other industry, commercial fishing has dominated Astoria throughout its history. Salmon canneries lined the waterfront at the turn of the 20th century. Albacore and longline shark fishing put dinner on the table in the 1930s and 1940s. In the modern era, commercial fishing has turned to sole, lingcod, rockfish, flounder, and other bottom fish. If it's not enough to watch these commercial operations from the dock, try joining a charter.

Tiki Charters (350 Industry St., 503/325-7818, www.tikicharter.com) will take you out for salmon, halibut, bottom fish, and sturgeon,

---

THE *PETER IREDALE*

One of the best known of the hundreds of ships wrecked on the Oregon coast over the centuries is the British schooner *Peter Iredale*. This 278-foot four-master, fashioned of steel plates on an iron frame, was built in Liverpool in 1890 and came to its untimely end on the beach south of Clatsop Spit on October 25, 1906. En route from Mexico to pick up a load of wheat on the Columbia River, the vessel ran aground during high seas and a northwesterly squall. All hands were rescued, and with little damage to the hull, hopes initially ran high that the ship could be towed back to sea and salvaged. That effort proved fruitless, and eventually the ship was written off as a total loss. Today, nearly a century later, the remains of her rusting skeleton protrude from the sands of Fort Stevens State Park as a familiar sight to most who have traveled the north coast. Signs within Fort Stevens State Park lead the way to a parking area close to the wreck.

depending on the season. Trips depart from the dock near the former Red Lion Inn. Given the retail price of fresh salmon, you could theoretically pay for a charter trip by landing a single fish. **Gale Force Guides** (trips depart from Warrenton, 503/861-1494, www.galeforceguides.com) takes sport anglers fishing for salmon in either salt- or freshwater, depending on the season. Sturgeon and crabbing trips are also offered.

On your own, go after trout, bass, catfish, steelhead, and sturgeon in freshwater lakes, streams, and rivers. Lingcod, rockfish, surfperch, and other bottom fish can be pursued at sea, off jetties, or along ocean beaches.

Hiking

An in-town hike that's not too strenuous begins at 28th and Irving Streets, meandering up the hill to the Astoria Column. If you drive to the trailhead, park along 28th Street. It's about a one-mile walk to the top. En route is the **Cathedral Tree,** an old-growth fir with a sort of Gothic arch formed at its roots.

The **Oregon Coast Trail** starts (or ends) at Clatsop Spit, at the north end of **Fort Stevens State Park** (100 Peter Iredale Rd., Hammond, 503/861-1671 or 800/551-6949, www.oregonstateparks.org, $5 day use). The most northerly stretch extends south along the beach for 14 miles to Gearhart. It's a flat, easy walk, and your journey could well be highlighted by a sighting of the endangered silverspot butterfly. The species frequents just six sites, including four in Oregon; Clatsop County is one of them. The endangered status of the creature protects it by law and has stopped developers from building resorts on coastal meadows and dunes north of Gearhart. Look for a small orange butterfly with silvery spots on the undersides of its wings.

You might also encounter cars on the beach. This section of shoreline, inexplicably, is the longest stretch of coastline open to motor vehicles in Oregon. Call the **State Parks and Recreation Division** (800/551-6949) for an up-to-date report on trail conditions before starting out.

Fort Stevens State Park has nine miles of hiking trails through woods, wetlands, and dunes. One popular hike here is the two-mile loop around **Coffenbury Lake.**

In 2005, as part of the expansion of Lewis and Clark National Historical Park, the **Fort to Sea Trail** was created to link Fort Clatsop to the Pacific. The 6.5-mile trail follows the route through forest, fields, and dunes that the corps traveled as they explored and traded along the Pacific coast.

The Fort to Sea Trail starts from the visitors center at Fort Clatsop. The first 1.5 miles involve a gentle climb past many trees blown down in a big 2007 storm to the Clatsop Ridge, where on a clear day you can see through the trees to the Pacific Ocean. The ridge makes a fine destination for a short hike, but the really beautiful part of the trail is the hikers-only (no dogs) stretch from the overlook to the beach, where you'll pass through deep woods and forested pastures dotted with small lakes. The trail passes a tunnel underneath U.S. 101 and continues through dunes to the Sunset Beach-Fort to Sea Trail parking lot. From there, a one-mile path leads to the beach.

Unless you plan to return along the trail—which makes for a long day's hike—you'll need to arrange a pickup.

Water Parks

The **Astoria Aquatic Center** (20th St. and Marine Dr., 503/325-7027, www.astoriaparks.com, 5am-8pm Mon.-Fri., 9am-5pm Sat., 11am-5pm Sun., $6.50 adult, $4.50 children ages 2-17, $15 family) houses four pools, including a 100-foot waterslide with a 20-foot drop and a lazy-river current; a six-lane, 25-yard lap pool; an adult hydro spa pool; a kiddies' wading pool; locker rooms; and a variety of fitness equipment.

ENTERTAINMENT AND EVENTS

For the lowdown on all the happenings in and around Astoria, get your hands on a copy of *Hipfish,* Astoria's spirited monthly tabloid distributed free all over town.

LEWIS AND CLARK NATIONAL HISTORICAL PARK

On November 2, 2004, President George W. Bush signed a bill into law to create the 59th national park in the United States. The Lewis and Clark National and State Historical Parks honor explorers Meriwether Lewis and William Clark, whose journey in 1804-1806 paved the way for the U.S. settlement of the West. The park focuses on the sites at the mouth of the Columbia River, where the Corps of Discovery spent the famously wet winter of 1805.

The park is somewhat unusual in that it is essentially a rebranding of current National Park facilities and a federalization of current state parks. The new park includes a dozen sites linked to Lewis and Clark exploration, campsites, and lore. One of these, **Fort Clatsop National Memorial,** south of Astoria and where the Corps actually spent the winter, was already operated by the National Park Service, while **Cape Disappointment State Park** formerly Fort Canby State Park, on the Washington side of the Columbia, remains a Washington state park but is managed by the national park entity.

Besides these two existing facilities, units of the new national park include the **Fort to Sea Trail,** a path linking Fort Clatsop to the Pacific; **Clarks Dismal Nitch,** a notoriously wet campsite near the Washington base of the Astoria-Megler Bridge; **Station Camp,** another improvident campsite for the Corps; the **Salt Works** in Seaside, where the Corps boiled seawater to make salt; **Netul Landing,** the canoe launch area used by Lewis and Clark near Fort Clatsop; and a **memorial to Thomas Jefferson** yet to be constructed on the grounds of Cape Disappointment State Park.

The new national park also encompasses the existing **Fort Columbia State Park** in Washington, which preserves a turn-of-the-20th-century military encampment, and **Fort Stevens, Sunset Beach,** and **Ecola State Parks** in Oregon.

The national park designation changes little for these once disparate sites, at least in the near future. Fort Clatsop has been expanded to 1,500 acres, and the **Lewis and Clark Interpretive Center** at Fort Disappointment State Park was revamped. Visitors will mostly notice new and consistent signage throughout the park units. Ranger-guided hikes and living history reenactors promise to bring to life the famous, often very wet, events that took place here over 200 years ago.

Nightlife

Befitting of a vintage fishing port, Astoria has lots of old bars and watering holes. As tribute to Astoria's scrappy spirit, explore some of the city's classic bars. The **Portway** (422 W. Marine Dr., 503/325-2651) is the oldest bar in the oldest American settlement west of the Rockies. Though the present building dates from 1923, it's loaded with character and characters. Directly under the bridge, **Mary Todd's Workers Bar and Grill** (281 W. Marine Dr., 503/338-7291) is a classic old bar with a notable drink special: the Yucca. Also try the marvelously crispy onion rings. On the eastern edge of Astoria, the slightly disreputable-looking **Desdemona Club** (2997 Marine Dr., 503/325-8540) is in fact a friendly *Cheers*-type

pub that welcomes strangers with pool tables and good food. **Phyllis & Bob's Labor Temple Café & Bar** (939 Duane St., 503/325-0801) is the oldest communal union hall in the Pacific Northwest and is not to be missed. The clientele is a mix of longtime union activists, twenty-something artists, and rowdy young sailors, making for some interesting dynamics. The **Voodoo Room** (1114 Marine Dr., 503/325-2233, www.columbianvoodoo.com) is a dark and cluttered bar with hipsters, cocktails, and occasional live music.

All of Astoria's brewpubs are friendly places to start a conversation or settle in with a pint and decent pub grub to quietly muse on the world. **Fort George Brewery and Public House** (1483 Duane St., 503/325-7468, www.fortgeorgebrewery.com) has free live music on Sunday evenings.

The Arts

The handsome **Liberty Theatre** (1203 Commercial St., 503/325-5922, www.liberty-theater.org), whose colonnaded facades along Commercial and 12th Streets converge at the corner box office, is a vibrant symbol of Astoria's ongoing rejuvenation. The ornate Mediterranean-style building in the heart of downtown began its life in 1925 as a venue for silent films, vaudeville acts, and lectures. The theater continued as a first-run movie house, but after decades of neglect this grande dame was badly showing her age, and it looked as though the Liberty would eventually meet the sad wrecking ball fate of so many fine old movie palaces. Fortunately, though, a nonprofit organization undertook efforts to restore the theater to its original elegance and equip it to be a state-of-the-art performing arts center, and the Liberty currently hosts concerts, recitals, theater, and other events.

Astoria's long-running *Shanghaied in Astoria* (122 W. Bond St., 503/325-6104, www.shanghaiedinastoria.com, evenings Thurs.-Sat. mid-July-mid-Sept., $16-20), based on the town's dubious distinction as a notorious shanghai port during the late 1800s, is a good old-fashioned melodrama. Chase scenes, bar fights, and a liberal sprinkling of Scandinavian jokes will have you laughing in between applauding the hero and booing the villain. Performed with gusto by the Astor Street Opry Company, the show has been running since 1985, and has spawned a number of related shows: a "junior" *Shanghaied in Astoria* for kids, a once-yearly drag version, and the holiday season *Scrooged in Astoria.*

Cinema

The **Columbian Theater** (1102 Marine Dr., 503/325-3516, www.columbianvoodoo.com, 7pm, $4, $2 children ages 12 and under) sits adjacent to the Columbian Cafe and screens the big movies you may have missed a month earlier in their first run. Enjoy beer, wine, cocktails, pizza, and other munchies while you watch.

Astoria Gateway Cinema (1875 Marine Dr., 503/338-6575) is a modern movie multiplex, showing the usual stuff, where you can pass an afternoon trying to forget the often dismal weather.

Festivals and Events
FISHER POETS GATHERING

Modeled after Elko, Nevada's popular Cowboy Poets Gathering, the **Fisher Poets Gathering** (www.fisherpoets.org) provides a forum in which men and women involved in the fishing and other maritime industries share their poems, stories, songs, and artwork in a convivial seaport setting. The annual late February event, which dates back to 1998, draws writers and artists from up and down the Pacific coast and farther afield for readings, art shows, concerts, book signings, workshops, films, a silent auction, and other activities at pubs, galleries, theaters, and other venues around town. Participation isn't limited to fisherfolk but extends to anyone with a connection to maritime activity, and themes range from the rigors (and humor) of life on the water to environmental issues. Admission is by donation ($5) at the ticket booth of the **Columbian Theater** (1102 Marine Dr.). For more details and a full schedule, check the website.

ASTORIA-WARRENTON CRAB AND SEAFOOD FESTIVAL

The **Astoria-Warrenton Crab and Seafood Festival** (Clatsop County Fairgrounds, 503/325-6311 or 800/875-6807, 4pm-9pm Fri., 10am-8pm Sat., 11am-4pm Sun., $5-10 adults, children ages 5-12 half price), held the last weekend in April, is a hugely popular event that brings in crowds from miles around. Scores of booths feature a cornucopia of seafood and other eats, regional beers and Oregon wines, and arts and crafts. Activities include continuous entertainment, crab races, a petting zoo, and kids' activities. A traditional crab dinner caps off the evening. To get to the fairgrounds from Astoria, take Highway 202 for 4.5 miles to Walluski Loop Road and watch for signs. Parking is limited at the fairgrounds. Frequent shuttle service takes folks between the fairgrounds, park-and-ride lots, downtown, the Port of Astoria, and local hotels and campgrounds.

SCANDINAVIAN MIDSUMMER FESTIVAL

The legacy of the thousands of Scandinavians who arrived to work in area mills and canneries in the late 19th and early 20th centuries is still strong in Astoria. For many locals, the summer's biggest event is the **Scandinavian Midsummer Festival** (503/325-6311; www. astoriascanfest.com, $8 adults, $3 children ages 6-12), which usually takes place the third weekend of June, Friday through Sunday. Local Danes, Finns, Icelanders, Norwegians, and Swedes come together to celebrate their heritage; visitors and musicians from the Old Country keep the festivities authentic. Costumed dancers weave around a flowered midsummer pole (a fertility rite), burn a bonfire to destroy evil spirits, and have tugs-of-war pitting Scandinavian nationalities against each other. Food, dancing, crafts, musical concerts, and a parade bring the whole town out to the Clatsop County Fairgrounds on Walluski Loop Road just off Highway 202.

ASTORIA REGATTA WEEK

A tradition since 1894, **Astoria Regatta Week** is considered the Pacific Northwest's longest-running festival. Held on the waterfront in mid-August, the five-day event kicks off with the regatta queen's coronation and reception. Attractions include live entertainment, a grand street parade, historic home tours, ship tours and boat rides, sailboat and dragon boat races, a classic car show, a salmon barbecue, arts and crafts, food booths, a beer garden, and a twilight boat parade. For details and a schedule, contact the **Astoria Regatta Association** (503/325-6311 or 800/875-6807, www.astoriaregatta.org).

SHOPPING

On Sundays between early May to early October, follow local tradition and stroll leisurely up and down 12th Street between Marine Drive and Exchange Street for the **Astoria Sunday Market** (10am-3pm), where vendors offer farm-fresh produce, plants, crafts, and specialty foods.

A local store worth noting is **Finnware** (1116 Commercial St., 503/325-5720, www. finnware.com, 10am-5pm Mon.-Sat., 11am-4pm Sun.) which stocks Scandinavian crystal and glassware, jewelry, books, and kitchen tools. This is a store that takes its Finnish roots seriously.

Art Galleries

Astoria has a well-deserved reputation as an art center, with many downtown storefronts now serving as art galleries. Not to miss is **RiverSea Gallery** (1160 Commercial St., 503/325-1270, http://riverseagallery.com, 11am-5:30pm Mon.-Thurs., 11am-7pm Fri.-Sat., 11am-4pm Sun.), with a large and varied selection of work by local painters, glass artists, jewelry makers, and fine craftspeople. For a more quixotic art scene, go to **Imogen Gallery** (240 11th St., 503/325-1566, http://imogengallery.com, 11am-5pm Mon.-Tues. and Thurs.-Sat., 11am-4pm Sun.), dedicated to contemporary and conceptual art by local artists. **Lightbox Photographic Gallery** (1045 Marine Dr., 503/468-0238, http://lightbox-photographic.com, 10am-6 Tues.-Fri., 10am-5pm Sat.) is the region's gallery for fine art photography.

The second Saturday of each month is the **Astoria Art Walk** (5pm-9pm), when most galleries and shops in downtown stay open late.

Bookstores

Several bookstores in town invite serious browsing, buying, and intellectual stimulation. **Lucy's Books** (348 12th St., 503/325-4210, 10:30am-5:30pm Tues.-Sat., 11am-3pm Sun.) is a small but bighearted locally owned bookshop with an emphasis on Pacific Northwest regional subjects. On the next block, **Godfather's Books and Espresso** (1108 Commercial St.,

Everyone turns out for the Astoria Sunday Market.

503/325-8143, 8am-8pm Mon.-Sat., 9am-6pm Sun.) sells a mix of new and used books and has a case of excellent antique maps and prints depicting the Columbia River and north coast.

Local Food

Josephson's Smokehouse (106 Marine Dr., 503/325-2190, www.josephsons.com, 9am-6pm Mon.-Sat.) was established in 1920 in a false-front clapboard building near the waterfront. Josephson's is Oregon's most esteemed purveyor of gourmet smoked fish, producing Scandinavian cold-smoked salmon without dyes or preservatives. The smokehouse caters to mail-order clientele and fine restaurants. You can buy direct here at cheaper (but not cheap) prices than the mail-order rates. Pickled salmon, salmon jerky, sturgeon caviar, crab, oysters, and a variety of alder-smoked and canned fish are also sold here. On typically foggy days here in midwinter, there's nothing finer than a cup of Josephson's very thick clam chowder.

To shop the daily catch, which can include Dungeness crab, wild salmon, halibut, albacore tuna, sardines, sole, and rockfish, go to **Warrenton Deep Sea Fish Market** (45 NE Harbor Pl., Warrenton, 503/861-3911, 9am-5:30pm Mon.-Sat, 10am-4pm Sun.). They carry the largest selection of locally caught fish in the area, and you'll find a variety of smoked fish and seafood here as well.

ACCOMMODATIONS

With its wealth of large, elegant Victorian homes, it's not surprising that Astoria has more bed-and-breakfasts than any other town on the Oregon coast. The historic former homes of merchants, politicians, sea captains, and salmon canners number among them. In addition, a classic downtown hotel has been completely spiffed up and renovated, offering very comfortable rooms with vintage elegance. Several new hotels take advantage of wonderful riverfront views.

You'll also find about a dozen motels to choose from in and around Astoria, most of them located along U.S. 30, otherwise known as Marine Drive, in the northwest section of town. Most are fairly similar and don't have the charm that the town's B&Bs and hotels offer, but they're generally less expensive and are reasonably close to downtown.

The prices noted are for high season (summer) double-occupancy rooms. Rates fall by as much as half off-season.

$50-100

Astoria's **C Commodore** (258 14th St., 503/325-4747, http://commodoreastoria.com, $79-159) has simple but stylishly decorated rooms in a renovated downtown hotel. The least expensive rooms ("cabins") are just sleeping chambers with a sink, a flat-screen TV and DVD player, and an iPod docking station, with shared toilets and handsome tiled showers at the end of the hallway. Suite rooms are larger and include a private bathroom. The Commodore is very popular with hip young travelers, especially its coffee shop on the ground floor. Be aware that the Commodore is on a busy downtown corner, so if traffic noise will be a problem, bring earplugs.

Astoria has several motels that offer basic but clean rooms. Except on summer weekends, the following should have rooms available without reservations. On the eastern edge of Astoria, the **Crest Motel** (5366 Leif Erickson Dr./U.S. 30, 503/325-3141 or 800/421-3141, http://astoriacrestmotel.com, $66-112 depending on views) offers cliff-side river views, a coin-operated laundry, a whirlpool set in a gazebo overlooking the river, and pet-friendly rooms (with no extra fees). Two blocks from the West Mooring Basin and its charter docks, the **Astoria Dunes Motel** (288 W. Marine Dr., 503/325-7111 or 800/441-3319, http://astoriadunes-motel.com, $90-125) has an indoor heated pool and whirlpool tub. About 0.5 mile east of the Astoria-Megler Bridge, the **Rivershore Motel** (59 W. Marine Dr., 503/325-2921, www.astoriarivershoremotel.com, $75-100) has 43 rooms with coffeemakers, microwaves, refrigerators, and Internet access. Some rooms include kitchens.

A couple of blocks away from busy downtown streets, the **Rose River Inn B&B** (1510 Franklin Ave., 503/325-7175, www.roseriverinn.com, $95-150) offers two river-view suites and three guest rooms in a large cheerfully painted Victorian, decorated with European antiques and art and surrounded by a neatly tended garden. Each room includes a clawfoot tub, and the River Suite also has a Finnish sauna.

$100-150

Clementine's Bed and Breakfast (847 Exchange St., 800/521-6801, www.clementines-bb.com, $118-169, two-night min.), a handsome two-story home built in the Italianate style in 1888, stands in good company across the street from the Flavel House and is itself on Astoria's Historic Homes Walking Tour. From the gardens around the house come the fresh flowers that accent the guest rooms and common areas, as do the herbs that spice the delicious gourmet breakfasts. There are five rooms in the main house, all with feather beds and private bathrooms; upper-story rooms have private balconies with river views.

In addition to these guest rooms, two spacious sunny suites are available in the **Moose Temple Lodge** ($125-165), adjacent to the main house. Built in 1850, this is the oldest extant building in Astoria; it was the Moose Temple from 1900 to 1940 and later served as a Mormon church. Renovated with skylights, wood floors, fireplaces, small kitchens, and several beds, these are ideal for families or groups. Pets are welcome.

The **Benjamin Young Inn** (3652 Duane St., 503/325-6172, www.benjaminyounginn.com, $100-150) is an elegant 1888 Queen Anne-style mansion with four large guest rooms, all with private baths and great river views. The inn is in the eastern part of Astoria, away from the hubbub of downtown.

$150-200

Stay right downtown in the beautifully renovated **C Hotel Elliott** (357 12th St., 877/378-1924, www.hotelelliott.com, $149-259), a small boutique hotel that's an easy walk from good restaurants and the river. The Elliott first opened in 1924, and its current incarnation has preserved much of the original charm of its Craftsman-era details, including the mahogany-clad lobby, handcrafted cabinetry, and wood and marble fireplaces. An original banner painted across the hotel's north side proudly proclaims Hotel Elliott—Wonderful Beds. The new Elliott has made a point of living up to this claim, with goose-down pillows, luxurious 440-thread-count Egyptian cotton sheets, feather beds, and top-of-the-line mattresses to ensure a memorable slumber. In addition to standard rooms, the Elliott has a variety of suites, including the five-room Presidential Suite with access to a rooftop garden. The rooftop is open to all and is a fine place to enjoy a glass of wine and the sunset.

You can't top the views at the **Holiday Inn Express Hotel & Suites** (204 W. Marine Dr., 503/325-6222 or 888/898-6222, www.astoriahie.com, $180-200), directly under the Astoria-Megler Bridge. Guest rooms have a refrigerator, a microwave, a coffeemaker, a high-speed Internet connection, a TV, and a DVD player. Facilities include an indoor pool, a breakfast bar, a business center, and an exercise room. Pets are welcome.

Hampton Inn & Suites Astoria (201 39th St., 503/325-8888, $179-239) is Astoria's newest hotel and located east of downtown near Pier 39, so not really within walking distance of the city center. However, the Astoria Waterfront Trolley passes directly in front of the hotel, and you can ride it downtown and back during its operating season. The rooms are spacious and nicely furnished, and face directly onto the river. Amenities include a pool and business center, plus free breakfast.

Over $200

ⓒCannery Pier Hotel (10 Basin St., 503/325-4996 or 888/325-4996, www.cannerypierhotel.com, $269-350) is a modern luxury hotel on the former site of a historic cannery, jutting 600 feet out into the Columbia below the Astoria-Megler Bridge. The opulently furnished rooms have dramatic views, even from the shower; all

rooms have balconies, fireplaces, and beautiful hardwood floors. Complimentary continental breakfast is included in the rates, as are hors d'oeuvres and wine in the afternoon. There's also a day spa in the hotel, plus a Finnish sauna, a fitness room, and a hot tub.

Camping

Families flock to **Fort Stevens State Park** (100 Peter Iredale Rd., Hammond, reservations 800/452-5687, www.oregonstateparks.org, year-round, $21 tents, $27 RVs, $41 yurts, $86 cabins). With over 500 sites, the campground is the largest in the state park system, and it's incredibly popular. The park's many amenities and attractions make it the perfect base camp from which to take advantage of the region. Just be sure to avoid spring break (around Mar. 23-29) if you want to be spared the rites of spring enacted here by Oregon teenagers.

Across the road from the state park, **Astoria Warrenton Seaside KOA** (1100 NW Ridge Rd., Hammond, 503/861-2606 or 800/562-8506, www.astoriakoa.com, $25 tents, $38 RVs w/electric, $52 RVs full hookup, cabins $62 and up, $5 resort fee) is another sprawling campground. Amenities include an indoor pool and hot tub, a game room, miniature golf, and bike rentals.

FOOD

Over the years, Astoria has developed a reputation for excellent dining at fair prices. In addition to the restaurants and cafés listed here, you'll find do-it-yourself options at **Astoria's Sunday Market** on 12th Street between Marine Drive and Exchange Street and **Josephson's Smokehouse** (106 Marine Dr., 503/325-2190, www.josephsons.com, 9am-6pm Mon.-Sat.). A good stop for fresh produce, health food, and deli items is the **Astoria Co-op** (355 Exchange Street, 503/325-0027, 8am-8pm daily).

Astoria also features a number of food carts—there are several on both the east and west entrances to downtown. Most notable is **Bowfingers,** with really good fish-and-chips served out of a converted boat near the corner of Duane and 17th Streets.

Bakeries and Cafés

Stop by the **◖ Astoria Coffeehouse and Bistro** (245 11th St., 503/325-1787, 7am-9pm Sun.-Thurs., 7am-10pm Fri.-Sat., $13-22) for fresh breakfast pastries and coffee, salads and sandwiches, and home-cooked regional fare. It's an airy, friendly place to sit and read the paper, but if you're off to explore town, you can also just order a sandwich to go. In the evening, enjoy well-prepared comfort food such as meatloaf, cioppino, steak frites and Peruvian veggie stew.

At the collectively run **◖ Blue Scorcher Bakery Cafe** (1493 Duane St., 503/338-7473, 8am-5pm Mon.-Fri., 8am-4pm Sat.-Sun., $9), the motto is "joyful work, delicious food, and strong community," and it's all true. Settle in with a tasty veggie sandwich (if the tempeh Reuben is on the menu, don't turn up your nose at it) and watch the Astorians—any one of whom would make an excellent new friend—come and go. A personal favorite are cardamom almond rolls, an old-fashioned Swedish treat that's perfect with a cup of coffee on a brisk morning. A wide range of gluten-free pastries are offered on Friday. If it's all too healthy and wholesome for you, there's a brewpub next door.

American

A good, if rather standard, choice for families with kids, the Astoria outlet of **Pig 'N Pancake** (146 W. Bond St., 503/325-3144, 6am-9pm Sun.-Thurs., 6am-10pm Fri.-Sat., breakfast and lunch $7-10, dinner $10-18), a small north-coast chain (others are in Seaside and Cannon Beach), excels at big, filling breakfasts at reasonable prices. The specialty is homemade pancakes and waffles, available in a dozen variations, including potato pancakes, Swedish pancakes (thin and crispy with lingonberries), pecan-filled pancakes, and, of course, pigs in a blanket.

Eastern European

There aren't a lot of Bosnian restaurants around, and the **Drina Daisy** (915 Commercial St., 503/338-2912, www.drinadaisy.com, 11am-9pm Wed.-Sun., $11-23) is worth a stop to sample foods from an unfamiliar part of the world. The cuisine is a cross between Greek and Central European cooking. You can't go wrong with the appetizers or salads, many of which come with smoked sausages and filo-wrapped goodies.

Italian

For Astoria's top Italian food, go to **Fulio's Pastaria** (1149 Commercial St., 503/325-9001, 11am-close daily, $11-30) with excellent pasta, Tuscan-style steaks, and a good wine list in a lively and convivial dining room.

Mexican

There are a number of serviceable Mexican restaurants in Astoria (including, at last count, four food carts), but the locals' favorite is the hole-in-the-wall **Rio Café** (125 9th St., 503/325-2409, 11am-3pm Mon., 11am-8pm Tues.-Thurs., 11am-9pm Fri.-Sat., $10-18). Everything is fresh and made from scratch; the home-style cooking here packs more flavor than you'll find at many upscale Mexican restaurants.

Pacific Northwest

As widely appreciated as it is small, the **◖ Columbian Cafe** (1114 Marine Dr., 503/325-2233, 8am-2pm Mon.-Tues., 8am-2pm and 5pm-8pm Wed.-Thurs., 8am-2pm and 5pm-9pm Fri., 9am-2pm and 5pm-9pm Sat., 9am-2pm Sun., breakfast and lunch $7-10, dinner entrées $11-24) is where the meatless 1960s collides with Pacific Northwest cuisine. The menu changes according to season and the chef's whim (be daring and order the "chef's mercy") but generally includes a good selection of pastas, chilies, crepes, fresh catch of the day, and always a selection of homemade garlic, jalapeño, and red-pepper jellies. You may also enjoy the free-flowing political repartee with the staff and regulars in this cramped (several booths and a lunch counter) but friendly place. Breakfast is a highlight here. If this is your first visit to the Columbian Cafe, don't let the tiny, slightly seedy-looking venue put you off. Just barge in and take a seat—the servers will make you feel comfortable, and the rest is all culinary pleasure. Expect to be here for a while; the Columbian is not a quick in-and-out dining experience.

On downtown's most prominent corner, diagonally across from the Liberty Theatre, **Clemente's** (1198 Commercial St., 503/325-1067, 11am-3pm and 5pm-9pm Tues.-Sun., lunch $9-15, dinner entrées $16-26) serves fresh sustainably grown cuisine inspired by both the owner's Italian roots and the slow food movement. "From the Water" dishes include not only salmon but a tasty local albacore tuna and halibut. The restaurant's large windows and large paintings contribute to a sophisticated but casual atmosphere. A three-course prix fixe menu ($25) highlights whatever is fresh and local—a great value.

Another good restaurant with an inspiring motto ("Eat well, laugh often, and love much") is the easygoing **T. Paul's Urban Cafe** (1119 Commercial St., 503/338-5133, 11am-9pm Mon.-Sat., $9-19). The menu of hip diner food with fresh Pacific Northwest twists includes towering turkey sandwiches, bay shrimp ceviche, Caribbean jerk quesadillas, prawn pasta, and clam chowder. Quesadillas are the specialty, with about a dozen innovative varieties served. T. Paul's has a second downtown location, **《 The Supper Club** (360 12th St., 503/325-2545, 11am-9pm Mon.-Thurs., 11am-10pm Fri.-Sat., $12-28) with a wide-ranging menu, a rather swank dining room, and some of the most reliably delicious food in Astoria. Top choices are pasta dishes, burgers, salads, and fresh seafood. The tiny bar is the perfect spot for a cocktail.

Seafood

One of Astoria's more notable restaurants is **Silver Salmon Grille** (1105 Commercial St., 503/338-6640, 11am-9pm daily, $13-28) for fine dining in an atmosphere that's somewhat formal but not starchy. Attractive murals of the eponymous fish adorn the walls inside and out, and salmon takes pride of place on the dinner menu as well in a variety of preparations that

are fresh and cooked to perfection. Pasta dishes, seasonal seafood items such as razor clams, and several meat choices fill out the extensive menu. The wine list includes reasonably priced house wines made especially for the restaurant by Maryhill Winery in the Columbia Gorge. The bar here is one of the nicest in downtown Astoria, and it's a favorite of locals out on the town.

Settle in for some excellent seafood at **《 Bridgewater Bistro** (20 Basin St., 503/235-6777, 11am-close daily, $12-26), where you can graze on tapas (small plates menu 3pm-5pm), sample a four-course prix fixe meal ($45), or order regular-size or smaller entrées. The soaring ceiling and riverside setting of the historic building next to the Cannery Pier Hotel are almost as compelling as the food. (Note to long-time coast visitors: The Bridgewater is owned by the same folks who used to run the legendary Shoalwater Restaurant up on Washington's Long Beach Peninsula.)

At the end of 12th Street, directly overlooking the Columbia, **Baked Alaska** (1 12th St., 503/325-7414, 10am-11pm daily, $18-32) features a selection of small and large plates with modern, international inflections. Seared sea scallops are served with grilled peaches, shiso leaves, cider aioli and shaved hazelnuts, while prawn and Dungeness crab spaghettini comes with figs, capered brown butter, and fresh lovage. But about that name—yes, you can get baked Alaska here—the restaurant's twist on this classic dessert is basically a flaming ice cream sundae served on chocolate-chip cookies. The views rival the food, particularly in summer when there's deck seating. Baked Alaska now also operates a wood-fired pizzeria, and its pizzas are available in the dining room, bar, and to go.

Indian

《 Himani Indian Cuisine (1044 Marine Dr., 503/325-8171, www.himaniindian.com, 11am-3pm and 5pm-9pm Mon.-Fri., noon-3pm and 5pm-9pm Sat.-Sun, $9-20) serves a very wide selection of Indian cuisine, with a specialty in southern Indian dishes such as tandoori dishes (including tandoori salmon) and masala dosa. The naan breads are equally delicious. A buffet ($9) is available Monday-Friday for lunch, and also all day Sunday. Himani also serves food from its original stall at the Astoria Sunday Market.

Brewpubs

Astoria's oldest brewpub, the **Wet Dog Cafe** (144 11th St., 503/325-6975, 11am-9pm Sun.-Thurs., 11am-10pm Fri.-Sat., $9-20) is home to the Astoria Brewing Company, maker of excellent handcrafted microbrews. There's also a full bar and live music or entertainment Thursday-Saturday nights. The café is housed in a cavernous remodeled former waterfront warehouse, with good views of the river. The food is good basic pub grub: fish-and-chips, burgers (including seafood burgers), sandwiches, and salads.

The **Rogue Ales Public House** (100 39th St., 503/325-5964, 11am-10pm daily, $9-22) is east of downtown in the Hanthorn Pier development. The pub is set inside a wood-plank structure atop a former cannery pier and offers excellent ales plus burgers, pizza, and sandwiches. It's hard to get more Astorian than this. For beer snobs, the place to go is **Fort George Brewery and Public House** (1483 Duane St., 503/325-7468, www.fortgeorgebrewery.com, 11am-11pm Mon.-Thurs., 11am-midnight Fri.-Sat., noon-11pm Sun., $7-12), whose powerful ales have won it a reputation as one of Oregon's top breweries. The pub grub is a bit basic, but in 2013 a full-service restaurant opens on the pub's second floor. There's free live music every Sunday evening.

INFORMATION AND SERVICES

The **Astoria Chamber of Commerce** (111 W. Marine Dr., 503/325-6311 or 800/875-6807, www.oldoregon.com, 8am-6pm daily May-Sept., 9am-5pm Mon.-Fri. Oct.-Apr.) operates the Oregon Welcome Center at its offices, providing a plethora of brochures and maps for visitors to Astoria and other destinations on the north Oregon coast and southwest

© BILL MCRAE

jolly times at Fort George Brewery and Public House

Washington. The website has downloadable audio tours.

With 10,000 people, Astoria is the largest city and the media hub of the north coast. The local newspaper, the *Daily Astorian* (www.dailyastorian.com) is sold around town and worth a look if only to get the editorial slant of Steve Forrester. This former Washington correspondent's witty commentary on local, regional, and national events pulls no punches. The free monthly *Hipfish* is a publication in the great tradition of the alternative press of the 1960s. Whether you agree with its take on regional politics or not, the thoughtful and lively articles and complete entertainment listings will enhance your visit to the north coast.

Throughout the north coast, **KMUN** (91.9 FM in Astoria and Seaside, 89.5 FM in Cannon Beach) is a public radio station with excellent community-based programming. Folk, classical, jazz, and rock music, public affairs, radio drama, literature readings, children's bedtime stories, and National Public Radio news will keep your dial set on this frequency. A sister station, KCPB, broadcasts classical music in addition to NPR news.

The **Astoria Post Office** is located in the Federal Building at 750 Commercial Street. Useful numbers to know include the **county sheriff** (503/225-2061), the **Coast Guard** (2285 Airport Rd., Warrenton, 503/861-6220), and **Columbia Memorial Hospital** (2111 Exchange St., Astoria, 503/325-4321).

GETTING THERE AND AROUND

Amtrak Thruway Motorcoach Service (800/USA-RAIL or 800/872-7245, www.amtrak.com) runs two buses daily between the north coast and Portland Union Station. Board the coach in Astoria at the **Welcome Center** (111 W. Marine Dr.) or at the downtown transit center. After-hours tickets are available at the **Mini Mart** (95 W. Marine Dr., 503/325-4162). The bus stops on request at Seaside, Warrenton, and Gearhart.

Getting around Astoria can have its pitfalls for the unsuspecting. Potentially troublesome for visitors are the steep hills and the city's layout of seemingly random one-way streets. Holidays and summer weekends bring heavy traffic along U.S. 30, also known as Leif Erickson Drive (east end of town) and Marine Drive (center and west), Astoria's major traffic artery.

Car rentals are available from **Enterprise** (644 W. Marine Dr., 503/325-6500). For visitors willing to let go of their cars for a while, the Sunset Empire Transportation District, better known as **The Bus** (503/861-RIDE, 503/861-7433, or 800/776-6406, www.ridethebus.org, 40-60 min. Mon.-Sat.), provides reasonably frequent transportation around Astoria and along the coast to Warrenton, including to Gearhart, Seaside, and Cannon Beach, and the campgrounds at Fort Stevens State Park.

Seaside and Gearhart

Seaside is Oregon's quintessential, and oldest, family beach resort. The beach is long and flat, sheltered by a scenic headland, with lifeguards on duty during the summer months, beachside playground equipment, and a boardwalk winding through the dunes. Ice cream parlors, game arcades, eateries, and gift shops crowd shoulder to shoulder along the main drag, Broadway. The aromas of cotton candy and french fries lend a heady incense to the salt air, and the

clatter of bumper cars and other amusements can induce sensory overload. Atlantic City it's not—thank goodness—but on a crowded summer day the town evokes the feeling of a carnival midway by the sea. During spring break, when Pacific Northwest high school and college students arrive, the town's population of 6,200 can quadruple almost overnight.

South of town, the presence of clammers and waders in the shallows and surfers

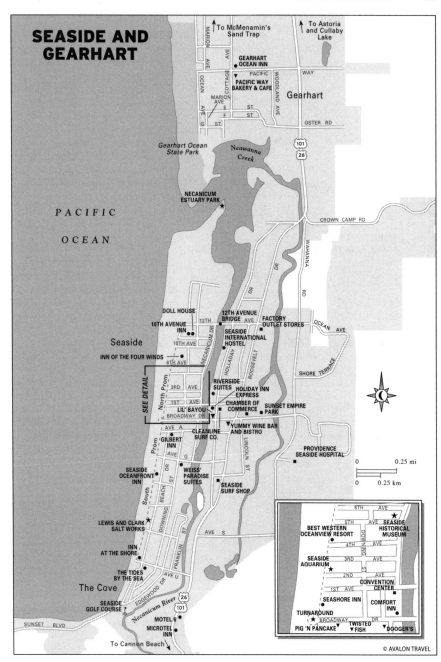

SEASIDE AND GEARHART

To McMenamin's Sand Trap

To Astoria and Cullaby Lake

GEARHART OCEAN INN

PACIFIC WAY BAKERY & CAFE

WAY

Gearhart

MARION AVE

OCEAN AVE

COTTAGE AVE

PACIFIC

WOODLAND AVE

MARION AVE

E ST

F ST

G ST

ST

ST

OSTER RD

101 26

PACIFIC

OCEAN

Gearhart Ocean State Park

Neawanna Creek

NECANICUM ESTUARY PARK

CROWN CAMP RD

WAHANNA DR

WAHANNA RD

DOLL HOUSE

10TH AVENUE INN

12TH

12TH AVENUE BRIDGE

AVE

FACTORY OUTLET STORES

Seaside

10TH AVE

SEASIDE INTERNATIONAL HOSTEL

NECANICUM DR

OCEAN AVE

INN OF THE FOUR WINDS

6TH AVE

HOLLADAY

ROOSEVELT

SHORE TERRACE

North Prom

3RD AVE

RIVERSIDE SUITES

HOLIDAY INN EXPRESS

SEE DETAIL

1ST AVE

LIL' BAYOU

BROADWAY DR

CHAMBER OF COMMERCE

SUNSET EMPIRE PARK

AVE A

YUMMY WINE BAR AND BISTRO

CLEANLINE SURF CO.

LINCOLN ST

PROVIDENCE SEASIDE HOSPITAL

Prom

GILBERT INN

AVE G

0   0.25 mi

0   0.25 km

South

BEACH DR

DOWNING DR

WEISS' PARADISE SUITES

SEASIDE OCEANFRONT INN

SEASIDE SURF SHOP

LEWIS AND CLARK SALT WORKS

FRANKLIN ST

AVE S

INN AT THE SHORE

THE TIDES BY THE SEA

AVE U

The Cove

SEASIDE GOLF COURSE

EDGEWOOD DR

Necanicum River

26 101

MOTEL 6

MICROTEL INN

SUNSET BLVD

To Cannon Beach

Detail

6TH AVE

5TH AVE

SEASIDE HISTORICAL MUSEUM

BEST WESTERN OCEANVIEW RESORT

4TH AVE

DOWNING

SEASIDE AQUARIUM

3RD AVE

2ND AVE

CONVENTION CENTER

1ST AVE

SEASHORE INN

COMFORT INN

TURNAROUND

BROADWAY DR

PIG 'N PANCAKE

TWISTED FISH

DOOGER'S

© AVALON TRAVEL

negotiating the swells also recalls the live-liness of a Southern California or Atlantic shorefront instead of the remote peacefulness of many Oregon beaches. East Coast visitors often liken Cannon Beach to Provincetown, Massachusetts, and Seaside to Coney Island, New York. Neighboring Gearhart, a mainly residential community (pop. 1,100) just to the north, has a few lodgings away from the bustle of Seaside as well as a venerable 18-hole golf course.

Located along the Necanicum River, in the shadow of majestic Tillamook Head, Seaside has attracted tourists since the early 1870s, when transportation magnate Ben Holladay sensed the potential for a resort hotel near the water. But better transportation was needed to get customers to the place. At that time, the way to get to Seaside was first by boat from Portland down the Columbia River to Skipanon (now Warrenton), and from there by carriage south to Seaside. To speed the connec-tion, Holladay later constructed a railroad line from Skipanon to Seaside.

To escape Portland's summer heat, fami-lies in the late 19th century would make the boat and railroad journey to spend their sum-mer in Seaside. Most men would go back to Portland to work during the week, return-ing to the coast on Friday to visit the family. Every weekend the families would gather at the railroad station to greet the men, then see them off again for the trip back to Portland. It wasn't long before the train became known as the "Daddy Train." As roads between Portland and the coast were constructed, the car took over, and the railroad carried its last dad in 1939.

In recent years, the town has become more than just a retreat for Portland families. Oregon's apostle of haute cuisine, the late James Beard, used to hold a celebrated cooking class here each summer. This opened the door for writers' retreats, art classes, and business con-ventions. If these occasions or a family outing should bring you to Seaside, you'll enjoy the spirit of fun if you don't mind plenty of com-pany on summer weekends.

SIGHTS
The Promenade and Broadway

Sightseeing in Seaside means bustling up and down Broadway and strolling leisurely along the Prom. This three-mile-long concrete walk-way, extending from Avenue U north to 12th Avenue, was initially constructed in 1908 to protect ocean properties from the waves. A pleasant walk alongside the beach, the board-walk offers a fine vantage point from which to contemplate the sand, surf, frolicking beach lovers, and the massive contours of 1,200-foot-high Tillamook Head to the south. The Prom is also popular for jogging, bicycle riding, and in-line skating.

Midway along the Prom is the **Turnaround,** a concrete-and-brick traffic circle that is the western terminus of Broadway. A bronze statue of Lewis and Clark gazing ever seaward pro-claims this point the end of the trail for their expedition, though in fact they explored a bit farther south, beyond Tillamook Head. Eight blocks south of the Turnaround, between Beach Drive and the Prom, is a replica of the Lewis and Clark salt cairn.

Heading east from the Turnaround, Broadway runs 0.5 mile to Roosevelt Avenue (U.S. 101) through a dizzying gamut of tourist attractions, arcades, restaurants, and bars. Along Broadway, in a four-block area west of U.S. 101 and bordered by the Necanicum River, 1st Avenue, and Avenue A, you'll find some fancy Victorian frame houses, a portion of the few old buildings that survived the 1912 fire that destroyed much of the town.

Today, the most notable sight in this busy section of Seaside is the enormous $73.3 mil-lion WorldMark Seaside (owned by Wyndham) time-share condo development containing nearly 300 units. Condos in this outsized structure aren't available for rent directly from Wyndham, though vacation property rental companies can handle sublets.

Seaside Historical Society Museum

If you tire of Broadway and the beach is

© BILL MCRAE

Pedal-powered surreys are popular on the Seaside Promenade.

too cold and wet, make your way to the **Seaside Historical Society Museum** (570 Necanicum Dr., 503/738-7065, www.seasidemuseum.org, 10am-4pm Mon.-Sat., noon-3pm Sun. late Mar.-Oct., noon-3pm Mon.-Sat., noon-3pm Sun. Nov.-late Mar.; $3 adults, $2 seniors, $1 students), housed in a classic seaside cottage six blocks north of Broadway, where Clatsop artifacts and exhibits on early tourism in Seaside impart more of a sense of history than anything else in town.

Seaside Aquarium

Right on the Prom north of the Turnaround is the **Seaside Aquarium** (200 N. Prom, 503/738-6211, 9am-7pm daily Mar.-Oct., 9am-5pm Wed.-Sun. Nov.-Feb., $7.50 adults, $6.25 seniors, $3.75 children ages 6-13). It's not quite the Oregon Coast Aquarium (find that in Newport), but if you're not going to make it that far south, it's an okay introduction to sealife for young children. Back in the era of the Daddy Train, this place served

as a natatorium but was converted to its current use in 1937. Today the pool is filled with raucously barking seals. In addition, a hundred species of marine life here include 20-ray sea stars, crabs, ferocious-looking wolf eels and moray eels, and octopuses.

Lewis and Clark Salt Works

Near the south end of the Prom at Lewis and Clark Way are the reconstructed salt works of Lewis and Clark. While camped at Fort Clatsop during the winter of 1805-1806, the captains sent a detachment south to find a place suitable for rendering salt from seawater. Their supply was nearly exhausted, and the precious commodity was a necessity for preserving and seasoning their food on the expedition's return journey. At the south end of present-day Seaside, five men built a cairn-like stone oven near a settlement of the Clatsop and Killamox people and set about boiling seawater nonstop for seven weeks to produce 3.5 bushels (about 314 pounds) of salt for the trip back east.

SPORTS AND RECREATION
Bicycling
Seaside has a bumper crop of places that rent bicycles, skates, and surreys, all for similar rates, about $10 per hour for a bike. The **Prom Bike Shop** (622 12th Ave., 503/738-8251, http://prombikeshop.com, 10:30am-5:30pm daily) is a full-service bike shop; rent cruisers or novelty bikes at **Wheel Fun Rentals Spoke 1** (21 N. Columbia St., 503/717-4337, 9am-sunset daily) or **Wheel Fun Rentals Spoke 2** (151 Ave. A, 503/738-7212, 9am-sunset daily).

Boating and Fishing
Just because you're smack-dab in the middle of a family resort town doesn't mean you can't enjoy some of nature's bounty; anglers can reel in trout, salmon, and steelhead from the Necanicum River right in the center of downtown. The **12th Avenue Bridge** is a popular spot for fishing and crabbing.

Cullaby Lake, on the east side of U.S. 101 about four miles north of Gearhart, offers fishing for crappies, bluegills, perch, catfish, and largemouth bass. At 88 acres, Cullaby is the largest of the many lakes on the Clatsop Plains. Two parks on the lake, **Carnahan Park** and **Cullaby Lake County Park,** have boat ramps, picnic areas, and other facilities. Cullaby is the only practical place to water-ski in the area.

A half mile west of Highway 101, **Sunset Beach Park** on Neacoxie Lake (also known as Sunset Lake) has a boat ramp, picnic tables, and a playground. Anglers come for warm-water fish species, plus the rainbow trout stocked in the spring. From Astoria, drive south 10 miles on Highway 101 and turn west on Sunset Beach Road.

At **Quatat Park** (503/440-1548), beside the Necanicum River in downtown Seaside, rent kayaks, canoes, and pedal boats for exploring the waterway.

Golf
Golfers can escape to public courses south of Seaside and north in the small town of Gearhart. At **Seaside Golf Club** (451 Ave. U,

503/738-5261), greens fees are $15-17 for nine holes. The **Highlands at Gearhart** (1 Highland Rd., Gearhart, 503/738-5248, www.highlandsgolfgearhart.com, $16 for nine holes) is another public nine-hole course, with ocean views from most holes. The British-links-style course at **Gearhart Golf Links** (1157 N. Marion St., Gearhart, 503/738-3538, www.gearhartgolflinks.com, $65-75 for 18 holes in summer) was established in 1882, making it one of the oldest on the West Coast and Oregon's oldest.

Hiking
From the south end of Seaside, walk in the footsteps of Lewis and Clark on an exhilarating hike over Tillamook Head. In January 1806, neighboring Native Americans told of a beached whale lying several miles south of their encampment. William Clark and a few companions, including Sacajawea, set off in an attempt to find it and trade for blubber and whale oil, which fueled the expedition's lanterns. Climbing Tillamook Head from the north, the party crested the promontory. Clark was moved enough by the view to later write about it in his journal:

> I beheld the grandest and most pleasing prospect which my eyes ever surveyed. Immediately in front of us is the ocean breaking in fury. To this boisterous scene the Columbia with its tributaries and studded on both sides with the Chinook and Clatsop villages forms a charming contrast, while beneath our feet are stretched the rich prairies.

They eventually found the whale, south of Tillamook Head. Ecola Point and State Park here are named for it, after the Chinook word for whale, *ecola* or *ekkoli.* By the time Clark arrived, however, the whale had been reduced to little more than a skeleton by the industrious Tillamooks, who used every part of the beast that they could harvest. Clark measured the leviathan at 105 feet, which, if accurate, could only mean it was a blue whale, the largest animal on earth and an extraordinary windfall for the Native Americans. He found the

Tillamooks busily engaged in boiling the blubber in a large wooden trough by means of hot stones. The oil, when extracted, was stored in bladders. He had to bargain hard for a share, and he wrote this of the negotiations:

> The Tillamooks, although they possessed large quantities of this blubber and oil, were so penurious that they disposed of it with great reluctance, and in small quantities only; insomuch that my utmost exertions, aided by the party, with the small stock of merchandise I had taken with me, were not able to procure more blubber than about 300 pounds and a few gallons of oil. Small as this stock is, I prize it highly; and thank Providence for directing the whale to us; and think Him much more kind to us than He was to Jonah having sent this monster to be swallowed by us, instead of swallowing of us, as Jonah's did.

Today, you can experience the view that so impressed Clark on the **Tillamook Head National Recreation Trail,** which runs seven miles through Ecola State Park. Prior to setting out, you could arrange to have a friend drive south to Indian Beach to pick you up at the end of this three- to five-hour trek (or you can be picked up another mile south at the Ecola Point parking lot). As you head up the forested trail on the north side of Tillamook Head, look back over the Seaside town site. In about 20 minutes, you'll be gazing down at the ocean from cliffs 1,000 feet above. A few hours later, you'll hike down onto Indian Beach.

To get to the trailhead from Seaside, drive south, following Avenue U past the golf course to Edgewood Street, and turn left; continue until you reach the parking lot at the end of the road.

Surfing

The best surfing spot in the Seaside area is the beach just south of town simply referred to as **The Cove,** directly north of Tillamook Head and reached from parking areas along Sunset Boulevard. While prevailing winds favor winter surfing rather than summer, this is in fact a popular destination year-round. Local surfers can be impatient with beginners, so this probably isn't a good spot for novices.

Seaside Surf Shop (1116 S. Roosevelt Dr., 503/717-1110, www.seasidesurfshop.com, 10am-6pm Mon.-Fri., 9am-6pm Sat., 9am-5pm Sun.) and **Cleanline Surf Co.** (60 N. Roosevelt Dr., 503/738-2061, www.cleanline-surf.com, 9am-6pm Mon.-Sat., 10am-6pm Sun.) rent and sell surfboards as well as wetsuits, boots, and flippers; Cleanline Surf also offers instruction. **Northwest Women's Surf Camps** (503/440-5782, www.nwwomenssurf-camps.com) will give you a bit of land training (the camp includes yoga to get you limbered up and in the right frame of mind) and then accompany you into the waves.

Swimming

Despite the lifeguard on duty in summer, swimming at Seaside's beach isn't the most comfortable, unless you're used to the North Sea. Gearhart boasts a quieter beach than Seaside's, although the water is every bit as cool. Warm-blooded swimmers can head to the facilities at **Sunset Empire Park** (1140 E. Broadway, Seaside, 503/738-3311, open daily), which includes three pools, waterslides, a 15-person hot tub, and fitness equipment.

Wildlife-Watching

Bird-watchers gather at **Necanicum Estuary Park,** at the 1900 block of North Holladay Drive across the street from Seaside High School. Local students have built a viewing platform, stairs to the beach, a boardwalk, and interpretive signs. Great blue and green herons and numerous migratory bird species flock to the grassy marshes and slow tidal waters near the mouth of the Necanicum River. During the fall and winter, buffleheads and mergansers shelter in the estuary, while in summer the waters are often thronged with pelicans. Occasionally, Roosevelt elk, black-tailed deer, river otters, beavers, mink, and muskrats can also be sighted.

ENTERTAINMENT AND EVENTS

Seaside predates any other town on the Oregon coast as a place built with good times in mind. A zoo and racetrack were among Seaside's first structures, and arcades are still thriving near the foot of Broadway. **Cannes Cinema** (U.S. 101 at 12th Ave.) is a five-screen multiplex showing first-run films.

The annual **Oregon Dixieland Jubilee** (800/738-6894, www.jazzseaside.com) takes place at the end of February. This event has been gaining momentum for more than 25 years and appeals to fans of Dixieland and traditional jazz. The town celebrates the **Fourth of July** with a parade, a picnic and social at the Seaside Historical Society Museum (570 Necanicum Dr.), and a big fireworks show on the beach.

In early September, **Wheels and Waves** (503/717-1914) brings over 500 classic hot rods and custom cars (1962 and earlier, please) to downtown and the **Civic and Convention Center** (1st Ave. at Necanicum Dr.).

SHOPPING

Seaside is a shopping hub not only for its own population but also for Cannon Beach, which oddly doesn't even have a real grocery store, let alone a shopping mall. A number of shopping centers line U.S. 101 as it passes through Seaside; the **Seaside Factory Outlet Center** (1111 N. Roosevelt Dr., 503/717-1603) has 25 discount stores, including outlets for Eddie Bauer and Nike.

ACCOMMODATIONS

Whatever your price range, you'll have to reserve ahead for a room in Seaside during the summer and on weekends and holidays (especially spring break). If you do, chances are you'll be able to find the specs you're looking for, given the area's array of lodgings and over 1,800 hotel rooms. The **Seaside Visitors Bureau's** helpful website (www.seasideor.com) provides comprehensive listings.

Generally speaking, there are three lodging areas in Seaside. First, there are several modern motels along busy U.S. 101, about eight blocks from the beach. If you're just passing through or waited too long to call for reservations, these offer inexpensive rooms, but little in the way of beachside charm. A second grouping of hotels is in the center of Seaside, along the Necanicum River. These have a quieter riverside setting but still aren't beachfront (though you won't have to cross U.S. 101 to get to the beach). Finally, there are numerous hotels that face directly onto the beach or are just a short stumble to the strand. Even here, there's quite a difference in price between rooms that face the beach and those that face the parking lot.

Under $50

The cheapest place in town is the quite nice **Seaside International Hostel** (930 N. Holladay Dr., 503/738-7911 or 888/994-0001, www.seasidehostel.net, dorm-style bunk $29 pp, private rooms $69), with special touches such as morning meditation and exercise classes. Unlike many hostels, it doesn't close down during the day and there's no curfew at night. There's an espresso bar on-site, and the Necanicum River runs through the backyard. Close by is the Necanicum Estuary Park.

$50-100

Out along U.S. 101 are two motels that provide good value and new rooms, but most people wouldn't consider them walking distance to the beach. **Motel 6** (2369 S. Roosevelt Dr., 503/738-6269 or 800/466-8356, $86-106), on U.S. 101 about 0.5 mile south of Broadway, isn't near the sand but does offer reasonably priced rooms. Just south is **Microtel Inns & Suites** (2455 S. Roosevelt Dr., 503/482-7666 or 866/482-7666, $96-136), with free breakfast waffles, free high-speed Internet, and guest laundry. These two motels on the southern entry to Seaside are closest to Cannon Beach.

$100-150

There's a clutch of motels south of the Broadway-Prom axis that offer easy beach access at fair prices—and a much quieter beachfront experience than town center. **The Tides**

by the Sea (2316 Beach Dr., 503/738-6317 or 800/548-2846, www.thetidesbythesea. com, $107-204) is an older motel that has converted its large guest rooms and cottages into condos. About a quarter of the units face onto the Prom, but those that don't are just seconds away from the beach. If you can live without an ocean view, you'll save a bundle here. Each of the units is different, but most have kitchens and fireplaces. In high season, there is a two-night minimum stay policy.

The rooms at **Seashore Inn** (60 N. Prom, 503/738-6368 or 888/738-6368, www.seashoreinnor.com, $129-229) are right in the thick of it along the Promenade. Half the guest rooms face the beach, but half don't. These rooms are just steps from the beach but are a fraction of the cost of rooms on the other side of the building. All guest rooms have microwaves and mini-refrigerators, and some have full kitchens and balconies. There's also an indoor pool in case the weather turns foul.

While motels dominate the lodging scene in Seaside, a few B&Bs and small inns offer an alternative. The **Gilbert Inn** (341 Beach Dr., 503/738-9770 or 800/410-9770, www.gilbertinn.com, $119-169) is a well-preserved 1892 Queen Anne just a block south of Broadway and a block from the beach. Period furnishings adorn the 10 guest rooms, which all have private bathrooms, down comforters, and other nice touches (though this seems like a classic B&B, no breakfast is served). The third-floor "Garret" sleeps up to four in a queen and two twin beds, with ocean views from the dormer window.

North of Broadway, the **10th Avenue Inn** (125 10th Ave., 503/738-0643 or 800/745-2378, www.10aveinn.com, $115-135) is a comfortable 1908 home built just a few steps from the beach. In the parlor a baby grand piano, a guitar, and other instruments are available for musically inclined guests. The three guest rooms have king-size beds, attached bathrooms, TVs, and small refrigerators. Next door and operated by the same folks is the **Doll House,** a sweet two-bedroom cottage ideal for four adults plus two or three children, with a

full kitchen and a deck with a barbecue grill. It goes for $890 per week in summer (minimum 1-week rental), and $160 per night off-season (2-night minimum).

Just north of the Necanicum River's mouth, Gearhart offers a respite from the bustle of Seaside. The ❰ **Gearhart Ocean Inn** (67 N. Cottage St., 503/738-7373, www.gearhartoceaninn.com, $145-240) offers a choice of 12 New England-style wooden cottages with comforters, wicker chairs, and throw rugs, and the beaches are a short walk away. The two-story deluxe units have kitchens and hardwood floors. Pets are allowed in some units. Especially during the off-season, this spruced-up old motor court is one of the best values on the north coast.

A charmingly refurbished lodging just three short blocks from the beach, ❰ **Weiss' Paradise Suites** (741 S. Downing St., 503/738-6691 or 800/738-6691, www.seasidesuites.com, $130-160) is south of the Broadway action but offers homey, recently upgraded units with lots of extras, including full kitchens, decks, two TVs, free DVDs, and robes. One-, two-, and three-bedroom suites are available.

$150-200

Well south of the bustling Broadway scene, the **Inn at the Shore** (2275 S. Prom, 503/738-3113 or 800/713-9914, www.innattheshore. com, $179-289) has nicely appointed rooms, each with a gas fireplace, a balcony, a wet bar, a microwave, a coffeemaker, a refrigerator, a flat-screen TV, and a DVD/VCR.

The four-story, shingle-sided **Seaside Oceanfront Inn** (581 S. Prom, 503/319-3300 or 800/772-7766, https://theseasideinn.com, $150-250) stands right on the beach, with its north gable skewered by a clock tower. Each of the 14 guest rooms is decorated in a unique theme—the clock tower room has a huge round bed in the center of the room, but other than that, they're pretty tasteful. Most have a spectacular ocean view, and pets are permitted in certain rooms. The on-site restaurant is very good.

Seaside's most stylish rooms are at the **(Inn of the Four Winds** (820 N. Prom, 503/738-9524 or 800/818-9524, www.innofthefourwinds.com, $129-259). This 14-room boutique hotel has very comfortable rooms furnished with taste and panache. Each guest room has a microwave, a coffeemaker, a refrigerator, a DVD player, a gas fireplace, and a deck or balcony with an ocean view. Best of all, the inn faces directly onto the beach eight blocks north of the frenetic Broadway strip.

In the center of Seaside, with balconies over the Necanicum River, the **Holiday Inn Express Hotel Suites Seaside Convention Center** (34 Holladay Dr., 503/717-8000, $171-235) has an indoor pool and spa, wireless high-speed Internet access, and rooms with fridges, microwaves, coffeemakers, and CD and DVD players. Rates include a complimentary breakfast bar.

Best Western Oceanview Resort (414 N. Prom, 503/738-3264 or 800/234-8439, www.oceanviewresort.com, $169-229) is a large hotel right on the beach near the center of town. Amenities include an on-site restaurant and lounge, a heated pool, and a spa; the majority of rooms face the ocean.

In the center of Seaside, right on the Necanicum River, the **Rivertides Suites** (102 N. Holladay Dr., 877/871-8433, www.rivertidesuites.com, $149-199) offers some of the most upscale accommodations in Seaside. All rooms have balconies, full kitchens, fine linens, and jetted tubs, plus complimentary breakfast, indoor pool and hot tub, exercise room, and great views from the rooftop viewing deck. In addition to the entry-level studio suites, there are also one- and two-bedroom suites.

Vacation Rentals

A good option for many travelers is one of the several dozen vacation rentals; options range from tiny cottages at less than $100 per night (minimum stays are often required, especially in summer) to large homes that can host groups of 10-12. Check with the **Seaside Visitors Bureau** (7 N. Roosevelt St., 503/738-3097 or 888/306-2326, www.seasideor.com, 8am-5pm

daily), or contact one of the rental agencies: **Beachhouse Vacation Rentals** (503/738-9068, www.beachhouse1.com), **Oceanside Vacation Rental** (503/738-7767 or 800/840-7764, www.oceanside1.com), or **Northwind Vacation Rentals** (503/738-5532 or 866/738-5532, www.northwindrentals.com).

Camping

One mile south of Seaside in a lush green meadow is **Circle Creek RV Park and Campground** (85658 U.S. 101, 503/738-6070, www.circlecreekrv.com, mid-Mar.-Oct., tents $24, RVs $40). The campground offers showers, a small store, picnic tables, and fire rings.

FOOD

While a stroll down Broadway might have you thinking that cotton candy, corn dogs, and saltwater taffy are the staples of Seaside cuisine, several eateries here can satisfy more refined palates as well.

American

If you're traveling with kids, you'll almost inevitably end up eating at **Pig 'N Pancake** (323 Broadway, 503/738-7243, 6am-9pm Sun.-Thurs., 6am-10pm Fri.-Sat., breakfast and lunch $7-10, dinner $10-18), where the Swedish pancakes and crab-and-cheese omelets are tops at breakfast, and the Frisbee-size cinnamon rolls will launch your blood sugar to new heights.

Cajun

A rarity in these parts, **(Lil' Bayou** (20 N. Holladay Dr., 503/717-0624, 5pm-9pm Wed.-Mon., $15-20) dishes up authentic muffulettas, jambalaya, blackened catfish, gumbo, and a host of other Cajun and Creole standards, right down to side dishes of collard greens, at reasonable prices. Finish off with a slice of sweet potato pecan pie or Aunt B's cheesecake.

Pacific Northwest

Maggie's (581 S. Prom, 503/738-6403, 8am-10:30am, 11am-3pm, 5pm-9pm daily, breakfast $3-10, lunch $7-12, dinner $17-20), tucked away in the Seaside Oceanfront Inn, serves carefully prepared meals, with dinners that include simple pasta dishes and a number of seafood choices such as hazelnut-crusted halibut and salmon burgers.

Should the frenetic ambience of Seaside on a holiday weekend begin to wear thin, try the 🄲 **Pacific Way Bakery and Cafe** in Gearhart (601 Pacific Way, 503/738-0245, bakery 7am-1pm Thurs.-Mon., restaurant 11am-3:30pm, 5pm-9pm Thurs.-Mon., dinner $10-30, dinner reservations recommended). Pasta, crusty pizzas, and seafood dishes (including thick seafood cioppino) as well as Dungeness crab sandwiches with aioli pop up at lunch and dinner. Rib eye steak and local razor clams are other frequent dinnertime highlights in the surprisingly urbane little café hidden behind a rustic old storefront. In the morning, the bakery side of the operation is *the* place to be for coffee and pastries.

Right in the heart of busy Broadway, **Twisted Fish** (311 Broadway, 503/738-3467, 11am-10pm daily, $10-30) is a Pacific Northwest-style steakhouse, with hand-cut steaks, fresh fish and seafood, pasta and Mediterranean-inflected dishes such as chicken and prawn picatta. All bread and desserts are made in-house; live music is offered on weekend evenings.

Seafood
Dooger's (505 Broadway, 503/738-3773, 11am-9pm daily, $11-20), which also has an outlet in Cannon Beach, is a popular Broadway mainstay known for its clam chowder. Although it's kind of a frumpy-looking place, it serves good seafood. Local clams and oysters, fresh Dungeness crab legs, sautéed shrimp, and marionberry cobbler are also the basis of Dooger's reputation.

Brewpubs and Wine Bars
Although Seaside isn't generally considered to be a hip town (hipsters, Astoria is your place), and in spite of its silly name, 🄲 **Yummy Wine Bar and Bistro** (831 Broadway, 503/738-3100, 3pm-10pm Thurs.-Mon., $17-23) has the right vibe of comfortable nonintimidating hipness mixed with good food, wine, art, and occasional live music. Order an assortment of small plates, such as ahi tuna tartare ($10) or prawn bruschetta ($13), or a full meal; happy hour runs 3pm-6pm and includes some small appetizers and good deals on house wine.

At the Gearhart Golf Links, the old clubhouse now houses **McMenamins Sand Trap** (1157 N. Marion Ave., 503/717-8150, 11am-10pm Mon.-Tues., 11am-11pm Wed.-Thurs., 11am-midnight Fri., 8am-midnight Sat., 8am-10pm Sun., $7-27); it has been decorated with the McMenamins' trademark whimsical artwork and serves the local chain's decent (not great, but always edible) upscale pub food.

INFORMATION AND SERVICES
The **Seaside Visitors Bureau** (7 N. Roosevelt St., 503/738-3097 or 888/306-2326, www.seasideor.com) is open 8am-5pm daily. **Providence Seaside Hospital** (725 S. Wahanna Rd., 503/717-7000) has 24-hour service and an emergency room.

GETTING THERE
Sunset Empire Transportation District operates **The Bus** (503/861-RIDE, 503/861-7433, or 800/776-6406, www.ridethebus.org) serving Cannon Beach, Seaside, Astoria-Warrenton, and points in between. **Amtrak** (800/872-7245, www.amtrak.com) throughway buses pass through twice daily on their run between Portland and Astoria.

Cannon Beach and Vicinity

In 1846, the USS *Shark* met its end on the Columbia River Bar. The ship broke apart, and a section of deck bearing cannons and an iron capstan drifted south, finally in 1894 washing ashore south of the current city limits at Arch Cape. And so this town got its name, which it adopted in 1922. In the winter of 2008, during an especially low tide, two additional cannons were revealed. Although their provenance has not been verified, they're also thought to be from the *Shark*. Although they are currently being cleaned and studied at Texas A&M University, these cannons are expected to end up at the Astoria maritime museum.

In 1873, stagecoach and railroad tycoon Ben Holladay helped create Oregon's first coastal tourist mecca, Seaside, while ignoring its attractive neighbor in the shadow of Haystack Rock. In the 20th century, Cannon Beach evolved into a bohemian alternative to the hustle and bustle of the family-oriented resort scene to the north. Before the recent era of development, this place was a quaint backwater attracting laid-back artists, summer home residents, and the overflow from Seaside.

Today, the low-key charm and atmosphere conducive to artistic expression have in some part been quashed by development and the attendant massive visitor influx and price increases. While such vital signs as a first-rate theater, a good bookstore, cheek-by-jowl art galleries, and fine restaurants are still in ample evidence, your view of them from the other side of the street might be blocked by a convoy of Winnebagos.

Nonetheless, the broad three-mile stretch of beach dominated by the impressive monolith of Haystack Rock still provides a contemplative experience. And if you're patient and resourceful enough to find a space for your wheels (try the free municipal lot one block east of the main street), the finest gallery-hopping, crafts, and shopping on the coast await. The city is small enough for strolling, and its location removed from U.S. 101 spares it the kind of traffic blight seen on the main drags of other coastal tourist towns.

Wood shingles and understated earth tones dominate the architecture of tastefully rendered galleries, bookstores, and bistros. Throngs of walkers along Hemlock Street, the main drag, also distinguish this burg from the typical coastal strip town whose heart and soul have been pierced by U.S. 101.

SIGHTS
◖ Haystack Rock

Haystack Rock looms large above the long, broad beach. This is the third-highest sea stack in the state, measuring 235 feet high. As part of the Oregon Islands National Wildlife Refuge, it has wilderness status and is off limits to climbing. Puffins and other seabirds nest on its steep faces, and intertidal organisms thrive in the tidepools around the base. The surrounding tidepools, within a radius of 300 yards from the base of the monolith, are designated a "marine garden"; they are open to exploration, but with strict no-collecting (of anything) and no-harassment (of any living organisms) protections in effect. Flanking the mountain are two rock formations known as the Needles. These spires had two other counterparts at the turn of the 20th century that have gradually been leveled by weathering and erosion. Old-timers will tell you that the government dynamited a trail to the top of Haystack in 1968 to keep people off this bird rookery. It also reduced the number of intrepid hikers trapped on the rock at high tide.

Volunteers from the **Haystack Rock Awareness Program** (503/436-1581) are often on the beach with displays, spotting scopes, and answers to many of your questions. Spend some time chatting with these folks, but don't forget to listen to the beach's own distinctive voices. You can't miss the cacophony of seabirds at sunset and, if you listen closely, the

winter phenomenon of "singing sands" created by wind blowing over the beach.

Beach access is available at the west end of any public east-west street. From downtown, Harrison Street works well; south of downtown, Tolovana Beach Wayside has a large parking area and easy beach access.

Cannon Beach History Center

Permanent exhibits at the small **Cannon Beach History Center** (1387 S. Spruce St., 503/436-9301, www.cbhistory.org, 11am-5pm Thurs.-Mon., free) chronicle the town's timeline, from prehistory to the modern expansion of tourism and recreation. The original eponymous cannon (the one found in 1894) from the ill-fated *Shark* is also on display here.

Ecola State Park

Ecola State Park (off U.S. 101, 800/551-6949, www.oregonstateparks.org, $5 day-use fee) is two miles north of Cannon Beach. Thick conifer forests line the access road to Ecola Point. This forested cliff has many trails leading down to the water. The view south takes in Haystack Rock and the overlapping peaks of the Coast Range extending to Neahkahnie Mountain. This is one of the most photographed views on the coast. Out to sea, the sight of sea lions basking on surf-drenched rocks (mid-Apr.-July) or migrating gray whales (Dec. and Mar.) and orcas (May) is seasonal highlights.

From Ecola Point, trails lead north to horseshoe-shaped **Indian Beach,** a favorite with surfers. Some prefer to drive the steep narrow road down to Indian Beach as a prelude to hiking up Tillamook Head, considered by Lewis and Clark the region's most beautiful viewpoint. The 2.5-mile Clatsop Loop Trail begins and ends at Indian Beach and climbs through Sitka spruce to a viewpoint. Ambitious hikers can do the first half of the loop, then continue another four miles north to Seaside.

The name Ecola means "whale" in Chinook and was first used as a place-name by William Clark, referring to a creek in the area. Lewis and Clark journals note a 105-foot beached whale found somewhere within present-day

© BILL MCRAE

Haystack Rock

Ecola Park's southern border at Crescent Beach. This area represents the southernmost extent of Lewis and Clark's coastal Oregon travels.

◖ Saddle Mountain State Natural Area

A good reason to head east from Cannon Beach is the hike up 3,283-foot Saddle Mountain at **Saddle Mountain State Natural Area** (off U.S. 26, 800/551-6949, www.oregonstateparks.org). On a clear day, hikers can see some 50 miles of the Oregon and Washington coastlines, including the Columbia River. Also possible are spectacular views of Mounts Rainier, St. Helens, and Hood, and miles of clear-cuts. On the upper part of the trail, plant species that pushed south from Alaska and Canada during the last ice age still thrive. The cool, moist climate here keeps them from dying out as they did at lower elevations. Some early blooms include pink coast fawn lily, monkeyflower, wild rose, wood violet, bleeding heart, oxalis, Indian paintbrush, and trillium. Cable handrails

provide safety on the narrow final 0.25-mile trail to the summit.

To get to the trailhead, take U.S. 26 from its junction with U.S. 101 for 10 miles and turn left on the prominently signed Saddle Mountain Road. (Although it's paved, this road is not suitable for RVs or wide-bodied vehicles.) After seven twisting miles, you'll come to the trailhead of the highest peak in this part of the Coast Range. The trail itself is steep and gains more than 1,600 feet in 2.5 miles. Wet conditions can make the going difficult (allow four hours round-trip) and the scenery en route is not always exceptional unless you look down for the lovely May-August wildflower display; the view from the top is worth the climb.

The campground ($5-10) at Saddle Mountain is tiny and rustic and offers a secluded option for campers not attracted to the busy family scene at nearby Fort Stevens State Park.

Beaches

Stunning beaches don't end with Cannon

Beach. Sandy expanses stretch seven miles south to the Arch Cape tunnel on U.S. 101, indicating the entrance to Oswald West State Park. Several of these beaches are reached via state park waysides. As you head south, views of **Hug Point State Recreation Site** (off U.S. 101, 800/551-6949, www.oregonstateparks. org) and pristine beaches will have you ready to pull over. In summer, this can be a good escape from the crowds at Cannon Beach. Time your visit to coincide with low tide, when all manner of marine life will be exposed in tidal pools. Also at low tide, you may see remains of an 800-foot-long Model T-sized road blasted into the base of Hug Point, an early precursor to U.S. 101. The cliffs are gouged with caves and crevasses that also invite exploring, but be mindful of the tides so that you don't find yourself stranded. Hug Point got its name in the days when stagecoaches used the beach as highways; they had to dash between the waves, hugging the jutting headland to get around.

SPORTS AND RECREATION
Bicycling
Mike's Bike Shop (248 N. Spruce St., Cannon Beach, 503/436-1266, 10am-6pm Thurs.-Tues., $8-12 per hour) rents mountain bikes, road bikes, beach cruisers, and three-wheeled recumbent "fun cycles," which zip up and down the hard-packed sand when the tide is out. Mike, who has run this shop since 1974, is a good guy who can help you figure out how to travel the coast car-free.

Horseback Riding
Sea Ranch Stables (415 Old U.S. 101, 503/436-2815, 9am-4:30pm daily mid-June-Labor Day, 9am-4:30pm weekends mid-May-mid-June, $70-130), at the north entrance to Cannon Beach off U.S. 101, offers a number of one- to two-hour guided rides, including night rides. Rides to Haystack Rock start at 9am, before the beach gets crowded.

Surfing
The area around Cannon Beach has several good surfing beaches. The most popular, and the best bet for beginners, is **Short Sands Beach,** at the end of the trail to the beach at Oswald West State Park, south of Arch Cape. It's a bit of a hike down to the beach, but the sheltered cove is a great place to spend the day, even if you're just bobbing around in the waves.

Another good spot for somewhat more advanced surfers (and surf kayakers) is **Indian Beach,** at **Ecola State Park** (off U.S. 101, 800/551-6949, www.oregonstateparks.org, $5 day-use fee). Up the road in Seaside, locals tend to control the surf breaks—if you're good enough to fit in, give it a go.

Rent a board and wetsuit at **Cleanline Surf** (171 Sunset Blvd., 503/436-9726).

ENTERTAINMENT AND EVENTS
Going strong since 1972, the **Coaster Theatre Playhouse** (108 N. Hemlock St., 503/436-1242, www.coastertheatre.com, $15-23) stages a varied bill of musicals, dramas, mysteries, comedies, concerts, and other entertainment. It's open year-round, in a building that started in the 1920s as a skating rink-turned-silent-movie house.

The half dozen or so other sand-sculpting contests that take place on the Oregon coast pale in comparison to Cannon Beach's annual **Sandcastle Day** (503/436-2623, call to confirm dates). In 1964 a tsunami washed out a bridge, and the isolated residents of Cannon Beach organized the first contest as a way to amuse their children. Now in its fifth decade, this is the state's oldest and most prestigious competition of its kind. Tens of thousands of spectators show up to watch 1,000-plus competitors fashion their sculptures with the aid of buckets, shovels, squirt guns, and any natural material found on the beach. The resulting sculptures are often amazingly complex and inventive. This event is free to spectators, but entrants pay a fee. Recent winners included Egyptian pyramids and a gigantic sea turtle. This collapsible art show usually coincides with the lowest-tide Saturday in June and takes place north of Haystack Rock. Building begins in the early morning; winners are announced at noon. The American Legion serves a big breakfast buffet ($7 adult, $5 children ages 6-12) at 1216 South Hemlock Street, open to all.

Writers, singers, composers, painters, and sculptors take over the town for the **Stormy Weather Arts Festival** (503/436-2623), usually held the first weekend of November. Events include music in the streets, plays, a Saturday afternoon Art Walk, and the Quick Draw, in which artists have one hour to paint, complete, and frame a piece while the audience watches. The art is then sold by auction.

Beginning in July, the city park at Spruce and 2nd Streets hosts **Concerts in the Park** (5pm-7pm Sun.), a series of jazz, rhythm and blues, and popular music at the bandstand.

SHOPPING

Much of the attraction of Cannon Beach is window shopping up and down Hemlock Street, which, in addition to galleries, is lined with clothing stores, gift shops, and other boutiques. Cannon Beach supports a fine kite

© BILL MCRAE

Cannon Beach's shopping district is like a maze.

store: **Once Upon a Breeze** (240 N. Spruce St., 503/436-1112) and one of the better bookstores on the coast, the **Cannon Beach Book Company** (130 N. Hemlock St., 503/436-1301, http://cannonbeachbooks.com); it's the place to pick up regional titles or a good novel (lots of mysteries) for that rainy weekend.

Art Galleries

Cannon Beach has long attracted artists and artisans, and here art lovers and purchasers will find nearly two dozen galleries and shops with high-quality works. Most of the Cannon Beach galleries and boutiques are concentrated along Hemlock Street, where you can hardly swing a Winsor & Newton No. 12 hogbristle brush without hitting one. Not surprisingly, the seashore itself is the subject and inspiration of many works you'll see here, with Haystack Rock frequently depicted in various media. The **Cannon Beach Information Center** (201 E. 2nd St., 503/436-2623, www.cannonbeach. org, 11am-5pm Mon.-Sat., 10am-4pm Sun.) has a guide to all the galleries in town, or you can just stroll and discover them for yourself.

At the north end of town, **Northwest by Northwest Gallery** (232 N. Spruce St., 503/436-0741, www.nwbynwgallery.com) showcases works by photographer Christopher Burkett, Native American ceramicist and bronze artist Lillian Pitt, and leading glass artists such as Duane Dahl. **White Bird Gallery** (251 N. Hemlock St., 503/436-2681, www. whitebirdgallery.com), founded in 1971 and one of Cannon Beach's oldest galleries, casts a wide net with paintings, sculpture, prints, photography, glass, ceramics, and jewelry. Nearby, the **Bronze Coast Gallery** (224 N. Hemlock St., 503/436-1055, www.bronzecoastgallery. com) shows both traditional Western bronzes and innovative bronze works and paintings that may appeal to those who aren't crazy about traditional Western art. In midtown, **Icefire Glassworks** (116 Gower St., 503/436-2359) is a working glass studio where you can watch glassblowers and artists shape their work and then shop for unique pieces in the gallery.

DragonFire Gallery (123 S. Hemlock St.,

503/436-1533) shows the work of a wide variety of artists; on Saturday afternoons throughout the summer, everyone is invited to come and meet gallery artists.

ACCOMMODATIONS

Cannon Beach has an abundance of small, locally owned lodgings, most of which rise above rusticity to the level of comfortable hominess. Many run $100-200 during the summer, but prices can drop as low as $60-80 during the off-season. If you're into luxury, Cannon Beach also offers some of Oregon's most opulent rooms.

$50-100

There aren't many inexpensive lodging options in Cannon Beach, but "mountain-view" rooms at the enormous **Tolovana Inn** (3400 S. Hemlock St., 503/436-2211 or 800/333-8890, www.tolovanainn.com, $79-105 mountain view, $169-269 ocean view, minimum stay in summer) hotel complex at the southern end of the Cannon Beach sprawl offer a good location at a fairly reasonable price. To make up for the rather cookie-cutter design and furnishings, you'll get a swimming pool, a spa, and a sauna, a number of restaurants sharing the same parking lots, and the beach right out the front door.

$100-150

About a one-minute walk to the beach, with friendly management and a great vibe, the **Blue Gull Inn** (632 S. Hemlock St., 503/436-2714 or 800/507-2714, www.bluegullinn.net, $139-209, two-night min. in summer) offers a choice between a beach house or less expensive motel units that come with housekeeping facilities. The modern cottages have in-room whirlpool tubs, fireplaces, and full kitchens. Cottages for larger groups are also available. Blue Gull Inn is one of several reliably comfortable and relatively inexpensive properties managed by **Haystack Lodgings,** which can be reached through the Blue Gull Inn website.

The **McBee Cottages** (888 S. Hemlock St., 503/436-0247 or 800/238-4107, www.mcbeecottages.com, $119-179) is a 1940s-era

motel with semidetached units that have been nicely renovated. The rooms are simple and certainly not expansive, but the McBee is nonetheless a favorite of many visitors looking for cozy accommodations, and it's just a minute from the beach and within walking distance of downtown. McBee accepts pets in several of its homey cottages.

For a homey atmosphere, try the **Argonauta Inn** or **The Waves Motel,** which share an office (188 W. 2nd St., 503/436-2205 or 800/822-2468, www.thewavescannonbeach.com). The Argonauta ($139-275) is made up of four houses in the middle of downtown and has five furnished units just 150 feet from the beach. A cluster of six beachfront buildings makes up The Waves ($139-289), with units to fit the needs of families, couples, or larger groups. These are not cookie-cutter units but the kind of individual lodgings you'd expect in Oregon.

The **Cannon Beach Hotel** (1116 Hemlock St., 503/436-1392 or 800/238-4107, www.cannonbeachhotel.com, $139-259) is a converted 1910 loggers' boardinghouse with 30 rooms and a small café and restaurant on the premises. The most expensive rooms have fireplaces, whirlpools, and partial ocean views. Meals are available in the restaurant adjacent to the lobby.

Just a few minutes' walk from downtown, **Ecola Creek Lodge** (208 E. 5th St., 503/436-2776 or 800/873-2749, www.ecolacreeklodge.com, $119-179) is a Cape Cod-style inn with 22 unique units set within four buildings. Accommodations range from simple queen-bed studios to two-bedroom suites. Special features include stained glass, lawns, fountains, flower gardens, and a lily pond. Les Shirley Park and Ecola Creek separate the lodge from the beach.

Over $200

The ◖ **Surfsand Resort** (148 W. Gower St., 503/436-2274 or 800/547-6100, www.surfsand.com, $200-319) offers a great combination of location and amenities, with Haystack Rock right out the door and spacious, nicely furnished suites. The resort has an indoor pool and spa and on-site massage services; pets are permitted in some rooms. The popular Wayfarer Restaurant is adjacent.

The handsome **Inn at Cannon Beach** (3215 S. Hemlock St., 503/436-9085 or 800/321-6304, www.atcannonbeach.com, $249-289, minimum stay requirements in summer) has large and stylish cottage-like rooms in a beautifully landscaped garden setting with a courtyard pond, just a block from the beach. All guest rooms include a gas fireplace, a fridge, a microwave, a coffeemaker, and a TV/VCR/DVD combo; some rooms can accommodate pets.

The fabulously expensive (for Oregon) **Stephanie Inn** (2740 S. Pacific St., 503/436-2221 or 800/633-3466, www.stephanie-inn.com, $499-589) offers attentive B&B-style service (breakfast buffet and evening wine gathering included), attention to detail, and luxury-level rooms with a low-key, not-too-fussy Oregonian touch. All guest rooms have balconies, fireplaces, wet bars, Jacuzzi tubs, fine linens, and all the extras you'd expect in an upscale resort hotel—including a fine dining restaurant. The Stephanie is a romantic adult-focused inn; children under 12 are not permitted.

The **Ocean Lodge** (2864 S. Pacific Dr., 503/436-2241 or 888/777-4047, www.the-oceanlodge.com, $239-389) feels like a long-established beach getaway, though in fact it was built recently. The high-end furnishings also give a clue that despite its venerable design, this rambling lodge isn't soaked in tradition. Rooms all have balconies, DVD players, fireplaces, microwaves, and refrigerators.

For a more private experience just steps from the ocean, the **White Heron Lodge** (356 N. Spruce St., 503/436-2205 or 800/822-2468, www.thewavescannonbeach.com, $309, three-night minimum stays in summer) comprises two fully furnished oceanfront Victorian-style homes, both of which sleep up to four. Each of the suites looks directly out on the Pacific. Wide sandy beaches and spacious front lawns make it a great location for families, especially those with small children. Located on a residential dead-end

street, the lodge is only one block from downtown Cannon Beach.

Three miles south of Cannon Beach in quiet Arch Cape, the **Arch Cape Inn** (31970 E. Ocean Ln., 503/436-2800 or 800/436-2848, www.archcapeinn.com, $238-369) is a bit over-the-top in its turreted castle-like design, but it's supremely luxurious. Although it's not on the beach, it's an easy walk, and several rooms have good ocean views. Friday or Saturday lodging requires one night's dinner reservations at the on-site restaurant (Thurs.-Mon. May-Oct., Fri.-Sat. year-round).

Vacation Rentals

Several local property management companies offer a large selection of furnished rentals ranging from grand oceanfront homes to quaint secluded cottages. **Cannon Beach Property Management** (3188 S. Hemlock St., 503/436-2021 or 877/386-3402, www.cbpm.com) and **Cannon Beach Vacation Rentals** (P.O. Box 723, Cannon Beach 97110, 866/436-0940, www.visitcb.com) both have good websites. During the summer, many beach houses are only available for weekly rentals.

Camping

Camping offers easier access to Cannon Beach's natural wonders at a bargain price. Although camping is not permitted on the beach or in Cannon Beach city parks, there are plenty of options for RV, tent, and outdoor enthusiasts.

The **Sea Ranch RV Park** (415 Fir St., 503/436-2815, www.cannon-beach.net/searanch, $33 tents, $38-43 RVs, $85-95 cabins) has grassy sites nestled among the trees, and is also home to horses, ducks, rabbits, and raccoons. It's open year-round with both full and partial hookups for RVs; campsites include a picnic table and a fire ring (firewood is sold on the premises) and access to restrooms with hot showers—all just three blocks from the beach and downtown. Pets are welcome but must be on a leash. Reservations are recommended.

For a more pampered RV-only experience, check out the **RV Resort at Cannon Beach**

(345 Elk Creek Rd., 503/436-2231 or 800/847-2231, www.cbrvresort.com, $32-44). Open year-round, the RV Resort has 100 full hook-ups, an indoor pool and spa, free cable TV, an on-site convenience store, a laundry facility, restrooms, and a meeting room.

Unlike most private campgrounds, the small family-run **Wright's for Camping** (334 Reservoir Rd., 503/436-2347, www.wrights-forcamping.com, $30-32) is geared toward tent campers. It's just east of U.S. 101 and has 20 sites with picnic tables and fire rings as well as restrooms and a laundry. Wright's is wheelchair accessible; leashed pets are allowed.

Roughly 20 miles east of Cannon Beach off U.S. 26 is **Saddle Mountain State Natural Area** (800/551-6949, www.oregonstateparks.org, Mar.-Oct., $5-10 tents, first-come, first-served), which offers 10 tent camping sites at the base of 3,283-foot Saddle Mountain, one of the highest peaks in Oregon's Coast Range. This more primitive and remote campground (although there are flush toilets and piped

water, in addition to picnic tables and fire pits) might just be the tonic if you're weary of the crowds along the beach.

FOOD

If you're on a budget, keep dining prices down at the **Mariner Market** (139 N. Hemlock St., 503/436-2442, 8am-9pm daily), a dimly lit old grocery that's fully stocked with fresh meat, fruit, vegetables, and deli items.

Bakeries and Cafés

Grab a cheese biscuit to go or sit down for a cup of coffee and a marionberry scone at **Waves of Grain Bakery** (3116 S. Hemlock St., 503/436-9600, 7am-3pm daily, $2-5), which is far and away the best bakery in town, with all the baked goods produced from scratch in-house. At times, you can also get soup.

Try the wood-paneled sky-lit **Lazy Susan Cafe** (126 N. Hemlock St., 503/436-2816, www.lazy-susan-cafe.com, 8am-3pm Sun.-Mon. and Wed.-Thurs., $7-13) for a great breakfast (waffles are a specialty) or satisfying lunch (salads are very good).

American

The local **Pig 'N Pancake** (223 S. Hemlock St., 503/436-2851, 7am-3pm daily, $6-12) has large picture windows overlooking a leafy ravine. Choose from 35 breakfast dishes served anytime, including homemade pancakes (which are very good and extremely popular—expect to wait). For lunch, try the soups, chowder, or halibut and chips.

The **Lumberyard Rotisserie and Grill** (264 3rd St., 503/436-0285, www.thelumberyard-grill.com, noon-9pm daily, $8-23) is a block away from busy downtown Cannon Beach, but this spacious restaurant offers high-quality food at good prices. The specialty is rotisserie chicken, but the pizza here is also good, as are such appetizers as the Dungeness crab and artichoke skillet. The Lumberyard is owned by the same company as the Stephanie Inn and the Surfsand Resort, and it has a similarly polished appearance.

Somewhat oddly, few of Cannon Beach's

© BILL MCRAE

Cannon Beach offers a wide range of food.

top restaurants have a view of the beach, so if excellent vistas of Haystack Rock and breaking waves are important to you, call to reserve a table at **The Wayfarer** (1190 Pacific Dr., 503/436-1108, 8am-9pm daily, dinner $17-30), tucked above a beach entrance at Gower Street. The food, which is good but not as memorable as the views, features classic steak and seafood main courses. The lounge here is a good spot for a drink.

Italian

The pizza at **Pizza a'Fetta** (231 N. Hemlock St., 503/436-0333, 11am-8pm Sun.-Thurs., 11am-9pm Fri.-Sat., slices $3-4, whole pies $20-33) is Cannon Beach's best, with a selection of to-go slices available at a takeout window. Or crowd into the always-busy dining room for your choice of pies, salads, minestrone soup, and Oregon microbrew beer and Italian wines.

Mediterranean

Cozy and refined, **The Bistro** (263 N. Hemlock St., 503/436-2661, 5pm-10pm daily, $20-25) is tucked back in a maze of shops and gardens in downtown Cannon Beach. The atmosphere is a bit stark, particularly after a rebuild from a recent fire, but the menu brings a taste of Provençe to traditional fish and seafood dishes—the seafood stew is a wonderful blend of Pacific Northwest fish and shellfish prepared with Mediterranean zest. The dining room is truly tiny and the food superlative, so reservations are mandatory.

◖ Newman's at 988 (988 S. Hemlock St., 503/436-1151, www.newmansat988. com, 5:30pm-9pm Tues.-Sat. Oct. 16-June 30; 5:30pm-9pm daily July-Oct. 15, $19-26) is a good special-occasion restaurant in a tiny house, with an elegant atmosphere and excellent food. The chef-owner takes great pride in using fresh local ingredients to prepare seasonal menus with French and Italian influences, featuring such dishes as seared duck breast with foie gras and truffles or lobster ravioli with marsala cream.

Irish

The **Irish Table** (1235 S. Hemlock St., 503/436-0708, 5:30pm-9pm Fri.-Tues., $11-22) makes the most of the Pacific Northwest bounty and hearty Irish cooking traditions, including meat pastries, grilled salmon, braised mussels, and variations on local lamb, including Irish lamb stew. The bar offers a wide selection of Scotch and Irish whiskies, plus Irish ales.

Pacific Northwest

Whether or not you're staying at the **Stephanie Inn** (2740 S. Pacific St., 503/436-2221 or 800/633-3466, www.stephanie-inn.com, 5pm-9pm nightly, $28-34, 4-course dinner $65), you are welcome to join guests in the dining room for creative Pacific Northwest cuisine. The atmosphere boasts mountain views, open wood beams, and a river-rock fireplace. Since guests get first shot at tables, those staying elsewhere should reserve well ahead of time.

For a much more casual dining experience, go to **Sweet Basil's Cafe** (271 N. Hemlock St., 503/436-1539, www.cafesweetbasils.com, 11am-10pm Wed.-Sun., $12-21), a tiny restaurant whose commitment is "natural, organic, wild." At lunch, enjoy mostly vegetarian sandwiches and salads. In the evening, linger in the wine bar, where tapas-style dishes are eclectic and creative—pork tenderloin with Bourbon sauce and seared duck breast with blueberries and pecan rice.

Seafood

Hankering for some authentic West Coast chowder? Head to **◖ Dooger's Seafood and Grill** (1371 S. Hemlock St., 503/436-2225, 8am-9pm daily, dinners $12-45) for seafood that's always fresh and delicious. Don't overlook Dooger's for breakfast—during crab season (mostly winter and spring) the crab Benedict is a real treat. **Mo's at Tolovana** (195 Warren Way, Tolovana Park, 503/436-1111, www.moschowder.com, 11am-8pm Mon.-Thurs., 11am-9pm Fri., 8am-9pm Sat., 8am-8pm Sun., $3-16) has great views; although its clam chowder is locally famous (perhaps because of fondness for Mo and her family), the food is not the big draw if you're looking for cutting-edge preparations.

In the fishing business for more than 25 years, **Ecola Seafoods** (208 N. Spruce St., 503/436-9130, 9am-9pm daily summer, 10am-7pm daily winter) features fresh-catch Dungeness crab and bay shrimp cocktails, as well as a decent clam chowder ($5). Or sample the smoked salmon and fish-and-chips. You'll find it across from the public parking lots and information center.

Brewpubs
Bill's Tavern (188 N. Hemlock St., 503/436-2202, 11:30am-10pm Thurs.-Tues., 4:30pm-10pm Wed., bar open later, $7-13), once a legendary watering hole, is now a more traditional brewpub. Sweet thick onion rings, good fries, one-third-pound burgers, sautéed prawns, and grilled oysters are on the bill of fare.

Farther south near Tolovana, the **Warren House Pub** (3301 S. Hemlock St., 503/436-1130, 10:30am-1am daily, $7-14) serves local beers from Bill's Tavern but in an English pub setting. The menu includes good smoked ribs, burgers, and seafood; in summer the backyard beer garden is a lovely spot to relax. Kids are allowed on the restaurant side of the pub.

INFORMATION AND SERVICES
The chamber of commerce operates the **Cannon Beach Information Center** (201 E. 2nd St., 503/436-2623, www.cannonbeach. org, 11am-5pm Mon.-Sat., 10am-4pm Sun.). This facility is close to the public restrooms (2nd St. and Spruce St.) and basketball and tennis courts.

Providence North Coast Clinic (171 N. Larch St., 503/717-7000) offers medical care and minor emergency services. It's located in Sandpiper Square behind the stores on the main drag.

Cooking Schools
After a day on the beach, spend an evening at **EVOO Cooking School** (188 S. Hemlock St., 503/436-8555, www.evoo.biz), where multi-course dinner classes ($79-120, includes dinner) are offered at least a couple of nights a week. Specialty classes on topics such as bread baking and cooking seafood are also offered.

GETTING THERE AND AROUND
From U.S. 101, there's a choice of four entrances to the beach loop (also known as U.S. 101 Alternate, a section of the old Oregon Coast Highway) to take you into town. As you wade into the town's shops, galleries, and restaurants, the beach loop becomes Hemlock Street, the main drag of Cannon Beach. Sunset Empire Transportation District operates **The Bus** (503/861-RIDE, 503/861-7433, or 800/776-6406, www.ridethebus.org), which serves Cannon Beach, Seaside, Astoria-Warrenton, and points in between. **Parking** can be hard to come by, especially on weekends, but you'll find public lots south of town at Tolovana Park and in town at Hemlock at 1st Street and on 2nd Street.

The **Cannon Beach Shuttle** runs every half hour on a 6.5-mile loop, from Les Shirley Park on the north end of town to Tolovana Park; it operates 10am-6pm daily, with extended summer hours. The fare is $1.

Amtrak Thruway Motorcoach Service (800/USA-RAIL or 800/872-7245, www. amtrak.com) runs two buses daily between Portland Union Station and Cannon Beach (continuing on to Seaside and Astoria). The bus stops at 1088 South Hemlock Street, across the street from the Cannon Beach Mercantile store.

Nehalem Bay Area

MANZANITA AND VICINITY

Just south of Arch Cape, Neahkahnie Mountain towers nearly 1,700 feet up from the edge of the sea. U.S. 101 climbs up and over its shoulder to an elevation of 700 feet, and the vistas from a half dozen pullouts (the highest along the Oregon coast) are spectacular—but do try to keep your eyes on the snaking road until you've parked your car.

This stretch of the highway, built by the Works Progress Administration in the 1930s, was constructed by blasting a roadbed from the rock face and buttressing it with stonework walls on the precarious cliffs. The fainthearted or acrophobic certainly couldn't have lasted long on this job. The handiwork of these road builders and masons can be admired at several pullouts, along with the breathtaking vista of Manzanita Beach, Nehalem Spit, and

old-growth tree along the trail in Oswald West State Park

some 20 miles south to Cape Meares. Much of Neahkahnie Mountain and its rugged coastline are preserved in Oswald West State Park, one of the state's finest.

Immediately to the south, huddled along an expansive curve of beach at the foot of Neahkahnie Mountain, quiet Manzanita (pop. 700) makes a pleasant stop for lunch or for the weekend. When adjacent coastal areas are fogbound, the seven-mile-long Manzanita Beach often enjoys sunshine because of the shelter of Neahkahnie Mountain. As one of the few towns along the north Oregon coast that's not located directly on U.S. 101, Manzanita feels more peaceful and secluded than most others; like Cannon Beach, it's also a relatively wealthy and stylish town.

Oswald West State Park

Most of Neahkahnie Mountain and the prominent headlands of Cape Falcon are encompassed within the 2,500-acre gem of **Oswald West State Park** (off U.S. 101, 800/551-6949, www.oregonstateparks.org). Whether or not you believe in the stories of lost pirate wealth buried somewhere on the mountain, there is real treasure today for all who venture here in search of the intangible currency of extraordinary natural beauty. The state park bears the name of Governor Oswald West, whose farsighted 1913 beach bill was instrumental in protecting Oregon's virgin shoreline. That same year, Neahkahnie Mountain was the site of another shipwreck in somewhat mysterious circumstances.

Several hiking trails weave through the park, including the 13 miles of the **Oregon Coast Trail** linking Arch Cape to the north with Manzanita. From the main parking lot on the east side of U.S. 101, a 0.5-mile trail follows Short Sands Creek to **Short Sands Beach,** a relatively sheltered beach that's popular with surfers year-round. Rainforests of hemlock, cedar, and gigantic Sitka spruce crowd the secluded boulder-strewn shoreline. From Short Sands Beach, hike north on the three-mile old-growth-lined **Cape Falcon Trail** to spectacular views.

From the trail to the beach, it's also possible to turn south and hike to **Neahkahnie Mountain** (4 miles one-way) with some stiff climbing. Shave about 1.3 miles off the hike by starting a mile south of the main Oswald West parking lot, where there's an access road to the Neahkahnie Mountain Summit Trail on the east side of the highway. It's not well marked; look for a subdivision on the golf course to the west. Drive up the gravel road 0.25 mile to the trailhead parking lot and begin a moderately difficult 1.5-mile ascent. Allow about 45 minutes to get to the top. The summit view south to Cape Meares and east to the Nehalem Valley ranks as one of the finest on the coast.

Visitors who remember camping among the old-growth trees at Oswald West should treasure the memory. Due to the instability of the ancient trees, the campground remains closed.

Accommodations

Manzanita is a small town without an abundance of lodgings. Advance reservations are a must, especially in summer, and many accommodations require two- to three-night stays during the high season and on some holidays. A good alternative to motels for families here are the rentals available from the several property management agencies in town. Among these is **Manzanita Beach Getaway** (503/368-2929 or 855/368-2929, www.manzanitabeachgetaway. com), with fully furnished homes to rent, running $110-225 per night (most require weekly rentals in July and August).

If you're looking for an upscale retreat, the cedar-clad **⟨ Inn at Manzanita** (67 Laneda Ave., 503/368-6754, www.innatmanzanita. com, $179-199), set in a Japanese-accented garden just a short walk from the beach, promises guests the three R's: recreation, relaxation, and romance. Each of its 13 wood-paneled guest rooms features a gas fireplace and a two-person spa; most rooms have a balcony, offering glimpses through the evergreens of the nearby

© DUNCAN MACK MURPHY

yoga at Short Sands Beach

beach. Fresh flowers daily, robes, and other amenities help you feel pampered. Despite being in the middle of town near restaurants and the beach, a feeling of luxurious seclusion prevails.

The remodeled **Ocean Inn** (32 Laneda Ave., 866/3687701 or 503/368-7701, www.ocean-innatmanzanita.com, $139-209) has large and comfortable condo-like rooms (most with full kitchens); several have wood stoves and two have patios. Most rooms have ocean views, and the beach is just moments away.

Six blocks from the beach, the six spacious, stylish, and airy cabins of **Coast Cabins** (635 Laneda Ave., 503/368-7113, www.coastcabins.com, $215-440, two-night minimum stays in summer and weekends) comfortably sleep one to two (although two-story Cabin 5 is designed for up to four people) and offer kitchenettes or full kitchens, satellite TV, and goose-down pillows and comforters. The Coast Cabins folks also rent out a few sophisticated one- and two-bedroom condos in downtown Manzanita.

For a more standard motel experience, the **Sunset Surf** (248 Ocean Rd., 503/368-5224 or 800/243-8035, www.sunsetsurfocean.com, $184-165) offers guest rooms (many with kitchens) in three oceanfront units that share an outdoor pool. Although rooms are basic, the setting is great.

Another reasonably priced older motel, the **Spindrift Inn** (114 Laneda Ave., 503/368-1001 or 877/368-1001, www.spindrift-inn.com, $80-110) has rooms that are nicer than the rather plain exterior. It's a very short walk to the beach.

Camping

Just south of Manzanita and occupying the entire sandy appendage of Nehalem Spit is scenic, sprawling **Nehalem Bay State Park** (800/452-5687, www.reserveamerica.com, year-round, $24 tents or RVs, $36 yurts, $5 day use for noncampers), a favorite with bikers, beachcombers, anglers, horse owners, and pilots (yes, there's a little airstrip and a fly-in campsite). Sandwiched between the bay and a beautiful four-mile beach stretching from

Manzanita to the mouth of the Nehalem River is a vast campground with hot showers. Sites are a little bit close together with few trees to screen the neighbors; dunes separate campers from the ocean. As big as this park is, it does fill up in summer, so reservations are recommended (particularly July-Aug.). To get there, turn south at Bayshore Junction just before U.S. 101 heads east into the town of Nehalem.

Food

House renters, budget diners, and picnickers can take advantage of the excellent produce and impressive (for a coastal market) grocery section at **Manzanita Grocery & Deli** (193 Laneda Ave., 503/368-5362, 8am-8pm daily). One block away, **Mother Nature's Natural Foods Store** (298 Laneda Ave., 503/368-5316, 10am-7pm Mon.-Sat.) stocks natural groceries, coffees and teas, bulk foods, wine, and beer.

Stop at **Manzanita News & Espresso** (500 Laneda Ave., 503/368-7450, 7:30am-2pm daily, $2-5) for coffee, a pastry, and a magazine (there are lots to choose from, and the selection is anything but generic).

The local bakery, **Bread and Ocean** (154 Laneda Ave., 503/368-5823, 7:30am-2pm Wed.-Sat., 8am-2pm Sun., $4-9), makes sandwiches as well as cinnamon rolls. The locals' favorite for hefty traditional breakfasts is **Big Wave Cafe** (822 Laneda Ave., 503/368-9283, 7am-9pm Fri.-Wed., 8am-9pm Thurs., $7-18), where you'll find Makin' Waves Eggs Benedict, dressed with spinach and chipotle-pepper hollandaise sauce.

Left Coast Siesta (288 Laneda Ave., 503/368-7997, 11:30am-8pm Mon.-Sat., noon-7pm Sun., closed Mon.-Tues. winter, $6-8) specializes in design-your-own burritos, the perfect takeout for a beach lunch or dinner. Options include spicy beef, spicy chicken, tequila-lime chicken, or black beans to fill a selection of flavored tortillas. It also serves tacos and enchiladas. And if you like it *caliente,* this is the place for you: Left Coast Siesta stocks a hot sauce bar with 200-plus different types of the hot stuff, many available to purchase by the jar.

Just a couple of blocks from the beach,

Marzano's (60 Laneda Ave., 503/368-3663, 4pm-8:30pm Sun.-Mon. and Thurs., 4pm-9pm Fri., noon-9pm Sat., large pies mostly $20-25) serves the area's best slices of gourmet pizza. The roasted vegetable pizza is recommended, and the smoked prosciutto with aged montegrappa cheese is another winner.

For relaxed fine dining, the best option is **Neah-Kah-Nie Bistro** (519 Laneda Ave., 503/368-2722, 11:30am-4pm and 5pm-8pm Tues.-Thurs and Sun., 5pm-9pm Fri.-Sat., $16-27), a small dining room serving local seafood and meats with up-to-date continental preparations. Halibut cheeks are sautéed in lemon butter, champagne, and capers, while grilled pork chops come with house-made pear chutney.

For drinks and light meals, try **Great Northern Garlic Company** (868 Laneda Ave., 503/368-7700, $6-18), a well-stocked wine bar that serves a broad selection of small plates, including caprese salad, cheese fondue, barbecue oysters, and seasonal fish specials such as just caught Dungeness crab. There's not a lot of room in the dining room, but in summer and early fall there is amble seating on the patio (gas heaters are available to take the chill off). This operation often closes in winter and early spring; call to confirm hours outside of May-Dec.

NEHALEM

Tiny Nehalem (pop. 205) occupies just a few blocks along U.S. 101 on the north bank of the Nehalem River. It's a lovely location with a few Old West-style storefronts. Sizable runs of spring and fall chinook salmon and winter steelhead make this a popular destination for anglers. In August, locals claim you could just about cross the river stepping from boat to boat when the fish are in. Just southwest of town, the county maintains a boat launch facility and dock, providing access to the river and to the bay downstream. The bay and slow-moving river also invite exploration by kayak and canoe; bring your own, or rent them in nearby Wheeler. Be sure to pack the binoculars: The Nehalem River is a good place to watch birds.

Wineries

The **Nehalem Bay Winery** (34965 Hwy. 53, 503/368-9463, www.nehalembaywinery.com) offers tastings and sales of its varietals (pinot noir, Gewürztraminer), as well as fruit and berry wines (including delicious blackberry). You can tour the grounds and picnic 10am-6pm daily or enjoy the tasting room's welcoming milieu. To get to the winery, look for the Highway 53 sign on U.S. 101 and head east 1.5 miles.

Accommodations

If you'd like to overnight close to the river—*on* the river—try the **Ripple Run Resort and Marina** (35165 U.S. 101 N., 503/368-3865 or 877/655-0623, www.ripplerunresort.com, $100-199). Choose among four one-of-a-kind floating lodgings, including a 35-foot barge that sleeps 4-6 for $135 nightly, or a 47-foot converted tug that sleeps two. If a night on the water doesn't entice you, opt for a room in a riverside cottage. All units include linens, towels, kitchenettes with dishes, gas barbecues, cable TV, and videos. Reservations are recommended.

Food

The 【 **Nehalem River Inn** (34910 Hwy. 53, 503/368-7708, hours vary, call for reservations, $27-31) is one of the best places on the coast to experience fresh and inventive Pacific Northwest cuisine. The inn's sophisticated menu blends Pacific Northwest seafood, game, locally grown organic produce, wild mushrooms, and other ingredients to create dishes that will turn the heads of even the most discriminating diners—such as Muscovy duck breast served with black truffle potato gnocchi or Piedmontese flat iron steak with creamy corn bread, spring onion, and whiskey jam. Complement your meal with a bottle from a well-selected wine list favoring Oregon wineries, including Nehalem River Inn's own private-label wines. Reservations are recommended.

On the highway in Nehalem, 【 **Wanda's** (12870 U.S. 101 N., 503/368-8100, 8am-2pm Fri.-Tues., $7-12) is a popular breakfast and

THE WRECK OF THE *GLENESSLIN*

The sea was calm and the winds mild along the north Oregon coast on the afternoon of October 1, 1913, when locals observed a square-rigged ship sailing perilously close to the Nehalem shore. The Liverpool-built three-master *Glenesslin*, bound for Portland, was one of a dying breed of large sailing ships on the high seas, which were quickly being replaced by steam-powered vessels. Built in 1885, it was a fine ship, and fast: Its 74-day passage from Portland, Oregon, to Port Elizabeth, South Africa, was never surpassed by another square-rigger. But on this day, in the twilight of sail, seasoned and reliable crews were scarce—the ship's first and second officers were but 22 years old—and inexperience led to disaster.

According to maritime author James A. Gibbs, in his fascinating *Shipwrecks of the Pacific Coast*, the *Glenesslin*, under full sail, suddenly turned east toward the base of Neahkahnie Mountain. Losing the wind under the lee of Cape Falcon, Gibbs theorizes, the ship lost headway and the crew was unable to bring it about. As it neared the shore, an underwater reef ripped open the ship's bottom plates. The crew shot a line to shore, and with the help of local rescuers, all 21 hands made it safely to land—many of them, it was said, under the influence of strong drink. As breakers pounded the stern, grinding the ship against the rocks, it soon began to break up. A Nehalem man bought the dying vessel for $100, but there was little hope of salvaging much.

In the lengthy official inquiry that followed, the captain and second mate were judged negligent in their duties, and the first mate was reprimanded. The ship's underwriter initially balked at covering the loss, claiming that the ship had been intentionally wrecked in a scheme to collect the insurance, but the insurer eventually paid up. It was a heartbreaking end for a beautiful and storied ship.

lunch spot with old-fashioned granny's attic decor and delicious omelets, tuna melt sandwiches, and baked goods. Stop in for a muffin if nothing else.

WHEELER

Wheeler (pop. 393) is a little town flanking the Nehalem River where most accommodations are low-cost efficiencies for visiting fisherfolk, but the 10 guest rooms of the **Wheeler on the Bay Lodge and Marina** (580 Marine Dr., 503/368-5858 or 800/469-3204, www.wheeleronthebay.com, $90-155), on U.S. 101 on the shore of Nehalem Bay, have more appeal. Most guest rooms have at least partial bay views, and several have jetted tubs. There's also a video store, kayak rentals, and on-site massage services, and they can help arrange fishing charters.

Guest rooms at **The Old Wheeler Hotel** (495 U.S. 101, 503/368-6000 or 877/653-4683, www.oldwheelerhotel.com, $119-165), a 1920s landmark across the road from the bay, may remind you of your great-aunt's guest room. They're old-fashioned in a very down-to-earth way. Although all guest rooms have private bathrooms, some bathrooms are down the hall from their rooms.

In a tiny cottage just off the main drag, the ◖ **Rising Star Cafe** (92 Rorvik St., 503/368-3990, noon-3pm and 5pm-8pm Wed.-Thurs. and Sat., 5pm-8pm Fri., 10am-3pm Sun., $13-26) is a sweet spot for excellent pasta, sandwiches, and chowder—some of the best on the coast. There are only seven tables in this popular restaurant, so call ahead for reservations. The food can be very good here (if the brandied bread pudding is on the menu, go for it), and the atmosphere is comfortable and friendly.

ROCKAWAY BEACH

This town of 1,380 was established as a summer resort in the 1920s by Portlanders who wanted a coastal getaway. And so it remains today—a quiet spot without much going on besides walks on the seven miles of sandy beach, a **Kite Festival** in mid-May, and an **Arts and Crafts Fair** in mid-August. Shallow **Lake Lytle,** on the east side of the highway, offers spring and early summer fishing for trout, bass, and crappie. While the town of Rockaway is singularly unattractive from U.S. 101—a lengthy stretch of tacky shops, modest motels, and big new condos—the beach is quite nice, anchored at the south by the impressive Twin Rocks formation. The **Visitor Information Center** (503/355-8108, www. rockawaybeach.net), lodged in a bright red caboose in the center of town, can fill you in on other goings-on.

Accommodations

Rockaway's motels are basic and family-oriented; if you are planning in advance, take a moment to check out the beach houses available for rent on the **chamber of commerce website** (www.rockawaybeach.net).

The following motels are on the ocean side of busy U.S. 101, which dominates this long string bean of a town. **Surfside Resort Motel** (101 NW 11th St., 503/355-2312 or 800/243-7786, www.surfsideocean.com, $79-85 with no ocean view, $89-129 ocean view) is a large beachfront complex with an indoor pool. Some guest rooms with kitchens are available; for $59, you can also rent a simple "sleeping room" with basic facilities (including bathroom) but no view. **Silver Sands Oceanfront Resort** (215 S. Pacific Ave., 503/355-2206 or 800/457-8972, www.oregonsilversands.com, $136-166) is also right on the beach, with fairly basic rooms (some kitchenettes), an indoor pool and hot tub, and a sauna.

About a mile south of town, **Twin Rocks Motel** (7925 Minehaha St., 503/355-2391 or 877/355-2391, www.twinrocksmotel.net, $177-199) is a small cluster of dog-friendly two-bedroom oceanfront cottages. If you're looking for a simple, quiet getaway with family or a couple of friends, this might be your place.

Food

Cow Belle Cafe (194 U.S. 101 S., 503/355-2441, 8am-2pm Thurs.-Sun., $8-14) is a locals' favorite for breakfast. The biscuits and gravy here are renowned, as is the bovine-rich decor. The **Beach Bite** (162 U.S. 101 S., 503/355-2073, 11am-9pm Mon.-Thurs., 11am-11pm Fri., 8am-11pm Sat., 8am-9pm Sun., $6-20) is one of the classier dining places in town (don't worry, flip-flops and a sweatshirt will get you by), featuring burgers and pasta.

Tillamook Bay

GARIBALDI

Tillamook Bay's commercial fishing fleet is concentrated in this little port town (pop. 970) near the north end of the bay. Garibaldi, named in 1879 by the local postmaster for the Italian patriot, is a fish-processing center: Crabs, shrimp, fresh salmon, lingcod, and bottom fish (halibut, cabezon, rockfish, and sea perch) are the specialties. At the marina, **Garibaldi Cannery** (606 Commercial Dr., 503/322-3344, 7am-6pm Mon.-Sat.) gets crab, fish, and other seafood right off the boats, so the selection is both low-priced and fresh. If you want it fresher, you'll have to catch it yourself.

In addition to dock fishing, guide and charter services offer salmon and halibut fishing, bird-watching, and whale-watching excursions. North of Garibaldi on U.S. 101, the bay entrance is a good place to see brown pelicans, harlequin ducks, oystercatchers, and guillemots. The Miami River marsh, south of town, is a bird-watching paradise at low tide, when ducks and shorebirds hunt for food.

Garibaldi Maritime Museum

The small but interesting **Garibaldi Maritime Museum** (112 Garibaldi Ave., 503/322-8411, www.garibaldimuseum.com, 10am-4pm Thurs.-Mon. April-Nov., $3 adults, $2.50 seniors and children ages 5-18) retells the history

© BILL MCRAE

Watch out for salty characters on the Garibaldi docks.

of this longtime fishing village. It also focuses on the late-18th-century sailing world and the British sea captain Robert Gray and his historical vessels, the *Lady Washington* and the *Columbia Rediviva,* which explored the Pacific Northwest in 1787 and 1792. Among the museum displays are models of these ships, an eight-foot-tall reproduction of the *Columbia* figurehead, a half model of the *Columbia* showing how the ship was provisioned for long voyages, as well as reproductions of period musical instruments and typical sailors' clothing.

Oregon Coast Explorer Trains

The **Oregon Coast Scenic Railroad** (503/842-8206, www.ocsr.net, basic tours $18 adults, $17 seniors, $10 children ages 3-10) operates a number of rail excursions on a train pulled by a 1910 Heisler Locomotive Works steam engine between Garibaldi and Rockaway Beach. The basic tour is 1.5 hours round-trip; trains depart Garibaldi at noon, 2pm, and 4pm with opportunities to board in Rockaway Beach at 1pm and 3pm. The train operates weekends only

Memorial Day-June and Labor Day-September, and daily July-August as well as assorted holidays throughout the year. Dinner trains are also offered.

Fishing

The town's fishing and crabbing piers attract visitors looking to catch their own. Rent fishing boats, crab traps, and other gear at the **Garibaldi Marina** (302 Mooring Basin Rd., 503/322-3312, www.garibaldimarina.com).

The **Miami River** and **Kilchis River,** which empty into Tillamook Bay south of Garibaldi, get the state's only two significant runs of chum salmon, a species much more common from Washington northward. There's a catch-and-release season for them mid-September-mid-November. Both rivers also get runs of spring chinook and are open for steelhead most of the year.

Several charter companies have offices at the marina. **Garibaldi Charters** (607 Garibaldi Ave., 503/322-0007, www.garibaldicharters. com) offers fishing excursions (a full day of

BAYOCEAN SPIT

At the western entrance to Tillamook Bay, a long narrow spit of land reaches north from Cape Meares nearly all the way to Garibaldi. Although today it's a good place for a long and sandy flat hike, it was once developed as the town of Bayocean, promoted as "the Atlantic City of the West."

In the early 1900s, two real estate developers, enchanted by the great views of the ocean, built a grand resort hotel on the spit and began selling lots. A giant natatorium—a heated saltwater surf pool—was built in 1914. Initially, the only access was by boat or ferry; in 1928 a road was built from Tillamook.

The town that grew on the four-mile-long spit was thriving when the inevitable erosion began to chip away at the peninsula. Houses slipped into the sea, and by the late 1930s most folks had packed up and left. By 1939 the natatorium had been swallowed up.

Since the early 1990s, the spit has been managed for protection and preservation of its ecosystem, which is dominated by beach grass and Scotch broom.

To reach Bayocean Spit from Tillamook, head west on the Three Capes Scenic Loop (3rd St. from downtown Tillamook) and travel three miles to the Bayocean Spit sign. Turn right and follow a gravel road 1.5 miles to the parking area.

---

salmon fishing runs about $105) and wildlife-viewing or whale-watching trips ($40 per person).

Accommodations and Camping

If you want to wake up on the docks, spend the night at **Harbor View Inn** (302 S. 7th St., 503/322-3251, www.harborviewfun.com, $79-95), a motel popular with fishers and sports enthusiasts. A more standard motel is the **Garibaldi House Inn** (502 Garibaldi Ave., 503/322-3338 or 877/322-6489, www.garibaldihouse.com, $119-139), which offers very pleasant rooms, as well as an indoor pool, hot tub, sauna, fitness room, and complimentary hot breakfast.

Both tent and RV campers are welcome at **Barview Jetty County Park** (503/322-3522, $15-30, reservations accepted), a large campground in the tiny community of Barview (2.5 miles north of Garibaldi) with easy access to the beach forming the north side of Tillamook Bay. Most of the sites are for tents, with a section reserved for hikers and bikers; hot showers are a welcome amenity.

Food

One of the joys of eating on the Oregon coast is getting really good fish-and-chips from rough-edged dives on the docks. In Garibaldi, the **Fisherman's Korner Restaurant** (306 Mooring Basin, 503/322-2033, 7:30am-3pm Thurs.-Mon., $6-12) is right on the wharf and offers absolutely fresh fish-and-chips and excellent clam chowder. Breakfasts here are massive—meant for hungry sailors.

If you're looking for pub grub, a good choice is **Ghost Hole Public House** (409 Garibaldi Ave., 503/322-2723, 11am-2:30am daily, $6-15) with good burgers and sandwiches and a friendly vibe.

Just north of Garibaldi, **Pirate's Cove Restaurant** (14170 U.S. 101 N., 503/322-2092, http://piratesonline.biz, noon-9pm Mon.-Tues., 8am-9pm Wed.-Sat., 8am-8pm Sun., dinner $10-30) is one of the better restaurants between Manzanita and Lincoln City, with a dramatic vista of the mouth of Tillamook Bay. Try the local oysters and razor clams. Lunches are a better deal than the rather expensive dinners.

Four miles south at the little enclave of Bay City is another temple to seafood. **Pacific Oyster** (5150 Oyster Bay Dr., 503/377-2323, 10am-7pm Sun.-Thurs., 10am-8pm Fri.-Sat., $5-16) is mostly an oyster-processing center, but it's also an excellent spot for a few oyster shooters or a quick meal. Although there are a variety of seafood choices, the main draw is the oysters, which here are both for eating and entertainment. As you eat, you can watch the oyster shuckers in action next door, as the dining area overlooks the oyster-processing area.

TILLAMOOK

Without much sun or surf, what could possibly draw enough visitors to the town of Tillamook (pop. 4,500) to make it one of Oregon's top three tourism attractions? Superficially speaking, cheese factories and a World War II blimp hangar, in a town flanked by mudflats and rain-soaked dairy country, shouldn't pull in more than a million tourists per year. But they do. And after a drive down U.S. 101 or along the scenic Three Capes Loop, you too will be mysteriously drawn to the huge white, blue, and gold building proffering bite-size samples of cheddar, not to mention ice cream.

Tillamook County is home to more than 26,000 cows, which easily outnumber the county's human population. They're the foundation of the Tillamook County Creamery Association's famous cheddar cheese and other dairy products, which generate about $85 million in annual sales—this dwarfs the region's other important contributors to the local economy, fishing and oyster farming.

In 1940-1942, partially in response to a Japanese submarine firing on Fort Stevens in Astoria, the U.S. Navy built two blimp hangars south of town, the two largest wooden structures ever built, according to *The Guinness Book of World Records.* One of five naval air stations on the Pacific coast, the Tillamook blimp guard patrolled the waters from northern California to the San Juan Islands and escorted ships into Puget Sound. While all kinds of blimp stories abound in Tillamook bars, only one wartime encounter has been documented. Declassified records confirm that blimps were involved in the sinking of what was believed to be two Japanese submarines off Cape Meares. In late May 1943, two of the high-flying craft, assisted by U.S. Navy subchasers and destroyers,

dropped several depth charges on the submarines, which are still lying on the ocean floor.

Until 1946, when the station was decommissioned, the naval presence here created a boomtown. Bars and businesses flourished, and civilian jobs were easy to come by. After the war years, Tillamook County returned to the economic trinity of "trees, cheese, and ocean breeze" that has sustained the region to the present day.

Tillamook Cheese Factory

With over a million visitors a year, the **Tillamook Cheese Factory** (4175 U.S. 101 N., 503/842-4481, www.tillamookcheese. com, 8am-6pm daily Labor Day-mid-June, 8am-8pm daily summer, free) is far and away the county's biggest drawing card. The plant welcomes visitors with a reproduction of the *Morningstar,* the schooner that transported locally made butter and cheese in the late 1800s and now adorns the label of every Tillamook product. The quaint vessel symbolizing Tillamook cheese-making's humble beginnings stands in contrast to the technology and sophistication that go into making this world-famous lunchbox staple today.

Inside the plant, a self-guided tour follows the movement of curds and whey to the "cheddaring table." Whey is drained from the curds, which are then cut and folded. These processes are coordinated by white-uniformed workers in a stadium-size factory. As you look down on the antiseptic scene from the glassed-in observation area, it's hard to imagine this as the birthplace of many a grilled cheese sandwich. Tastes of a few samples, however, prove it's true.

User-friendly informational placards and historical displays recount Tillamook Valley's dairy history from 1851, when settlers began importing cows. The problem then was how to ship the milk to San Francisco and Portland. Even though salting butter to preserve it allowed exportation, ships still faced the difficulty of negotiating the treacherous Tillamook bar. In 1894, Peter McIntosh

© BILL MCRAE

There's a reason that Tillamook is known for its cheese.

introduced techniques here to make cheddar cheese, whose long shelf life enabled it to be transported overland.

In the early 1900s, the Tillamook County Creamery Association absorbed smaller operations; the modern plant opened in 1949. Today, Tillamook produces tens of millions of pounds of cheese annually, including monterey jack, swiss, and multiple variations of the award-winning cheddar. Pepperoni, butter, cheese soup, milk, and other products are also available. There's a gift shop (more Holstein-themed tchotchkes than you've probably dreamed of) and a full-service restaurant, but the big attraction is the ice cream counter. Have a double-scoop chocolate peanut butter cone—worth every penny.

Blue Heron French Cheese Company

A quarter million people per year visit Tillamook County's *second*-most-popular

attraction, **Blue Heron French Cheese Company** (2001 Blue Heron Dr., 503/842-8282, www.blueheronoregon.com, 9am-6pm daily Labor Day-mid-June; 8am-8pm daily mid-June-Labor Day, free), a mile south of the Tillamook Cheese Factory. Housed in a large white barn, Blue Heron is famous for its brie-style cheese (though it's not produced on-site). In addition to cheeses and other gourmet foods, the shop sells gift baskets; over 250 varieties of Oregon wines are available in the wine-tasting room. A deli serves lunches of homemade soups and salads. For kids, there's a petting farm with the usual barnyard suspects.

Tillamook Air Museum

South of town off U.S. 101, you can't possibly miss the enormous Quonset hut-like building east of the highway. The world-class aircraft collection of the **Tillamook Air Museum** (6030 Hangar Rd., 503/842-1130, www.tillamookair.com, 9am-5pm daily, $12 adults, $11 seniors, $8 children ages 6-17) is housed in and around Hangar B of the decommissioned Tillamook Naval Air Station. At 1,072 feet long, 206 feet wide, and 192 feet high, it's the largest wooden structure in the world, and it's worth the price of admission just to experience the enormity of it. During World War II, this and another gargantuan hangar on the site (which burned down in 1992) sheltered eight K-class blimps, each 242 feet long.

Inside the seven-acre structure, you can learn about the role the big blimps played during wartime as well as how they are used today. In addition, there's a large collection of World War II fighter planes (many one-of-a-kind models) as well as photos and artifacts from the naval air station days. Be sure to check out the cyclo-crane, a combination blimp, plane, and helicopter. This was devised in the 1980s to aid in remote logging operations; it ended up an $8 million bust.

To get there from downtown, take U.S. 101 south two miles, make a left at the flashing yellow light, and follow the signs. If you want to see the historic aircraft in Tillamook's hangars,

© BILL MCRAE

The Tilamook Air Museum is housed in a World War II hangar.

then do so soon. The air museum will move to Madras, in central Oregon, by 2016.

Tillamook County Pioneer Museum

East of the highway in the heart of downtown, **Tillamook County Pioneer Museum** (2106 2nd St., 503/842-4553, www.tcpm.org, 10am-4pm Tues.-Sun., $4 adults, $3 seniors, $1 children ages 7-10) is famous for its taxidermy exhibits as well as memorabilia from pioneer households. Particularly intriguing are hunks of ancient beeswax with odd inscriptions recovered from near Neahkahnie Mountain, which are thought to be remnants from 18th-century shipwrecks. The old courtroom on the second floor has one of the best displays of natural history in the state. There are many beautiful dioramas, plus shells, insects, and nests. The Beals Memorial Room houses a large rock, mineral, and fossil collection.

Latimer Quilt and Textile Center

The collection at the **Latimer Quilt and Textile Center** (2105 Wilson River Loop Rd., www.latimerquiltandtextile.com, 503/842-8622, 10am-5pm Mon.-Sat., noon-4pm Sun. Apr.-Oct., 10am-4pm Mon.-Sat. Nov.-Mar., $3) includes quilts from the 1850s to the present as well as looms, spinning wheels, and a variety of woven items. On Friday, you can see weavers at work; lessons can be arranged by calling ahead. The center, housed in a restored school, is just south and east of the cheese factory.

Munson Creek Falls

The highest waterfall in the Oregon Coast Range is lovely **Munson Creek Falls,** which drops 266 feet over mossy cliffs surrounded by an old-growth forest. A steep 0.25-mile trail leads to the base of the falls, while another slightly longer trail leads to a higher viewpoint; wooden walkways clinging to the cliff lead to a small viewing platform. This is a spectacle in all seasons, but come in winter when the falls pour down with greater fury.

To reach the falls, seven miles south of Tillamook turn east from U.S. 101 on Munson

THE LOST TREASURE OF NEAHKAHNIE MOUNTAIN

Is there pirate gold on Neahkahnie Mountain? Local native legends tell of Spanish pirates burying a treasure here. One story relates that the crew of a shipwrecked Manila galleon salvaged its cargo of gold and beeswax (a valuable commodity in trade with Asia) by burying it in the side of the mountain. To deter natives from going to the site, the pirates killed a black man and buried him on top of the cargo. While this account taken from native histories has never been substantiated, a piece of crudely inscribed beeswax retrieved from the Neahkahnie region carbon-dated AD 1500-1700 (on display at the Tillamook County Pioneer Museum) keeps speculation alive. Further intrigue was added by the 1993 discovery of an ancient wooden rigging block. Found in the mud at the mouth of the Nehalem River, it was determined by a Spanish maritime expert to have been from a Manila galleon during that same time period. Lewis and Clark's 1805 reports of a Chinook with red hair, and similar accounts from the Vancouver Expedition's 1792 encounter with a redheaded native who claimed his late father had been a shipwrecked Spanish sailor, would tend to corroborate the shipwreck and treasure stories passed down in oral histories.

Creek Road and drive 1.5 miles on the very narrow, bumpy dirt access road that leads to the parking lot. Note that motor homes and trailers cannot get into the park; the lot is too small.

Tillamook State Forest

A series of intense forest fires in the 1930s and 1940s burned vast amounts of land in the northern Coast Range. Most of this land was owned by private timber companies, who walked away from the seemingly worthless "Tillamook Burn," leaving property rights to revert to the counties, who then handed the land over to the state. A massive replanting effort ensued, and in 1973 the Tillamook Burn became the **Tillamook State Forest.** In 2006 the Tillamook Forest Center opened in a soaring timbered building in the middle of the once-burned, now-lush forest. Be sure to stop in to see the short movie about the area's history; the vivid fire scenes are a bit frightening—a sensation that's enhanced when the smell of smoke is released into the auditorium. Don't leave without walking out through the center's back door, crossing the footbridge, and taking at least a short hike, where you'll see an assortment of native wildflowers, shrubs, and trees. If you head west from the bridge, Wilson Falls is about two miles away.

If a short hike outside the Forest Center leaves you hankering for more, head east along Highway 6 to the Kings Mountain trailhead. On a clear day (ha!) there are good views from the top. Several more trails start at the summit of the Coast Range. The campgrounds along Highway 6, including Jones Creek, which is right next to the **Tillamook Forest Center** (45500 Wilson River Hwy., 503/815-6800 or 866/930-4646, www.tillamookforestcenter. org, 10am-5pm daily Memorial Day-Labor Day, reduced hours spring and fall, closed in winter, free), are popular with off-road vehicle drivers, who have their own trail network back in the hills.

Hiking

The Tillamook State Forest offers plenty of recreational opportunities. From a distance, the forest seems like a tree plantation, but hidden waterfalls, old railroad trestles from the days of logging trains, and moss-covered oaks in the Salmonberry River Canyon will convince you otherwise. Bird-watchers and mushroom pickers can easily penetrate this thicket thanks to 1,000 miles of maintained roads and old railroad grades.

Two challenging trails off Highway 6, **Kings Mountain** (25 miles east of Tillamook) and **Elk Mountain** (28 miles east of Tillamook) climb through lands affected by the Tillamook Burn, but with scenic views throughout. Thanks to salvage logging in the wake of the disaster and subsequent replanting, myriad trails crisscross forests of Douglas and noble fir, hemlock, and red alder. Stop at the visitor center for maps and trail descriptions.

Fishing

Among Oregon anglers, Tillamook County is known for its steelhead and salmon. Motorists along U.S. 101 can tell the fall chinook run has arrived when fishing boats cluster outside the Tillamook Bay entrance at Garibaldi. As the season wears on, the fish—affectionately called "hogs" because they sometimes weigh in at more than 50 pounds—make their way inland up the five coastal rivers—the Trask, Wilson, Tillamook, Kilchis, and Miami—that flow into Tillamook Bay. At their peak, the runs create such competition for favorite holes that the process of sparring for them is jocularly referred to as "combat fishing," as fishing boats anchor up gunwale to gunwale to form a fish-stopping palisade called a "hogline." Smokehouses and gas stations dot the outer reaches of the bay to cater to this fall influx.

The **Guide Shop Inc.** (12140 Wilson River Hwy., Tillamook, 503/842-3474, www.guide-shop.com) can arrange for a full day of fishing for chinook and silver salmon, steelhead, sturgeon, or trout; rates are about $150 per person for one to four anglers. Nearby Garibaldi is home base for several other charter operations.

Golf

Golfers choose between two public courses in Tillamook. Near the cheese factory and east of U.S. 101, find nine-hole **Bay Breeze Golf Course** (2325 Latimer Rd., Tillamook, 503/842-1166, 8am-6pm Mon.-Fri., 8am-7pm Sat.-Sun., $10-15 for 9 holes). Another two miles north, **Alderbrook Golf Course** (7300 Alderbrook Rd., Tillamook, 503/842-6413, www.alderbrookgolfcourse.com, 9am-dusk, $30-45 for 18 holes) has 18 holes.

Wildlife-Viewing

Bird-watchers flock to Tillamook Bay June-November to view pelicans, sandpipers, tufted puffins, blue herons, and a variety of shorebirds. Prime time is before high tide, but step lively because this waterway was originally called "quicksand bay."

Accommodations

Most travelers seem to pass through Tillamook on their way to someplace else, and there are plenty of chain motels available all along the busy U.S. 101 strip north of town. A good local choice along this strip is **Ashley Inn** (1722 N. Makinster Rd., 503/842-7599 or 800/299-4817, www.ashleyinntillamook.com, $120-140), close to the cheese factory. Rooms have a refrigerator, a microwave, an iron and ironing board, a coffeemaker, and cable TV. Amenities include an indoor pool, a sauna, and a hot tub, plus a complimentary continental breakfast.

There's not a lot going on in downtown Tillamook, but if you'd like to stay in the center of things, as opposed to the lengthy and busy commercial strip north of town, then book a room at the **Mar-Clair Inn** (11 Main Ave., 503/842-7571 or 800/331-6857, www.marclair.com, $79-99), a pleasant motor court tucked just off 101 with an outdoor pool and a restaurant.

Food

To sample the county's freshest produce, visit the **Tillamook Farmers Market** in downtown Tillamook. It runs every Saturday, mid-June-late September, at the corner of 2nd Street and Laurel Avenue.

The **Farmhouse Cafe** (8am-6pm daily Labor Day-mid-June, 8am-8pm daily summer, $4-8) at the Tillamook Cheese Factory serves breakfast and lunch. The deli at the **Blue Heron French Cheese Company** (2001 Blue Heron Dr., 503/842-8282, www.blueheronoregon.com, 9am-6pm daily Labor Day-mid-June, 8am-8pm daily summer) fixes sandwiches, soups, and salads daily; in polls conducted by the local paper, this is one of the locals' favorite lunch spots. **La Mexicana** (2203 3rd St., 503/842-2101, 11am-9pm daily, $8-16) is the town's best Mexican restaurant.

This restaurant, housed in a vintage home on the edge of downtown, goes way beyond tacos and burritos, preparing local fish and seafood with south-of-the-border zest and finesse.

In downtown Tillamook, attempts to open fine dining restaurants have faltered in recent years, but one promising spot is **⟨ Pacific Restaurant** (2102 1st St., 503/354-2350, http://pacificrestaurant.info, 11:30am-9pm Thurs.-Tues., $12-29) with an eclectic menu featuring local seafood and seasonal produce. The exterior of the restaurant (right downtown) is very unassuming, but the food—including pasta, salads, salmon, and chowders—is very well prepared. Also downtown is **Fat Dog Pizza** (116 Main St., 503/354-2283, 11:30am-9pm Sun.-Thurs., 11:30am-10pm Fri.-Sat., $15). Pizzas feature house-made dough (the Fat Dog Special is for meat lovers), and the submarine sandwiches, called Zeppelins in honor of Tillamook's

dirigible history, are tasty. For burgers and microbrews, try **Corky's Bar & Grill** (204½ Main St. 503/842-6960, 11am-2:30am Tues.-Sun., $8-15).

On the west side of U.S. 101, between the two cheese meccas, lunchtime do-it-yourselfers might check the locally raised and cured meat and smoked salmon at **Debbie D's Sausage Factory** (503/842-2622).

Take your time to savor a cup of tea at **La Tea Da Tea Room** (904 Main Ave., 503/842-5447, 11am-4pm Mon.-Sat. summer, 11am-4pm Tues.-Sat. winter, high tea $21). Go for the full high tea or settle for scones, soup, or little tea sandwiches.

Information

The **Tillamook Chamber of Commerce** (3705 U.S. 101 N., 503/842-7525, www.tillamook-chamber.org, 9am-5pm Mon.-Fri.) is located across the parking lot from the cheese factory.

Three Capes Scenic Loop

The Three Capes Scenic Loop, a 35-mile byway off U.S. 101 between Tillamook and Pacific City, stays close to the ocean, which U.S. 101 does not. And although the beauty of Capes Meares, Lookout, and Kiwanda certainly justifies leaving the main highway, it would be an overstatement to portray this drive as a thrill-a-minute detour on the order of the south coast's Boardman State Park or the central coast's Otter Crest Loop. Instead of fronting the ocean, the road connecting the capes winds mostly through dairy country, small beach towns, and second-growth forest. What's special here are the three capes themselves, and unless you get out of the car and walk on the trails, you'll miss the aesthetic appeal and distinctiveness of each headland's ecosystem. The wave-battered bluffs of Cape Kiwanda, the precipitous overlooks along the Cape Lookout Highway, and the curious Octopus Tree at Cape Meares are the perfect antidotes to the inland towns along

this stretch of U.S. 101. The majority of the Three Capes lodging and dining options are clustered in Netarts and Oceanside and at the other end in Pacific City. In between, it's mostly sand dunes, isolated beaches, rainforest, and pasture. To reach the Three Capes Scenic Loop from the north, turn west at Tillamook and follow signs to Cape Meares. From the south, follow signs north of Neskowin to Pacific City.

CAPE MEARES STATE SCENIC VIEWPOINT

With stunning views, picnic tables, a newly restored lighthouse, and a uniquely contorted tree a short walk from the parking lot, **Cape Meares State Scenic Viewpoint** is the most effortless site to visit on the Three Capes Loop. It was named for English navigator John Meares, who mapped many points along this coast in a 1788 voyage. The famed **Octopus Tree** is less than 0.25 mile up a forested hill. The tentacle-like

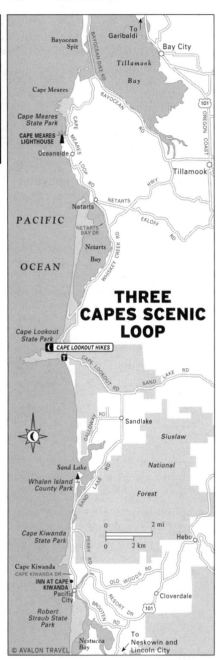

extensions of this Sitka spruce have also been compared to candelabra arms.

The 45-foot diameter of its base supports five-foot-thick trunks, each of which by itself is large enough to be a single tree. Scientists have propounded several theories for the cause of its unusual shape, including everything from wind and weather to insects damaging the spruce when it was young. A Native American legend about the spruce contends that it was shaped this way so that the branches could hold the canoes of a chief's dead family. Supposedly, the bodies were buried near the tree. This was a traditional practice among the tribes of the area, who referred to species formed thusly as "council trees."

Beyond the tree you can look south at Oceanside and Three Arch Rocks Wildlife Refuge. The sweep of Pacific shore and off-shore monoliths makes a fitting beginning (or finale, if you're driving from the south) to your sojourn along the Three Capes Scenic Loop, but be sure also to stroll the short paved trail down to the lighthouse, which begins at the parking lot and provides dramatic views of an offshore wildlife refuge, **Cape Meares Rocks.** Bring binoculars to see tufted puffins, pelagic cormorants, seals, and sea lions. The landward portion of the refuge protects rare old-growth evergreens.

The restored interior of **Cape Meares Lighthouse** (503/842-2244, 11am-4pm daily Apr.-Oct., free) was built in 1890. This beacon was replaced as a functioning light in 1963 by the automated facility behind it, and it now houses a gift shop. A free tour is occasionally offered by volunteers who might tell you about how the lighthouse was built here by mistake and perhaps offer a peek into the prismatic Fresnel lenses.

OCEANSIDE

The road between Cape Meares and Netarts heads into the beach house community of Oceanside (pop. about 340). Many of the homes are built into the cliff overlooking the ocean, Sausalito style. This maze of very steep, very narrow streets reaches its apex atop

Cape Meares Lighthouse

Maxwell Point. You can peer several hundred feet down at **Three Arch Rocks Wildlife Refuge** (www.fws.gov), part-time home to one of the continent's largest and most varied collections of shorebirds. A herd of sea lions also populates this trio of sea stacks from time to time.

Accommodations and Food

There aren't many lodging options in Oceanside. While low prices and a window on the water can be found at **Ocean Front Cabins** (1610 Pacific Ave., 503/842-6081 or 888/845-8470, www.oceanfrontcabins.com, $70-125), the older, smallish guest rooms here might give upscale travelers pause. Nonetheless, for as little as $70 for a sleeping unit without a kitchenette—or $125 for a two-bed room with a full kitchen—you'll find yourself literally a stone's throw from Oceanside's beachcombing and dining highlights. Pets are accepted in some cabins.

For a more stylish lodging, consider **Thyme and Tide B&B** (5015 Grand Ave.,

503/842-5527, www.thyme-and-tide.com, $150-160), with two handsome rooms with ocean views and a location between Netarts and Oceanside.

Another good lodging option is **Bender Vacation Rental Properties** (503/233-4363, www.benderproperties.com/beachrentals. html), boasting six units with cliff-side ocean views, large private decks, and full kitchens (except for one unit). Other amenities include fireplaces, TVs, VCRs, and microwaves. Pets are welcome at most locations. For $80-125 per night with a two-night minimum, this is a great deal.

A popular draw for hungry Three Capes travelers, ◖ **Roseanna's Oceanside Cafe** (1490 Pacific Ave. NW, 503/842-7351, www. roseannascafe.com, 9am-9pm daily, call to confirm winter hours, $11-19) garners high marks from just about everyone. At first, the weatherbeaten cedar-shake exterior might lead you to expect an old general store, as indeed it was decades ago. Once you're inside, however, the ornate decor leaves little doubt that this place takes its new identity seriously. From an elevated perch above the breakers, you'll be treated to expertly prepared local oysters, fresh salmon, a bevy of chicken dishes, and interesting pastas, such as gorgonzola and pear with penne noodles. Be sure to save room for blackberry cobbler; order it warm so the Tillamook Vanilla Bean ice cream on top melts down the sides, and watch the waves over a long cup of coffee.

Blue Agate Cafe (1610 Pacific Ave., 503/815-2596, 8am-5pm Mon. and Thurs., 8am-6pm Sat.-Sun., $7-15), is a happening little eatery in the center of Oceanside with fun breakfasts (try the Dungeness crab scramble), sandwiches, pasta, and excellent fish tacos.

NETARTS

Netarts (pop. about 750) has an enviable location overlooking Netarts Bay and the Pacific beyond. Along with nearby Oceanside, it's the closest coastal settlement to Tillamook and makes for a fine quiet getaway. Netarts Bay and seven-mile-long Netarts Spit are popular with clam diggers and crabbers, who can

© BILL MCRAE

© BILL MCRAE

Oceanside's Blue Agate Cafe

launch boats from Netarts Landing at the northeast corner of the bay. **Netarts Bay RV Park and Marina** (2260 Bilyeu St., 503/842-7774) and **Big Spruce RV Park** (4850 Netarts Hwy. W., 503/842-7443) rent motorboats and crabbing supplies.

Accommodations and Food

The **Terimore** (5105 Crab Ave., 503/842-4623 or 800/635-1821, www.terimoremotel.com, motel rooms $74-95, cabins $72-99) is situated a short walk from the water at the north end of Netarts Bay. Other than some units with fireplaces and kitchens, there are few frills, but for fair rates you'll find yourself close to the water, within easy driving distance of the Cape Lookout Trail, and a beach walk away from Roseanna's, the best restaurant on the Three Capes Scenic Loop.

For more up-to-date comforts, **Edgewater Motel and Vacation Rentals** (1st St. and Crab Ave., 503/842-1300 or 888/425-1050, www.oregoncoastmotels.com, $279) offers four luxury two-bedroom rentals directly above Netarts

Bay. Each unit has two massive stone fireplaces (one in the master bedroom, one in the "great room"), a 650-gallon Jacuzzi tub, two balconies, and a well-equipped kitchen. Each unit sleeps up to eight people (with two queen-size foldout couches). The views can't be beat. If you don't require this level of sophistication, there are also vintage cabins and cottages on the same property, each with kitchens and TVs with a DVD player, and some have fireplaces ($100-200).

You'll find several lunch and dinner spots to choose from. The view of Cape Lookout is tops at **The Schooner** (2065 Netarts Bay Rd., 503/842-4988, 11am-8pm Mon.-Thurs., 7am-9pm Fri.-Sat., 7am-8pm Sun. $10-25), and the food is a nice surprise also. Stop by for some steamer clams, fresh oysters, or tasty wood-fired pizza.

Sugarfoot's (4740 Netarts Highway W., 503/354-2422, 11am-7pm Tues.-Thurs., 11am-8pm Fri.-Sat., $8-10) offers well-prepared comfort food both to eat on premises and to go. You'll find fresh local oysters, fried Spam sliders, Italian subs, lots of veggie sandwiches, wraps, and the house specialty burger with a turkey and black bean patty. This is a friendly spot with really tasty, rather unorthodox casual dining options.

CAPE LOOKOUT STATE PARK

One of the scenic highlights of the Three Capes route, **Cape Lookout State Park** (off U.S. 101, www.oregonstateparks.org, $5 day use) juts out nearly a mile from the mainland, like a finger pointing out to sea. The cliffs along the south side of the cape rise 800 feet from the Pacific's pounding waves. The best way to take in the vista and the thrill of the location is on foot.

◖ Hiking

Hiking to the end of mile-wide Cape Lookout is one of the top coast hikes in Oregon. The trail begins either at the campground, where it climbs 2.5 miles up to a ridgetop trailhead with a parking lot, or from the Three Capes road at a well-signed trailhead. An orientation map at the trailhead details the options. The main 2.5-mile trail out to the end, along the narrowing finger of land, can give hikers the impression that they're on the prow of a giant ship suspended 500 feet above the ocean on all sides. Here, more than anywhere else on the Oregon coast, you get the sense of being on the edge of the continent. Giant spruce, western red cedars, and hemlocks surround the gently hilly trail to the tip of the cape. In March, Cape Lookout is a popular vantage point for whale-watching. June through August, a bevy of wildflowers and birds further enhance the rolling terrain en route to the tip of this headland, and in late summer red huckleberries line the path.

Halfway to the overlook, there are views north to Cape Meares over the Netarts sand spit. Even if you settle for a mere 15-minute stroll down the trail, you can look southward beyond Haystack Rock to Cascade Head. Right about where the trees open up, look for a bronze plaque commemorating the crash of a World War II plane and nearly a dozen casualties, which is embedded in the rock wall bordering the right-hand (north) side of the

trail at eye level. If you're unable to take this hike, two unmarked turnouts along the Three Capes road between the sand dunes and Cape Lookout parking lot let you survey the terrain south to Cape Kiwanda. Don't be surprised if you see hang gliders and paragliders.

Another popular trail in the state park heads north from the campground through a variety of estuarine habitats along the sand spit separating Netarts Bay from the Pacific. It's a popular site for agate hunters, clammers, and crabbers.

Camping

At the southern end of Netarts Spit is the state park's **campground and beach extension** (13000 Whiskey Creek Rd. W., 503/842-4981 for information, 800/452-5687 or www.reserveamerica.com for reservations, $5-76), which also encompasses the entire cape and the seven-mile-long Netarts Spit within its boundaries. The campground has 173 tent sites ($15-19) and 38 full-hookup sites ($20-24), as well as 13 yurts ($36), three cabins (with bathrooms, a kitchen, and a TV/VCR, $56-76), and a hiker-biker camp ($5); discounts apply October-April. Some yurts accept pets ($10 fee). Amenities include showers, flush toilets, and evening programs. Reservations and a deposit are almost always needed at this popular campground.

South of Cape Lookout, the terrain suddenly changes. Extensive sand dunes surrounding the Sand Lake Estuary suddenly appear, drowning the forest in sand. The dunes and beach attract squadrons of dune buggy enthusiasts. Camping is available year-round at **Sand Beach Campground** (5 miles south of Cape Lookout on Galloway Rd., 503/392-3161 or 877/444-6777, $16, reservations at www.recreation.gov), a part of the Siuslaw National Forest, with has basic sites for tenters and RVs. This dramatic area is also popular with hikers.

PACIFIC CITY AND CAPE KIWANDA

As you approach the shore in Pacific City, the sight of **Haystack Rock** will immediately grab your attention. At 327 feet, this sea stack is nearly 100 feet taller than the similarly named rock in Cannon Beach. Standing a mile offshore, this monolith has a brooding, enigmatic quality that constantly draws the eye to it. Look closely, and you'll understand why some folks called it Teacup Rock.

The tawny sandstone escarpment of Cape Kiwanda juts half a mile out to sea from Pacific City and frames the north end of the beach. In storm-tossed waters, this cape is the undisputed king of rock-and-roll, if you go by coffee table books and calendar photos. While other sandstone promontories on the north coast have been ground into sandy beaches by the pounding surf, it's been theorized that Kiwanda has endured thanks to the buffer of Haystack Rock. In any case, hang gliding aficionados are glad the cape is here. They scale its shoulders and set themselves aloft off the north face to glide above the beach and dunes.

The small town of Pacific City, with about 1,000 residents, is at the base of Cape Kiwanda. It attracts growing numbers of vacationers and retirees but remains true to its 19th-century origins as a working fishing village. In addition to the knockout seascapes and recreation, if you come here at the right times of day, you may be treated to a unique spectacle—the launch or return of the **dory fleet.**

It's a tradition dating back to the 1920s, when gillnetting was banned on the Nestucca River to protect the dwindling salmon runs. To retain their livelihood, commercial fishers began to haul flat-bottomed double-ended dories down to the beach on horse-drawn wagons, then row out through the surf to fish. These days, trucks and trailers get the boats to and from the beach, and outboard motors have replaced oar power, enabling the dories to get 50 miles out to sea. If you come around 6am, you can watch them taking off. The fleet's late afternoon return attracts a crowd that arrives to see the dory operators skidding their craft as far as possible up the beach to the waiting boat trailers. Others meet the dories to buy salmon and tuna.

In mid-July, **Dory Days** celebrate the area's fleet. The three-day fete includes craft and food

booths, a pancake breakfast, a fishing derby, and other activities. For more information, call the **chamber of commerce** (503/965-6161). If you want to join the anglers for a summertime ocean fishing trip on a dory, contact **Haystack Fishing** (888/965-7555), across from the beach near the Inn at Cape Kiwanda.

In addition, the Pacific City area is besieged by surfers, who enjoy some of the longest waves on the Oregon coast. **Robert Straub State Park,** just south of town, offers access to Nestucca Bay and to the dunes and a long uninterrupted stretch of beach. Pacific City surfers should use *extreme* caution when the dories are returning to the beach.

Accommodations

The nicest motel on the Three Capes Scenic Loop is the large ◖ **Inn at Cape Kiwanda** (33105 Cape Kiwanda Dr., 503/965-6366 or 888/965-7001, www.yourlittlebeachtown.com/inn, $189-229). All rooms face a beautiful beach and Cape Kiwanda's giant sand dune. If it's too rainy to go outside, fireplaces and spacious well-appointed rooms make for great storm-watching. Whirlpool tub rooms are available, and pets are permitted in some rooms.

For a more historic experience, head to the ◖ **Craftsman B&B** (35255 4th St., 503/965-4574, www.craftsmanbb.com, $150-180), an exquisitely refurbished Craftsman-style home with very stylish guest rooms. Built in 1921 (and perhaps Pacific City's oldest home), this B&B is a monument to sensitive historic preservation and also a very friendly, comfortable place to stay. All four guest rooms have private baths and are decorated according to the styles of Arts and Crafts luminaries such as Gustav Stickley, Charles Rennie Macintosh, and William Morris.

Camping

About 4.5 miles north of Pacific City on the Three Capes Loop Road, the **Clay Meyers Natural Area at Whalen Island** (4.5 miles north of Pacific City on Sandlake Rd., 503/965-6085, www.co.tillamook.or.us, $10-15) has a small campground run by Tillamook County. It's an open sandy spot with a boat launch and flush toilets; nearby hiking trails traverse wetlands and provide a great look at the coastal Sand Lake Estuary.

Food

A popular and well-known Pacific City hangout is the **(** **Pelican Pub and Brewery** (33180 Cape Kiwanda Dr., 503/965-7007, 8am-close daily, $6-23). Set in a most enviable spot right on the beach opposite Cape Kiwanda and Haystack Rock, this place boasts the best coastal view of any brewpub in Oregon. Buttermilk-beer pancakes, dory-caught fish-and-chips, pizzas, "shark bites," tasty chili, and IPA-poached salmon are some of the standouts. The pub's brews, including Tsunami Stout, Doryman's Dark Ale, India Pelican Ale, and MacPelican's Scottish Style Ale, have garnered stacks of awards.

Delicate Palate Bistro (35280 Brooten Rd., 503/965-6464, www.delicatepalate.com, 5pm-close Wed.-Sun., $17-25) is a classy little place where the chef brings a deft touch to classics— think pan-seared wild salmon with artichoke ragout or bouillabaisse made with a coconut curry broth and served with soba noodles—and the meals are backed up by an excellent wine list (or a long martini menu, if you prefer). The deck, which overlooks the local airstrip, is open for dining when weather allows.

Also on Brooten Road toward the north end of town, find the **(** **Grateful Bread Bakery** (34085 Brooten Rd., 503/965-7337, 8am-4pm Thurs.-Mon., $5-9), where the challah bread, carrot cake, marionberry strudel, and other homemade baked goods deserve special mention. The full breakfast menu offers a range of tasty omelets served with oven-roasted spuds at great prices. Lunch sandwiches include a wide range of vegetarian options.

Neskowin and Cascade Head

NESKOWIN

The tiny vacation village of Neskowin (rhymes with "let's go in," pop. 170) has a quiet appeal based on a beautiful beach and a golf course in the shadow of 1,500-foot-high Cascade Head. It's the polar opposite of busy Lincoln City, 15 miles south. There's not much to do here but relax on the uncrowded beach and enjoy the views of Cascade Head and the dark beauty of **Proposal Rock,** a stony, forested hillock that stands right at the edge of the surf, with Neskowin Creek curving around it. The feature was named by Neskowin's first postmistress, whose daughter received a marriage proposal nearby. Neskowin has the reputation as a beach town for old-money, in-the-know Portland families.

Sleepy Neskowin has only one art gallery, and it's a good one. **Hawk Creek Gallery** (48460 U.S. 101 S., 503/392-3879, www. hawkcreekgallery.com, 11am-5pm daily summer, 11am-5pm Sat.-Sun. spring and fall) is the

studio and showroom for the works of painter Michael Schlicting, who exhibits his work internationally but has made the Hawk Creek Gallery his home base since 1978.

Neskowin Marsh Golf Course (48405 Hawk St., 503/392-3377, $18 for nine holes) has streams and water hazards adding a challenge to most of the nine greens.

Accommodations

Proposal Rock Inn (48988 U.S. 101 S., 503/392-3115, www.proposalrockneskowin. com, rooms $62-127, suites $125-240) backs up on Hawk Creek and commands a fine view of the beach and the eponymous rock. Two-room oceanview suites with a full kitchen fetch higher prices than the standard non-oceanview guest rooms, but all are right on the beach.

The nine two-bedroom condo units at **The Chelan** (48750 Breakers Blvd., 503/392-3270, www.rentoregoncoast.com, $125-245) are comfier than the boxy stucco exterior suggests, with

© BILL MCRAE

Neskowin's Hawk Creek Cafe is a top spot for breakfast.

fireplaces, kitchens, views, and direct access to the beach.

To rent a home in the Neskowin or Pacific City area, contact the property management firm **Neskowin Vacation Rentals** (503/392-4850, http://neskowinvacationrentals.com).

Food

Neskowin's only restaurant, fortunately, serves great food at moderate prices. Waits can be long at the tiny **Hawk Creek Cafe** (4505 Salem Ave., 503/392-3838, 8am-9pm Thurs.-Sun., 11am-9pm Mon.-Wed., $12-23), but it's the only game in town and has good food. Count on filling omelets for breakfast; sandwiches (about $10), burgers, and wood-fired pizza ($16-18) for lunch; and grilled fish and steaks for dinner.

CASCADE HEAD
Cascade Head Scenic Research Area

About 10 miles north of Lincoln City, the 11,890-acre Cascade Head Experimental Forest

was set aside in 1934 for scientific study of typical coastal Sitka spruce and western hemlock forests found along the Oregon coast. In 1974 Congress established the 9,670-acre **Cascade Head Scenic Research Area** (www.fsl.orst.edu/chef), which includes the western half of the forest, several prairie headlands, and the Salmon River estuary. In 1980 the entire area was designated a biosphere reserve as part of the United Nations Biosphere Reserve system.

The headlands, reaching as high as 1,800 feet, are unusual for their extensive prairies still dominated by native grasses: red fescue, wild rye, and Pacific reedgrass. The Nechesney Indians, who inhabited the area as long as 12,000 years ago, purposely burned forest tracts around Cascade Head probably to provide browse for deer and to reduce the possibility of larger uncontrollable blazes. These human-made alterations are complemented by the inherent dryness of south-facing slopes that receive increased exposure to the sun. In contrast to these grasslands, the northern part of the headland is the domain of giant spruces and firs because it catches the brunt of the heavy rainfalls and lingering fogs. Endemic wildflowers include coastal paintbrush, goldenrod, streambank lupine, rare hairy checkermallow, and blue violet, a plant critical to the survival of the Oregon silverspot butterfly, a threatened species found in only six locations. Deer, elk, coyotes, snowshoe hare, and the Pacific giant salamander find refuge here, while bald eagles, great horned owls, and peregrine falcons may be seen hunting above the grassy slopes. Today, in addition to its biological importance, the area is a mecca for some 6,000 hikers annually and for anglers who target the salmon and steelhead runs on the Salmon River.

On the north side of the Salmon River, turn west from U.S. 101 onto **Three Rocks Road** for a scenic driving detour on the south side of Cascade Head. The paved road curves about 2.5 miles above the wetlands and widening channel of the Salmon River estuary, passes Savage Road, and ends at a parking area and boat launch at Knight County Park. From the park, the road turns to gravel and narrows (not suitable for RVs or trailers) and continues about another 0.5 mile to its end at a spectacular overlook across the estuary.

HIKING

Cascade Head offers some outstanding scenic hikes, with rainforest pathways and wildflower meadows giving way to dramatic ocean views.

A short but brisk hike to the top of the headland on a **Nature Conservancy trail** begins near Knight County Park. Leave your car at the park and walk 0.5 mile up Savage Road to the trailhead. It's 1.7 miles one-way, with a 1,100-foot elevation gain. No dogs or bicycles are allowed on the trail, which is open year-round.

Two trails are accessible from Cascade Head Road (Forest Rd. 1861), a gravel road that is open seasonally (July 16-Dec. 31) that heads west off U.S. 101 about three miles north of Three Rocks Road, near the highway summit of Cascade Head. Travel this road four miles west of U.S. 101 to the **Hart's Cove Trailhead.** The first part of the trail runs through arching red alder treetops and 250-year-old Sitka spruces with five-foot diameters. The understory of mosses and ferns is nourished by 100-inch rainfalls. Next, the trail emerges into open grasslands. The five-mile round-trip hike loses 900 feet in elevation on its way to an oceanfront meadow overlooking Hart's Cove, where the barking of sea lions might greet you. This trail can have plenty of mud, so boots are recommended as you tromp through the rainforest.

An easier trail accessible from Cascade Head Road heads to a viewpoint on the Nature Conservancy's preserve. (Again, no dogs or bikes are allowed on Nature Conservancy land.) The one-mile trail starts about 3.5 miles west of U.S. 101 and heads to a big meadow and an ocean overlook. It's possible to continue from the overlook, heading downhill to join up with the lower Nature Conservancy trail described above.

The **Cascade Head Trail** runs six miles roughly parallel to the highway, with a south trailhead near the intersection of Three Rocks Road and U.S. 101 and a north trailhead at Falls Creek, on U.S. 101 about one mile south of Neskowin. It passes through old-growth forest and is entirely inland, without the spectacular ocean views of other trails in the area.

Sitka Center for Art and Ecology

The region in the shadow of Cascade Head can be explored in even greater depth thanks to the **Sitka Center for Art and Ecology** (56605 Sitka Dr., Otis, 541/994-5485, www.sitkacenter.org, 8:30am-4:30pm Mon.-Fri.), located off Savage Road on the south side of the headland. Classes are offered June-August focusing on art and nature, with an emphasis on the strong relationship between the two. Experts in everything from local plant communities to Siletz Indian baskets conduct outdoor workshops on the grounds of Cascade Head Ranch. Classes can last from a couple of days to a week, and fees vary accordingly.

CENTRAL COAST

Oregon's central coast, from Lincoln City to Reedsport and Winchester Bay, embraces such contrasts that it's difficult to generalize about the region.

In the north, Lincoln City's dense mix of lodgings and shopping, combined with its Native American casinos, generates the coast's worst traffic jams, especially on holidays and weekends. The sprawling town isn't everyone's first choice for a quiet getaway, but it's a longtime favorite with families. Depoe Bay—built around the world's smallest navigable natural harbor—is headquarters for the coast's busiest whale-watching fleet—and one of the largest and most sprawling condo developments.

A necklace of small state parks adorns the shore every couple of miles all the way from southern Lincoln City southward; inland, the Siuslaw National Forest safeguards several wilderness areas and groves of rare old-growth coastal forest, beckoning hikers to explore the primeval landscapes. Just north of Newport, Yaquina Head Outstanding Natural Area offers excellent vantage points for up close whale-watching and bird-watching, plus tidepools accessible to wheelchair users.

The bustling harbor at Newport is home to the state's largest commercial fishing fleet and second-largest recreational fleet, which runs charters year-round for rockfish and seasonally for salmon, tuna, and halibut. Newport also boasts the state-of-the-art Oregon Coast Aquarium, former residence of Keiko the

HIGHLIGHTS

◖ **Oregon Coast Aquarium:** Explore the life of Oregon's shores and oceans at this excellent aquarium (page 116).

◖ **Yaquina Head Outstanding Natural Area:** A soaring lighthouse stands above a tidepool-studded inlet at this small park, the quintessence of the Oregon coast (page 118).

◖ **Whale-Watching:** *Thar she blows!* Newport is a great departure point for gray whale-watching tours (page 120).

◖ **Cape Perpetua:** One of the most dramatic natural areas along the Oregon coast, Cape Perpetua is a top spot for hiking and exploring tidepools (page 130).

◖ **Sea Lion Caves:** Take an elevator ride down to the caves at cliff's bottom to get a close look at the Steller sea lion rookery (page 137).

◖ **Heceta Head Lighthouse and Devil's Elbow:** Climb to the top of this whitewashed lighthouse for wonderful views—or stay in the lighthouse keeper's house, now a B&B (page 137).

◖ **John Dellenback Trail:** Explore 400-foot dunes in the Oregon Dunes National Recreation Area. It's like trekking the Sahara (page 150).

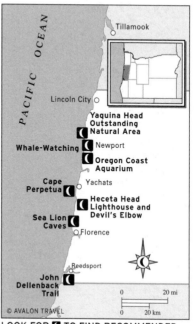

© AVALON TRAVEL

LOOK FOR ◖ TO FIND RECOMMENDED SIGHTS, ACTIVITIES, DINING, AND LODGING.

beloved orca, and the bohemian resort community of Nye Beach, which has been attracting tourists since the 19th century.

Just south of Yachats, the panoramic view from Cape Perpetua can, on a clear day, extend 75 miles in each direction. Down at sea level, the tidepools here are some of the most fascinating on the coast. At Sea Lion Caves, a touristy but unique experience between Yachats and Florence, the world's largest sea cave is the only mainland rookery of Steller sea lions in the lower 48 states. Close by, photographers spend more time trying to capture the perfect image of Heceta Head Lighthouse than any other sight along the entire coast.

PLANNING YOUR TIME

It's easy to spend a few days exploring the central coast. Although **Lincoln City** has abundant hotel rooms and is a good fallback during busy times of the year, tiny **Depoe Bay** is a great place to spend a night, perhaps with an early rise to take a fishing or whale-watching trip. And though **Newport** is a big city by Oregon coast standards, it's definitely worth spending a couple of nights here. In fact, if you're looking for a base for central coast explorations, Newport is well situated to visit sites from Lincoln City down to Florence. While in Newport, you may simply want to poke around the Nye Beach and Bayfront neighborhoods,

CENTRAL COAST

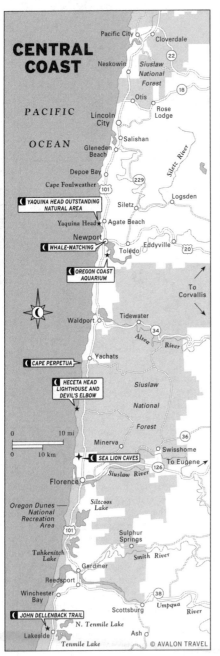

beachcomb on Agate Beach, and check out the tidepools and lighthouse at the Yaquina Head Outstanding Natural Area; or you might decide to devote a day to the Oregon Coast Aquarium and the nearby Oregon State University Hatfield Marine Science Center.

Personally, when we have the opportunity to plunk down at the coast for a long weekend, we almost always head to **Yachats** to enjoy the low-key atmosphere, the incredible natural beauty, and the good restaurants of this tiny town. If you are touring the coast, we think it (and the incredible Cape Perpetua coastline just south) is worth a full day and night of your time.

Florence is a short hop from Yachats and is a good alternative if you'd rather stay in a slightly larger town with a lively Old Town and easy access to the north end of the Oregon Dunes National Recreation Area, a fantastic landscape of dazzling white sand mountains and jewel lakes stretched along nearly 50 miles of shoreline.

Although anglers may want to stay at **Winchester Bay,** for most coast travelers this little town is a good stop for fish-and-chips, but not an overnight destination. Nearby, **Reedsport** is in the heart of the dune country and a good place to camp while exploring the dunes, but it does not have a huge wealth of fancy hotels and restaurants.

Lincoln City

Back in 1964, five burgs that straddled seven miles of beachfront between Siletz Bay and the Salmon River came together and incorporated as Lincoln City. In commemoration, a 14-foot bronze statue of Abraham Lincoln was donated to the city by an Illinois sculptor. *The Lank Lawyer Reading in His Saddle While His Horse Grazes* originally occupied a city park; today the statue stands in a nondescript lot at NE 22nd Street and Quay Avenue. Look for the sign on U.S. 101 near the Dairy Queen.

In the following decades, what were discrete towns have grown and melded into an uninterrupted conurbation with a population of about 8,000 (which can balloon to 30,000 on a busy weekend). While the resulting sprawl and heavy traffic on U.S. 101 can be maddening at times, once you get off the highway, Lincoln City has

some charming neighborhoods (check out the Taft area at the south end of town); wide sandy beaches; superlative wildlife-viewing around Siletz Bay; the large freshwater Devils Lake; and two Native American casinos. Add prime kite-flying, some of the coast's better restaurants, and bibliophilic and antiquing haunts, and it's clear that there's more to the area than the pull of saltwater taffy and outlet malls.

SIGHTS AND RECREATION
Lincoln City Beach

Lincoln City boasts seven uninterrupted miles of sandy beach. From Siletz Bay north to Road's End State Recreation Area, there are more than a dozen access points. You can head west from U.S. 101 on just about any side street to get there, though high coastal bluffs lining the north-central portion of town may mean a climb down (and back up) long flights of stairs cut into the cliff. For something approaching solitude on a crowded day, follow Logan Road west from the highway near the north end of town to **Road's End State Recreation Area;** tidepools and a secluded cove add to the allure. This stretch is also popular with windsurfers.

Tidepool explorers should also check out the **rock formations** at SW 11th Street (Canyon Drive Park), NW 15th Street, and SW 32nd Street.

The **D River Wayside,** a small park on the beach in more or less the middle of town, is a state park property where you can watch what locals claim is the "world's shortest river" empty into the ocean. Flowing just 120 feet from its source, Devils Lake, to its mouth at the Pacific, it's short, all right; despite its unspectacular appearance, it was a cause célèbre when *The Guinness Book of World Records* withdrew the D's claim to fame in favor of a Montana waterway, the Roe. Local schoolkids rallied to the D's defense with an amended measurement, but the Roe, at a mere 53 feet long, carries the *Guinness* imprimatur as the shortest river. In

KESEY'S LEGACY

Two miles south of Lincoln City, you'll come to the turnoff for Highway 229 along the Siletz River. If you drive down the north side of the river about 1.25 miles, on the opposite shore you'll note a Victorian-ish house that was built to last. It was constructed for the movie version of *Sometimes a Great Notion.* The 1971 film, a so-so adaptation of Ken Kesey's memorable novel, starred Paul Newman, Lee Remick, Henry Fonda, and Michael Sarrazin. The plot concerns the never-say-die spirit of an antiunion timber baron, his not-always-supportive family, and life in the mythical Coast Range logging community of Wakonda. A huge porch once fronted the riverbank, heavily reinforced against the elements. It was taken down in the decade after the movie was made, but it lives on in the pages of the book. Much of the movie was shot in this area, with café scenes taking place at Mo's on Newport's bay front. Other scenes were shot near Florence.

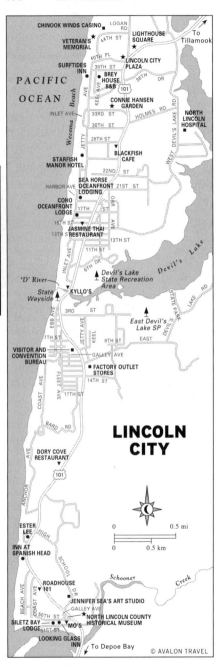

addition to seeing the D River flow from "D" Lake into "D" ocean, you can fly a kite on the beach. It's one of the easier beach access points between stretches of high motel-topped bluffs, so it can get a little crowded.

Another convenient beach access is off SW 51st Street at the south end of town, just before **Siletz Bay.** A large parking area here in what's known as the Taft District stands beside the driftwood-strewn shore of the bay, where you can often see a group of harbor seals chasing their dinner or coming in for a closer look at you. It's a short walk to the ocean.

Time was when it was common for storms and currents to wash up that ultimate beach-comber's prize—**glass fishing floats**—on the Oregon coast. Lincoln City improves the beachcomber's odds by distributing over 2,000 glass floats along its beaches mid-October-Memorial Day. Handcrafted by Pacific Northwest glass artists, each of the colorful floats is signed and numbered and placed by volunteers on the beaches above the high-tide line. If you find one, it's yours to keep; you can call or stop in at the visitor center for a certificate and information about the artist who created it.

Devils Lake

Devils Lake, just east of the highway, is the recreation center of Lincoln City. In addition to windsurfing and hydroplaning, you can fish here—the lake is stocked with hatchery trout, and there's also a population of wild coho salmon (catch-and-release only) as well as lampreys. There's also good bird-watching on and around this shallow 678-acre lake, which attracts flocks of migratory geese, ducks, and other waterfowl. Species to look for include canvasbacks, Canada geese, widgeons, gadwalls, grebes, and mallards. Bald eagles and ospreys nest in the trees bordering the lake.

The lake takes its name from a local Native American legend. The story goes that when Siletz warriors paddled a canoe across the lake one moonlit night, a tentacled beast erupted from the still water and pulled the men under. It's said that boaters today who cross the moon's reflection in the middle of the lake tempt the same fate, but the lake's devil has remained silent for years.

Of the five access points, East Devils Lake Road off U.S. 101 northeast of town offers a scenic route around the lake's east side before rejoining U.S. 101 near the day-use portion of the state park at the south end of the lake. To reach the camping area of **Devils Lake State Recreation Area,** take NE 6th Drive east from U.S. 101, about 0.25 mile north of the D River. The day-use area has a boat ramp, and there's a moorage dock across the lake adjacent to the campground.

Mountain bikes, canoes, fishing boats, and Jet Skis can be rented at the **Blue Heron Landing** (4006 W. Devils Lake Rd., 541/994-4708, www.blueheronlanding.net).

Drift Creek Falls

Although it requires a drive inland, it's worth heading about 10 miles east to hike **Drift Creek Falls** (503/392-3161, $5 NW Forest Pass to park). The relatively easy but steadily downhill

© JUDY JEWELL

Head east from Lincoln City to find Drift Creek Falls.

1.5-mile trail passes through a forest with mostly second growth, a little old growth, lots of big stumps, and an understory of lovely native plants, and it leads to a dramatic 240-foot-high suspension bridge overlooking the 75-foot falls. The bridge, built in 1998, is as much an attraction as the falls—it sways a little bit as you walk out to view the falls. From the bridge, the trail continues another 0.25 mile to the base of the falls.

From Oregon State Road 18, turn south at Rose Lodge onto Bear Creek Road (which becomes Forest Road 17) and follow it for about nine miles. At the fork with Schooner Creek Road, be sure to go left (uphill); a rustic sign notes that it's the way to "Drift Creek Camp."

From U.S. 101, turn east onto Drift Creek Road (at the south end of Lincoln City), then south onto South Drift Creek Road and east onto Forest Road 17. Follow Forest Road 17 for about 10 miles.

Siletz River

The **Siletz Bay National Wildlife Refuge** preserves coastal estuaries and wetlands on either side of U.S. 101 at the south end of Lincoln City. The skeleton trees here are reminders of times when the salt marsh was diked to provide pasture for dairy cows. Now these snags are used by red-tailed hawks, bald eagles, and other birds of prey. The wetlands provide habitat for great blue herons, egrets, and other waterbirds.

During the summer, refuge rangers lead a small number of **paddle trips** along the Siletz estuaries. Trips are free, but participants must register well beforehand (541/270-0610) and provide their own canoe or kayak. **Siletz Moorage** (82 Siletz Hwy., 541/996-3671) rents kayaks ($25 for 4 hours) from its location on the north bank of the river just east of the highway.

Casinos

One of the biggest draws in town is the **Chinook Winds Casino** (1777 NW 44th St., 541/996-5825 or 888/244-6665, www.chinookwindscasino.com, open 24 hours daily), operated by the Confederated Tribes of Siletz

Indians, near the north end of town. In addition to slots, blackjack, poker, Keno, bingo, craps, and roulette, the casino has two on-site restaurants and a busy schedule of big-name (or formerly big-name) entertainment.

About 25 miles east of Lincoln City is the state's number-one visitor attraction, **Spirit Mountain Casino** (21700 SW Salmon River Hwy., Grand Ronde, 800/760-7977, http://spiritmountain.com, open 24 hours daily), operated by the Confederated Tribes of Grand Ronde. Games of chance include slots, craps, blackjack, poker, Keno, and bingo. No matter what you think of the casino, it should be noted that the Grand Ronde people have done a great job at getting their tribal status officially reinstated after the U.S. government officially terminated the tribe in 1954, leaving it with not much more than the tribal cemetery and a shed. They have amassed land and established a community fund that is a substantial supporter of nonprofit organizations in Oregon—6 percent of the casino's proceeds go into this charitable fund.

North Lincoln County Historical Museum

The modest **North Lincoln County Historical Museum** (4907 SW U.S. 101, 541/996-6614, www.northlincolncountyhistoricalmuseum. com, noon-5pm Wed.-Sun. May 15-Oct. 15 and Wed.-Sat. Oct. 16-Dec. 14 and Feb. 1-May 14, free) tells the story of this area through exhibits of old-time logging machinery, homesteading tools, fishing, military life, and Native American history. A highlight is the great collection of Japanese glass fishing floats.

Connie Hansen Garden

Tucked into the neighborhood between busy U.S. 101 and the beach, the **Connie Hansen Garden** (1931 NW 33rd St., 541/994-6338, www.conniehansengarden.com, dawn-dusk daily, free) is a great example of a coastal rainforest garden. The late Connie Hansen bought the land because its dampness seemed well suited to growing irises, her favorite plants, but

she soon expanded her vision, working with the site's ecology and her own artistic talents to create a horticultural showcase. Guided tours are available for a small fee with advance notice, and a gift shop is open 10am-2pm Tuesday and Saturday.

Glass Art

Spend a rainy day learning to blow a glass float or paperweight at the **Jennifer Sears Art Studio** (4821 SW U.S. 101, 541/996-2569, www.jennifersearsglassart.com, 10am-6pm daily, classes $65-135, reservations recommended). Kids ages 8-10 may participate with parental supervision. Be sure to wear closed-toe shoes and no fleece!

About four miles south of town, near Salishan, you can watch the glass blowers at **Alder House** (611 Immonen Rd., 541/994-6485, www.alderhouse.com, 10am-5pm daily May-Thanksgiving weekend) and buy floats, paperweights, or other glass creations at very reasonable prices. Call ahead to confirm opening hours.

Golf

The area's most prestigious golf resort is seven miles south of Lincoln City at Gleneden Beach. **Salishan Spa and Golf Resort** (7760 N. U.S. 101, Gleneden Beach, 541/764-3632 or 800/890-8037, www.salishan.com, $89-119 for 18 holes) is an award-winning 18-hole course set in the foothills of the Coast Range and bordered by Siletz Bay and the sea. This challenging 6,470-yard, par-71, championship layout course was redesigned by Oregon golf superstar Peter Jacobsen and includes stunning ocean views. Keep in mind that this is a Scottish links course, where the roughs are really rough.

The 18-hole **Chinook Winds Golf Resort** (3245 NE 50th St., 541/994-8442, http://chinookwindscasino.com, $35-40 for 18 holes) is set in hilly (and frequently windy) terrain amidst towering coastal mountains on the edge of Lincoln City, this course is another venture of the Chinook Winds Casino, operated by the Confederated Tribes of Siletz Indians. The golf course spans just 5,000 yards with men's par 65 and women's 72.

ENTERTAINMENT AND EVENTS

Housed within the renovated Gleneden Brick and Tile Factory, five miles south of Lincoln City in Gleneden Beach, **Eden Hall** (6645 Gleneden Beach Loop Rd., 541/764-3826 performance info, 541/764-3825 restaurant, www.edenhall.com) stages live theater and hosts an impressively eclectic roster of regional and touring musicians. This spacious airy warehouse has an excellent sound system and is a wonderful place to take in a concert, with an emphasis on jazz, folk, and blues. Enjoy lunch or dinner at the adjacent Side Door Café.

The Arts

Lincoln City's homegrown theater company, **Theatre West** (3536 SE U.S. 101, 541/994-5663, www.theatrewest.com), stages half a dozen productions each year, with an emphasis on comedies plus musicals and drama. Visit the website for a list of current plays and their synopses.

Cinema

Catch first-run flicks at the **Bijou Theatre** (1624 NE U.S. 101, 541/994-8255), an old-time movie house dating back to the 1930s, making it a rare old survivor around here. The six-screen **Regal Cinemas** (3755 SE High School Dr., 541/994-7649), just east of U.S. 101 in the south end of town, is its modern competitor.

Festivals and Events

Lincoln City calls itself the kite capital of the world, pointing to its position midway between the pole and the equator, which gives the area predictable wind patterns. The town holds not one but two kite fiestas at the D River Wayside each year. The summer **Kite Festival** (541/994-3070 or 800/452-2151) takes place the last weekend in June; the fall festival is held the second weekend in October. The event is famous for giant spin socks, some as long as 150 feet.

SHOPPING

To sample the work of area artists, check out the **Ryan Gallery** (4270 N. U.S. 101, 541/994-5391, www.ryanartgallery.com). South of town at Salishan, the **Lawrence Gallery** (7755 U.S. 101 N., 541/764-2318, www.lawrencegallery.net) is a high-end gallery that's lots of fun to visit.

With some 65 shops, the **Tanger Outlet Center** (1500 SE East Devils Lake Rd., 541/996-5000), near the south end of town, is the largest outlet mall on the Oregon coast and has become something of a regional destination. Shops here include the ones you'd expect—Coach, Chico's, Eddie Bauer—plus the Oregon-based **Pendleton Woolen Mills** (541/994-2496, www.pendleton-usa.com).

Northwest Winds (130 SE U.S. 101, 541/994-1004) sells and repairs kites just across the highway from the D River Wayside, Lincoln City's kite-flying hub.

ACCOMMODATIONS

Lincoln City has more hotel rooms than any other coastal Oregon city. There are plenty to choose from, and many are very similar—basic hotel rooms within walking distance of the beach. However, there are some distinctions. Unless severely constrained by budget, one would not purposefully choose to stay on the east side of U.S. 101, necessitating an unpleasant fording of that great vehicular river just to walk to the beach, so, with one exception (Salishan), all the following hotels are on the beach side of the highway. Also, just because a hotel is new doesn't mean that it's preferred over older models. Many vintage hotels and motels have the best locations, and their slightly worn-in atmosphere is perfect for a summer holiday.

$50-100

The **Ester Lee** (3803 SW U.S. 101, 541/996-3606 or 888/996-3606, www.esterlee.com, $97-117) is a decades-old family motel complex, with some cottages on a bluff above miles of beachfront. All rooms have ocean views and fireplaces; some have kitchens and hot tubs.

CENTRAL COAST

Pets are allowed in some of the cottage units, most of which have kitchens and fireplaces. It's not a fancy place, but it's clean and pleasant with a great location and a good value.

$100-150

The **Siletz Bay Lodge** (1012 SW 51st St., 541/996-6111 or 888/430-2100, www.siletzbaylodge.com, $128-148), on the north end of Siletz Bay on a driftwood-strewn beach, is a family-friendly and wheelchair-accessible (with elevators) lodging in a location ideal for birdwatching and viewing seals. About half of the standard rooms of this older hotel have balconies, with delightful views of the bay and the sunset over Salishan Spit. In-room amenities include microwaves, refrigerators, and coffeemakers, and a continental breakfast is offered.

For a small oceanfront luxury hotel near the popular D River Wayside, the **Shearwater Inn** (120 NW Inlet Ct., 541/994-4121 or 800/869-8069, www.theshearwaterinn.com, $129-279) offers 30 units with balconies and gas fireplaces. Guests meet in the lobby every afternoon to sample Oregon wine. The hotel provides concierge and massage services, a continental breakfast, and accepts pets. The building is also wheelchair accessible.

A longtime Lincoln City motel, the **Coho Oceanfront Lodge** (1635 NW Harbor Ave., 541/994-3684 or 800/848-7006, www.thecoholodge.com, $144-220), has undergone a multimillion-dollar renovation; guest rooms have a sleek and sophisticated modern look. A DVD library, an indoor pool, a hot tub, and a sauna are available for guests to use; pets are allowed in some rooms.

Another place that has had a makeover is the **Surftides Inn** (2945 NW Jetty Ave., 541/994-2191 or 800/452-2159, www.surftidesinn.com, $140-240 for updated oceanview rooms), a large complex hugging the beach at the northern edge of Lincoln City. All of the oceanfront guest rooms have balconies and most have fireplaces. The guest rooms' redecoration has given the place a welcome freshening up; all rooms include a small refrigerator, a microwave oven, and a coffeemaker, as well as cable TV with a

DVD player. The inn has an indoor pool, a decent restaurant, a lounge, and meeting rooms. Prices vary by view; ask about partial or noview rooms for up to 30 percent in savings. Pets are accepted in some rooms.

On the bluff above the beach, with fine views and easy access to the sand, **Sea Horse Oceanfront Lodging** (2039 NW Harbor Dr., 541/994-2101 or 800/662-2101, www.seahorsemotel.com, $119-249) has a dizzying selection of lodging options, from simple motel rooms to cottages, houses, and two- and three-bedroom units, all in an extensive and quiet oceanfront compound. While it's a bit hard to generalize, most rooms have kitchens, some have fireplaces, and all guests are welcome at the breakfast bar, indoor pool, and outdoor hot tub, which overlooks the beach. There are a handful of discounted partial or no-view rooms available. This friendly and venerable operation is one of the reasons Lincoln City is so popular with families.

Another good spot on the north end of Siletz Bay in Lincoln City's historic Taft area is the **Looking Glass Inn** (861 SW 51 St., 541/996-3996 or 800/843-4940, www.lookingglassinn.com, $114-129), an attractive place that would be quiet and tucked away if it weren't for the busy Mo's restaurant just across the road. Most rooms have kitchenettes, and most are dog-friendly.

Close to the beach at the north end of town, **Brey House B&B** (3725 NW Keel Ave., 541/994-7123, www.breyhouse.com, $109-159) is one of the oldest bed-and-breakfast inns on the Oregon coast, a three-story Cape Cod-style home built in 1940 with four bedrooms, all with private baths and entrances. The excellent breakfast is served in a light-filled room overlooking the ocean. Rooms are for adults only.

$150-200

More a small boutique hotel than the typical sprawling motel complex that typifies Lincoln City, ◖**Starfish Manor Hotel** (2735 NW Inlet Ave., 541/996-9300 or 800/972-6155, www.onthebeachfront.com, $179-399) has just 17 oceanfront guest rooms and suites perched above the beach. All units have large ocean-view whirlpool tubs, fireplaces, oceanfront decks, kitchenettes, tasteful furnishings, and fine linens. Some units have two bedrooms. The Starfish is in a quiet part of town, perfect for a romantic getaway. The folks who own the Starfish have two other small boutique hotels with even more upscale suites; see the Starfish website for links.

If you've been fantasizing about rolling out of bed, slipping on your robe and walking out—coffee in hand—onto a semiprivate stretch of beach, then the **Inn at Spanish Head** (4009 SW U.S. 101, 541/996-2161 or 800/452-8127, www.spanishhead.com, $159-249) may be your best bet. Oregon's only resort hotel right on the beach, the inn takes its place—large and looming—against the backdrop of rugged cliffs. Whether a suite, studio, or bed-room unit, every room has an ocean view. On-site amenities include Fathoms, the 10th-floor restaurant-bar, a fireplace lounge, meeting rooms, a heated outdoor pool, saunas, a spa, and an exercise room.

Over $200

When asked to choose *the* place to stay on the Oregon coast, most Oregonians would have the **C Salishan Spa and Golf Resort** (7760 N. U.S. 101, Gleneden Beach, 541/764-3600 or 800/452-2300, www.salishan.com, $212-292), a few miles south of Lincoln City, on their short list.

While there are distant Siletz Bay views, Salishan isn't a beachfront resort, and most folks quickly learn to appreciate the peace of the forest and the golf course. This paradigm shift is facilitated by art and landscape architecture that convey the vision of John Gray, who built Salishan and such other Pacific Northwest properties as Skamania Lodge (on the Washington side of the Columbia Gorge) and Sunriver (south of Bend) from native materials with respect for the surrounding environment.

Even if you don't stay here, the grounds and facilities are worth a look. The art gallery is free and features works by top Oregon artists; also check out master woodcarver Leroy Setziol's

CENTRAL COAST

© JUDY JEWELL

coastal estuary near Salishan Spa and Golf Resort

bas-relief panels in the dining room. In addition to the recreational and aesthetic appeal of the resort, the dining room contributes to Salishan's lofty reputation. The forested trails behind the golf course showcase the rainforested foothills of the Coast Range and the waterfowl near Siletz Bay. Across the street, the Salishan Marketplace features first-rate galleries and a good bookstore, Allegory Books.

In high season, Salishan attracts well-heeled nature lovers, corporate expense-account clientele, folks enjoying a special occasion, and serious golfers. You'll also find everyday folks and seminar attendees on winter weekend specials at half the summertime rates. Ask about multiday packages for big savings on your room rate.

Vacation Rentals

To rent vacation homes throughout Lincoln County, contact the **Lincoln City Visitor and Convention Bureau** (800/452-2151, www.oregoncoast.org), or try **Pacific Retreats** (541/994-4833 or 800/473-4833, www.pacificretreats.com), which features a selection of vacation home rentals.

Camping

Devils Lake State Recreation Area (1452 NE 6th St., 541/994-2002 information, 800/452-5687 reservations, www.reserveamerica.com, $21 tents, $28 RVs, $40 yurts, $6 hiker-biker) is the main public campground in Lincoln City, with 54 tent sites, 28 RV sites with full hookups, 10 yurts, and a hiker/biker camp. This campground is right in town, just off U.S. 101 at the northeast end of town, so it's hardly a quiet wilderness retreat, but it does provide easy access to swimming or boating on Devils Lake.

The **Salmon River RV Park** (6029 Salmon River Hwy., 541/994-3116, www.salmonriverrvp.com, $20 tents, $23-30 RVs) is a good spot for anglers; it's on the Salmon River near the town of Otis. The **Lincoln City KOA** (5298 NE Park Ln., 541/994-2961 or 800/562-3316, www.koa.com, $27 tents, $33-37 RVs, $48 cabins) is also just a little ways inland, near the northeast corner of Devils Lake. At the south end of town, **Coyote Rock** (1676 Siletz Hwy.,

541/996-6824, www.coyote-rock.com, $21 tents, $29-35 RVs, $46 "tree house" cabins) has a nice setting where the Siletz River meets its bay. All of these campgrounds, including the state park, have showers.

FOOD

Lincoln City offers many dining options, most of them very busy and family-dining focused. There are several fine dining and ethnic options, however, and the general quality of food is high.

American

If you're en route to the wine country or the Willamette Valley or just want a respite from resort traffic, a place that appeals to everybody is **❚ Otis Cafe** (1259 Salmon River Hwy., 541/994-2813, www.otiscafe.com, 7am-3pm Mon.-Wed., 7am-8pm Thurs.-Sun., $5-13), at the Otis Junction on Highway 18 five miles northeast of Lincoln City. Innovative variations on American road food have earned the Otis a devoted following (stop by to read the enthusiastic review by a satisfied *New York Times* reporter). Long waits on the porch are the rule on weekend mornings, though it's worth it for thick-crusted molasses bread, buttermilk waffles, and hash browns under a crust of melted Rogue Valley white cheddar. Even if it's not mealtime, stop in for a slice of outstanding pie.

Two Native American gaming casinos are located within 25 miles of one another and offer dining alternatives to the coast-bound traveler. Both **Chinook Winds** (1777 NW 44th St., 541/966-5825 or 888/244-6665), and **Spirit Mountain** (21700 SW Salmon River Hwy., Grand Ronde, 800/760-7977), about 25 miles east of Lincoln City on Highway 22 in Grand Ronde, have many dining options. Each offers generous full buffets for breakfast, lunch, and dinner, and both have full-service fine dining restaurants offering moderate to expensive ($18-35) prices. Both casinos have nightly buffets in the $15-20 range. Chinook Winds' ocean views are also worth noting. Both casinos have outlets for 24-hour dining.

Asian

Jasmine Thai Restaurant (1437 NW U.S. 101, 541/994-2022, 11am-3pm and 4pm-9pm Mon.-Fri., noon-9pm Sat.-Sun., $9-14) serves well-prepared traditional Thai cuisine. An extensive menu includes a number of seafood specialties, as well as daily specials that takes advantage of seasonal vegetables and other local produce.

In the outlet mall, **Momiji** (1500 SE Devils Lake Rd., 541/996-8886, 10am-9pm daily, sushi rolls $4-14) offers both Chinese and Japanese cooking, but the reason this restaurant is so popular is the excellent sushi rolls and sashimi. You're welcome to watch at the bar as the sushi is made, eat family-style in the restaurant, or get your order to go.

Pacific Northwest

Some of coastal Oregon's top dining experiences are found just south of Lincoln City. The reasonable prices at the Salishan Lodge's **Sun Room Restaurant** (7760 N. U.S. 101, Gleneden Beach, www.salishan.com, 6:30am-10pm daily, $11-23) are a welcome surprise. This casual restaurant might be less elaborate and half the price of Salishan's signature **Dining Room** (5pm-9:30pm daily, $28-59), but its cuisine comes from the same kitchen. While prime steaks and other meats are the specialty in the Dining Room, fresh local seafood, such as halibut, crab, scallops, and salmon, are also featured. The wine list here is one of the largest in the state.

The **Ⓒ Blackfish Cafe** (2733 NW U.S. 101, 541/996-1007, www.blackfishcafe.com, 11:30am-close Wed.-Mon., $12-24) is a great find. Presided over by former Salishan Resort executive chef Rob Pounding, who has longstanding relationships with local farmers, anglers, and mushroom foragers, the Blackfish Cafe, in the tradition of James Beard, is dedicated to fairly priced and delicious regional cooking. The emphasis is on what's fresh, homegrown, and creative—grilled Willamette Valley pork brisket rubbed with coriander and cumin and troll-caught chinook salmon with fennel-lime butter. There is no shortage of humbler fare either, such as the self-proclaimed best clam chowder on the coast, Pacific City dory-caught fish-and-chips, and amazing fish tacos.

The **Bay House** (5911 SW U.S. 101, 541/996-3222, www.thebayhouse.org, 5:30pm-close Wed.-Sun., $27-40) combines oceanfront views with exquisite Pacific Northwest cuisine. Grilled local albacore tuna is served with black olives and avocado coulis, and the signature crab cakes come with saffron aioli. A $59 five-course tasting menu is available, but must be ordered by everyone at the table. For a more casual and less expensive light dinner, eat from the small plates menu in the lounge. In either dining area, oenophiles will want to look at the wine list, praised by *Wine Spectator*.

A half mile south of Salishan (five miles equidistant from Depoe Bay and Lincoln City) is a Gleneden Beach eatery with considerable appeal. The **Side Door Café** (6675 Gleneden Beach Loop, 541/764-3825, http://edenhall.com, 11:30am-9pm Wed.-Mon., $20-31) combines a gourmet restaurant with a musical venue. The airy yet cozy-feeling dining room features a menu where honey mustard and herb-rubbed salmon with marionberry glaze exemplifies the offerings.

Seafood

If coastal restaurants are eating a hole in your wallet, there's always tried-and-true **Mo's** (860 SW 51st St., 541/996-2535, www.moschowder.com, 10:30am-9pm Sun.-Thurs., 10:30am-10pm Fri., 8am-9pm Sat., $4-15). As at all Mo's locations, the view is great and the seafood more than serviceable.

The chowder is a little tastier at the **Dory Cove Restaurant** (2981 SW U.S. 101, 541/557-4000, www.dorycove.com, 11:30am-8pm Sun.-Thurs., 11:30am-9pm Fri.-Sat., $5-23), but the views from this simple restaurant are out onto the highway. Rest assured that the focus is on the food—good old-fashioned deep-fried and sautéed seafood main courses (halibut fish-and-chips are recommended) and homemade pies.

Kyllo's (1110 NW 1st Court, 541/994-3179,

www.kyllosrestaurant.com, 11:30am-9pm daily, $9-25) specializes in broiled, sautéed, and baked seafood, plus excellent homemade desserts and Oregon microbrews and wines. The restaurant is visible from U.S. 101 as you drive by the D River Wayside. With views of the water on all sides, this restaurant is a good place to linger, though waits can be long in the evening as no reservations are taken.

Brewpubs

The **Lighthouse Brew Pub** (4157 U.S. 101 N., 541/994-7238, 11am-10pm Sat.-Tues. and Thurs., 11am-11pm Wed., 11am-midnight Fri., $9-20) is a welcome rehash of the successful McMenamins formula. Just look for a light-house replica in a parking lot on the northwest side of U.S. 101 across from McDonald's. Pizza, burgers, sandwiches, and salads can be washed down with McMenamins' own ales as well as hard cider and wine.

The venerable **Roadhouse 101** (4649 SW U.S. 101, 541/994-7729, www.roadhouse101.com, 11:30am-10pm Sun.-Wed., 11:30am-midnight Thurs., 11:30am-1:30am Fri.-Sat., $8-20) has added Rusty Truck Brewing to its already rockin' establishment, with a selection of house-made ales and a "south of the border" lager. The Roadhouse features hearty American-style food, frequent live music, and a lively crowd ready to party.

INFORMATION

The **Lincoln City Visitor Center** (540 NE U.S. 101, 541/994-3302 or 800/452-2151, www.oregoncoast.org, 10am-4pm Mon.-Sat.) has a website that's full of helpful information.

The **Central Oregon Coast Association** (541/265-2064 or 800/767-2064, www.coast-visitor.com) also maintains a useful website with details on Lincoln City and the rest of coastal Lincoln County.

GETTING THERE AND AROUND

Lincoln County Transit (541/265-4900, www.co.lincoln.or.us/transit) buses stop in town for service Monday-Saturday. The line goes as far south as Yachats and does not run on major holidays.

Peak traffic times in Lincoln City can result in 25,000 cars a day crawling through town. As an alternative to rush hour on U.S. 101, you could try detouring on NE West Devils Lake Road or NE East Devils Lake Road, which bypass the worst congestion.

Depoe Bay

In his classic travel tale *Blue Highways,* William Least Heat-Moon characterized Depoe Bay thusly:

> Depoe Bay used to be a picturesque fish-ing village; now it was just picturesque. The fish houses, but for one seasonal com-pany, were gone, the fleet gone, and in their stead had come sport fishing boats and souvenir ashtray and T-shirt shops.

To be fair, tourists have come here since the establishment of the town. In fact, for all intents and purposes, the town didn't really exist until the completion of the Roosevelt Highway (U.S. 101) in 1927, which opened the area up to car travelers. Prior to that time, the area had been occupied mainly by a few members of the Siletz people. One worked at the U.S. Army depot and called himself Charlie Depot. The town was named after him, eventually taking on the current spelling.

Regardless of what you think of the busy commercial strip and the enormous time-share resort along the highway, the scenic appeal of Depoe's location is impossible to ignore. The rocky outer bay, flanked by headlands to the north and south, is pierced by a narrow channel through the basalt cliffs leading to the inner harbor. It's home to an active sportfishing fleet

© JUDY JEWELL

CENTRAL COAST

Boats maneuver in and out of Depoe Bay's tiny harbor.

as well as the whale-watching charters that have earned Depoe Bay its distinction as the whale-watching capital of the state.

SIGHTS AND RECREATION
The Bayfront and Harbor

Depoe Bay is situated along a truly beautiful coastline that cannot be fully appreciated from the highway. A quarter-mile-long seawall and promenade invite a stroll. For a panorama of the harbor, continue along the sidewalks across the gracefully arching concrete bridge, designed by Conde McCullough and built in 1927. Other nice perspectives are offered from residential streets west of U.S. 101; try Ellingson Street, south of the bridge, and Sunset Street, at the north end of the bay. Two "spouting horns," natural blowholes in the rocks north of the harbor entrance, can send plumes of spray 60 feet into the air when the tide and waves are right.

East of the bridge is Depoe Bay's claim to international fame, the world's smallest navigable natural harbor. This boat basin is also exceptional because it's a harbor within a harbor.

This topography is the result of wave action cutting into the basalt over eons until a 50-foot passageway leading to a six-acre inland lagoon was created. In addition to whale-watching, folks congregate on the bridge between the ocean and the harbor to watch boats maneuver into the enclosure. Depoe Bay's harbor was scenic enough to be selected as the site from which Jack Nicholson commandeered a yacht for his mental patient crew in the film *One Flew Over the Cuckoo's Nest.*

Whale Watching Center

Stop in at the **Whale Watching Center** (119 SW U.S. 101, 541/765-3304, www.oregon-stateparks.org, 9am-5pm daily summer, 10am-4pm Wed.-Sun. winter, free) where volunteers can help you spot whales and answer your questions about them. The center, right on the seawall, is an ideal viewing spot. Peak viewing times are mid-December-January, when whales are migrating south; late March-early June, when they're traveling north (mothers and babies generally come later in the season);

and mid-July-early November, when resident whales feed off the coast. The least likely times to see whales from the central Oregon coast are mid-November-mid-December and mid-January-mid-March.

Whale, Sea Life & Shark Museum

The private **Whale, Sea Life & Shark Museum** (234 S. U.S. 101, 541/912-6734, www.oregon-whales.com, 9am-5pm daily summer, 10am-4pm Wed.-Sun. winter, $5 adults, $3 children ages 4-10) on the harbor side of the highway, 100 feet south of the bridge, is run in conjunction with whale-watching tours in Zodiac craft. Carrie Newell, a marine biologist, runs both the museum and the tours ($30 for one hour, $50 for two hours). The museum, which is free with a whale-watching trip, features models of marine mammals, a large collection of shark jaws, and lots of photos of whales.

Boiler Bay State Scenic Viewpoint

Boiler Bay, half a mile north of Depoe Bay, is so named because of the boiler left from the 1910 wreck of the *J. Marhoffer*. The ship caught fire three miles offshore and drifted into the bay. The remains of the boiler are visible at low tide. This rock-rimmed bay is a favorite spot for rock fishing, birding, and whale-watching. A trail leads down to some excellent tidepools.

Whale Cove

This picturesque bay half a mile south of Depoe Bay has been scooped out of the sandstone bluffs. The tranquility of this calendar photo come to life is deceptive. There's considerable evidence to suggest that this tiny embayment—and not California's Marin County—was the site of Francis Drake's 1579 landing, but the jury is still out. During Prohibition, bootleggers used the protected cove as a clandestine port.

Rocky Creek State Scenic Viewpoint (800/551-6949, www.oregonstateparks.org) overlooks Whale Cove. There are picnic tables, and it's a good spot for whale-watching, but there's no beach access.

Otter Crest Loop

The rocky bluffs of this coastal stretch take on an even more dramatic aspect as you leave the highway at the **Otter Crest Loop,** a winding three-mile section of the old Coast Highway, two miles south of Depoe Bay. The northernmost part of the loop, down as far as Cape Foulweather, is one-way southbound, with a generous bike lane.

From atop **Cape Foulweather,** the visibility can extend 40 miles on a clear day. The view south to Yaquina Head and its lighthouse is a photographer's fantasy of headlands, coves, and offshore monoliths. Bronze plaques in the parking lot tell of Captain Cook naming the 500-foot-high headland during a bout with storm-tossed seas on March 7, 1778.

The Lookout (milepost 131.5 U.S. 101, 541/765-2270, www.lookoutgiftshop.com, 9am-5pm daily), a gift shop on the north side of the promontory, is a good place to buy Japanese fishing floats for a few bucks. The million-dollar view from inside the shop is easily one of the most spectacular windows on the ocean to be found anywhere.

Another mile south, in the hamlet of **Otter Rock,** you'll find another of the Oregon coast's several diabolically named natural features, the **Devil's Punchbowl.** The urn-like sandstone formation, filled with swirling water, has been sculpted by centuries of waves flooding into what had been a cave until its roof collapsed. The inexorable process continues today, thanks to the ebb and flow of the Pacific through two openings in the cauldron wall. A state park viewpoint gives you a ringside seat for this frothy confrontation between rock and tide. When the water recedes, you can see purple sea urchins and starfish in the tidepools of the **Marine Gardens** 100 feet to the north.

To the south of the Punchbowl vantage point are picnic tables and a wooden walkway down to the beach. Close by in tiny Otter Rock you'll find a small **Mo's** restaurant (122 1st St., 541/765-2442, 11am-8pm Mon.-Sat., 11am-6pm Sun., $4-16). Next door, the **Flying Dutchman Winery** (915 1st St., 541/765-2553, 11am-6pm daily) makes limited batches of

DRAKE'S LOST HARBOR?

In 1996 the media exploded with stories raising the possibility that the tiny hamlet of Whale
Cove, two miles south of Depoe Bay, could sup-
plant Plymouth Rock as the birthplace of a nation. Rotting timbers from what is theorized to
have been a stockade built by Sir Francis Drake
in 1579 were unearthed in an area where stories
have long circulated that the English privateer
made landfall.

Over the years, these notions have been fueled by several tantalizing pieces of evidence:
an unsigned ship's log from Drake's voyage in a
museum in England that identified 44 degrees
north latitude—the same as Whale Cove—as a
landing site; an English shilling dating from
1560 found on the central Oregon coast in
1982; a photo from the 1930s showing a local
resident with a distinctly English sword he unearthed; and a ship's cutlass found in Newport
in the early 19th century bearing the markings
of a 16th-century English arsenal. Moreover,
excavations of a nearby Indian village thought
to have been buried in 1600 turned up brass
items, blades, and Venetian beads.

An amateur British historian, Bob Ward,
makes a compelling case for Whale Cove as
the place where Drake spent five weeks in the
summer of 1579. In his flagship *Golden Hynde*,
the only one of his five-ship fleet to survive the
stormy straits around Cape Horn, Drake ha-
rassed Spanish settlements throughout Latin
America and plundered Spanish ships wherever
he met them. Sailing west from Mexico on its
return to England via the Cape of Good Hope,
the treasure-laden *Golden Hynde* was beset
by storms, and Drake had to retreat to land to
make repairs. Conventional history has held
that he made landfall around San Francisco,
most likely on the Marin County coast.

Ward, however, believes that Drake continued his voyage farther north and sailed into
the Strait of Juan de Fuca, thinking he had
found the fabled Northwest Passage. Turning
around before he realized his mistake, Drake
then headed south down the Washington and
Oregon coasts, where he found a sandy cove in
which to drop anchor and make repairs before
the long journey home.

On Drake's return to England after four
years at sea, news of his exploits were sup-
pressed. Queen Elizabeth confiscated the logs
and charts, and it would be 10 years before an
official account of the voyage would be published. Then, Drake's New Albion was described
as being around 38 degrees north latitude (in
northern California), in an attempt, Ward believes, to fool the Spanish into thinking the
Northwest Passage was much farther south.

After Elizabeth's death in 1603, however,
new charts began to appear that placed the
landing site much farther north, and early 17th-
century charts show a small shallow bay labeled
Novus Albionis (New Albion) that is an uncan-
nily accurate depiction of Whale Cove.

Since the initial blizzard of publicity, there
has been no final word from the archaeologists and historians involved in corroborating
these claims. Because most history books have
placed New Albion, Drake's fabled lost settlement, near San Francisco, researchers will not
be too quick to claim otherwise without defini-
tive research.

handcrafted wines from grapes grown in southern Oregon and the Willamette Valley (grapes
won't ripen on the coast).

Back on U.S. 101, a mile's drive south brings
you to Beverly Beach State Park.

Fishing and Whale-Watching Charters

With the ocean minutes from Depoe Bay's
port, catching a salmon or seeing a whale is
possible as soon as you leave the harbor. Most
charter operators here offer both fishing and
whale-watching excursions. Bottom-fishing
trips average $75 for a five-hour run, salmon
fishing (available only when salmon season is
open) about $130 for a seven- or eight-hour
day; whale-watching excursions run $15-25
per person per hour.

Dockside Charters (541/765-2545 or
800/733-8915, docksidedepoebay.com) offers

CENTRAL COAST

1.5-hour whale-watching trips aboard its 50-foot excursion boat for $16 per adult and one-hour trips on Zodiacs for $25 per adult. **Tradewinds Charters** (541/765-2345 or 800/445-8730, www.tradewindscharters.com) hosts one- and two-hour trips December-May. Rates run $18-30 per adult.

Surfing

If you're itching to actually get into the water and catch a few waves, the beach at **Otter Rock,** a few miles south of Depoe Bay, is a good place to surf. Park in the lot at Devil's Punchbowl and walk down the long flight of steps to the beach, which is relatively protected and has a large area where beginners tend to hang out. (There's also a section that gets bigger waves and better surfers.)

ENTERTANMENT AND EVENTS

The **Depoe Bay Classic Wooden Boat Show, Crab Feed, and Ducky Derby** is held the third weekend in April. Several dozen wooden craft,

the beach at Otter Rock

© JUDY JEWELL

both restored and newly constructed vessels, including kayaks, skiffs, dinghies, and larger fishing boats, are displayed in the harbor and the adjacent Depoe Bay City Park. Rowing races, boatbuilding workshops, crab races, and other activities are scheduled. The big Crab Feed, held 10am-5pm both Saturday and Sunday, sees some 1,500 pounds of crab plus side dishes devoured at the Community Hall; it costs $12-18 for a crab dinner. The Ducky Derby is a raffle in which you purchase "tickets" in the form of rubber duckies that race down the harbor's feeder stream vying for prizes. For more information, contact the **Depoe Bay Chamber of Commerce** (223 SW U.S. 101, 541/765-2889 or 877/485-8348, www.depoebaychamber.org).

The **Fleet of Flowers** happens each Memorial Day in the harbor to honor those lost at sea and in military service. Thousands come to witness a blanket of blossoms cast upon the waters.

The **Depoe Bay Salmon Bake** takes place on the third Saturday of September (10am-5pm) at Depoe Bay City Park, flanking the rear of the boat basin. Some 3,000 pounds of fresh ocean fish are caught, cooked Native American-style on alder stakes over an open fire, and served with all the trimmings, to be savored to the accompaniment of live entertainment. The cost is $20 adults, $10 children. It always seems to rain on the day of this event, but that's life on the Oregon coast.

ACCOMMODATIONS

Lodgings in popular Depoe Bay require advance reservations on most weekends and holidays.

The **Inn at Arch Rock** (70 NW Sunset St., 541/765-2560 or 800/767-1835, www.innatarchrock.com, $89-309) is a cluster of white clapboard buildings that overlook Depoe Bay from a cliff-top perch at the north end of town. Most rooms have ocean views and are in the $140-200 range; a non-oceanview room goes for $89. Pets are permitted in several rooms.

Harbor Lights Inn (235 SE Bay View Ave., 541/765-2322 or 800/228-0448, www.

theharborlightsinn.com, $129-189), a small inn overlooking the harbor, has the distinct advantage of being distant from U.S. 101. Perched above the marina and the Coast Guard station, this homey inn affords views of sea otters, ducks, and geese while the whale-watching and fishing boats come and go. All rooms have a harbor view; rates include a hot breakfast. Small pets are allowed with prior approval.

The 🎔 **Channel House** (35 Ellingson St., 541/765-2140 or 800/447-2140, www.channelhouse.com, rooms $140-330) features both standard B&B rooms and spacious suites boasting expansive dramatic views of the ocean, private decks with outdoor whirlpool tubs (in the majority of rooms), fireplaces, plush robes, and other amenities. This bluff-top B&B (there isn't a beach below, just miles of ocean and surrounding cliffs) may not look prepossessing from the outside, but inside, the place is all windows and angles. Imagine *Architectural Digest* in a nautical theme. This is one of the best places on the Oregon coast to commune with whales, passing boats, winter storms, and the setting sun. A continental breakfast with tasty baked goods in an ocean-side dining area is included in the rates.

About a mile south of town, perched above scenic Whale Cove, find the boxy new **Whale Cove Inn** (2345 S. U.S. 101, 541/765-4300 or 800/628-3409, www.whalecoveinn.com, $395-795), a small boutique hotel that's a sister hotel to the Channel House. Here you can lounge in the hot tub on your private deck or on the Tempur-Pedic mattress in your bedroom alcove (all accommodations are in spacious suites, the top-end suites sleep six). Fine dining is available in the hotel restaurant, Restaurant Beck. This is as high-end as the Oregon coast gets; kids 16 and older are welcome, but pets are not.

About three miles south of Depoe Bay, at one of the most scenic spots on the central coast, is the **Inn at Otter Crest** (301 Otter Crest Loop, Otter Rock, 541/765-2111 or 800/452-2101, www.innatottercrest.com, $110-329), a large condo resort perched near the sandstone bluffs at the ocean's edge. Hotel rooms have two queen-size beds, a refrigerator, a coffeemaker, and a private deck with picture windows. Studios have a queen-size Murphy bed (or a regular bed), a full kitchen, a fireplace, and a dining area; larger one- and two-bedroom suites are also available.

The **Surfrider Resort** (3115 NW U.S. 101, 541/764-2311 or 800/662-2378, www.surfriderresort.com, $99-135) is a few miles north of Depoe Bay on picturesque Fogarty Creek's rockbound coast. Oceanfront suites and rooms have decks; some feature whirlpool tubs, kitchens, and fireplaces. A good restaurant, an indoor pool, and midweek specials are also noteworthy.

FOOD

Of Depoe Bay's several restaurants, **Tidal Raves** (279 NW U.S. 101, 541/765-2995, www.tidalraves.com, 11am-9pm daily, $12-25) has the best combination of flavor, views, and casual ambience. A number of seafood dishes take on an Asian twist, such as Thai barbecued shrimp or udon noodles with sesame-crusted scallops. A pasta dish features crab, shrimp, lingcod, snapper, and more on a bed of linguine with pesto. The Dungeness crab casserole is also noteworthy for its flavor as well as its cholesterol level-improving properties.

🎔 **Restaurant Beck** (2345 S. U.S. 101, 541/765-3220, restaurantbeck.com, 5pm-9pm daily, $27-30), in the Whale Cove Inn south of town, is Depoe Bay's only really elegant restaurant. It has a great view and excellent food, much of which originates on nearby farms. Be prepared to experiment in a way that's not too scary: Pork belly confit and pickled sea beans are paired with whole-grain mustard ice cream; rockfish is served with snap peas, crisp anchovy spine, shaved asparagus, wild fennel vinaigrette, and buttermilk gel. Seasonal ingredients figure prominently; in June, Rainier cherries pair with ancho chilies atop a lamb loin.

INFORMATION

On the east side of the highway, opposite the seawall, the **Depoe Bay Chamber of Commerce** (223 SW U.S. 101, 541/765-2889 or 877/485-8348, www.depoebaychamber.org) offers literature about the town and the central coast in general.

GETTING THERE

On weekdays and Saturday, **Lincoln County Transit** (541/265-4900, www.co.lincoln.or.us/transit) runs buses four times daily, north to Lincoln City and south to Yachats.

Newport

In January 1852, a storm grounded the schooner *Juliet* near Yaquina (pronounced yah-KWIN-nah) Bay, where her captain and crew were stranded for two months. When they finally made their way inland to the Willamette Valley, they reported their discovery of an abundance of tiny sweet-tasting oysters in the bay. Within a decade, commercial oyster farms were established—the first major impetus to growth and settlement in Newport. The tasty morsels that delighted diners in San Francisco and at New York City's Waldorf-Astoria Hotel are almost gone now, but the oyster industry continues by harvesting introduced species.

In 2011, Newport (pop. 10,000) became the National Oceanic and Atmospheric Administration's Pacific Marine Operations Center, managing a fleet of NOAA research ships. During the summer, these ships are usually out at sea conducting oceanographic research, but when they're in port, the large white vessels are easy to spot in the harbor.

The port also bustles with the activity of Oregon's largest commercial fishing fleet and

Newport's bayfront is a working port; walk down to the docks and buy fish off the boat.

CENTRAL COAST

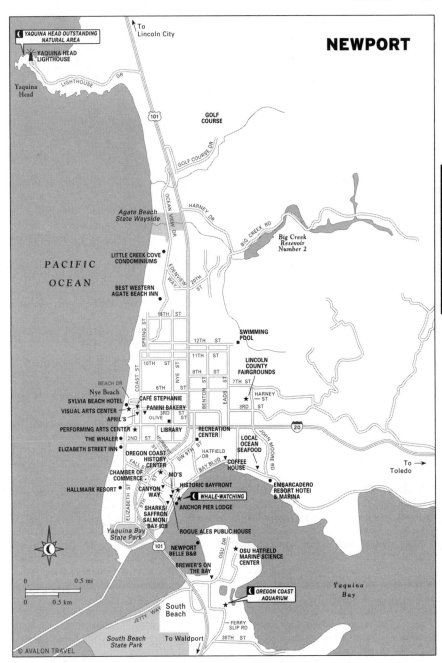

NEWPORT

To Lincoln City

YAQUINA HEAD OUTSTANDING NATURAL AREA

YAQUINA HEAD LIGHTHOUSE

Yaquina Head

LIGHTHOUSE DR

101

GOLF COURSE

GOLF COURSE DR

HARNEY DR

BIG CREEK RD

Big Creek Resevoir Number 2

Agate Beach State Wayside

LITTLE CREEK COVE CONDOMINIUMS

EDENVIEW WAY

26TH ST

PACIFIC OCEAN

BEST WESTERN AGATE BEACH INN

SPRING ST

16TH ST

OCEAN VIEW DR

SWIMMING POOL

12TH ST

11TH ST

NYE ST

8TH ST

LINCOLN COUNTY FAIRGROUNDS

BENTON ST

EADS ST

7TH ST

10TH ST

COAST ST

6TH ST

BEACH DR

Nye Beach

SYLVIA BEACH HOTEL

VISUAL ARTS CENTER

APRIL'S

CAFÉ STEPHANIE

PANINI BAKERY

3RD ST

OLIVE ST

HARNEY ST

3RD ST

20

PERFORMING ARTS CENTER

THE WHALER

ELIZABETH STREET INN

2ND ST

LIBRARY

RECREATION CENTER

OREGON COAST HISTORY CENTER

FALL ST

SW 9TH ST

HATFIELD DR

LOCAL OCEAN SEAFOOD

JOHN MOORE RD

To Toledo

CHAMBER OF COMMERCE

MO'S

BAY BLVD

COFFEE HOUSE

HALLMARK RESORT

ELIZABETH ST

CANYON WAY

HISTORIC BAYFRONT

WHALE-WATCHING

EMBARCADERO RESORT HOTEL & MARINA

SHARKS/ SAFFRON SALMON/ BAY 839

ANCHOR PIER LODGE

Yaquina Bay State Park

ROGUE ALES PUBLIC HOUSE

101

NEWPORT BELLE B&B

OSU DR

OSU HATFIELD MARINE SCIENCE CENTER

Yaquina Bay

BREWER'S ON THE BAY

N

0   0.5 mi

0   0.5 km

OREGON COAST AQUARIUM

JETTY WAY

South Beach

FERRY SLIP RD

35TH ST

South Beach State Park

To Waldport

© AVALON TRAVEL

second-largest recreational fleet. Factories to process *surimi* (a fish paste popular in Japan) and whiting have provided jobs, and a state-of-the-art aquarium that once housed Keiko the whale (from *Free Willy*) brings in the tourists. Wildlife observation facilities and decent access to tidal pools north of town at Yaquina Head make this park a highlight of the coast. The shops, galleries, and restaurants along Newport's historic bay front, together with the Performing Arts Center and quieter charm of Nye Beach, keep up a tourism tradition that goes back to when this town was the "honeymoon capital of Oregon."

SIGHTS
🄲 Oregon Coast Aquarium

There are 6,000 miles of water between the Oregon coast and Japan—the largest stretch of open ocean on earth. You can hear *our* side of the story at the **Oregon Coast Aquarium** (2820 SE Ferry Slip Rd., 541/867-3474, www.aquarium.org, 9am-6pm daily Memorial Day weekend-Labor Day weekend, 10am-5pm daily Labor Day-Memorial Day, closed Christmas Day, $18.95 adults, $16.95 seniors and youth 13-17, $11.95 children ages 3-12), one of the state's most popular attractions.

One of the gems of the aquarium is Passages of the Deep, a 200-foot-long acrylic tunnel offering 360-degree underwater views in three diverse habitats, from Orford Reef to Halibut Flats to Open Sea, where you're surrounded by free-swimming sharks. The jellyfish exhibit is a surprising highlight; it showcases several dozen kinds of jellyfish in an almost psychedelic display. If jellyfish aren't weird enough for you, check out the Oddwater exhibit, which looks at bizarre adaptations made by sea creatures.

At the large Jetty exhibit, visitors look through a window into a 35,000-gallon tank to watch white sturgeon and coho and chinook salmon swimming among large basalt boulders that simulate a coastal jetty, such as these anadromous fish might pass through in the wild on their upriver journey to their spawning grounds.

Of the several hundred species of Pacific Northwest fish, birds, and mammals on display in the rest of the facility, don't miss the sea otters, wolf eel, leopard sharks, lion's mane jellyfish, and tufted puffins. Kids will enjoy the sea cave with simulated wave action and resident octopus. Simulations of indigenous ecosystems help visitors immerse themselves in the region's biology.

In addition to gaining a heightened understanding of the coast biome, you might also come away with something from the museum shop's first-rate collection of regional books and oceanographic tomes or perhaps a crystal or gemstone. The on-site Mermaid Cafe emphasizes such Oregon fare as Tillamook dairy products, seasonal fruits, and seafood. Advance tickets (available online) are recommended on weekends, major holidays, and during the summer. To get there from U.S. 101 south of the Yaquina Bay Bridge, turn east on OSU Drive or 32nd Street, and follow Ferry Slip Road to the parking lot.

Oregon State University Hatfield Marine Science Center

Just south of the Yaquina Bay Bridge, head east on the road that parallels the bay to the **OSU Hatfield Marine Science Center** (2030 SE Marine Science Dr., 541/867-0100, http://hmsc.oregonstate.edu, 10am-5pm daily summer, 10am-4pm Thurs.-Mon. winter, 10am-4pm daily spring and winter break Whale Watch weeks, $5 donation suggested). This research and education facility is a low-key but interesting complement to the very popular Oregon Coast Aquarium, located half a mile south. At the door to greet you is an octopus in an open tank pointing the way to oceanography exhibits and a "hands-on" area where you can experience the feel of starfish, anemones, and other sea creatures. The back hallway has educational dioramas, and a theater shows marine science films throughout the day. If you proceed left from the octopus tank, you'll see tanks with different sea ecosystems. Beyond the walls of the museum, guided field trips (mostly Mon. summer; a fee is charged) explore estuary, beach, and coastal forest habitats (check with the front desk or the website for details). Perhaps the biggest thrill is watching the octopus eat—it's fed at 1pm each Monday, Thursday, and Saturday.

Oregon Coast History Center

For a glimpse into the rich past of Lincoln County, stop at the **Oregon Coast History Center** (545 SW 9th St., 541/265-7509, www.oregoncoast.history.museum, 11am-4pm Tues.-Sun. $5 adults, $3 children ages 3-12), which incorporates the Log Cabin Museum and the adjacent Queen Anne-style Burrows House, a former boardinghouse built in 1895. It's a half block east of the chamber of commerce on U.S. 101. The logging, farming, pioneer life, and maritime exhibits (particularly Newport shipwrecks) are interesting, but the Siletz baskets and other Native American artifacts steal the show.

Here you can learn the heartbreaking story of the hardships—forced displacement, inadequate housing, insufficient food, and poor medical facilities—that plagued the diverse Native American groups that made up the Confederated Siletz Reservation.

The historical society also runs the new **Pacific Maritime & Heritage Center** (333 SE Bay Blvd., 11am-4pm Thurs.-Sun. $5 adults, $3 children ages 3-12), which occupies a huge old mansion overlooking the Bayfront. Local residents have donated everything from ships' wheels to vintage surfboards to this museum, which is worth visiting for the setting and the building alone.

Bayfront District

Newport's Old Town Bayfront District can be easy to miss if you're not alert. At the north end of the Yaquina Bay Bridge, look for the signs pointing off U.S. 101 that lead you down the hill to Bay Boulevard, the Bayfront's main drag. Alternatively, turn southeast off the highway a few blocks north onto Hurbert Street; this runs into Canyon Way, which ends at Bay Boulevard. On summer weekends, forget about parking anywhere near here unless you arrive early. Spots close by the boulevard can often be found, however, along Canyon Way, the hillside access route to downtown.

Until 1936, ferries shuttled people and vehicles to and from Newport's waterfront. With the completion of the Yaquina Bay Bridge that year, however, traffic bypassed the Old Town area. Commerce and development moved to the highway corridor, and the Bayfront faded in importance. Within the last couple of decades, the pendulum has swung back, and the Bayfront District is now one of Newport's prime attractions, with some of its best restaurants and watering holes, shopping, and tourist facilities.

One of the first things that'll strike you about the Bayfront today is that it's still a working neighborhood, not a sanitized re-creation of a real seaport. Chowder houses, galleries, and shops stand shoulder to shoulder with fish-processing plants and canneries, and the air is filled with the cries of fishmongers and the harmonious discord of sea lions and harbor seals. On the waterfront, sport anglers step off charter boats with their catches, and vessels laden with everything from wood products to whale-watching tourists ply the bay. Unfortunately, the severe catch limits and cost of equipment make this less of a working port every year. In deference to the Oregon commercial fishers and other endangered species, wall murals on the Bayfront memorialize fishing boats and whales.

Yaquina Bay State Recreation Site

In 1871 a lighthouse was built here on a bluff overlooking the mouth of Yaquina Bay, and the lighthouse keeper, his wife, and seven children moved into the two-story wood-frame structure. It soon became apparent, however, that the location was not ideal, as the light could not be seen by ships approaching the harbor from the north. The station was abandoned after just three years once the nearby light at Yaquina Head was completed. The building was slated for demolition in 1934, when local residents formed the Lincoln County Historical Society

© BILL MCRAE

CENTRAL COAST

Newport's Nye Beach neighborhood is home to good restaurants and shops.

connecting the two neighborhoods, and soon "summer people" were filling the cedar cottages. In the next century, thanks to an improved river-and-land route from Corvallis, health faddists (who came for hot seawater baths in the sanatorium) and honeymooners soon joined the mix.

A mile north from the Bayfront, to the west of U.S. 101 (look for signs on the highway), this onetime favorite retreat for wealthy Portlanders has undergone a revival in recent years. Rough times and rougher weather had reduced luxurious beach houses here to a cluster of weather-beaten shacks until a performing arts center went up in 1988. On the heels of the development of this first-rate cultural facility, the conversion of a 1910 hotel into a kind of literary hostel encouraged other restorations and plenty of new construction. Culture vultures, beach lovers, and people watchers now flock to Nye Beach, which feels a world away from the Coast Highway commercial strip just a few blocks to the east.

◖ Yaquina Head Outstanding Natural Area

Five miles north of Newport, rocky Yaquina Head juts out to sea. Tools dating back 5,000 years have been unearthed at Yaquina Head. Many were made from elk and deer antlers and bone, as well as stone. Clam and mussel shells from middens in the area evidence a diet rich in shellfish for the area's ancient inhabitants.

Today, much of the headland is encompassed in the **Yaquina Head Outstanding Natural Area** (750 NW Lighthouse Dr., 541/574-3100, www.blm.gov, $7 per vehicle), managed by the federal Bureau of Land Management. "Outstanding" is indeed the word for this place; a visitor could easily spend several hours exploring all the site has to offer.

At its outer tip stands **Yaquina Head Lighthouse** (guided tours 10am-4pm Thurs.-Tues., weather permitting), the coast's tallest beacon. In the early 1870s, materials intended for construction of a lighthouse several miles north at Otter Crest were mistakenly delivered here. The 93-foot tower began operation

to preserve it. In 1997 the government decided to turn Yaquina Bay's beacon back on.

Today, the handsome restored structure and surrounding grounds make up **Yaquina Bay State Recreation Site** (541/574-3129 or 800/551-6949, www.oregonstateparks.org, noon-4pm daily, free), in a beautiful location at the north end of the Yaquina Bay Bridge. The last wooden lighthouse on the Oregon coast is also the oldest building in Newport. The living quarters, replete with period furnishings, are open to the public. Be sure to ask the volunteers about the resident ghost.

From the parking area, you have an excellent photo op of the bay and the bridge. The park is a good place to have a picnic, or you can descend the trails to the beach and dig for razor clams or hunt for agates and petrified wood.

Nye Beach

The 1890s-era tourism boom that came to Newport's Bayfront spilled over into Nye Beach. In 1891 the city built a wooden sidewalk in 1873, replacing the poorly located lighthouse south of here at the mouth of Newport's harbor. Walk up the 114 cast-iron steps for a spectacular panorama of the headland and surrounding coast.

Below, an observation deck provides views of seals, sea lions, gray whales, and seabirds. Of the half dozen varieties of pelagic birds that cluster on Colony Rock—a large monolith in the shallows 200 yards offshore—the tufted puffin is the most colorful. It's sometimes called a sea parrot because of its large yellow-orange bill. Puffins arrive here in April and are most visible early in the day on the rock's grassy patches. The most ubiquitous species are common murres, pigeon guillemots, and cormorants. The murre's white breasts and bellies contrast with their darker bills and elongated backs. The guillemots resemble pigeons with white wing patches and bright red webbed feet. The cormorants look like prehistoric pelicans.

Down a flight of steps from the observation area is Cobble Beach, covered with surprisingly round stones. At low tides, the tidepools at Cobble Beach are teeming with sea stars, purple urchins, anemones, and hermit crabs.

East of the lighthouse, the large **Interpretive Center** (541/574-3116, 9:30am-5pm daily summer, 10am-5pm fall and spring, 10am-4pm winter) features exhibits on local ecosystems, Native American culture, and historical artifacts such as a 19th-century lighthouse keeper's journal. Other highlights include a life-size replica of the Fresnel lens that shines from the top of the nearby lighthouse, a sea cave simulation with a life-size mural of a California gray whale (accompanied by an exhibit detailing its migratory pattern), statues of birds and harbor seals, and information on tidepool inhabitants.

Although the tidepools in an abandoned basalt quarry on the south side of the headland have now largely filled with sand, the short but steep paved path down to Quarry Cove has some great views of the headland, and frequently, good close-up views of sea lions.

Beaches

The beach at **Yaquina Bay State Recreation Site** (541/574-3129 or 800/551-6949, www.oregonstateparks.org) is accessible via a trail from the bluff-top parking area. This is a popular spot for clam digging and agate hunting. There's also easy beach access from the Nye Beach neighborhood, with a large parking lot at the end of NW Beach St. Two miles south of the Yaquina Bay Bridge, **South Beach State Park** (541/867-4715 or 800/551-6949, www.oregonstateparks.org) draws beachcombers, anglers, campers, and picnickers to its miles of broad sandy beach.

North of town along U.S. 101, **Agate Beach** is a broad swath of coastline famed for its agate-hunting opportunities and its views of nearby Yaquina Head. In addition to the semiprecious stones, the contemplative appeal of Agate Beach inspired no less a figure than Ernest Bloch, the noted Swiss composer, who lived here from 1940 until his death in 1959. Famed violinist Yehudi Menuhin spoke of Bloch and the locale thusly: "Agate Beach is a wild forlorn stretch of coastline looking down upon waves coming in all the way from Asia to break on the shore, a place which suited the grandeur and intensity of Bloch's character."

Moolack Beach, two miles north of Yaquina Head, is a favorite with kite flyers and agate hunters. **Beverly Beach,** 1.5 miles farther north, is a place where 20-million-year-old fossils have been found in the sandstone cliffs above the shore. Beverly Beach also attracts waders, unique for Oregon's chilly waters. Offshore sandbars temper the waves and the weather, so it's not as rough or as cold as many coastal locales. This long stretch of sand (panoramic photos are best taken from Yaquina Head Lighthouse looking north) is connected via an under-highway passage to a large state park campground.

SPORTS AND RECREATION
Fishing

Newport is one of the top spots on the coast for charter fishing, and opportunities abound at the home port of Oregon's second-largest recreational fleet. Bottom fishing (year-round), tuna fishing (Aug.-Oct.), crabbing (year-round), and salmon and halibut fishing (seasonal) are all possible. Typical rates here are $75 for a half day of bottom fishing, $100 for a full day; $130 for an eight-hour chinook salmon outing; $225 for 12 hours of tuna fishing; and $180 for an all-day halibut charter.

In addition to a full menu of fishing excursions, most Newport operators also offer whale-watching charters. **Newport Marina Store and Charters** (2212 OSU Dr., South Beach, 541/867-4470, www.nmscharters.com) offers two-hour whale-watching trips for $30 per person. Two other local operators with similar trips and prices are **Newport Tradewinds** (653 SW Bay Blvd., 541/265-2101 or 800/676-7819, www.newporttradewinds.com) and **Captain's Reel Charters** (343 SW Bay Blvd., 541/265-7441 or 800/865-7441, www.captainsreel.com).

For those who prefer to take matters into their own hands, the clamming and Dungeness crabbing are superlative in Yaquina Bay. If you haven't done this before, local tackle shops, such as the Newport Marina Store in South Beach, rent crab pots or rings and offer instruction. The best time to dig clams is at an extremely low tide. At that time, look for clammers grabbing up cockles in the shallows of the bay. Tide tables are available from the chamber of commerce and many local businesses; they're also easy to find online.

Golf

The public course closest to Newport is nine-hole **Agate Beach Golf Course** (4100 North Coast Hwy., 541/265-7331, www.agatebeach-golf.net, year-round, $36 for 18 holes), just north of town. Just the views of Yaquina Head are worth a visit.

Kayaking

Join a ranger-led kayak tour at **South Beach State Park** (South Beach State Park Hospitality Center, 541/867-6590, Thurs.-Mon. July-Aug., $20, reservations recommended). Kayaks, paddles, and life vests are supplied for the two-hour tours, which set off from Ona Beach, six miles south of South Beach, and travel along Beaver Creek. Paddlers have a chance to see lots of wildlife, including great blue herons, immature bald eagles, turkey vultures, and signs of beavers, such as their lodges. Kayakers on evening tours have a pretty good chance of actually seeing beavers. This is pretty gentle paddling, but not suitable for children under age six; kids under 18 must be accompanied by an adult.

◖ Whale-Watching

The best company on the coast in terms of state-of-the-art equipment and natural history interpretation is **Marine Discovery Tours** (345 SW Bay Blvd., 541/265-6200 or 800/903-2628, www.marinediscovery.com, $36 adults, $34 seniors, $18 children ages 4-13). The two-hour SeaLife tour is narrated by naturalist guides and includes, depending on the time of year, whale-, seal-, and bird-watching, an oyster bed tour, estuary and ocean exploration, and a harbor tour. The 65-foot *Discovery* features video cameras that magnify the fascinating interplay between smaller life-forms, but the real attractions can be appreciated by the naked eye. Landlubbers will especially relish the full crab pots pulled up from the deep and the resident pod of whales often visible north of Yaquina Bay off Yaquina Head.

AGATE HUNTING

Hunting for agates after winter storms is a passion at several Oregon beaches, particularly around Newport. Deep in the earth, metals, oxides, and silicates fused together to create this type of quartz. Red, amber, blue, and other tones sometimes form stripes or spots in the translucent rocks. One of the best places to find these treasures is on the beach near the Best Western Agate Beach Hotel, not surprisingly called Agate Beach. Nearby Moolack Beach and the beach at Seal Rock, north of Waldport, as well as area estuaries and streambeds, are more spots worth a look October-May.

During the prime whale-watching weeks of late December and late March, volunteers from Whale Watching Spoken Here staff the **Don A. Davis City Kiosk** in Nye Beach to answer questions and help you spot whales.

ENTERTAINMENT AND EVENTS

Overlooking the sea in Nye Beach, the **Newport Performing Arts Center** (777 W. Olive St., 541/265-2787, www.coastarts.org), the Oregon coast's largest performance venue, hosts local and national entertainment in the 400-seat Alice Silverman Theatre and the smaller Studio Theatre. At the same address is the **Oregon Coast Council for the Arts,** which puts out a free monthly newsletter and has ticket information on the PAC venues. It also has updates on the **Newport Visual Arts Center** (777 NW Beach Dr., 541/265-6540), right above the beach two blocks north at the Nye Beach turnaround. Two floors and two galleries—**Runyan Gallery** (11am-5pm Tues.-Sun.) and the **Upstairs Gallery** (noon-4pm Tues.-Sat.)—offer art education programs and exhibition space for paintings, sculpture, and other works, often with a maritime theme. All exhibits are free.

In addition to its impressive schedule of music, dance, drama, and other arts, the Performing Arts Center screens a series of imported and art films—the ones you probably won't find at the multiplex **Newport Cinema** (5836 N. Coast Hwy., 541/265-2111).

In the Bayfront District, **Mariner Square** (250 SW Bay Blvd., 541/265-2206, 9am-8pm July-Aug., 10am-6pm June and Sept., usually 10am-5pm Oct.-May, $11.99 per attraction adults, $6.99 children) is a complex of three attractions that mostly appeal to kids: **Ripley's Believe It or Not!, The Waxworks,** and the **Undersea Gardens.** Discounts are offered to hardy souls who want to take in all three.

Festivals and Events

The biggest bash (and one of the largest events of its kind in the country) is late February's **Newport Seafood and Wine Festival** (541/265-8801 or 800/262-7844, www.seafoodandwine.com, $5-15), which features dozens of food booths and scores of Oregon wineries serving up palate pleasers, along with music and crafts, at the **South Beach Marina** (across Yaquina Bay from the Bayfront). A huge tent joins the exhibition hall, wherein festival-goers wash down delights from the deep with Oregon vintages. The event is open only to the 21-and-over crowd.

The second event of note is **Loyalty Days and Sea Fair** (541/961-1466, www.loyaltydays.com, free) in early May. What began during the Depression as the Crab Festival, intended to stimulate the market for Dungeness crab, was recast during the depths of the Red Scare of the 1950s as a public expression of patriotism. Although that aspect still undergirds the events, it's really just a big community party stretching over four days, with carnival rides, veterans' events, bike races, and a parade.

ACCOMMODATIONS
$100-150

For location, you can't beat **The Whaler** (155 SW Elizabeth St., 541/265-9261 or 800/433-9444, www.whalernewport.com, $117-177). Each of the 73 rooms has a view, and some have fireplaces, wet bars, and private balconies. Guests can use the pool and exercise facilities; continental breakfast is served. Dogs are permitted in some guest rooms.

Stay on the Bayfront at **Anchor Pier Lodge** (345 SW Bay Blvd., 541/265-7829, www.marinediscovery.com, $125-199), up a long flight of stairs from street level, where you'll truly be living "above the store" (there's a gift shop down below). The rooms are simple, with wood-plank floors, but tastefully and individually decorated. Although the Bayfront can be a little noisy with carousing people and sea lions, the inn provides earplugs. Rooms that overlook the bay have balconies; they're the ones to go for.

The extremely popular **Embarcadero Resort** (1000 SE Bay Blvd., 541/265-8521 or 800/547-4779, www.embarcadero-resort.com, $109-299) is bay-front but not beachfront; it overlooks Yaquina Bay and the soaring bay bridge, arguably one of the best views in Oregon. The Embarcadero has an assortment of suites and townhouses (including many timeshare units) with full kitchens and fireplaces. Facilities include an indoor pool, a sauna, two outdoor hot tubs, a restaurant and bar, a private dock, and boat rentals.

If you want to get away from it all, **Little Creek Cove Condominiums** (3641 NW Oceanview Dr., 541/265-8587 or 800/294-8025, www.littlecreekcove.com, $129-259) is a small condo resort that might be what you're looking for. Little Creek Cove resort is two miles north of Newport, perched just above an isolated stretch of beach. You have a choice of studio, one-, and two-bedroom units, each with a private deck, a full kitchen, and a fireplace.

North of town and above a great stretch of beach, the **Moolack Shores Motel** (8835 N. U.S. 101, 541/265-2326, http://moolackshores. com, $105-149) is a quiet spot, even though its parking area is just off the highway. The rooms are individually decorated and more than a little bit quirky, but most have good ocean views, and the beach is just down a long flight of wooden stairs from the motel.

You may not find any riverboat gamblers aboard the **Newport Belle Bed & Breakfast** (2126 SE OSU Dr., 541/867-6290, www.newportbelle.com, closed Nov.-Jan., $150-165), a recently constructed sternwheeler designed as a floating inn, but this 97-foot-long B&B moored on the H Dock of the Newport Marina evokes the ambience of the sternwheeler heyday. Choose from five generous staterooms, each with its own personality and private bath. Most have fabulous vistas of the bustling marina and bridge area. In the evening, guests can retire to their staterooms, enjoy the open afterdeck, or socialize in the main salon, where a gourmet breakfast is served every morning. No children or smoking; pets are allowed in one room. Soft-soled shoes are required.

$150-200

The **C Sylvia Beach Hotel** (267 NW Cliff St., 541/265-5428, www.sylviabeachhotel.

com, $115-220), a favorite of many Oregonians, combines the camaraderie of a hostel with the intimate charm of a bed-and-breakfast. Built in the era when the Corvallis-to-Yaquina Bay train and seven-seater Studebaker touring cars from Portland ferried the summer folks to Nye Beach, the hotel and its National Historic Landmark designation and literary theme have attracted an enthusiastic following. The 20 guest rooms, named after different authors, are furnished with decor evocative of each respective literary legacy. The Edgar Allan Poe Room, for instance, has a pendulum guillotine blade and stuffed ravens, while the Agatha Christie Room drops such clues as shoes underneath the curtains and capsules marked "Poison" in the medicine cabinet.

Most of the rooms ("best-sellers") run $160, with several oceanfront suites ("classics") featuring a fireplace and a deck going for $220. "Novels" go for $115 (no ocean view, but still quite charming). All rates include a full breakfast and reflect double occupancy. At breakfast, you have a choice of entrées and share a table with eight other guests, so misanthropes beware! No smoking, pets, or radios are allowed on the premises, and small children are discouraged.

To get there, turn off U.S. 101 onto NW 3rd Street and follow it down to the beach, where NW 3rd and Cliff Streets meet. Look for a large four-story dark green vintage wooden structure with a red roof on a bluff above the surf.

Elizabeth Street Inn (232 SW Elizabeth St., 541/265-9400 or 877/265-9400, www. elizabethstreetinn.com, $169-209), in the Nye Beach neighborhood, sits on a bluff overlooking the ocean. All of the spacious rooms in this newer property face the ocean and have private balconies. They come fully equipped with fireplaces, refrigerators, microwaves, and coffeemakers. Guests also get a complimentary continental breakfast and have use of the indoor pool, spa, and fitness room. Pets are permitted in some rooms.

The **Hallmark Resort** (744 SW Elizabeth St., 541/265-2600 or 888/448-4449, www. hallmarkinns.com, $159-209) is a large hotel

CENTRAL COAST

© BILL MCRAE

The Sylvia Beach Hotel is a much-loved Newport landmark.

complex sitting atop the Newport bluffs, looking westward over the Pacific and miles of sandy beach. Of the many modern hotels that share this vista, the Hallmark is one of the nicest, with large well-maintained guest rooms. Facilities include an indoor pool, a spa, and a restaurant. Many guest rooms are pet-friendly.

The **Best Western Plus Agate Beach Inn** (3019 N. Coast Hwy., 541/265-9411 or 800/547-3310, www.newportbestwestern.com, $165, nonview rooms $135) is a tall oceanfront hotel with a fine view overlooking Yaquina Head Lighthouse and Agate Beach. The rooms are comfortable standard-issue hotel rooms, and although it's a little bit of a hike down to the beach, it is one of Newport's best beaches. A sports bar and a restaurant are on-site. Pets are permitted in some guest rooms.

Camping

The campgrounds at Beverly Beach State Park and South Beach State Park are among the most popular on the Oregon coast. Their proximity to Newport, the absence of other camping in the area, and the special features of each explain their appeal.

Beverly Beach State Park (541/265-9278 or 800/452-5687 information, 800/452-5687 or www.reserveamerica.com reservations, $21 tents, $26 RVs, $40 yurts, $6 hiker/biker) is huge multiloop campground set seven miles north of Newport on the east side of the highway in a mossy glade. A pedestrian tunnel passes under the highway and leads to a long wide beach that is unfortunately directly bordered by the road. Devil's Punchbowl and Otter Crest are one and two miles up the highway, respectively.

It's just a hop over the sand dunes to the beach at **South Beach State Park** (541/867-4715 or 800/551-6949 information, 800/452-5687 or www.reserveamerica.com reservations, $21 tents, $27 RVs, $40 yurts, $6 hiker/biker), just south of the Yaquina Bay Bridge. The long beach has opportunities for fishing, agate hunting, windsurfing (for experts), horseback riding, and hiking; sign up in advance

(541/867-6500) for kayak tours of nearby Beaver Creek.

FOOD
This is a town for serious diners—folks who know good food and don't mind paying a tad more for it. It's also the kind of place where wharf-side vendors supply fresh fish on the cheap. Mid-May through October, you can pick up the freshest garden produce the area has to offer, plus baked goods, honey, and other delectables at the Lincoln County Small Farmers' Association's **Saturday Farmers Market,** held in the parking area of the **Newport City Hall** (U.S. 101 and Angle St., 9am-1pm, May-Oct.).

About seven miles east of the Bayfront, the **Oregon Oyster Farms** (6878 Yaquina Bay Rd., 541/265-5078, 9am-5pm daily) is the only remaining commercial outlet for Yaquina Bay oysters. Visitors are welcome to observe the farming and processing of these succulent shellfish. Try oysters on the half-shell, or sample smoked oysters on a stick. To get there, follow Bay Boulevard east six miles from the Embarcadero Resort.

Bakeries and Cafés
Down along the Bayfront is a wonderful breakfast haunt, the **Coffee House** (156 SW Bay Blvd., 541/265-6263, www.thecoffeehouse-newport.com, 7am-3pm daily, $6-16). Scones, muffins, and such creative brunch fare as a wild mushroom omelet, crab cakes Florentine, various crepes, meat pasties, and oysters lightly breaded with Japanese panko breadcrumbs are complemented by well-made espresso drinks. In fair weather, the outside deck is a relaxing spot for soaking up some rays while you gaze out on the harbor.

In the Nye Beach neighborhood, a charming spot for breakfast (including a good breakfast burrito) and lunch sandwiches is **Café Stephanie** (411 Coast St., 541/265-8082, 7:30am-3pm daily, $6-11), a bustling cubbyhole with friendly service. Here both breakfast and lunch are served all day long; consider starting your day with a bowl of smoked salmon chowder.

Nearby, the tiny **◖Panini Bakery** (232 NW Coast St., 541/265-5033, 7am-7pm Thurs.-Mon., $5-12 sandwiches) is a great spot for a chocolate panini, a ginger scone, a slice of pizza, and the local vibe. It's the best bakery in town and has a few tables. The Panini folks have also opened **Panini Wood Fire Oven** (432 SW Bay Blvd., 541/574-2272, 11am-10pm Wed.-Sun., $5 slice), a hole-in-the-wall joint tucked into a somewhat tacky mall down on the Bayfront. Great pizza, nice vibe, plus beer and desserts.

Italian
◖ April's at Nye Beach (749 NW 3rd St., 541/265-6855, http://aprilsatnyebeach.com, 5pm-9pm Wed.-Sun., $16-28) is a small stylish café just across the street from the Sylvia Beach Hotel. Roast duck with port sauce is a standout in a creative Mediterranean-influenced menu. House-made bruschetta and steamed clams with spicy sausage are excellent appetizers. In the summer, many vegetables come from the owners' farm. For dessert, have an éclair dipped in chocolate ganache and topped with slivered almonds. Affordable wines by the glass add to one of Newport's best dining experiences.

Pacific Northwest
You don't have to be a guest to have a meal at the **Tables of Content** (267 NW Cliff St., 541/265-5428, www.sylviabeachhotel.com, seatings at 7pm daily summer, 6pm Sun.-Thurs. and 7pm Fri.-Sat. winter, four-course prix fixe $25), the excellent restaurant at the Sylvia Beach Hotel. There's a nice view of the breakers, good company, and it's a good value for creatively prepared Pacific Northwest cuisine. Each night features several entrée selections with an appetizer, salad, bread, beverages (alcohol not included), and dessert. Diners share tables and are encouraged to break the ice with a game called Two Truths and a Lie, in which they regale each other with several stories, the object being to distinguish which one is untrue. Reservations are mandatory.

Seafood

If you're hankering for a broad selection of fresh local seafood but don't need a fancy dining room to enjoy it in, **(Local Ocean Seafoods** (213 SE Bay Blvd., 541/574-7959, http://localocean.net, 11am-9pm Sun.-Thurs., 11am-9:30pm Fri.-Sat., $6-28) is the place for you. Part fish market, part seafood grill, this bright and bustling restaurant spotlights sustainably caught fish, offering impeccably fresh fish and a lively atmosphere. Each item in the fish case is identified by name, where it was caught, how it was harvested, and who caught it. The menu items change depending on what's fresh, and though you can count on great fish-and-chips here, you may want to try the house-specialty fish tacos or albacore tuna kebabs.

Right on the bay front, with windows overlooking the active fishing port, **(Saffron Salmon** (859 SW Bay Blvd., 541/265-8921, http://saffronsalmon.com, 11:30am-2:15pm and 5pm-8:30pm Thurs.-Tues., $12-26) is one of Newport's finest choices for expertly prepared, sophisticated seafood. As you'd expect, the specialty is fresh wild salmon, grilled and served with basil-pine nut butter and quinoa, while calamari are sautéed with olive oil and red cabbage. There's also a good selection of organic steaks and rack of lamb.

Also in the old-town harbor area, **Sharks Seafood Bar & Steamer Co.** (852 SW Bay Blvd., 541/574-0590, http://sharksseafoodbar.com, 4pm-9pm Sun.-Wed., 4pm-9:30pm Fri.-Sat., $10-25) specializes in steamed seafood. But don't worry—this isn't tasteless health food. The Catalina bouillabaisse packs a wallop—1.5 pounds of seafood in every spice-filled bowl. You'll also find a savory seafood gumbo, oyster stew, and a mix of stewed and sautéed fish called a pan roast. Fresh fish gets the steam treatment—in season, try halibut, salmon, and rockfish steamed and served with the chef's special sauces. Sharks is also a fun, quirky place; the proprietors provide not just dinner but also a show. Be sure to sidle up to the bar in front of the cooking area to watch the chef in action.

The Newport Bayfront is where Mohava Niemi first opened the original **Mo's** (622 SW Bay Blvd., 541/265-2979, 11am-9pm daily, $4-16) several decades ago. When word got out about the good food and low prices, Mo's small homey place soon had more business than it could handle. In response to the overflow, **Mo's Annex** (657 SW Bay Blvd., 541/265-7512, 11am-9pm daily, $4-16) was created across the street. While both establishments feature such favorites as oyster stew and peanut butter cream pie, the Annex bay windows have the best view. Note that most discerning seafood lovers steer away from Mo's, except when moved by loyalty to a local institution.

There are ample opportunities to buy fresh fish or crab along the bay front in Newport. About a half-mile south of the bridge, the **South Beach Fish Market** (3640 S. U.S. 101, 541/867-6800, 8am-8pm daily, $8-12) sells fresh fish, cooked and uncooked; 90 percent of what they sell comes from the Newport fishing fleet. It's a good place for the family to stop for fish-and-chips after a visit to the aquarium.

Spanish

Right on the bay front, **Bay 839** (839 SW Bay Blvd., 541/265-2839, 11am-11pm Sun.-Thurs., 11am-midnight Fri.-Sat., $6-12) is a cocktail and tapas bar in a former fish processing plant. With great views onto the water, the restaurant is also open late for drinks and food. Favorites include crab cakes, sliders, local Yaquina oysters, red chili fish sandwiches, and whatever is fresh from the fishing boats.

Asian

Although most Asian restaurants on the coast are merely serviceable, a good spot for anything from kimchee to ramen to pho is **Noodle Cafe** (837 SW Bay Blvd., 541/574-6688, 11am-2:30pm and 4:30pm-9pm Mon.-Tues., Thurs.-Sat., 11am-2:30pm Sun., $7-20). The noodles are homemade and the restaurant makes good use of seafood.

Brewpubs

Rogue Ales Public House (748 SW Bay Blvd., 541/265-3188, 11am-midnight Mon.-Wed.,

Sat., 11am-1am Thurs.-Fri., $7-15) is along the bay in Old Town, serving seafood salads, shrimp-melt sandwiches, pizza, fish-and-chips, and seasonal fish dishes. In addition to the renowned Rogue ales, there's Rogue's draft root beer, a creamy concoction laced with honey and vanilla. Another Rogue Ales brewery, called **Brewers on the Bay** (2320 OSU Dr., 541/867-3660, 11am-9pm Sun.-Thurs., 11am-10pm Fri.-Sat., $7-15), is across Yaquina Bay near the Oregon Coast Aquarium. This is where the actual brewing is now done; tours are available weekdays at 3pm.

Rogue's third local outlet is the **Rogue House of Spirits** (2122 Marine Science Dr., 541/867-3670, 4pm-8pm Fri., noon-8pm Sat., noon-6pm Sun.), a distillery pub that produces rum, gin, vodka, and whiskey. The menu here is less extensive than at Rogue's brewpubs, and features excellent cheese from Central Point, Oregon's Rogue Creamery. Tours are offered at 4pm daily.

INFORMATION

The **Greater Newport Chamber of Commerce** (555 SW U.S. 101, 541/265-8801 or 800/262-7844, www.newportchamber.org, 8:30am-5pm Mon.-Fri.) has lots of literature, but the most helpful website for a visitor is the chamber's visitor website: http://discovernewport.com. The **Central Oregon Coast Association** (541/265-2064 or 800/767-2064, www.coastvisitor.com) maintains a useful website with details on Newport and the rest of Lincoln County.

A public radio station, **KLCO**, a local repeater station for Eugene's KLCC, is heard on your dial at 90.5 FM. The **Newport Public Library** (541/265-2153, 10am-9pm Mon.-Wed., 10am-6pm Thurs.-Sat., and noon-5pm Sun.) is at 35 NW Nye Street. The **post office** (310 SW 2nd St., 541/265-5542) is one block west of the highway.

Samaritan Pacific Communities Hospital (930 SW Abbey St., 541/265-2244) is the central coast's only major hospital.

GETTING THERE AND AROUND

Newport is one of the few places on the Oregon coast that can be reached by public transportation. **Valley Retriever** (541/265-2253) buses connect Newport with Corvallis, Portland, and Bend Sunday-Friday. **Lincoln County Transit** (541/265-4900, www.co.lincoln.or.us/transit) runs buses several times daily Monday-Saturday, north to Lincoln City and south to Yachats, with numerous stops en route through Newport.

A **shuttle bus** (http://discovernewport.com, 8am-5:30pm daily) travels up and down the length of Newport on streets just east and west of U.S. 101, going as far south as the Newport Business Plaza in South Beach and north to NE 73rd Street. The wheelchair-accessible bus is equipped with a bike rack. It's free for those with a pass from their Newport hotel and $1 for others. The route is not straightforward; it helps to have a map and schedule (www.newportchamber.org).

Newport's car rental agency of choice is **Enterprise Rent-A-Car** (533 E. Olive St., 541/574-1999).

Waldport and Vicinity

Originally a stronghold of the Alsea Native Americans, Waldport also has had incarnations as a gold rush town, salmon-canning center, and lumber port. This town of about 2,000, whose name means "forest port" in German, is pretty quiet today, with a nondescript main drag that gives no hint of the surrounding beaches and prime fishing and crabbing spots. An influx of retirees in the early 2000s spurred new home construction, particularly on the Alsea spit across from the town, but this place is still decidedly low-key. For those passing through, Waldport provides a low-cost alternative to the big-name destinations; you won't have to fight for a parking spot or make reservations months in advance.

SIGHTS AND RECREATION
Alsea Bay Bridge Historical Interpretive Center

The small museum and visitors center known as the **Alsea Bay Bridge Historical Interpretive Center** (620 NW Spring St., 541/563-2002, 9am-5pm daily summer, 9am-4pm Tues.-Sat. fall-spring, free), operated by the Oregon Parks and Recreation Department and Waldport Chamber of Commerce, stands along the highway on the south side of the river. Exhibits here tell the story of how the sleek 1991 bridge replaced the aging Conde McCullough span across the bay, which has since been demolished. Displays about transportation methods along the central coast since the 1800s, information on the Alsea Native American people, and a telescope trained on the seals and waterfowl on the bay are worth a quick stop. In addition, during the summer Oregon Parks and Recreation guides lead bridge tours daily at 2pm Friday-Monday and give clamming and crabbing demonstrations (locations and times vary according to the tides; see website for calendar).

Seal Rock State Recreation Site

Four miles north of Waldport, **Seal Rock** (800/551-6949, day use only) attracts beachcombers and agate hunters, as well as folks who come to explore the tidepools and observe the seals on offshore rocks. The park's name derives from a seal-shaped rock in the cluster of interesting formations in the tidewater. The picnic area is set in a shady area behind the sandy beach. During Christmas and spring breaks, the volunteers of Whale Watching Spoken Here are on hand to help visitors spot passing grays 10am-1pm.

Ona Beach State Park

Ona Beach State Park (800/551-6949, day use only) a couple of miles north of Seal Rock, is a beguiling park on the west side of the highway. Attractions include a forested picnic area with a 0.25-mile trail and a footbridge over Beaver Creek leading to a fine stretch of beach.

Beaver Creek State Natural Area

The **Beaver Creek State Natural Area** lies two miles east of Ona Beach, up Beaver Creek Road. This coastal wetland area has good paddling (ranger-led kayak tours are organized by staff at South Beach State Park Hospitality Center, 541/867-6590, 8:30am Thurs.-Mon., 6pm Thurs. July-Aug., $16, reservations required) and wildlife-watching, both from the creek and from a viewing blind that's just a short walk from the road. If you're not prepared to paddle, a seven-mile network of hiking trails starts at the visitor center.

Drift Creek Wilderness

Seven miles east of Waldport are the nearly 5,800 acres of the **Drift Creek Wilderness,** which protects the Coast Range's largest remaining stands of old-growth rainforest. Here you can see giant Sitka spruce and western hemlock hundreds of years old, nourished by

CENTRAL COAST

CENTRAL COAST

© JUDY JEWELL

Seal Rock State Recreation Site

up to 120 inches of rain per year. These trees are the "climax forest" in the Douglas fir ecosystem. They seldom reach old-growth status because the timber industry tends to replant only fir seedlings after logging operations. There is also perhaps the largest population of spotted owls in the state, along with bald eagles, Roosevelt elk, and black bears. Drift Creek sustains wild runs of chinook, steelhead, and coho salmon, which come up the Alsea River.

Steep ridges and their drainages, as well as small meadows, make up the topography, which is accessed via a couple of hiking trails. The trailhead closest to Waldport is the 3.5-mile **Harris Ranch Trail,** which descends 1,200 feet to a meadow near Drift Creek. The local access to Harris Ranch Trail and the conjoining Horse Creek Trail is via Highway 34; turn north off 34 at the Alsea River crossing seven miles east of Waldport. Here, pick up Risely Creek Road (Forest Service Rd. 3446) and Forest Service Road 346 to the trailhead.

Fishing

Waldport's recreational raison d'être is fishing. World-class clamming and Dungeness crabbing in Alsea Bay and the Alsea River's famous salmon, steelhead, and cutthroat trout runs account for a high percentage of visits to the area. Before commercial fishing on the river was shut down in 1957, as much as 137,000 pounds of chinook were netted in a season. The wild fall chinook run remains healthy and starts up in late August. Catch-and-release for sea-run cutthroats starts in mid-August, while steelhead are in the river December-March. Crabbers without boats can take advantage of the Port of Waldport docks.

Gene-O's Guide Service (541/563-3171) calls on four decades of experience to help you reel in salmon and steelhead. **Dock of the Bay Marina** (1245 NE Mill St., 541/563-2003) rents and sells crabbing and fishing supplies and can guide you to the best spots.

Golf

Crestview Hills Golf Course (1680 Crestline Dr., 541/563-3020, www.crestviewgolfclub. com, year-round, $22 for 9 holes) is a public nine-hole course one mile south of Waldport.

ACCOMMODATIONS
$50-100

Midway between Waldport and Yachats, the **Terry-a-While Motel** (7160 SW U.S. 101, 541/563-3377, www.terry-a-while.com, $60-200) has simple guest rooms that range in style from modern to vintage and in size from basic budget motel size to two-bedroom units with kitchens. Although the guest rooms are not extravagantly furnished, they all have decks with nice views.

The vintage **Cape Cod Cottages** (4150 SW U.S. 101, 541/563-2106, www.capecod-cottagesonline.com, $85-150) offer one- and two-bedroom oceanfront units with complete kitchens, cozy fireplaces, cable television, spectacular views, and private decks. A three-night minimum stay is required in summer.

The **Alsi Resort** (902 NW Bayshore Dr., 541/563-7700, http://alsiresort.com, $79-169) is partly a large beach hotel and partly a retreat center—although when we visited in early summer of 2013, it was mostly a place in transition, with new management, a new vision (of a place where "food, community, and nature meet"), and new staff. Half of the 84 rooms enjoy sweeping views of the bay, bridge, and town (the hotel is not beachfront). Although the hotel has a dining room, and previously had a very good restaurant, no food service was being offered when we were there. Pets are allowed in some guest rooms.

$100-150

The historic **Cliff House** (1450 Adahi Rd., 541/563-2506, www.cliffhouseoregon.com, $125-225) may appear rustic, but in fact this is a lovingly restored historic home, and the location can't be beat. Four guest rooms, some with whirlpools, are decorated with antiques; even the woodstoves are period. No pets are

allowed, and children are best left home with the grandparents or a sitter.

Camping

Two excellent campgrounds sit about four miles south of Waldport on U.S. 101 along the beach. **Beachside State Park** (541/563-3220 or 800/551-6949 information, 800/452-5687 or www.reserveamerica.com reservations, $21 tents, $26 RVs, $40 yurts) is near a half mile of beach not far from Alsea Bay and Alsea River. This is a paradise for rock fishers, surfcasters, clammers, and crabbers. Beachside fills up fast, so reserve early for space Memorial Day-Labor Day.

A half mile down U.S. 101, the Siuslaw National Forest's **Tillicum Beach** (877/444-6777 or www.recreation.gov, $24, reservations strongly recommended in summer) is set right along the ocean. Forest Service roads from here access Coast Range fishing streams. You'll also appreciate the strip of vegetation blocking the cool evening winds that whip up off the ocean.

Should Beachside and Tillicum be filled to overflowing, you might want to set up a base camp in the Coast Range along Highway 34—especially if you have fishing or hiking in the Drift Creek Wilderness in mind. Just go east of Waldport 17 miles on Highway 34 to the Siuslaw National Forest's **Blackberry Campground** (877/444-6777 or www.recreation.gov reservations, $22). The 33 sites are open year-round; most are right on the river. A boat ramp, flush toilets, and piped water are on-site.

FOOD

Dining options in Waldport are limited. For good homemade food (think meat loaf sandwiches or fish-and-chips) and a great setting, head seven miles up the Alsea River to **Jamie's Dockside Diner** (7164 E. Alsea Hwy., 541/528-3880, 7am-3pm Thurs.-Tues., $8-12). Don't be afraid when you see that this floating restaurant is accessed via a trailer park; during salmon-fishing season most of the business comes in by boat, and hungry anglers jam the little restaurant.

INFORMATION

The Waldport Chamber of Commerce operates a **visitors center** (620 NW Spring St., 541/563-2133, www.waldport-chamber. com, 9am-5pm daily) in the Alsea Bay Bridge Historical Interpretive Center, just south of the river. The **Siuslaw National Forest-Waldport Ranger Station** (1130 Forestry Ln., 541/563-3211) can provide information on area camping and hiking, including the trails in the Drift Creek Wilderness.

GETTING THERE

Highway 34 runs east from Waldport, following the Alsea River for several miles before veering northeast to Corvallis, about 65 miles away. This is one of the prettiest (and slowest) routes between the coast and the Willamette Valley.

The **Lincoln County Transit** (541/265-4900, www.co.lincoln.or.us/transit) buses run four times a day Monday-Saturday between Yachats and Newport.

Yachats and Cape Perpetua

Yachats (pronounced YAH-hots) is derived from an Alsea word meaning "dark waters at the foot of the mountain." The phrase aptly describes the location of this picturesque resort village of 690 people, clustered on the hillsides and coastal shelf beside the Yachats River mouth in the shadow of Cape Perpetua. Word of mouth has helped to spread the popularity of Yachats as a place for a quiet getaway and a base for enjoying the 2,700-acre Cape Perpetua Scenic Area and nearby beaches.

SIGHTS AND RECREATION

◖ Cape Perpetua

The most notable sight near Yachats, indeed on the whole central coast, is the view from 803-foot-high Cape Perpetua. The name derives from Captain Cook's sighting of the promontory on March 7, 1778, St. Perpetua's Day. It's too bad the British explorer didn't make landfall here to enjoy one of the world's preeminent coastal panoramas. Oregon's highest paved public road this close to the shoreline affords 150 miles of north-to-south visibility from the top of the headland. On a clear day, you can also see 39 miles out to sea.

Prior to hiking the 23 miles of foot trails or driving to the top of the cape, stop off at the **Cape Perpetua Visitor Center** (541/547-3289, 10am-5pm mid-June-Aug., 10am-4pm daily Sept.-mid-June, $5 per car or Northwest Forest Pass), three miles south of Yachats on the east

side of the highway. A picture window framing a bird's-eye view of rockbound coast, along with exhibits on forestry and marine life, begin your introduction to the region. Cataclysms such as the forest fire of 1846, the monsoons and 138-mph winds unleashed by the 1962 Columbus Day Storm, and 1964 Hurricane Frieda are artfully explained by exhibits. An excellent 15-minute film about Oregon's intertidal biome will also hold your interest.

HIKING

Personnel at the desk have maps and pamphlets about such trails as Cook's Ridge, Riggin' Slinger, and Giant Spruce, as well as directions for the auto tour to the summit, from which you can take the 0.25-mile **Whispering Spruce Trail** through the grounds of a former World War II Coast Guard lookout built by the Civilian Conservation Corps (CCC) in 1933. The southern views from the crest take in the highway and headlands as far as Coos Bay. Halfway along the path, you'll come to a Works Progress Administration-built rock hut called the West Shelter that makes a lofty perch for whale-watching, one of the best spots on the entire coast. Beyond this ridgetop aerie the curtain of trees parts to reveal fantastic views of the shoreline between Yachats and Cape Foulweather.

To begin your auto ascent, from the visitor center drive 100 yards north on U.S. 101 and look for the steep winding spur road (Forest Service Rd. 55) on the right. As you climb, you'll notice large Sitka spruce trees abutting the road. Halfway up the two-mile route, you'll come to a Y in the road. Take a hard left and follow the road another mile to the top of Cape Perpetua. If you miss the left turn and go straight ahead, you'll soon find yourself on a 22-mile loop through the Coast Range to Yachats. Along the way, placards annotate forest ecology.

If you'd rather hike to the top of the cape, the awe-inspiring 1.5-mile **Saint Perpetua Trail** from the Cape Perpetua visitors center to the summit is of moderate difficulty, gaining 600 feet in elevation. En route, placards explain the role of wind, erosion, and fire in forest succession in this mixed-conifer ecosystem.

The actual cape is only half the attraction at Cape Perpetua. At least as fascinating are the rocky coast and its tidepools, churns, and spouting horns of water. Just north of the turnoff for the top of Cape Perpetua (Forest Service Rd. 55) and U.S. 101 is the turnout for **Devil's Churn,** on the west side of the highway. Here the tides have cut a deep fissure in a basalt embankment on the shore. You can observe the action from a vertigo-inducing overlook high above or take the easy switchbacking trail down to the water's edge. While watching the white-water torrents in this foaming cistern, beware of "sneaker waves," particularly if you venture beyond the boundaries of the **Trail of the Restless Waters.** The highlights here are the spouting horns and acres of tidepools. All along this stretch of the coast, many trees appear to be leaning away from the ocean as if bent by storms. This illusion is caused by salt-laden westerlies drying out and killing the buds on the exposed side of the tree, leaving growth only on the leeward branches.

Another hike from the Cape Perpetua visitors center goes down to a geological blowhole (called a spouting horn), where seawater is funneled between rocks and explodes into spray. This is the **Captain Cook Trail,** which runs six miles through a dense wind-carved forest and the remains of an old CCC camp under

CENTRAL COAST

© JUDY JEWELL

Birders spend the morning at the Yachats State Recreation Area.

© JUDY JEWELL

It's easy to find a beach of your own around Yachats.

U.S. 101 to an ancient lava deposit on the shore. Given enough wave action, water bubbles up through fissures in the basalt. There are also Native American shell middens built up 300-2,000 years ago in the area.

State Parks and Coastal Waysides

In this part of the coast, state parks and viewpoints abound with attractions. There's so much to see here that keeping your eyes on the road in this heavily traveled section is a challenge.

A mile north of Yachats, **Smelt Sands State Recreation Site** gives access to tidepools and the 0.75-mile 804 Trail, which follows the rocky shore to a broad sandy beach to the north. In Yachats, turn west onto 2nd Street to loop around wave-battered **Yachats State Recreation Area,** overlooking Yachats Bay. The route heads north along the ocean, where it becomes Marine Drive. After going through a residential community, it eventually takes an easterly turn to reconnect with U.S. 101.

On the south bank of the Yachats River is a short but beautiful beach loop off U.S. 101 (going south, look for the "Beach Access" sign). The road runs between the landscaped grounds of beach houses and resorts on one side and the foamy sea on the other. A wide beach, tidepools, and blowholes on the bank by the river's mouth are a special treat.

A mile south of Cape Perpetua, **Neptune State Park** has a beautiful beach and is near the 9,300-acre **Cummins Creek Wilderness** east of U.S. 101. Just north of Neptune Park, Forest Service Road 1050 leads east to the Cummins Creek Trailhead. A half-mile south, gravelly Forest Service Road 1051 can take you to a point where a moderately difficult 2.5-mile hike leads to Cummins Ridge Trailhead. This pathway has some of the last remaining coastal old-growth Sitka spruce stands. Get maps and detailed directions for these and other area trails at the Cape Perpetua visitor center.

Close by, there's a chance to explore tidepools and sometimes observe harbor seals at **Strawberry Hill.** Scenic shorelines can also be found in the next few miles farther south at **Stonesfield Beach State Recreation Site** and **Muriel O. Ponsler State Scenic Viewpoint.**

ENTERTAINMENT AND EVENTS

This little village seems to be busy with some festival or other event just about every weekend. For a full schedule, see the local chamber of commerce website (www.yachats.org). What follows are some highlights.

Spring brings two arts and crafts festivals to the **Yachats Commons** (U.S. 101 and W. 4th St.): In late March, the chamber-sponsored **Original Yachats Arts and Crafts Fair** (541/547-3530 or 800/929-0477, free) exhibits the work of some 75 Pacific Northwest artists and artisans.

Yachats pulls out all the stops for the **Fourth of July.** Events include the short and silly La De Da Parade at noon, a pie and ice cream social, lots of live music, and a fireworks show on the bay when darkness falls.

During the Yachats **Fish Fry,** held the second Saturday of July, deep-fried cod and snapper are served on the grounds of **Yachats Commons Picnic Shelter** (on 5th St. at U.S. 101). Yachats used to be one of the few places in the world blessed with a run of oceangoing smelt, but they have declined drastically due to changing ocean conditions, and the town's erstwhile smelt fry has morphed into a fish fry. For $10 you get fish and a variety of side dishes and a beverage ($6 for children ages 12 and younger). Or choose a sausage plate for $5. What you're really paying for is a classic small-town festival where you get to rub elbows with a spirited community. More info is available from the chamber of commerce.

The same weekend, the **Yachats Music Festival** takes place several blocks north at the **Presbyterian Church** (360 W. 7th St., 510/845-4444). The lineup features classical virtuosi and vocalists from the San Francisco Bay Area for evening concerts and a Sunday matinee performance.

A relatively new but popular event here is the **Yachats Village Mushroom Fest**

(541/547-3530 or 800/929-0477), held the third weekend in October. Native mushrooms abound in the temperate rainforests of the Cape Perpetua region, and fall is the season to harvest them. Chef John Ullman started the Yachats event, inspired by similar festivals in Italy. Activities over the weekend include the Friday-night Yachats Rainforest Fungi Feast, mushroom-cooking demonstrations, guided mushroom walks at Cape Perpetua visitor center, and the last farmers market of the season.

SHOPPING

Yachats has long been a center for artists and bohemians, and for proof of this you need go no further than **Earthworks Gallery** (2222 U.S. 101 N., 541/547-4300, http://earthworksgalleries.net, 10am-5pm daily). This excellent gallery displays the work of local painters, glass artists, and jewelers, as well as high-quality crafts. **Touchstone Gallery** (2118 U.S. 101 N., 541/547-4121, 10am-5pm daily) is another gallery with unique Pacific Northwest arts and crafts.

ACCOMMODATIONS
$50-100

Facing onto the beach loop south of town, the **Yachats Inn** (331 U.S. 101, 541/547-3456 or 888/270-3456, www.yachatsinn.com, $89-140) offers basic summer shelter with unfussy rooms that have little decks and TVs but no phones, though some have kitchens and fireplaces. There's great access to the beach. Unless you have a dog along, the best bets here are the newly constructed suites, which have full kitchens and fireplaces. The indoor pool overlooks the beach.

For those looking for budget prices close to the center of town, try **Rock Park Cottages** (431 W. 2nd St., 541/547-3214 or 541/343-4382, www.rockparkcottages.com, $75-85), adjacent to Yachats State Recreation Area. Consisting of five rustic cottages arranged around a courtyard, Rock Park has to be one of the better bargains on the coast. The kitchens are well equipped, and the vintage cottages couldn't be better located.

Another good old-fashioned budget choice, **Deane's Oceanfront Lodge** (7365 U.S. 101, 541/547-3321, www.deaneslodge.com, $89-119) is about halfway between Yachats and Waldport. The rooms are well-kept but not fancy; the least expensive don't share the great ocean views afforded by the top-end rooms. Pets are permitted in some rooms.

The **Dublin House Motel** (U.S. 101 and 7th St., 541/547-3703 or 866/922-4287, www.dublinhousemotel.com, $64-94) offers standard motel rooms and ocean views, each room having a microwave, a refrigerator, a coffeemaker, and cable TV; some kitchen units are also available. The indoor heated pool is especially nice in the winter months.

$100-150

A little north of the town center, the imposing **Adobe Resort** (155 U.S. 101 N., 541/547-3141 or 800/522-3623, www.adoberesort.com, $124-235 for ocean view, $85 for hillside view) overlooks Smelt Sands Beach. Although the Adobe isn't what you'd call luxurious, it is one of the few full-service resorts in the area, with an on-site restaurant. All units have refrigerators, microwaves, satellite TV, DVD players, and a phone with voice mail. Pets are accepted in some guest rooms. Two-bedroom hot tub suites are 1,400 square feet and have all the comforts of a small home.

$150-200

A mile north of Yachats, above a thrust of wave-pounded tidepools, **⬤ Overleaf Lodge** (280 Overleaf Lodge Ln., 541/547-4880 or 800/338-0507, www.overleaflodge.com, $195-500) offers the newest and nicest rooms in the Yachats area. Most guest rooms have balconies, hot tubs, and fireplaces, and all have fantastic views. Rates include a breakfast buffet plus access to a fitness area. A 3,000-square-foot spa has treatment rooms, steam rooms, and saunas, plus oceanview hot tubs. Adjacent to the lodge are six newly built cottages tucked into the forest. With 2-4 bedrooms, these charming units with Craftsman-style decor have full

kitchens and everything a family or small group will need for a great beach vacation.

The secluded **Sea Quest Inn** (95354 U.S. 101, Ten Mile Creek, 541/547-3782 or 800/341-4878, www.seaquestinn.com, $180-325) is an antique-filled but contemporary inn of cedar and glass, with private entrances, seven miles south of Yachats. The innkeeper puts out a good breakfast, the wraparound deck affords superlative views of the beach, and telescopes and binoculars are always on hand for spotting whales and other marine life. Sea Quest is not appropriate for pets or children under 12 years of age; it is not handicapped accessible.

Vacation Rentals

If you'd rather settle into a house, check out **Yachats Village Rentals** (541/547-3501 or 888/288-5077, www.97498.com), which offers a varied stable of vacation homes ($140-350) for long- or short-term rental.

Camping

Set along Cape Creek in the Cape Perpetua Scenic Area, the Forest Service's **Cape Perpetua Campground** (877/444-6777 or www.recreation.gov reservations, May-Sept., $24), with 38 sites for tents, trailers, or motor homes up to 22 feet long, is a great home base for exploring the wonderful Cape Perpetua area. Picnic tables and grills are provided. Flush toilets and piped water are available.

FOOD

For a town its size, Yachats has particularly good restaurant choices.

Bakeries and Cafés

Start the day at **Green Salmon Bakery and Cafe** (220 U.S. 101, 541/547-3077, 7:30am-2pm Tues.-Sun., $2-10) for fresh breads and very good pastries plus soup and sandwiches for lunch. This lively café, which has a number of environmentally friendly practices, such as using collected rainwater to mop the floors, doubles as a hangout for the local alternative community. Lines can be long and slow-moving at the counter, so come equipped with patience.

American

The carefully restored but fun-loving **C Drift Inn Pub** (124 U.S. 101 N., 541/547-4477, 8am-10pm daily summer, 8am-9pm daily winter, $6-23) offers seafood dishes, crunchy salads, fish-and-chips, and other well-prepared pub grub in a relaxed, fun-loving atmosphere. There's often really good live music here, making this a lively spot whether you're here to eat or to quaff a pint or two. Families are welcome.

Italian

Heidi's (84 Beach St., 541/547-4409, 4pm-9pm Wed.-Sun., $12-18) is a quintessential Yachats business. This tiny Italian café serves brick-oven-baked pizza and homey Italian comfort food, including cioppino and butternut squash lasagna, in a modest little space that fronts the bay. Everything is homemade and served with charm and care. Takeout and dinner delivery are also available.

Pacific Northwest

The simply decorated bay-view **Ona Restaurant** (131 U.S. 101 N., 541/547-6627, www.onarestaurant.com, 11am-9pm Mon.-Thurs., 11am-10pm Fri.-Sat., $15-30) serves seasonal cuisine such as grilled fresh seafood, rib eye steaks, and fresh pasta. For appetizers, you can choose between local oysters, shrimp, clams, and crab cakes. Ona has a good happy hour (4pm-6pm Sun.-Thurs.), which is a good time to check out their offerings without emptying your wallet.

On a bluff overlooking Smelt Sands Beach is the glass-enclosed **Adobe Resort** (1555 U.S. 101 N., 541/547-3141, 8am-2:30pm and 5pm-9pm Mon.-Sat., 9am-1pm and 5pm-9pm Sun., $15-27). Two side-by-side semicircular dining rooms, with windows on the crashing surf, are a great place to start the day for breakfast or end it with a romantic evening meal, with such favorites as pan-fried oysters, salmon, and steaks. Ask about the loft, where elevated coastal views provide photo ops; this is the perfect place to nurse a drink. A Sunday champagne brunch is served.

Seafood

If you are looking for the quintessential fresh seafood experience, go to tiny **Luna Sea Fish House** (153 NW U.S. 101, 541/547-4794, www.lunaseafishhouse.com, 8am-9pm daily summer, 8am-8pm daily winter, $7-16) a fish restaurant owned by a local fisherman. Don't let the simple decor put you off; the food here is *good*. Using local ingredients, and particularly locally caught (never farmed) fish, Luna Sea offers superlative fish-and-chips and fish tacos. Breakfast omelets are also top-notch.

INFORMATION

The **Yachats Area Chamber of Commerce** (241 U.S. 101, 541/547-3530 or 800/929-0477, www.yachats.org, 10am-4pm daily mid-Mar.-Sept., Fri.-Sun. Oct.-mid-Mar.) has a central location on the highway (next to Clark's Market) and an enthusiastic staff. Ask them about fishing, rockhounding, bird-watching, and beachcombing in the area.

The **Central Oregon Coast Association** (541/265-2064 or 800/767-2064, www.coastvisitor.com) maintains a useful website with details on Yachats and the rest of coastal Lincoln County.

GETTING THERE

The bus stop is also in the parking lot of the **Clark's Market** complex (U.S. 101 and W. 2nd St.). Here you can catch **Lincoln County Transit** buses (541/265-4900, www.co.lincoln.or.us/transit), which run four times a day Monday-Saturday between Yachats and Newport, with a link to Lincoln City.

CENTRAL COAST

Florence and Vicinity

If you study the map of the central Oregon coast, you'll see that Florence is oriented along the Siuslaw River; a spit of dunes reaches up from the south, barring quick access from downtown to the ocean. But don't dismiss this riverfront town for its lack of oceanfront real estate; the views onto the river are plenty scenic, and Old Town is charming and easy to navigate on foot.

Florence began shortly after the California gold rush of 1849 put a premium on the lumber and produce shipped out via the Siuslaw River estuary. Several decades later, the town's name was inspired by a remnant from a French shipwreck that floated ashore, bearing the ship's name, *Florence*. The townspeople either recognized an omen when they saw it or just couldn't come up with anything better.

SIGHTS

If first and last impressions are enduring, Florence is truly blessed. A short way to the north of town, U.S. 101 passes over Heceta Head, with great views onto the lighthouse there. As you leave the city to the south, a graceful bridge over the Siuslaw ushers you away.

The Siuslaw River Bridge is an impressive example of Conde McCullough's Works Progress Administration-built spans. The Egyptian obelisks and art deco styling of McCullough's designs are complemented by the views to the west of the coruscating sand dunes. To the east, the riverside panorama of Florence's Old Town beckons for further investigation.

Old Town itself is a tasteful restoration, with all manner of shops and restaurants and an

Florence's elegant McCullough Bridge spans the Siuslaw River.

© BILL MCRAE

inviting boardwalk along the river. The quickest access to the beach and dunes is south of the bridge via South Jetty Road.

(Sea Lion Caves

Eleven miles north of Florence, you can descend into the world's largest sea cave to observe the only U.S. mainland rookery of Steller sea lions (*Eumetopias jubatus*). **Sea Lion Caves** (91560 U.S. 101, 541/547-3111, www. sealioncaves.com, 9am-7pm daily, closed Thanksgiving and Christmas, $14 adults, $13 seniors, $8 children ages 5-12, children 4 and under free) is home to a herd that averages 200 individuals, although the numbers change from season to season. These animals occupy the cave during the fall and winter, which are thus the prime visitation times. The Steller sea lions you'll see at those times are cows, yearlings, and immature bulls. In spring and summer, they breed and raise their young on the rock ledges just outside the cave. In addition, California sea lions (*Zalophus californianus*), common all along the Pacific Coast, are found at Sea Lion Caves from late fall to early spring.

Enter Sea Lion Caves through the gift shop on U.S. 101. A steep downhill walk reveals stunning perspectives of the coastal cliffs as well as several kinds of gulls and cormorants that nest here. The final leg of the descent is by an elevator that drops an additional 208 feet. After stepping off the lift into the cave, your eyes adjust to the gloomy subterranean light, and you'll see sea lions on the rock shelves amid the surging water inside the enormous cave. Flash photography is forbidden, so study your camera's settings if you want to take pictures inside. You have a better chance of seeing these animals inside during fall and winter. A set of stairs leads up to a view of Heceta Head Lighthouse through an opening in the cave.

Steller sea lions were referred to as *lobos marinos* (sea wolves) in early Spanish mariners' accounts of their 16th-century West Coast voyages, and their doglike yelps might explain why. You'll notice several shades of color in the herd, which has to do with the progressive lightening of their coats with age. Males sometimes weigh more than a ton and dominate the scene with macho posturings to scare off rivals for harems of as many as two dozen cows. Their protection as an endangered species enrages many commercial anglers, who claim that the sea lions take a significant bite out of fishing revenues by preying on salmon. In any case, the close-up view of these huge sea mammals in the cavernous enclaves of their natural habitat should not be missed—despite an odor not unlike sweat-soaked sneakers.

If you can't observe the animals to your satisfaction in the cave, go 0.25 mile north of the concession entrance to the "rockwork" turnout, where the herd sometimes populates the rocky ledges several hundred feet below. It's also a good place to snap a shot of the picturesque Heceta Head Lighthouse across the cove to the north from the turnout.

(Heceta Head Lighthouse and Devil's Elbow

Twelve miles north of Florence, **Heceta Head Lighthouse** (866/547-3696, tours 11am-5pm daily May-Sept., 11am-3pm Fri.-Mon. Mar.-Apr. and Oct., $5 day-use fee) is dramatically situated above a lovely cove at the mouth of Cape Creek and wedged into the flanks of 1,000-foot-high Heceta Head. The whitewashed lighthouse was completed in 1894, and beautifully restored in 2012; it's still in use, beaming the strongest light on the Oregon coast from its perch 205 feet above the pounding surf. A little below the lighthouse is Heceta House, where the lighthouse keepers used to live. Today, it serves both as an **interpretive center** (noon-5pm Mon.-Thurs. Memorial Day-Labor Day) and the **Heceta Head Lighthouse B&B** (92072 U.S. 101, 541/547-3696 or 866/547-3696, www.hecetalighthouse. com, $209-315). An easy half-mile trail leads up from the lighthouse's picnic and parking area to the tower. Other than the day-use fee, admission and tours are free.

Just south of the lighthouse, the graceful arc of Conde McCullough's Cape Creek Bridge spans a chasm more than 200 feet deep. From the lighthouse parking lot, a trail leads down

© JUDY JEWELL

CENTRAL COAST

Heceta Head Lighthouse

to where Cap Creek meets the beach at **Devil's Elbow State Park.** Be conscious of tides here if you climb along the rocks adjoining the beach.

Heceta Head is said to be the most photographed lighthouse in the country; that may be difficult to verify, but it's impossible to quibble with the magnificent sight of the gleaming white tower and outbuildings on the headland, particularly when viewed from a set of highway pullouts just south of the bridge. The vistas from the lighthouse and network of trails on the headland are no less dramatic: See murres, tufted puffins, and other seabirds, as well as sea lions, on the rock islands below; bald eagles soaring overhead; and in spring, northbound female gray whales and their calves as they pass close to shore. A trail leading to the north side of Heceta Head offers views to Cape Perpetua, 10 miles to the north.

Darlingtonia Botanical Gardens

Three miles north up the Coast Highway from Florence, in an area noted for dune access and freshwater lakes, are the **Darlingtonia**

Botanical Gardens (five miles north of Florence on the east side of U.S. 101, 800/551-6949, www.oregonstateparks.org, free). In a sylvan grove of spruce and alder are a series of wooden platforms that guide you through a bog where carnivorous *Darlingtonia californica* plants thrive. Shaped like a serpent's head, the darlingtonia is variously referred to as the cobra orchid, cobra lily, or pitcher plant.

The plant produces a sweet smell that invites insects to crawl through an opening into a hollow chamber beneath the plant's hood. Inside, thin transparent "windows" allow light to shine inside the chamber, confusing the bug as to where the exit is. As the insect crawls around in search of an escape, downward-pointing hairs within the enclosure inhibit its movement to freedom. Eventually, the tired-out bug falls to the bottom of the stem, where it is digested. The plant needs the nutrients from the trapped insects to compensate for the lack of sustenance supplied by its small root system. If you still have an appetite after witnessing this carnage, you might want to enjoy lunch at one of the shaded picnic tables.

Siuslaw Pioneer Museum

To fill yourself in on the early history of Florence and the Siuslaw River Valley, and to get some notion of Native American and pioneer life, spend an hour or so at the **Siuslaw Pioneer Museum** (278 Maple St., 541/997-7884, www.siuslawpioneermuseum.com, noon-4pm daily May-Sept., noon-4pm Tues.-Sun. Feb.-Apr. and Oct.-Dec., $3 adults, children ages 16 and under free). You'll find it in Old Town in a renovated school building from 1905. Along with exhibits on early logging and farming, read an account of how the U.S. government double-crossed the Siuslaw people, who sold their land to the feds and never received the promised recompense. The museum can also set you loose on a walking tour of historic Old Town buildings.

Jessie M. Honeyman Memorial State Park

Jessie M. Honeyman Memorial State Park

(84505 U.S. 101 S., 541/997-3641 information, 800/452-5687 reservations, $5 day-use fee or Oregon Coast Passport), three miles south of Florence, has a spectacular dune-scape and then some. Come here in May when the rhododendrons bloom along the short, sinuous road heading to the parking lot. A short walk west of the lot brings you to a 150-foot-high dune overlooking Cleawox Lake. From the top of this dune, look westward across the expanse of sand, marsh, and remnants of forest at the blue Pacific some two miles away. This is also a popular place to camp.

South Jetty

The northern boundary of the Oregon Dunes National Recreation Area is at the **South Jetty** ($5 per car or Northwest Forest Pass), where the Siuslaw River flows into the Pacific Ocean. May-September and on all weekends and holidays, the beach at the South Jetty is closed to motor vehicles, and even though there are no marked trails, it's a great place to explore the dunes in near solitude. The road into the jetty has several staging areas for off-highway vehicles; during the summer months, the area south of the road is open to motor vehicles. South Jetty Road is 0.5 mile south of the Siuslaw River Bridge.

SPORTS AND RECREATION

Huckleberry picking is an attraction just outside Florence. Some prime pickings are found about five miles north of Florence along the Sutton Creek Trail, which begins in the Sutton campground just off U.S. 101. During late summer or fall, these berries flourish below the dense canopy of shore pines.

Hiking

You'll find incredibly scenic hiking in the area around **Carl G. Washburne State Park,** 14 miles north of Florence on U.S. 101. At the southern end of the park is the **Hobbit Trail,** which winds 0.4 mile through dense forest thickets of pine, fir, and rhododendrons to the three-mile-long beach. From the same trailhead, another path takes off uphill to the

Heceta Head Lighthouse. In its 1.75-mile run, the trail gains quite a bit of elevation and passes some outstanding viewpoints. Also starting at the same U.S. 101 parking area, the **China Creek Trail** (a.k.a. the Valley Trail) runs 1.7 miles on the east side of the highway through a series of elk meadows to the Washburne campground. The parking area for all these hikes is on the east side of U.S. 101. It's also possible to park in the day-use lot across the highway from the campground, catch the Valley Trail near the campground entrance, and hike to the Hobbit and Heceta Head Trails.

Up the North Fork of the Siuslaw River is the **Pawn Old-Growth Trail,** a half-mile pathway through 9-foot-thick, 275-foot-tall Douglas fir and hemlock trees that are several hundred years old. The trailhead, at the confluence of the North Fork of the Siuslaw and Taylor's Creek, is a good place to see salmon spawning in the fall and observe water ouzels (also called dippers). The trail follows the creek and offers interpretive placards along the way. At one point in the trail, visitors walk through fallen Douglas fir logs 21 feet in diameter. Placards explain the science of tree rings. From Florence, take Highway 126 east for 1 mile, then turn north onto Forest Road 5070 and take it 12 miles to Forest Road 5084; stay right and go another five miles to the trailhead.

An excellent and not terribly difficult introduction to dune hiking can be found about 10 miles south of Florence at the **Oregon Dunes Day-Use Area** ($5 day-use fee). The **Overlook Beach Trail** runs for about a mile from a viewing platform to the beach. Follow the blue-topped wooden posts that mark the trail through the sand. To turn this into a more strenuous 3.5-mile loop, continue one mile south along the beach and head back inland (again following the posts) along the more rugged **Tahkenitch Creek Loop.** Find the turnoff from U.S. 101 near milepost 201.

Another good place to explore the dunes is along **Carter Dunes Trail** and **Taylor Dunes Trail.** Carter Dunes Trail starts near Carter Lake and heads west 1.5 miles to the beach. The first half of the mile-long Taylor Dunes

CENTRAL COAST

© BILL MCRAE

A guided dune buggy tour is the easiest way to experience the Oregon Dunes.

Trail is wheelchair accessible; the trail passes some of the oldest (and gnarliest) conifers in the area. Both of these trails are good places to view wildlife, especially in the winter and spring, when the dunes take on wetland characteristics. The two trails link up, forming a Y rather than a loop. The turnoff for both trails is 7.5 miles south of Florence. Carter Lake also has a campground.

Hike the **Waxmyrtle Trail** along the Siltcoos River; the 1.5-mile trail travels along the estuary and ends up at the beach. The trail is closed March 15-September 15 to protect nesting snowy plover. This is a good spot for bird-watching. Find the trailhead near the Waxmyrtle campground about eight miles south of Florence at the Siltcoos Recreation Area.

Dune Rides

Ride into the dunes with the folks from **Sand Dunes Frontier** (83960 U.S. 101, 541/997-3544, http://sanddunesfrontier.com). Half-hour-long, 20-person dune buggy rides cost $12 for adults and $10 for children ages 4-11 years old. Protective goggles are provided, along with a driver. At the same location **Torex ATV Rentals** (541/997-5363, $50-150 per hour) rents vehicles for travel in specially designated areas within the Oregon Dunes National Recreation Area. Go in the morning when the sand tends to blow around less.

Fishing

Oregon's largest coastal lake, 3,100-acre **Siltcoos Lake,** six miles south of Florence, offers excellent fishing and other recreation. The lake is stocked with rainbow trout in the spring, and steelhead, salmon (the lake is closed to coho fishing), and sea-run cutthroat trout move from the ocean into the lake via the short Siltcoos River in late summer and fall, but the real excitement here is the fishing for warm-water species, which is some of the best in the Pacific Northwest. Bluegill, crappie, yellow perch, and brown bullhead action is good through the summer, while fishing for largemouth bass can be good year-round. Access points include several public and private boat ramps on the lake, as well as a wheelchair-accessible fishing pier at Westlake Resort.

Golf

Ocean Dunes Golf Links (3345 Munsel Lake Rd., 541/997-3232, $28 for 9 holes, $48 for 18 holes), part of the Three Rivers Casino complex, lets you tee off with sand dunes (some more than 60 feet tall) as a backdrop. The manicured 18-hole course has a driving range, a full pro shop, and equipment rentals on-site. For the ultimate in golfing by the dunes, however, try **Sandpines Golf Course** (1201 35th St., 541/997-1940, www.sandpines.com, $70 for 18 holes, $55 for Oregon and Washington residents). To get there, go west off U.S. 101 on 35th Street. In May and June rhododendrons line this drive, which heads into dune country as you move toward the sea. Follow the signs until you see a water tower not far from the pro shop. A par-72 7,190-yard course, Sandpines's layout features fairways lined with lakes, Douglas firs, and beach grass on gently undulating terrain; the inward nine holes are traditional links style. Coastal winds that kick up in the afternoon can figure prominently in your shot selection.

Horseback Riding

Riding across the dunes into the sunset on a trusty steed sounds like a fantasy, but you can do it thanks to **C&M Stables** (90241 U.S. 101, 541/997-7540, www.oregonhorsebackriding.com, 10am-5pm daily). Rates range $55-110 per person for trips of 1-2 hours (with discounts for larger parties). The stables are open daily and are located near 14 miles of horse trails that wind through the forest on a bluff above the beach. With beach rides, dune trail excursions, and sunset trips, there's something for everybody.

Sandboarding

Dude, it's a natural! Wax up a board, strap it onto your bare feet, and carve your way down the dunes. On the outskirts of Florence, you can rent a board and try out the rails and

jumps at **Sand Master Park** (5351 U.S. 101, 541/997-6006, www.sandmasterpark.com, 9:30am-6:30pm daily June-mid-Sept., 10am-5pm Mon.-Tues. and Thurs.-Sat., noon-5pm Sun. Mar.-May and mid-Sept.-mid-Jan., board rentals from $16 includes admission). If you're more of a do-it-yourselfer, a number of roadside shops rent sandboards, and the dunes are certainly plentiful.

Water Sports

Although only the hardiest swimmers go into the ocean without wetsuits, **Cleawox** and **Woahink Lakes** warm up sufficiently to make summertime swimming enjoyable. Cleawox, the smaller of the two, is especially well suited for swimming. Woahink, which has a boat ramp and canoe rentals, is good for paddling. Both lakes are within Honeyman State Park, three miles south of Florence ($5 per vehicle day-use fee).

Surfers head to the beaches at South Jetty; the waves are best when small—they can often become overwhelming and unsuitable for novices. Look for more protection from the wind at the mouth of the river.

South of Florence, in the Oregon Dunes National Recreation Area, the **Siltcoos River** invites kayakers and canoeists to explore the two-mile stretch between Siltcoos Lake and the sea. Meandering two miles through dunes, forest, and estuary, the Siltcoos is a gentle Class I paddle with no white water or rapids, although a small dam midway must be portaged. Wildlife that you may encounter along the way include mink, raccoons, otters, beavers, and even bears. In the estuary, sea lions and harbor seals are common. Rent a canoe or kayak form **Siltcoos Lake Resort** (82855 Fir St., Westlake, 541/999-6941, www.siltcooslakeresort.com, $45 per day).

ENTERTAINMENT AND EVENTS

For current information on Florence area events, contact the **Florence Chamber of Commerce** (541/997-3128, www.florence-chamber.com).

DUNE COUNTRY: COOS BAY TO FLORENCE

Even though the 47-mile stretch of U.S. 101 between Coos Bay and Florence does not overlook the ocean, your eyes will be drawn constantly westward to the largest and most extensive oceanfront dunes in the world.

How did they come to exist in a coastal topography otherwise dominated by rocky bluffs? A combination of factors created this landscape over the past 12,000 years, but the principal agents are the Coos, Siuslaw, and Umpqua Rivers. The sand and sediment transported to the sea by these waterways are deposited by waves on the flat shallow beaches. Prevailing westerlies move the particulate matter exposed by the tide eastward up to several yards per year. Over the millennia, the dunes have grown huge, with some topping 500 feet.

Constantly on the move, the shifting sands have engulfed ancient forests, a fact occasionally corroborated by hikers as they stumble on the top of an exposed snag. The cross-section of sand-swept woodlands seen from U.S. 101 demonstrates that this inundation is still occurring. Nonetheless, the motorist gets the impression that the trees are winning the battle because the dunes are only intermittently visible from the road.

The Oregon Dunes National Recreation Area (NRA) is home to more than 400 species of flora and fauna, but the only dangerous animal within this ecosystem is possibly the American teenager. This species migrates here during summer vacation to assault the dunes with a variety of all-terrain vehicles. Of the 31,500 acres within the NRA, nearly half are designated open sand and riding trails for off-highway vehicles such as dune buggies.

GETTING ORIENTED

Reedsport and the nearby fishing village of Winchester Bay have carved out identities as refueling and supply depots for excursions into Oregon's Sahara-by-the-Sea. A great place to start your explorations is the **Oregon Dunes NRA Visitor Information Center** (885 U.S. 101, Reedsport, 541/271-6100, www. fs.usda.gov/siuslaw), at the junction of the Coast Highway and Highway 38. In addition to the printed information on hiking, camping, and recreation, the Siuslaw Forest Service personnel are very helpful.

Note that a $5 day-use fee is charged per vehicle at most facilities and access points within the NRA. You can purchase an annual pass at the Dunes Visitor Center for $30.

Because the dunes are difficult to see from the highway in many places, the most commonly asked question in the visitors center is "Where are the dunes?" To answer that question for everybody, the National Forest Service opened **Oregon Dunes Overlook** just south of Carter Lake, midway between Florence and Reedsport, at the point where the dunes come closest to U.S. 101. In addition to four levels of railing-enclosed platforms connected by wooden walkways, there are trails down to the sand. It's only about 0.25 mile to the dunes and then 1 mile through sand and wetlands to the beach.

You can hike a loop beginning where the sand gives way to willows. Bear right en route to the beach. Once there, walk south 1.5 miles. A wooden post marks where the trail resumes. It then traverses a footbridge going through trees onto sand, completing the loop. If you go in February, this loop has great bird-watching potential. A day-use fee is charged for cars.

During the third weekend of May, Florence celebrates the **Rhododendron Festival** coinciding with the blooming of these flowers, which proliferate in the area. It's a tradition that goes back to 1908, when the festival was started as a way to draw attention and commerce to the area. A parade, carnival, flower show, 5K and 10K "Rhody Run," and the crowning of Queen Rhododendra are highlights of the festivities. This is a very popular event, attracting more than 15,000 visitors each year.

Fourth of July celebrations include live outdoor music and a barbecue in Old Town, and a fireworks display over the river.

Other sites, listed from south to north, for easy introduction to the dune topography are: Spinreel Campground, Umpqua Dunes Trail, Honeyman State Park, and Florence's South Jetty.

RECREATION IN THE DUNES

There are three excellent state parks and a dozen Siuslaw National Forest Campgrounds within the NRA. Although joyriding in noisy dune buggies and other off-road vehicles doesn't lack devotees, the best way to appreciate the interface of ecosystems is on foot. Dunes exceeding 500 feet in height, wetland breeding grounds for waterfowl and other animals, evergreen forests, and deserted beaches can be encountered in a march to the sea. Numerous designated hiking trails, ranging from easy half-mile loops to six-mile round-trips, give visitors a chance to star in their own version of *Lawrence of Arabia* as they moonwalk through this earthbound Sea of Tranquility. The soundtrack is provided by the 247 species of birds—along with your heartbeat—as you scale these elephantine anthills. Deserted beaches and secret swimming holes are among the many rewards of the journey.

Before setting out, pick up the *Hiking Trails Recreation Opportunity Guide* from the Oregon Dunes NRA Visitor Center. This and other publications will correct the superficial impression that the dunes are just a domain for all-terrain vehicles and day hikers.

To ensure a *bon voyage*, it's important to understand this terrain. Carry plenty of water and dress in layers—there are hot spots in dune valleys and ocean breezes at higher elevations. Expect cool summers and wet mild winters. Although rainfall can average more than 70 inches per year (with 75 percent of it falling Mar.-Nov.), a string of dry 50-60°F days in February is not uncommon. Another surprise is summertime morning fog, brought in by hot weather inland. These fogs, together with the inevitable confusion caused by dunes that don't look much different from each other, make a compass necessary. The lack of defined trails also compels such measures as marking your return route in the sand with a stick. Binoculars can help with visual orientation, not to mention the bird-watching opportunities galore.

© JUDY JEWELL

It's a slow 1.25-mile walk to the beach from Oregon Dunes Overlook.

Authors, publishers, and readers gather at the **Florence Festival of Books** (541/997-1994) at the Florence Events Center the last weekend of September.

For general entertainment, the tribes run **Three Rivers Casino** (5647 Hwy. 126, 541/997-7529). Along with the slots and game tables, there's a hotel and golf course.

ACCOMMODATIONS

As just about everywhere else, there are budget motels on the main drag, but to experience the coast fully, try one of the romantic getaways between Florence and Yachats. There are a number of notable B&Bs north of town, some of which are detailed as follows or earlier in this chapter.

Unless otherwise noted, prices listed are for high-season doubles.

$50-100

One of the best bargains in town is the **Lighthouse Inn** (155 U.S. 101, 541/997-3221 or 866/997-3221, http://lighthouseinn-florence.com, $84-143), a Cape Cod-style two-story motel on the highway close to the bridge and convenient to Old Town. With neatly kept rooms decorated with bric-a-brac and other homey touches, it may give you the feeling that you're spending the night at your grandmother's house. There are no in-room kitchens, but a common refrigerator and a microwave are available for guest use. Most guest rooms have a queen- or king-size bed and sleep two; some are considered suites, with two rooms and a connecting bath, sleeping up to five guests. A few rooms are designated as pet-friendly.

Just around the corner from Old Town, and across the highway from the Lighthouse Inn, the pet-friendly **Old Town Inn** (170 U.S. 101 N., 541/997-7131 or 800/301-6494, www.old-town-inn.com, $99) provides guests with spacious rooms a short walk away from the river and Old Town. Although this motel is on U.S. 101, the guest rooms are fairly quiet.

If it's not important for you to be an easy walk from Old Town, consider staying three miles south of town at the charming and pet-friendly **◖ Park Motel** (85034 U.S. 101, 541/997-2634 or 800/392-0441, www.park-motelflorence.com, $69-138), a classic mom-and-pop place set well back from the highway in a stand of Douglas firs. The guest rooms are paneled in knotty pine and come in a variety of sizes and configurations, including a few cabins, making it a good place for families or groups of friends.

$100-150

For a river experience, try the **◖ River House Motel** (1202 Bay St., 541/997-3933 or 888/824-2454, www.riverhouseflorence.com, $119-179). It's worth paying extra for a riverfront balcony ($149). This newer and attractive motel, which also has good views of the Siuslaw River Bridge, is just two blocks away from the heart of Old Town.

$150-200

◖ The Edwin K B&B (1155 Bay St., 541/997-8360 or 800/833-9465, www.edwink.com, $160-185) has six guest rooms, all with private bathrooms, and is just two blocks from Old Town, across the street from the Siuslaw River. River views, period antiques, and multicourse breakfasts with locally famous soufflés and home-baked breads served on fine china have established this gracious 1914 home as Florence's preeminent B&B. Add a private courtyard and waterfall in back, tea and sherry in the afternoon, and a restful atmosphere, and you'll understand the need to reserve well in advance.

On the south bank of the river, just across the bridge from Old Town, the **Best Western Pier Point Inn** (85625 U.S. 101, 541/997-7191 or 800/425-6736, www.bwpierpointinn.com, $189-199) offers spacious rooms, great bay views, sand-dune hiking across the street, and a complimentary hot breakfast. Rates at this large and classy motel drop by about half in the off-season.

At Heceta Beach, on the northern edge of Florence, **Driftwood Shores Resort** (88416 1st Ave., 541/997-8263 or 800/422-5091, www.driftwoodshores.com, $122-264) is unique among Florence lodgings in that it is oceanside. It is also a huge complex, and in a pretty isolated area, far from Old Town and restaurants (except the resort restaurant). All rooms face the ocean and have decks or patios, as well as microwaves and refrigerators (some suites have full kitchens).

Over $200

Twelve miles north of Florence and just a short walk from Heceta Head Lighthouse is **Heceta Head Lighthouse B&B** (92072 U.S. 101, 541/547-3696 or 866/547-3696,

© JUDY JEWELL

CENTRAL COAST

Guests at the Heceta Head Lighthouse B&B stay in the former house of the lighthouse keeper.

www.hecetalighthouse.com, $209-315), built in 1893. It used to be the lighthouse keeper's home; today, it's a B&B with antique furnishings and vintage photos, which help re-create the lives of the keepers of the flame. Among the six bedrooms, the two Mariners' rooms command the finest views. The current caretakers maintain a garden on the grounds, as did the actual lighthouse keepers of yesteryear, and they use some of the produce to turn out amazing seven-course breakfasts, glorious 90-minute affairs replete with such dishes as d'Anjou pear with chevre and Oregon honey and vol-au-vent stuffed with eggs, chives, and asparagus. The innkeepers are more likely to tell you about resident ghosts during breakfast than right before bedtime.

Vacation Rentals

Elson Shields Property Management (3298 U.S. 101, 541/997-6235, www.florencerentals.com) offers vacation home rentals in the Florence and Oregon Dunes area.

Camping

There are excellent campgrounds around Florence, several with recreational opportunities comparable to those at the nearby Oregon Dunes National Recreation Area but with more varied scenery.

Carl G. Washburne State Park (93111 U.S. 101 N., 541/547-3416 information, 800/452-5687 yurt reservations, year-round, $21 tents, $26 RVs, $39 yurts, $5 hiker-biker spaces) is popular with Oregonians because of its proximity to beaches, tidepools, Sea Lion Caves, and hiking trails. The seven walk-in tent sites are secluded and the 56 full-hookup sites have electricity and water; like almost all state park campgrounds, there are showers. Reservations are not accepted for regular sites, but the park's two yurts can be reserved. It's 14 miles north of Florence on U.S. 101 (three miles past Sea Lion Caves), then one mile west on a park road. This state park offers a number of good hiking trails and three miles of relatively isolated beach.

Three miles south of Florence's McCullough

Bridge and on both sides of U.S. 101 is **Honeyman State Park** (84505 U.S. 101 S., 541/997-3641 information, 800/452-5687 reservations, $21-39). This exceedingly popular campground gets very crowded in the summer—reservations are a must—but it empties out enough during spring and autumn to make a stay here worthwhile. The park has two large freshwater lakes, formed by mountain streams that flow toward the Pacific but are trapped by sand dunes. Ask about canoe rentals to savor the serenity of Cleawox Lake. Fishing, swimming, hiking, and dune buggies are available nearby, so there's always something to do. Sandboarding down the incredible dunes is also a popular activity here. In spring, pink rhododendrons line the highway and park roads. There are 187 tent sites with the basics ($21), 121 electrical-hookup and 47 full-hookup ($26), and 10 yurts ($39). Facilities include showers, a playground, and interpretive events. Advance reservations are accepted Memorial Day-Labor Day.

These large state park campgrounds are deservedly popular with families but can get to be bustling. If you're looking for something smaller and low-key (with flush toilets but no showers) then two Siuslaw National Forest Service campgrounds just north of Florence might be the ticket. **Sutton Campground** (877/444-6777 or www.recreation.gov, $22 regular site, $26 with electricity) is four miles north of Florence, and in addition to 80 campsites amid the dunes, it features a darlingtonia bog and a hiking trail network. In high summer season, about a quarter of the sites can be reserved; the rest are available on a first-come, first-served basis.

Just another mile north is **Alder Dune Campground** (877/444-6777 or www.recreation.gov, $22) with two lakes with swimming beaches and trout fishing. Hiking trails lead out into the dunes and reach the Pacific beaches. During summer high season, all of the campground's 39 sites can be reserved. For more information on these campgrounds, contact the **Siuslaw National Forest** (541/750-7000, www.fs.fed.us).

FOOD

The majority of Florence restaurants are along the Old Town waterfront. Walk along Bay Street and discover dozens of dining options, from casual to upscale.

Bakeries and Cafés

Under the bridge in Old Town, **Siuslaw River Coffee Roasters** (1240 Bay St., 541/997-3443, www.coffeeoregon.com, 7am-5pm daily, $2-6) serves good coffee and pastries. There's a little deck out back overlooking the river, and lots of books and hobnobbing inside.

If you're visiting on a rainy afternoon, a good place to while away the time is **Lovejoy's Tea Room** (129 Nopal St., 541/997-0502, lovejoysrestaurant.com, 11am-6pm daily, $8-16), owned by the founder of a famed San Francisco tearoom. Dine on a Cornish pasty or sausage roll ($8) or go for high tea service ($15.95).

For a fresh-baked muffin, slice of banana bread, or scone and a chat with a friendly baker,

© JUDY JEWELL

Take your coffee out back of Siuslaw River Coffee Roasters for good views of the river.

search out the **Shed Bakery** (182 Laurel St., 541/590-0712, www.beccabakesit.com, 10am-6pm Thurs.-Sat. and Mon.-Tues., $2-4). The tiny bakery is off a large parking lot, tucked behind a beauty salon.

American
It doesn't look like much from the front, but the best reason to seek out the **Traveler's Cove** (1362 Bay St., 541/997-6845, 9am-9pm daily, $9-20) is the lovely back patio, with tables directly over the river. The food here is eclectic, with homemade clam chowder, tempting salads and sandwiches, and a number of Mexican dishes. Fresh Dungeness crab makes an appearance here with crab quiche, crab enchiladas, and "crabby" Caesar salad.

Italian
A good place to take a break from chowder (though not necessarily seafood) is **Pomodori Ristorante** (1415 7th St., 541/902-2525, www.lapomodori.com, 11:30am-2pm and 5pm-9pm Tues.-Fri., 5pm-9pm Sat., $14-21), an intimate northern Italian restaurant in a converted house. Specialties include fresh shrimp and halibut and pasta, as well as a pork chop stuffed with shrimp, pancetta, scallions, and tomatoes.

Down in Old Town, eat everything from breakfast to pizza at **1285 Restobar** (1285 Bay St., 541/902-8338, 9am-10pm daily, $8-17), a lively trattoria with a focus on seafood entrées. And although the breakfast menu has many traditional American dishes, why pass on the chance to have breakfast pizza, topped with an egg?

Pacific Northwest
The Oregon coast isn't really known for adventurous fine dining, but a handful of hip eateries are spicing up the scene. At the edge of Old Town, the **◖ Homegrown Public House** (294 Laurel St., 541/997-4886, www.homegrown-pub.com, 11:30am-close Tues.-Sat. and 11am-3pm Sun., $8-17) is an easygoing place for a beer and a snack or a full meal. As the name implies, much of the food is locally grown or gathered (try the summer chanterelles if they're available) and seasonal.

Seafood
No one will ever accuse the **◖ Waterfront Depot** (1252 Bay St., 541/902-9100, www.the-waterfrontdepot.com, 4pm-10:30pm nightly, $12-18) of lacking in personality; it's a friendly bustling place with good views out onto the river and lovely filtered evening light. This historic structure was formerly the rail station at nearby Mapleton before it was barged down the Siuslaw River to its current riverfront location. Ask for a table or sit at the bar, where you're likely to be next to a local regular in for the restaurant's signature dish, saucy crab-encrusted halibut fillet. For lighter appetites, try ordering from the tapas menu, which, like all the offerings, is written on a chalkboard up on the wall.

In Old Town, the local **Mo's** (1436 Bay St., 541/997-2185, 11am-9pm, $9-15) is the largest outlet of this famed Oregon chowder house, and its fresh fish, fast service, fair prices, and Siuslaw River frontage make it this neighborhood's most popular restaurant.

The **Bridgewater Fish House and Zebra Bar** (1297 Bay St., Old Town, 541/997-9405, 11am-10pm Wed.-Mon., $17-36) is what passes for fine dining in Old Town. But with its rattan furniture and tropical motif, it's much less stuffy than most white-tablecloth establishments. Fresh fish, often with a Cajun flair, dominates the menu, which is so wide-ranging that almost everyone can find something to his or her liking.

Dessert
After dinner, have dessert at one of the two locations of **BJ's Ice Cream Parlor** (2930 U.S. 101 or 1441 Bay St., 541/997-7286, 10am-11pm daily summer, 11am-10pm daily winter, $2-6). BJ's churns out hundreds of flavors, with 48 on display at any given time, famous all over Oregon. Full fountain service, ice cream cakes, cheesecakes, gourmet frozen yogurt, and pies complement the cones and cups.

INFORMATION AND SERVICES
The **Florence Area Chamber of Commerce** (290 U.S. 101, 541/997-3128, www.

CENTRAL COAST

florencechamber.com, 9am-5pm Mon.-Fri.), is three blocks north of the Siuslaw River Bridge.

Peace Harbor Hospital (400 9th St., Florence, 541/997-8412) is open 24 hours, with a handful of specialists and an emergency room. The **post office** (770 Maple St., 541/997-2533), near the junction of Highway 126 and U.S. 101, is close to the library.

GETTING THERE

Porter Stage Lines (541/269-7183, www. amtrak.com) offers daily bus service between Coos Bay in the south and Eugene to the east. These buses can be booked online through Amtrak's reservation service. Eugene offers both Greyhound and Amtrak service, as well as air links to the rest of the country from Mahlon Sweet Field Airport (EUG).

Reedsport and Winchester Bay

If you're going fishing or coming back from a dunes hike, you'll appreciate a hot meal and a clean low-priced motel room in Reedsport. Otherwise, this town of 5,000 people might seem like a strange mirage of cut-rate motels, taverns, and burger joints in the midst of the Oregon Dunes National Recreation Area. Reedsport is not a tourist town, to put it politely. But there's lots of fascinating recreation available in the Oregon Dunes NRA that encircles the town, and the Umpqua River is itself a destination for anglers.

Jedediah Smith explored this country in 1828 after the Hudson's Bay Company's Peter Skene Ogden theorized that the Umpqua River—the largest river between San Francisco Bay and the Columbia—might be the fabled Northwest Passage. It wasn't, of course, but this river is still one of the great fishing streams of the state. Zane Grey avoided writing about it, lavishing the publicity instead on the Rogue to divert people from his favorite steelhead spots.

Cargo ships from Scottsburg, a hamlet some 17 miles upriver from Reedsport, supplied San Francisco markets with meat, milk, and produce between 1856 and the early 20th century. In its 1850s heyday, Scottsburg was larger than Portland, with some 5,000 residents, before an 1861 flood destroyed much of the town.

Two miles north of Reedsport, the little burg of Gardiner was created in the wake of a shipwreck. The *Bostonian* (owned by a Mr.

Gardiner) was dashed against the rocks at the mouth of the Umpqua in 1856, and from its remnants the first wood-frame structure in this area was built. It was soon joined by other white-painted homes and facilities for a port on the Umpqua. This "white city by the sea" declined in importance when the highway elevated Reedsport to regional hub status, and lost more punch when its huge lumber mill was closed, and then demolished.

Three miles southwest of Reedsport, Salmon Harbor Marina in **Winchester Bay** (pop. 1,000), a busy port for commercial sportfishing at the mouth of the Umpqua, has given the whole area new life in recent years, following hard times precipitated by the decline in timber revenues. In many ways, Winchester Bay is the more interesting destination of the two side-by-side towns, with its busy harbor and collage of waterfront bars and restaurants.

SIGHTS
Umpqua Discovery Center

In Reedsport's Old Town on the south bank of the river, the **Umpqua Discovery Center** (409 Riverfront Way, 541/271-4816, www.umpqua-discoverycenter.com, 9:30am-5pm Mon.-Sat., 11am-4pm Sun. mid-Mar.-mid-Oct., 10am-4pm Mon.-Sat., 11am-4pm Sun. mid-Oct.-mid-Mar., $8 adults, $4 children ages 6-15) interprets the regional human and natural history through multimedia programs, dioramas, scale models, and helpful staff. The gift store is stuffed with local goodies. The boardwalk and

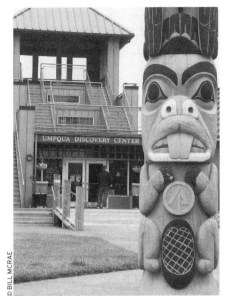

© BILL MCRAE

The Umpqua Discovery Center is on the Reedsport waterfront.

observation tower give a good view of the broad lower reaches of the Umpqua. In summer, free Thursday evening concerts are staged, and the center is the site of the September Tsalila festival.

Dean Creek Elk Viewing Area

Three miles east of Reedsport, and stretching three miles along the south side of Highway 38, the **Dean Creek Elk Viewing Area** (48819 Hwy. 38, Reedsport, www.blm.gov, 541/756-0100) provides parking areas and viewing platforms for observing the herd of some 120 wild Roosevelt elk that roam this 1,100-acre preserve. The elk move out of the forest to graze the preserve's marshy pastures, sometimes coming quite close to the highway. Elk can reach 1,100 pounds at maturity, and the majestic rack on a fully grown bull can spread three feet across. Early mornings and just before dusk are the most promising times to look for them; during hot weather and storms the elk tend to stay within the cover of the woods.

Umpqua Lighthouse State Park

Less than one mile south of Winchester Bay is **Umpqua Lighthouse State Park** (460 Lighthouse Rd., Winchester Bay, 541/271-4118, www.umpqualighthouse.org, 10am-4pm daily May-Oct., $3). Tour the red-capped 1894 **lighthouse** (1020 Lighthouse Rd., 541/271-4471, 10am-4pm daily May-Oct., $3) or admire it from the roadside. Next door, in a former Coast Guard building, the park's **visitors center and museum** has marine and timber exhibits; this is also where tours begin. Directly opposite the lighthouse, overlooking the mouth of the Umpqua and oceanfront dunes, is a whale-watching platform with a plaque explaining where, when, and what to look for.

Lake Marie, just south near the camping area, has a swimming beach and is stocked with rainbow trout. A one-mile forest trail around the lake makes for an easy hike. A trail from the campground leads to the highest dunes in the United States (elev. 545 feet), west of Clear Lake.

SPORTS AND RECREATION
Fishing

Winchester Bay and the tidewater reaches of the lower Umpqua River comprise Oregon's top coastal sturgeon fishery and one of the best areas for striped bass, particularly near the mouth of the Smith River, which enters the Umpqua just east of Reedsport. The best action for the Umpqua's spring chinook tends to be inland, below Scottsburg. Fall chinook enter the bay July-September. Other notable fisheries here are the huge runs of shad, which peak May-June, and smallmouth bass offer action upstream from Reedsport. Crabbing and clamming are also popular and productive pastimes in Winchester Bay and the lower reaches of the river. Every year August 1-mid-September, tagged crabs are released into the water in and around Winchester Bay, one of them worth a cash prize of $5,000 to whomever catches it.

Fishing charter services operating in the area include **Living Waters** (541/584-2295, www.fishinglivingwaters.com), **Strike Zone**

Charters (541/361-0194, www.strikezonecharters.com), and **River's End Guide Service** (541/271-3125, www.umpquafishing.com).

Hiking
◖ JOHN DELLENBACK TRAIL

This spectacular dunes landscape can be found 10.5 miles south of Reedsport, 0.25 mile south of the Eel Creek Campground near Lakeside. After you emerge from a 0.5-mile hike through coastal evergreen forest, you'll be greeted by dunes 300-400 feet high. It's said that dunes near here can approach 500 feet high and one mile long after a windblown buildup. The trail, marked by blue-banded wooden posts, continues another 2.5 miles to the beach. Dune hiking can be a bit disorienting. If you lose the trail, climb to the top of the tallest dune and scan for the trail markers.

A shorter and easier one-mile loop trail leads through woodlands to the dunes for a quick introduction to this landscape.

Skate Park

Near the south end of Reedsport in Lions Park is a world-class **skate park** (U.S. 101 and S. 22nd St.). Here you'll find a funnel-shaped full pipe and a 360-degree full loop as well as many more approachable features.

Water Sports

Ten miles south of Reedsport, the sleepy resort town of **Lakeside** hosted visits from Bob Hope, Bing Crosby, and the Ink Spots, among other luminaries, back in its 1930s and 1940s heyday. Today, it's still a popular destination, primarily for its proximity to the sprawling many-armed Tenmile and North Tenmile Lakes. These large shallow lakes offer waterskiing and excellent fishing for stocked rainbow trout and warm-water species, including crappie, yellow perch, bluegill, and lunker largemouth bass, which can grow up to 10 pounds. A 0.25-mile channel connects the two lakes, and a county park on Tenmile Lake has a paved boat ramp, fishing docks, a sandy swimming beach, and a picnic area.

ENTERTAINMENT AND EVENTS

Every June, over Father's Day weekend, chainsaw sculptors compete for $10,000 in prizes as they transform pieces of raw western red cedar into grizzly bears, giant salmon, and other rustic works of art during the **Chainsaw Sculpture Championships** (www.odcsc.com) at the Rainbow Plaza in Old Town Reedsport, near North 2nd Street and Greenwood Avenue.

Contact the **Reedsport Chamber of Commerce** (541/271-3495 or 800/247-2155, www.reedsportcc.org) for more information on events and festivals in the area.

ACCOMMODATIONS
$50-100

Of the half-dozen old-fashioned motor court motels that flank U.S. 101 in Reedsport, the **Fir Grove Motel** (2178 Winchester Ave., 541/271-4848, $58) is basic but clean.

Just off Highway 101 on the road to Winchester Bay, **Salmon Harbor Landing** (265 8th St., Winchester Bay, 541/271-3742, www.salmonharborlanding.com, $59-69) is a simple, but clean and friendly, motel. This is a good place to stay if you don't need fancy amenities but enjoy a personal touch. Each room is individually decorated, with many of the owner's antiques featured.

Anglers, or anyone who'd rather be in a location off the main drag, should consider the **Winchester Bay Motel** (4th St. and Broadway, Winchester Bay, 541/271-4871 or 800/246-1462, www.winbayinn.com, $69-96), just across from the docks. Guest rooms are basic but clean. Even though this is a large sprawling complex, be sure to reserve ahead of time in fishing season. Pets are permitted in some guest rooms.

Another clean and convenient place for anglers, crabbers, and storm-watchers is the **Harbor View Motel** (540 Beach Blvd., Winchester Bay, 541/271-3352, $50-70), a small place with easy access to charter boats.

$150-200

The **Best Western Plus Salbasgeon Inn**

(1400 U.S. 101, 541/271-4831 or 800/528-1234, $145-172) is Reedsport's largest and most full-service hotel, on U.S. 101 just south of the Umpqua River bridge. Amenities include an indoor pool, a fitness center, guest laundry, and a hot tub. Continental breakfast is complimentary.

Camping

Choices abound in this recreation-rich area. Just south of Winchester Bay is **Umpqua Lighthouse State Park** (460 Lighthouse Rd., Winchester Bay, 541/271-4118 information, 800/452-5687 reservations, $19-76). The campground alongside Lake Marie has firewood, flush toilets, showers, picnic tables, electricity, and piped water. The 20 RV sites go for $24; the 24 tent sites are $19; two basic yurts are $36; six deluxe yurts (with shower, small kitchen, refrigerator, microwave, and TV/VCR) are $76; and two rustic cabins are $39. The lake offers fishing, boating, and swimming. Trails from the campground lead to the highest dunes in the United States (elev. 545 feet), west of Clear Lake.

William A. Tugman State Park (541/759-3604 information, 800/452-5687 reservations) is eight miles south of Reedsport, in the heart of dune country. This larger campground, with 115 sites, has a similar range of creature comforts, prices, and recreation. It sits on the west shore of Eel Lake, east of U.S. 101 across from the widest point of the dunes, two miles to the sea.

Windy Cove Campground (541/271-4138) is a county park with 24 full-hookup sites ($24) and four other sites with electric service only ($15). Located on the south side of Salmon Harbor Drive, across from the Winchester Bay marina, it has restrooms, picnic tables, grass, and paved site pads. No reservations are accepted. It is legal to drive your off-highway vehicle (OHV) from this campground directly to the dunes, but that requires a couple of miles' drive on the pavement.

About nine miles south of Reedsport, set along Eel Creek near Eel and Tenmile Lakes,

is **Eel Creek Campground** (877/444-6777 reservations, www.recreation.gov, mid-May-Sept., $20), a Siuslaw National Forest facility with 51 basic tent and RV sites; reservations are advised. The Umpqua Dunes Trail offers access to the dunes and the beach.

Eight miles north of Reedsport, the **Tahkenitch Campground** (877/444-6777 reservations, www.recreation.gov, mid-May-Sept., $20) is another Forest Service facility set among ancient Douglas firs and conveniently located near Tahkenitch and other lakes, dunes, and ocean beaches. A network of trails branch out through the dunes, along Tahkenitch Lake, and to the beach.

If you're coming to the dunes to play in the sand, consider spending the night at the all-in-one **Discovery Point Resort** (242 Discovery Point Ln., 541/271-3443, www.discoverypointresort.com, $16 tents, $31-34 RVs) near Winchester Bay. The resort offers OHV enthusiasts dune access and all-terrain vehicle (ATV) rentals, and provides condos, one- to three-bedroom cabins (which sleep up to six, $275), 60 RV spaces, and tent sites. To get there from Reedsport, head two miles south on U.S. 101 to Winchester Bay, then turn right at Pelican Market onto Salmon Harbor Drive. Go one mile, and you'll see Discovery Point Resort on the left. Reservations are strongly recommended.

FOOD

Seek not cuisine in Reedsport. Standard American fare is the norm in this hardscrabble town. The best bets for seafood are the wharfside restaurants in Winchester Bay.

Reedsport

A popular place on U.S. 101 is **Don's Main Street Restaurant** (2115 Winchester Ave., 541/271-2032, 8am-8pm daily, $7-13), with burgers, fried chicken, and a parlor serving local Umpqua ice cream. This is the locals' favorite place for pies.

The **Schooner Inn Café** (423 Riverfront Way, 541/271-3945, 10am-3pm daily, lunch

CENTRAL COAST

$8-10), on the boardwalk next door to the Discovery Center, has a pleasant riverside patio and a good selection of delicious salads and sandwiches. This is a quiet spot for an al fresco lunch overlooking the Umpqua.

Winchester Bay

For the best fresh seafood in the dune country, head down to the Salmon Harbor Marina at Winchester Bay, where there are a number of casual seafood restaurants within easily strolling distance.

The friendly staff at the **Sportsmen's Cannery and Smokehouse** (182 Bay Front Loop, 541/271-3293, shop 9am-5pm daily) hosts a weekend seafood barbecue (4pm-7pm Fri., 11am-7pm Sat.-Sun., $12-18) that features salmon, halibut, and crab (and whatever else is fresh) and all the trimmings. Don't expect indoor seating for this meal—you'll eat at picnic tables set up in the parking lot. Peek inside and you may see cannery employees cutting up the day's catch. Visit the adjoining shop to purchase fresh, smoked, or canned fish; they'll even smoke your catch for you.

Another good bets for fresh seafood in an authentic dockside setting is **Fishpatrick's Crabby Cafe** (196 Bay Front Loop, 541/271-3474, 11am-3pm Sun. and Wed., 11am-8pm Thurs.-Sat., $8-25), which offers excellent fish-and-chips, crab, and fish sandwiches in a woodsy dining room.

© BILL MCRAE

Winchester Bay is an excellent place to eat fresh seafood.

INFORMATION

The **Oregon Dunes National Recreation Area Visitor Information Center** (885 U.S. 101, Reedsport, 541/271-6100, www.fs.usda.gov/siuslaw) and **Reedsport Chamber of Commerce** (541/271-3495 or 800/247-2155, www.reedsportcc.org) share a building at the junction of U.S. 101 and Highway 38. It's open 8am-4:30pm weekdays year-round and 8am-4:30pm weekends mid-July-early September.

SOUTH COAST

Stretching from the Coos Bay area to the California border, the southern Oregon coast is far from the population centers of Oregon's interior valleys, but the south coast amply rewards visitors who make the effort to get here. The foothills of the Klamath Mountains tumble down the narrow coastal plain and fall off in precipitous headlands at the ocean's edge. Close to shore, the waters are a rocky garden of sea stacks and islets that are home to uncounted flocks of pelagic birds. With half a dozen wild rivers slicing through the mountains to the sea, the south coast is famed for its outstanding salmon fishing, especially on charters from the harbors of Charleston, Gold Beach, Bandon, and Brookings.

In addition, the southern region is blessed with the fairest weather on the Oregon coast and generally gets the most sunshine, the least rain, and the warmest temperatures—attributes as appealing to visitors as to the area's many retirees and other transplants.

Scenic highlights of the south coast include the weather-beaten bluffs and formal gardens at Cape Arago and Shore Acres State Parks, the gorgeous scenery of Boardman and Harris Beach State Parks, and just about every inch of the drive between Brookings and Port Orford.

In addition to fishing, recreational opportunities are seemingly endless: Outstanding courses draws golfers to Bandon (*Golf* magazine hailed Bandon Dunes as one of the country's top three courses) and Brookings (with the Salmon Run Golf Course alongside the Chetco River); some of the coast's top windsurfing and kiting are near Cape Sebastian; and popular

© BILL MCRAE

HIGHLIGHTS

(Shore Acres State Park: The regal manor house is gone, but the formal gardens from a onetime private estate still thrive above an especially rugged stretch of beach (page 159).

(South Slough National Estuarine Research Reserve: Here, where freshwater meets saltwater, is a nutrient-rich environment that supports many wildlife species. Hike or paddle, but either way, pay attention to the tides (page 160).

(Bandon Historical Society Museum: Learn all about cranberries, native cultures, and frontier coastal history at this well-curated regional museum (page 170).

(Bandon Dunes Golf Resort: This links-style course on the coastal headlands is evocative of Scotland. There are four golf courses, each expertly designed in a gorgeous setting (page 173).

(Humbug Mountain: The three-mile trail to the top of Humbug Mountain passes a spectacular array of native plants. Even if the promised mountaintop view is shrouded in fog, it's a great hike (page 181).

(Cape Blanco State Park and Hughes House: This is the only lighthouse in Oregon that allows visitors into the lantern room, with its massive Fresnel lens (page 181).

(Cape Sebastian: Hike up Cape Sebastian for a front-row seat for springtime whale-watching (page 186).

(Rogue River Jet-Boat Ride: Even die-hard paddlers won't regret succumbing to a jet-boat tour up the Rogue River. Boaters often get to see ospreys and eagles fishing along this stretch of river (page 187).

(Samuel H. Boardman State Scenic Corridor: North of Brookings, the road winds hundreds of feet above the surf, allowing you to peer down at one of the most dramatic meetings of rock and tide in the world (page 196).

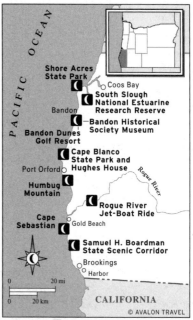

© AVALON TRAVEL

LOOK FOR (TO FIND RECOMMENDED SIGHTS, ACTIVITIES, DINING, AND LODGING.

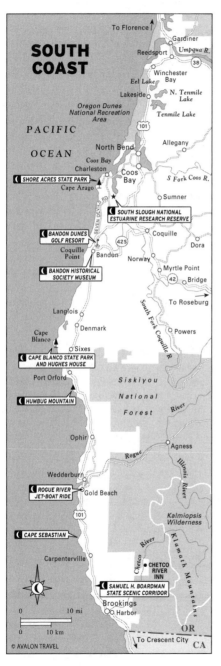

SOUTH
COAST

PACIFIC

OCEAN

jet-boat tours run up the Rogue River from Gold Beach.

PLANNING YOUR TIME

Plan to spend at least a day or two exploring the **Coos Bay-Bandon** region. Coos Bay is the only real city along the southern coast, and like Tillamook to the north, it's a gateway to some spectacular areas but pretty workaday itself. Be sure to head west and south from town to explore the wonderful shoreline parks at Sunset Bay and Cape Arago.

Don't overlook the coastal wetlands, especially the coastal estuary at **South Slough National Estuarine Research Reserve,** south of Coos Bay. **Bandon Marsh National Wildlife Refuge** protects the largest remaining tract of salt marsh within the Coquille River estuary. Major habitats include undisturbed salt marsh, mudflat, Sitka spruce, and alder riparian communities, which provide resting and feeding areas for migratory waterfowl, shore and wading birds, and raptors.

Of course, **Bandon** is now best known for its world-class Bandon Dunes Golf Resort, but the old downtown area still hums to its counterculture vibes. Bandon's beachfront, along with the Coos Bay sand spit, the beaches on the western side of Humbug Mountain, and the isolated shorelines of Boardman State Park are choice beachcombing spots.

Port Orford is often overlooked, but it's one of our favorite spots, with great ocean vistas from town and lots of hiking at nearby Humbug Mountain. It also doesn't hurt that there's good eating here. It's worth at least an afternoon stop.

Jet-boat tours start in **Gold Beach** and head up the Rogue River, offering those with just a morning to spare the chance to explore stunning river vistas—and perhaps help deliver the mail. Between Gold Beach and Brookings, save some serious time to explore beaches sequestered between steep cliffs and pounding surf at the 11-mile-long **Boardman State Scenic Corridor.**

Charleston, Coos Bay, and North Bend

The towns around the harbor of Coos Bay—Charleston, Coos Bay, and North Bend—refer to themselves collectively as the Bay Area. In contrast to its namesake in California, the Oregon version is not exactly the Athens of the coast. Nonetheless, visitors will be impressed by the area's beautiful beaches, the largest oceanfront dunes in North America, and three wonderfully scenic and historic state parks. Because much of this natural beauty is on the periphery of the industrialized core of the Bay Area, away from U.S. 101, it's easy to miss. All that many motorists see upon entering Coos Bay/North Bend on the Coast Highway are the dockside lumber mills and foreign vessels anchored at the onetime site of the world's largest lumber port.

The little town of Charleston (pop. 700) to the southwest makes few pretenses of being anything other than what it really is—a bustling commercial fishing port. Processing plants here can or cold-pack tuna, salmon, crab, oysters, shrimp, and other kinds of seafood. The town might occasionally smell of fish, but the few restaurants and lodgings here are good values, and the town is the gateway to a trio of extraordinary state parks: Sunset Bay, Shore Acres, and Cape Arago.

To reach Charleston from points south, or to head south from town, take the **Seven Devils Road,** which has its southern terminus about three miles north of Bandon. This route runs 13 miles past forests, a few clear-cuts, and an estuarine preserve.

SIGHTS
Coos Bay Harbor
A good place to take in the bustling bay front is the **Coos Bay Boardwalk** (U.S. 101 and Anderson Ave.) where you can check out the oceangoing freighters, visit a restored tugboat, and learn of the harbor's history courtesy of interpretive placards. A 400-gallon saltwater aquarium holds fish and other marine life of Coos Bay. This is the largest coastal harbor

between San Francisco and Puget Sound (more than 100 deepwater vessels call each year), and it's fun to watch the ships docking and the portside wood-chip piles growing by dozens of feet overnight. Wood chips are Oregon's primary forest-product export—raw log exports (which formerly made Coos Bay the world's busiest lumber shipment center) are now prohibited.

Coos Art Museum
The **Coos Art Museum** (235 Anderson Ave., Coos Bay, 541/267-3901, www.coosart.org, 10am-4pm Tues.-Fri., 1pm-4pm Sat., $5 adults, $2 seniors and students), in downtown Coos Bay, is the Oregon coast's only art museum and features primarily 20th-century and contemporary works by American artists, including pieces by Robert Rauschenberg and Larry Rivers. Etchings, woodcuts, serigraphs, and other prints make up a large part of the permanent collection, which includes several of Janet Turner's richly detailed depictions of birds in natural settings. Other highlights include Kirk Lybecker's photo-realistic watercolors. Don't miss the Prefontaine Room on the second floor of the museum. Photos, trophies, medals, and other memorabilia of native-son world-class runner Steve Prefontaine illustrate his credo: "I want to make something beautiful when I run."

In addition to the permanent collection, recurring events worth detouring for are the May-July juried show of artists from the Western states, and the Maritime Art Exhibit, August-September.

Coos County Historical and Maritime Museum
The **Coos County Historical and Maritime Museum** (1220 Sherman Ave., North Bend, 541/756-6320, www.cooshistory.org, 10am-4pm Tues.-Sat., $5 adults, $2 seniors and students, free ages 12 and under) is near the south end of the Conde McCullough Bridge,

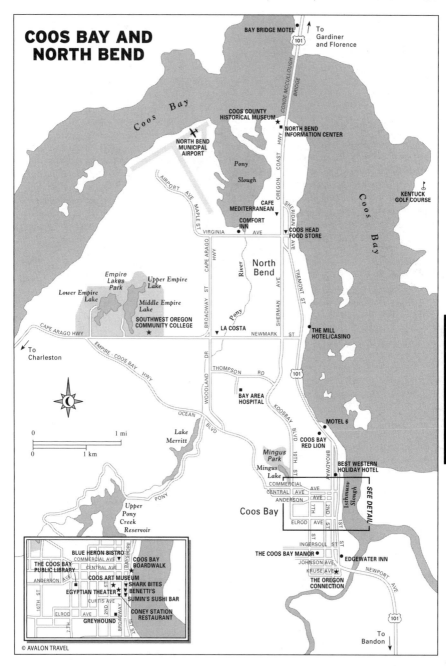

COOS BAY AND NORTH BEND

BAY BRIDGE MOTEL
101
To Gardiner and Florence

Coos Bay

CONDE MCCULLOUGH BRIDGE

COOS COUNTY HISTORICAL MUSEUM
★
NORTH BEND INFORMATION CENTER

NORTH BEND MUNICIPAL AIRPORT

AIRPORT AVE

MAPLE ST

Pony Slough

OREGON COAST HWY

SHERIDAN AVE

KENTUCK GOLF COURSE

Coos Bay

CAFE MEDITERRANEAN
▼

COMFORT INN

VIRGINIA AVE

COOS HEAD FOOD STORE

CAPE ARAGO HWY

BROADWAY ST

River

North Bend

Pony

TREMONT ST

Empire Lakes Park

Upper Empire Lake

Lower Empire Lake

Middle Empire Lake

SOUTHWEST OREGON COMMUNITY COLLEGE
★

LA COSTA ■

SHERMAN AVE

NEWMARK ST

THE MILL HOTEL/CASINO ★

CAPE ARAGO HWY

EMPIRE - COOS BAY HWY

To Charleston

WOODLAND DR

THOMPSON RD

101

BAY AREA HOSPITAL ■

KOOSBAY BLVD

OCEAN BLVD

Lake Merritt

MOTEL 6 ●

COOS BAY RED LION ■

Mingus Park

Mingus Lake

10TH ST

BROADWAY

BEST WESTERN HOLIDAY HOTEL ●

0   1 mi
0   1 km

Upper Pony Creek Reservoir

PONY

COMMERCIAL

CENTRAL AVE AVE

ANDERSON AVE

Coos Bay

2ND ST

1ST ST

Isthmus Slough

7TH ST

ELROD AVE

SEE DETAIL

INGERSOLL ST

THE COOS BAY MANOR ●

JOHNSON AVE

KRUSE AVE

EDGEWATER INN ●

THE OREGON CONNECTION ★

NEWPORT AVE

101

To Bandon

[Detail inset]

BLUE HERON BISTRO ■

THE COOS BAY PUBLIC LIBRARY ■

COMMERCIAL AVE ▼

CENTRAL AVE

BAYSHORE

COOS BAY BOARDWALK

ANDERSON AVE

COOS ART MUSEUM ■

EGYPTIAN THEATER ★

SHARK BITES ▼

BENETTI'S ▼

SUMIN'S SUSHI BAR ▼

CURTIS AVE

CONEY STATION RESTAURANT

ELROD AVE

GREYHOUND ●

10TH ST

J TH ST

2ND ST

1ST ST

BROADWAY

SOUTH COAST

© BILL MCRAE

The Coos Bay Boardwalk is an open-air maritime museum.

one of several distinctive Depression-era spans by Oregon's master bridge-builder. The museum houses more than the usual bric-a-brac from earlier eras, thanks largely to the region's heritage as a shipping center. An early-1900s Regina music box, a piano shipped around Cape Horn, miniature boat models, and a jade Chinese plaque, as well as Coos Indian beadwork and other artifacts, make this collection especially memorable. Outside, old-time logging equipment and a 1920s steam train are also worth a look.

Sunset Bay State Park

The Cape Arago Highway west of Charleston leads to some of the most dramatic beaches and interesting state parks on the coast. Among the several beaches on the road to Cape Arago, the strand at **Sunset Bay State Park** (13030 Cape Arago Hwy., 541/888-4902 information, 800/452-5687 reservations) is the big attraction because its sheltered shallow cove, encircled by sandstone bluffs, is warm and calm enough for swimming, a rarity in the Pacific Ocean north

of Santa Barbara, California. In addition to swimmers, divers, surfers, kayakers, and boaters, many people come here to watch the sunset. Local legend tells that pirates hid out in this well-protected cove.

A spectacular four-mile cliff-side segment of the **Oregon Coast Trail** runs from Sunset Beach south to Cape Arago. Good views of **Cape Arago Lighthouse** across the water can be seen along this route. Listen for its unique foghorn. For a short hike, follow the signs from the mouth of Big Creek to the viewpoint overlooking Sunset Bay.

The Cape Arago Lighthouse is on Chief Island and was linked to the mainland by a steel-truss bridge. For the local Coos Indians, Chief Island and the adjacent shoreline were a traditional burial ground, though after the building of the first lighthouse in 1866, the Coast Guard no longer allowed native burials. However, the island continued to have a sacred significance for the Coos.

A total of three different structures have served as the lighthouse on Chief Island. Then,

the craggy coastline at Sunset Bay State Park

8am-sunset year-round, $5 per vehicle or Oregon Coast Passport), the grandeur of nature is complemented by human endeavor. The park is set on the grounds of lumber magnate and entrepreneur Louis J. Simpson's early-1900s mansion, which began as a summer home in 1906 and grew into a three-story mansion complete with an indoor heated swimming pool and large ballroom. Originally a Christmas present to his wife, Shore Acres became the showplace of the Oregon coast, with formal and Japanese gardens eventually added to the 743-acre estate. After a 1921 fire, a second, larger (two stories high and 224 feet long) incarnation of Simpson's "shack by the beach" was built. Over the following years the building fell into disrepair; the house and grounds were ceded to the state in 1942. Because of the high cost of upkeep, the mansion had to be razed, but the gardens have been lovingly maintained.

The gardens are compelling attractions, but the headland's rim is more dramatic. Perched near the edge of the bluff, on the site formerly occupied by the mansion, a glass-enclosed observation shelter makes a perfect vantage point from which to watch for whales or marvel at the crashing waves. When there's a storm, the waves really slam into the sandstone reefs and cliffs, hurling up tremendous fountains of spray. It's not uncommon to feel the spray atop the 75-foot promontory. The history of the Simpson family is really the history of the Bay Area, and their story is captioned beneath period photos in the observation gazebo and in the garden in a small enclosure at the west end of the floral displays.

In the seven acres of neatly tended gardens, set back from the sea, the international botanical bounty culled by Simpson clipper ships and schooners is still in its glory, complemented by award-winning roses, rhododendrons, tulips, and azaleas. A restored gardener's cottage with antique furnishings stands at the back of the formal gardens. It's open for special occasions and during the winter holidays. Also in the gardens, note the copper egret sculptures at the

after 140 years of service, on January 1, 2006, the lighthouse was decommissioned. Oregon's congressional delegation in 2008 successfully maneuvered to transfer Chief Island, the adjacent shoreline, and the Cape Arago Lighthouse to the Confederated Tribes of the Coos, Lower Umpqua, and Siuslaw Indians. As part of the agreement, the Native Americans have pledged to maintain the lighthouse and make it available "to the general public for educational, park, recreational, cultural, or historic preservation purposes at times and under conditions determined to be reasonable by the Secretary of the Interior." The island will again primarily be used as a burial ground, though the tribes have also discussed building an interpretive center on the mainland. However, the bridge to Chief Island has been removed, and the lighthouse and Chief Island are currently not open to the public.

◖ Shore Acres State Park

Less than one mile south of Sunset Bay at **Shore Acres State Park** (541/888-3732,

COOS BAY SHIPWRECKS

The *Captain Lincoln*, whose grounding on the treacherous North Spit of Coos Bay led to settlement of the area, would not be the last ship to meet its end on these dangerous shores. In 1910, the *Czarina* foundered in heavy seas on the bar; 24 people were killed in one of the worst shipwrecks on Oregon's south coast. The *Claremont* and the *Santa Clara* both wrecked on the bar in 1915, and the *Sujameco* grounded on Horsfall Beach in 1929. Although most of the ship was removed during salvage operations, iron projections can sometimes still be seen in the sand at low tide.

The most recent and infamous shipwreck here, though, was the February 4, 1999, grounding of the 640-foot wood-chip carrier *New Carissa*, on the North Spit. After the Coast Guard firebombed the freighter in an attempt to burn off the 150,000 gallons of fuel oil on board, the vessel broke into two parts. After weeks of failed attempts, the bow section was finally towed out to sea and sunk in 10,000 feet of water by a Navy torpedo. Most of the stern was finally removed, but a section of it remained mired in the sand on the North Spit, just beyond the surf, until 2008. During the shipwreck and months of salvage efforts, the hulk leaked some 70,000 gallons of oil, which killed an estimated 2,400 seabirds and destroyed oyster beds. The media circus that sprang up around the site generated a temporary economic boomlet for the region, but the long-term ecological damage is still to be determined.

pond and the greenhouse for rare plants from warmer climes.

From Thanksgiving through New Year's, during the annual **Holiday Lights and Open House** (4pm-10pm daily), the gardens are decorated with 250,000 colored lights and other holiday touches. The gardener's cottage opens and serves free refreshments during this time.

If you bear right and follow the pond's contours toward the ocean, you'll come to the **Simpson Beach Trail.** Follow it north for cliffside views of the rock-studded shallows below. Southward, the trail goes downhill to a scene of exceptional beauty. From the vantage point of a small beach, you can watch waves crash into rocks with such force that the white spray appears to hang suspended in the air. Pursuits for the active traveler include exploring tidepools and caves as well as springtime swimming in a cove, formed by winter storms, on the south side of the beach. In summer, thimbleberries and salal growing along the trail down to the beach can provide sustenance for these activities.

Cape Arago State Park

A little more than one mile south of Shore Acres is **Cape Arago State Park** (800/551-6949, day-use only, free), at the end of the Cape Arago Highway. Locals have made much of the fact that this was a possible landing site of the English explorer Sir Francis Drake in 1579, and they put a plaque here commemorating him.

Beachcombers can make their own discoveries in the numerous tidepools, some of the best on the coast. The south cove trail (find it past the picnic shelter) runs down to a sandy beach and the better tidepools. The north cove trail leads to more tidepools, good spots for fishing, and views of the colonies of seals and sea lions at Shell Island, including the most northerly breeding colony of enormous elephant seals. Their huge pups, when just a month old, may already weigh 300-400 pounds. Note that the north trail closes March 1-June 30 to protect seal pups. The picnic tables on the headlands command beautiful ocean panoramas and are superbly placed for whale-watching.

(South Slough National Estuarine Research Reserve

Estuaries, where freshwater and saltwater interface, form some of the richest ecosystems on earth, capable of producing five times

© BILL MCRAE

The gardens at Shore Acres State Park are well-tended and surprisingly elegant.

more plant material than a cornfield of comparable size while supporting great numbers of fish, birds, and other wildlife. The South Slough of Coos Bay is the largest such web of life on the Oregon coast. The **South Slough National Estuarine Reserve Interpretive Center** (61907 Seven Devils Rd., 541/888-5558, www.oregon.gov, 10am-4:30pm daily Memorial Day-Labor Day, free), four miles south of Charleston, will help you coordinate a canoe trip through the estuary and offers guided hikes as well.

The center looks out over several estuarine arms of Coos Bay, the largest harbor between San Francisco Bay and Puget Sound. These vital wetlands nurture a variety of life-forms, detailed by the placards captioning the center's exhibits. The coastal ecosystem is presented by the "10-minute trail" behind the interpretive center. The various conifers and the understory are clearly labeled along the gently sloping half-mile loop. Branch trails lead down toward the water for an up-close view of the estuary.

Down by the slough, you may see elk grazing in marshy meadows and bald eagles circling above, while *Homo sapiens* harvest oysters and shrimp in these waters.

Beginning near the visitors center is the easy three-mile **estuary study trail,** which follows Hidden Creek from the wooded uplands down the valley to a boardwalk that winds through fresh- and saltwater marshes and leads to several wildlife observation points.

Whiskey Run Beach
Midway between Charleston and Bandon is the quiet beach at **Whiskey Run,** whose ore-bearing sands spread gold fever down the south coast in the early 1850s. As many as 2,000 miners worked here until a storm washed away the deposit. Other forms of beachcombing at Whiskey Run and on the beaches to the north are still thriving, however. Agate-hunting after a season of winter storms and clamming at low tide make these solitary shorelines ideal places to forget worldly concerns. To get there, turn west from the lightly traveled Seven Devils Road onto Whiskey Run Road, and drive 1.5 miles to this county park. Just to the north you'll find Seven Devils State Wayside. Vehicles are permitted on the beach at Whiskey Run; Seven Devils is reserved for foot traffic.

Horsfall Beach and the North Spit
On the spit north of North Bend, the Oregon Dunes taper down to wide, sandy beaches and wetlands. **Horsfall Beach** is extremely popular with ATV riders, but it's also a good place to enjoy nature. It's also worth exploring on foot, especially in the winter, when storms can expose old shipwrecks.

Myrtlewood
To see Oregon coast folk art in the making, visit the **Oregon Connection** (1125 S. 1st St., Coos Bay, 541/267-7804, www,oregonconnection. com, 9am-5:30pm Mon.-Sat., 11am-4pm Sun.), just off U.S. 101 at the south end of Coos Bay. The myrtlewood factory tour shows you how a myrtlewood log gets fashioned into

Horsfall Beach is popular with ATV riders.

bowls, clocks, tables, and other utensils. No admission is charged for this 25-minute guided run through a working factory. After you're done, the store is a delight, with Oregon gourmet foods and crafts supplementing the quality woodwork.

Five miles north of North Bend, **The Real Oregon Gift** (3955 U.S. 101, 541/756-2220, www.realoregongift.com, 9am-5pm Mon.-Sat., 9:30am-4:30pm Sun.) is another large myrtlewood factory and showroom.

SPORTS AND RECREATION

Wavecrest Discoveries (541/267-4027, http://wavecrestdiscoveries.com) offers a cornucopia of guided outdoor activities around the Bay Area and beyond, including clamming and tidepooling excursions, sea kayaking, dune and estuary tours, and more.

Fishing

Spring chinook salmon, which sometimes exceed 30 pounds and are renowned as an unrivaled dining treat, offer prime fishing in Coos Bay. However, their population levels and fishing rules vary from year to year. Mid-August-November, Isthmus Slough sees a good return of fin-clipped hatchery cohos. In saltwater, chinook and coho are usually found in good numbers within a one- to two-mile radius of the mouth of Coos Bay May-September, although the legal season varies; carefully check the regulations. Remnant striped bass are still occasionally caught in Coos Bay's sloughs and upper tidewater, but their numbers are diminishing.

Coos Bay is also one of the premier areas for crabbing and clamming. The Charleston Fishing Pier is a productive spot for crabs, while the best clamming spots are found along the bay side of the North Spit.

Fishing charters, bay cruises, whale-watching, and the like can be arranged through a number of charter outfits based at the Charleston Boat Basin. **Betty Kay Charters** (541/888-9021 or 800/752-6303, www.bettykaycharters.com) charges typical per-person prices: $75 for five hours of rock fishing; $140

© BILL MCRAE

THE MYRTLEWOOD TREE

When exploring the southern Oregon coast, you'll soon discover that myrtlewood is very popular hereabouts—nearly every town has a myrtlewood factory or showroom that peddles bowls, sculpture, furniture, and other products fashioned from this rare and unusual wood.

Myrtlewood is a member of the Lauraceae family of small trees and is a relative of the camphor, bay, and sassafras trees. Like these trees, the leaves and wood of the tree have a pungent odor. The myrtlewood tree grows only in a small area of southern Oregon and northern California, and it is large enough to harvest only after 100-150 years of growth. The wood is highly patterned, with the grain forming erratic bands of differing color in a single block of wood.

Myrtlewood is particularly popular for turn-ing into bowls—salad and serving bowls make a lovely gift or keepsake of a trip to coastal Oregon. However, the tree and its wood have been used for myriad other functional and decorative purposes for many years.

Hudson's Bay Company trappers used myrtlewood leaves to brew tea as a remedy for chills. In 1869 the golden spike marking the completion of the nation's first transcontinental railroad (near Promontory, Utah) was driven into a highly polished myrtlewood tie. Novelist Jack London was so taken by the beauty of the wood's swirling grain that he ordered an entire suite of furniture.

During the Depression, the city of North Bend issued myrtlewood coins after the only bank in town failed. The coins ranged $0.50-10 in value and are still redeemable, although they are worth far more as collectors' items.

SOUTH COAST

for seven hours of salmon fishing; $200 for 12 hours of tuna or halibut fishing; and $40 for a two-hour bay cruise, whale-watching, or ecotour.

Golf

Tee up in a lovely setting at **Sunset Bay Golf Course** (11001 Cape Arago Hwy., Charleston, 541/888-9301, $18 weekends, $15 weekdays), a nine-holer close to Sunset Bay State Park.

Hiking

Although most hikers head to the coast, especially the four-mile stretch of the **Oregon Coast Trail** between Sunset Bay and Cape Arago, for a nice trail with spectacular views, it's also worth looking inland. Twenty-five miles northeast of Coos Bay in the Coast Range is **Golden and Silver Falls State Park** (800/551-6949). Two spectacular waterfalls are showcased in this little-known gem of a park. Getting here involves driving east of Coos Bay along the Coos River, crossing to its north bank, and continuing along the Millicoma River through the community of Allegany. To find your way from Coos Bay, look for the Allegany/Eastside exit off U.S. 101. Beyond Allegany, continue up the East Fork of the Millicoma River to its junction with Glenn Creek, which ultimately leads to the park. The narrow winding gravel roads make this half-hour trip unsuitable for a wide-body vehicle.

You can reach each waterfall by way of two 0.5-mile trails. The 100-foot cataracts lie about one mile apart, and although both are about the same height, each has a distinct character. For most of the year, Silver Falls is more visually arresting because it flows in a near semicircle around a knob near its top. During or just after the winter rains, however, the thunderous sound of Golden Falls makes it the more awe-inspiring of the two. Along the trails, look for the beautifully delicate maidenhair fern.

Kayaking

From a canoe or sea kayak, as you pass tide flats, salt marshes, forested areas, and open water, you can really begin to grasp the richness of the estuarine habitat at the **South Slough National Estuarine**

Research Reserve (541/888-5558, www.
oregon.gov). The estuary here has two main
branches, offering plenty of territory for a day
of exploration.

Although the waters are placid, they are
strongly influenced by the tides—be sure to
consult tide tables when you plan an outing.
Wind can also affect your trip: Know that in
the spring and summer, the prevailing winds
are from the northwest; in the winter they're
from the southwest. At all times of year, the
wind blows hardest in the afternoon.

Kayaks can be rented just outside of
Charleston at **High Tide Rentals** (91124 Cape
Arago Hwy., 541/888-3664).

Surfing and Swimming

The best spot on the Oregon coast for swimming is **Sunset Bay State Park** (13030 Cape
Arago Hwy., Coos Bay, 541/888-4902). The
water is warm enough for most adults and gentle enough for most kids.

Surfing is best just northeast of Sunset
Bay, at **Bastendorff Beach County Park**
(63379 Bastendorff Beach Rd., Charleston,
541/888-5353).

ENTERTAINMENT AND EVENTS

The first event of note in summer is the **Oregon
Coast Music Festival** (541/267-0938 or
877/897-9350, www.oregoncoastmusic.com),
which runs for two weeks in mid-July and has
been bringing music to the coast since 1978.
Coos Bay is the central venue for these classical, jazz, pop, and world music concerts, but
Bandon, North Bend, Charleston, and other
neighboring burgs host some performances as
well. Tickets to some events are free, with tickets to the majority of events under $20.

In late August, the ubiquitous Oregon blackberry is celebrated with the **Blackberry Arts
Festival** (541/269-0215). Food and wine-tasting booths, a juried arts-and-crafts show, and
entertainers fill the **Coos Bay Mall** (Central
Ave. in downtown Coos Bay).

Polish up the spotting scope and head to
the Oregon Institute of Marine Biology in

Charleston during the last weekend of August
to see migratory shorebirds with the **Oregon
Shorebird Festival** (541/867-4550 or 541/756-
5688). Guided trips on land and water are offered; a boat trip out to see albatrosses and
other seldom-seen species that frequent the
open ocean is a highlight. Other excursions
visit the Bandon Marsh National Wildlife
Refuge and Coos Bay to see plovers, loons, and
a variety of other shorebirds.

In mid-September, perhaps the best-known
Bay Area sports celebrity, Steve Prefontaine, is
honored with a 10K race and two-mile walk
in the annual **Prefontaine Memorial Run**
(541/269-1103, www.prefontainerun.com).
Prefontaine was a world-class runner whose
gutsy style of running and record performances
made him a major sports personality until his
premature death at age 24 in 1974. Many top-
flight runners pay homage by taking part in
the race. Events begin and end at the runner's
alma mater, **Marshfield High School** (4th St.
and Anderson Ave., Coos Bay).

Occupying the former bay-side site of the
Weyerhaeuser mill alongside U.S. 101 in
North Bend, the **Mill Casino** (3201 Tremont
Ave., North Bend, 541/756-8800 or 800/953-
4800, www.themillcasino.com) is operated by
the Coquille Indian Tribe. Open 24 hours a
day, the casino offers blackjack, lots o' slots,
poker, and bingo. A large hotel, lounge, and
several restaurants are on-site.

ACCOMMODATIONS AND CAMPING

Most of the lodgings in Coos Bay and North
Bend stretch along busy U.S. 101, and most
are of the mid-century motor-court variety,
but the majority are well-maintained and rep-
resent good value. Another option is staying
in Charleston, particularly if your destination
includes local state parks, ocean beaches, or
South Slough. Charleston lodgings aren't fan-
cier, but you'll stay near the fishing marina,
not the highway.

Coos Bay

If you're just looking for a basic clean room,

the local **Motel 6** (1445 Bayshore Dr., 541/267-7171, $72-92) is well maintained and offers a number of kitchen units. Close to downtown, the **Best Western Holiday Hotel** (411 N. Bayshore Dr., 541/269-5111 or 800/228-8655, $132-159) is within walking distance of city center restaurants and offers a pool, hot tub, and hot breakfast buffet. Pets are welcome.

A more upscale alternative is the **Coos Bay Red Lion** (1313 N. Bayshore Dr., 541/267-4141, www.redlion.com, $119-139), which offers large guest rooms with extras such as an outdoor pool, a fitness center, and a bar and restaurant. A complimentary shuttle runs guests to and from the airport.

The Coos Bay Manor (955 5th St., 800/269-1224, www.coosbaymanor.com, $135-220, full breakfast included) is a grand high-ceilinged colonial-style home with eye-popping river views from the open-air second-floor breakfast balcony. The B&B's five spacious rooms have distinctive decor; two of the rooms can be combined to make a suite for families.

The waterfront **Edgewater Inn** (275 E. Johnson Ave., 541/267-0423 or 800/233-0423, www.theedgewaterinn.com, $100-135) has loads of perks in addition to its location off the highway facing the working waterfront. With 82 spacious rooms, many with views and kitchens, the hotel also offers fitness and tanning rooms, an indoor pool, a spa and sauna, and complimentary breakfast.

Even though the crowds at **Sunset Bay State Park** (13030 Cape Arago Hwy., Coos Bay, 541/888-4902 or 800/452-5687, www.reserveamerica.com for reservations, $5-36) can make it seem like a trailer park in midsummer, the proximity of Oregon's only major swimming beach on the ocean keeps occupants of the 66 tent sites ($19) and 65 trailer sites ($24) happy. The eight yurts go for $36 each, and primitive hiker-biker sites are $5 each. Facilities include the standard state park showers, and there is a boat launch at the north end of the beach. This site, three miles southwest of Charleston, is popular with anglers, who can cast into the rocky intertidal

area for cabezon and sea bass. It's also a good base camp for hikers.

Northwest of the Bay Area—2.5 miles north of the McCullough Bridge—is the Trans-Pacific Parkway, a causeway west across the water leading to Coos Bay's North Spit and the south end of the Oregon Dunes National Recreation Area, with four **Forest Service campgrounds** (541/271-6000 or 877/444-6777, www.recreation.gov, year-round, $20) and expansive dunes that draw ATV enthusiasts. The main **Horsfall Campground** is popular with crowds of noisy ATVs and RVs. It's the only campground on the spit with showers. For more quiet and privacy, continue another mile on Horsfall Beach Road to **Bluebill Lake.** There isn't ATV dune access from this campground, and it tends to attract trekkers who use their feet to explore. Ask the campground hosts about area trails and the nearby oyster farm for the ultimate in campfire fare. Close by, **Horsfall Beach Campground** is in the dunes next to the beach. ATV access and beachcombing are popular activities. A half mile away, **Wild Mare Horse Camp** has beach and dune access and a dozen primitive campsites, each with a single or double horse corral.

North Bend

One of the best values in the area is **Bay Bridge Motel** (33 Coast Hwy., 541/765-3151 or 800/557-3156, $90-112), a small motel just north of the McCullough Bridge, with good views of the bay from the higher-priced rooms.

Another option is the **Quality Inn & Suites Coos Bay** (1503 Virginia Ave., 541/756-3191, www.coosbayinn.com, $110-134), just five blocks from U.S. 101. With 96 units and the standard chain-hotel amenities, this hotel provides a quiet escape.

◖ **The Mill Hotel** (3201 Tremont Ave., 541/756-8800 or 800/953-4800, www.themillcasino.com, $133-160) is just south of the Mill Casino along the waterfront in a new seven-story tower and a building that once housed a plywood mill. Owned and operated by the Coquille (pronounced ko-KWELL in the local dialect) Indian Tribe, the hotel seeks to express its owners' patrimony: The exterior of this three-story hotel is the same cedar that the Coquille people used to build their plank houses, and the fireplace in the lobby is made of Coquille River rocks. The canoe displayed behind the front desk was carved by tribal members and is part of an interpretive display that tells the story of the Coquilles. Guest rooms are very nicely furnished, and waterfront views from the tower are especially dramatic. And, of course, all the pleasures of a modern casino are just a few feet away. In addition to gaming, the casino has a good restaurant, shops, and a performance center.

Charleston

There are a few basic motels in Charleston. If you'd like to catch your own dinner, the **Plainview Motel** (91904 Cape Arago Hwy., 541/888-5166 or 800/962-2815, http://plainviewmotel.com, $74-90) provides guests with crab rings and fishing poles or will set you up on a guided fishing trip. This small older motel has 12 pet-friendly units, some with kitchens. Pets cost an extra $10.

Bastendorff Beach County Park (63379 Bastendorff Beach Rd., Charleston, 541/888-5353, $16-30) is a conveniently and beautifully located park two miles west of Charleston just off the Cape Arago Highway. It's open for camping year-round, with RV and tent sites ($16-20, less off-season), as well as cabins ($30) and some hiker-biker sites. Campsites have drinking water, woodstoves, flush toilets, and hot showers (for an extra $2). Fishing, hiking, and a nice stretch of beach are the recreational attractions, plus there's a good playground for toddlers.

FOOD

Oregon's Bay Area has many eateries where your nutritional needs can be met, if not in fine style then at least at the right price. With a couple of notable exceptions, in both Coos Bay and North Bend, you won't find it easy to dine on seafood—in these hardworking towns, eating well seems to require heartier fare. For fresh

seafood, you're advised to head to the docks in Charleston.

Coos Bay

Nearly all the following are located along a two-block section of busy Broadway, which is the name given to southbound U.S. 101 as it passes through downtown Coos Bay. So just park the car and check out which of the following looks good.

The **Blue Heron Bistro** (110 W. Commercial Ave., 541/267-3933, 11am-9pm Mon.-Fri., noon-9pm Sat., noon-8pm Sun., $15-20) is in the heart of downtown Coos Bay—with its Bavarian-style half-timbered exterior, you can't miss it. The specialty is traditional German cooking, such as sauerbraten, schnitzel, and sausages, although fresh salmon and seafood are also featured.

For old-school Italian food, try **Benetti's** (290 S. Broadway, 541/267-6066, 5pm-9pm Sun.-Thurs., 5pm-10pm Fri.-Sat., $8-25). Choose between pasta dishes such as spaghetti with house-made meatballs, chicken parmigiana, or a grilled steak.

The **Coney Station Restaurant** (295 S. Broadway, 541/269-6948, 11am-midnight daily, $8-22) combines features of a pub and steak house, with good burgers, sandwiches by day, and grilled chicken, beef, and ribs by night. The bar features over 20 regional brews on tap.

One good spot for seafood in Coos Bay is ◖ **Shark Bites** (240 S. Broadway, 541/266-7582, 11am-9pm Mon.-Sat., $7-15), a hip little eatery with a droll sense of humor and good, freshly prepared food, with several local seafood options. A variety of wraps and sandwiches, including a very tasty halibut burger, as well as pasta and fish tacos, are favorites—best of all, prices are fair and quality is high.

Another place to get your seafood hit is **Sumin's Sushi Bar** (298 S. Broadway, 541/267-0119, 11am-8pm daily, $4-18), a friendly Asian food outpost with a selection of Chinese, Japanese, and Korean food. The quality is high, particularly for the sushi and hand rolls—try the Coos Bay Roll, with salmon, salmon skin, crabmeat, and spinach.

If you're visiting the waterfront boardwalk and feel the hankering for seafood, stop by **Fisherman Seafood Market** (200 S. Bayshore Dr., 541/267-2722, 10:30am-7pm Mon.-Sat., $6-12), a boat anchored off the boardwalk that serves as a seafood store for a local fishing family, plus a casual spot for (mostly) carry-out seafood sandwiches, fish-and-chips, and chowder.

North Bend

If you've had enough of the standard coastal fare, try **❰ Cafe Mediterranean** (1860 Union St., 541/756-2299, www.cafemediterranean. net, 11am-9pm Mon.-Sat., $7-16) for Middle Eastern-style Mediterranean food, including a locally famed lentil soup, in a friendly relaxed setting. This is a good spot for sharing a mezze platter, a Greek salad, and some kebabs. The Food Network's Rachael Ray stopped by for a Chicken Shawerma sandwich when she was filming in the area.

For another break from chowder, try **La Costa** (1930 Newport St., 541/751-0066, 11:30am-9pm Tues.-Thurs., 11am-10pm Fri.-Sat., noon-8 Sun., $8-17), with Peruvian and Mexican food fired up on the grill.

The **Mill Casino** (3201 Tremont Ave., 541/756-8800 or 800/953-4800, www.themillcasino.com) has a total of five dining options, including the **Timbers Café** (24 hours daily, $8-22), with burgers, sandwiches, and other light dining options. The more upscale **Plank Room** (7am-10pm Sun.-Thurs., 7am-11pm Fri.-Sat., $12-28) offers three meals daily in a waterfront dining room. At the **Saw Blade** (4pm-9pm Fri.-Sat., $25 adults, $12.50 children ages 11 and under), a seafood buffet is offered on weekend evenings.

Natural-food fans converge at **Coos Head Food Store** (1960 Sherman Ave., 541/756-7264, 9am-7pm Mon.-Fri., 10am-6pm Sat., noon-5pm Sun.), which has the largest selection of certified organic produce and food on the south coast.

Charleston

You can't go too far wrong looking for a fresh seafood meal down at the docks—a number of casual restaurants (some are more like shacks) cluster here, including one spot where the crab cooker is always on.

The Sea Basket (63502 Kingfisher Rd., 541/888-5711, 7am-8pm daily, $8-16) typifies the good seafood, fast service, and fair prices you expect on the docks. Oysters are especially tasty in this restaurant, with noted breeding farms close by. It is also famous for its Bigman burgers. The fluorescent glare above the cafeteria-style tables frequented by anglers in work-blackened denims may not count much for atmosphere, but you'll leave satisfied.

Close by, the classier **Portside** (63383 Kingfisher Rd., Charleston Boat Basin, 541/888-5544, 11:30am-11pm daily, $11-34) has a wide menu of rather old-fashioned seafood specialties, but the selection is broad and you're sure to find something to your liking.

Just before the Charleston Bridge, the **Fisherman's Grotto** (91149 Cape Arago Hwy., 541/888-3251, 11am-8pm daily, $9-23) is a good place for fish-and-chips, seafood dinners such as grilled salmon or stuffed sole, or a plate of pasta (including seafood pasta). If you're an oyster lover, you'll certainly want to visit **Qualman's** (4898 Crown Point Rd., 541/888-3145, 10am-5:30pm daily), which sells incredibly fresh oysters from its nearby beds. Just look for the signs on the north side of the Charleston Bridge on the east side of the highway.

Part sports bar, part seafood restaurant, **❰ Miller's at the Cove** (63346 Boat Basin Rd., 541/808-2904, 11am-midnight daily, $9-14) has seafood every bit as fresh as it should be. Don't expect anything fancy, just delicious crab Louis or fish tacos. Kids are allowed until 9pm.

INFORMATION AND SERVICES

The **Bay Area Chamber of Commerce** (50 E. Central Ave., Coos Bay, 541/269-0215 or 800/824-8486, www.oregonsbayarea.org, 9am-5pm Mon.-Fri., 10am-4pm Sat.) is five blocks west of U.S. 101 off Commercial Avenue.

The Coos Bay World (www.theworld-link.com) is the largest daily paper on the

SOUTH COAST

south coast. The **Coos Bay Public Library** (525 W. Anderson Ave., Coos Bay, 541/267-1101) is open 10am-7pm Monday-Thursday and noon-6pm Friday-Saturday.

For health care and emergencies, the **Bay Area Hospital** (1775 Thompson Rd., Coos Bay, 541/269-8111), 0.5 mile west of U.S. 101 via Newmark Street, is the south coast's largest medical facility.

GETTING THERE AND AROUND

Improvements to OR 42 make it possible to get to and from Roseburg, 87 miles from Coos Bay, in less than two hours.

Porter Stage Lines (541/269-7183, www. porterstageline.com) operates daily bus service between Coos Bay and Eugene via Reedsport and Florence. Eugene has Amtrak and regular Greyhound service, as well as an airport served by national carriers. **Coastal Express** buses (800/921-2871, www.currypublictransit.org), operated by Curry County Transport, run on weekdays between North Bend and Brookings to the south.

The **Southwest Oregon Regional Airport** (OTH), at the north end of North Bend, offers flights to Portland and San Francisco.

Public transportation in the Bay Area is limited; one bus line, **Coos County Area Transit** (541/267-7111, www.coostransit.org), makes a loop in Coos Bay and North Bend.

Bandon and Vicinity

Between Coos Bay and Bandon, U.S. 101 veers inland through forests and bucolic farmland. The highway reencounters the Pacific at Bandon, near the mouth of the Coquille River.

Bandon (pop. 3,100) is characterized by the style and grace of an earlier era, especially in Old Town, a picturesque collection of shops, galleries, and restaurants, fronting onto a bustling waterfront.

Although logging, fishing, dairy products, and the harvest of cranberries have been the traditional mainstays of the local economy, in the early part of the 20th century Bandon also enjoyed its first tourism boom. In addition to being a summer retreat from the heat of the Willamette Valley, it was a port of call for thousands of San Francisco-Seattle steamship passengers. This era inspired such tourist venues as the Silver Spray dance hall and a natatorium with a saltwater swimming pool. The golden age that began with the advent of large-scale steamship traffic in 1900, however, came to an abrupt end following a devastating fire in 1936 that destroyed most of the town. The blaze was started by the easily ignitable gorse weed, imported from Ireland (as was the town's name) in the mid-1800s. Dramatic descriptions of the townspeople fighting the flames with their backs to the sea earned the incident a citation as one of the top 10 news stories of the year.

The face-lift given Old Town decades later, and the subsequent tourist influx, conjured for many the image of the mythical phoenix rising from its ashes to fly again. Today, Bandon is a curious mixture of provincial backwater, destination golf resort, and artists' colony. Backpack-toting travelers coexist happily with the large population of retirees, artisans, golfers from around the world, and locals who seem to have cornered the market on late-model pickups with gun racks.

SIGHTS

One of the appealing things about Bandon is that most of its attractions are within walking distance of each other. In addition, on the periphery of town is a varied array of things to see and do.

Old Town

Bandon's **Old Town**, much of which dates from after the 1936 fire, is a half-dozen blocks of shops, cafés, and galleries squeezed in between the harbor and a steep bluff. The renovated

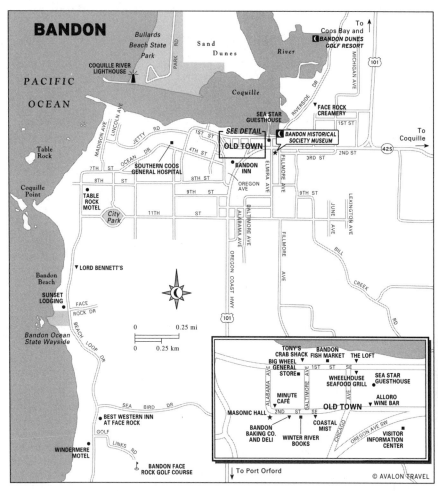

BANDON

PACIFIC

OCEAN

Bullards
Beach State
Park

COQUILLE RIVER
LIGHTHOUSE

Sand
Dunes

Coquille

River

To
Coos Bay and
BANDON DUNES
GOLF RESORT

To
Coquille

FACE ROCK
CREAMERY

1ST ST

SEA STAR
GUESTHOUSE

SEE DETAIL

OLD TOWN

BANDON HISTORICAL
SOCIETY MUSEUM

3RD ST   2ND ST

BANDON
INN

OREGON
AVE

SOUTHERN COOS
GENERAL HOSPITAL

9TH ST

TABLE
ROCK
MOTEL

City
Park

11TH   ST

LORD BENNETT'S

Bandon
Beach

SUNSET
LODGING

FACE
ROCK DR

Bandon Ocean
State Wayside

Table
Rock

Coquille
Point

BEACH   LOOP   DR

SEA   BIRD   DR

BEST WESTERN INN
AT FACE ROCK

GOLF

WINDERMERE
MOTEL

LINKS   RD

BANDON FACE
ROCK GOLF COURSE

0   0.25 mi
0   0.25 km

To Port Orford

© AVALON TRAVEL

Detail — OLD TOWN

TONY'S
CRAB SHACK

BANDON
FISH MARKET   THE LOFT

BIG WHEEL
GENERAL
STORE

WHEELHOUSE
SEAFOOD GRILL

SEA STAR
GUESTHOUSE

MINUTE
CAFÉ

ALLORO
WINE BAR

OLD TOWN

MASONIC HALL

BANDON
BAKING CO.
AND DELI

WINTER RIVER
BOOKS

COASTAL
MIST

VISITOR
INFORMATION
CENTER

waterfront invites relaxed strolling, and crabbers and anglers pull in catches right off the city docks. The small commercial fleet based here pursues salmon and tuna offshore.

Preservation buffs should check out **Masonic Hall** (2nd St. and Alabama St.), one of the few buildings to have survived Bandon's 1914 and 1936 blazes. A photo in the historical museum shows the same building and surrounding structures on Alabama Street (then called Atwater) circa 1914. The photo depicts boardwalks leading to a woolen mill, old storefronts,

a theater, and the Bandon Popular Hotel and Restaurant, outside which a horse and buggy await. The scene today has changed dramatically, but nonetheless an early-1900s charm still pervades the neighborhood.

Throughout Old Town are artists and artisans pursuing their crafts and selling their wares. The **2nd Street Gallery** (210 2nd St., 541/347-4133, http://secondstreetgallery.net, 10am-5:30pm daily) has a little of everything, from functional and art pottery to blown glass to paintings and sculptures. **WinterRiver**

SOUTH COAST

BOGGED DOWN WITH CRANBERRIES

From the vantage point of U.S. 101 between Port Orford and 10 miles north of Bandon, you'll notice what appears to be reddish-tinged ground in flood-irrigated fields. If you get closer, you'll see cranberries—small evergreen bushes that creep along the ground and send out runners that take root. Along the runners, upright branches 6-8 inches long hold pink flowers and, later, deep red fruit.

These berries are cultivated in bogs to satisfy their tremendous need for water and to protect them against insects and winter cold. Bandon leads Oregon in this crop, with an output ranking third in the nation. Oregon berries are often used in cranberry juice production by Ocean Spray because of their deep red pigment and high vitamin C content.

Oregon bogs were producing wild cranberries when Lewis and Clark first traded with the Indians for them in 1805. Shortly thereafter, cultivated bogs were developed in Massachusetts, which, like Oregon, has acidic soils with lots of organic materials conducive to berry production. By the time of the California gold rush of 1849, East Coast growing and harvesting techniques had transformed Bandon's marshes into commercial cranberry bogs. In the years to come, much of the modern equipment for harvesting these bogs was developed in Bandon. Wet-picking, for instance, is facilitated by the water reel, which is rotated to create eddies on the bog to shake berries off the vines. After they float to the surface, the cranberries are pushed by long booms toward a submerged hopper. They are then transferred by conveyor belt onto trucks. Walking through the bogs without trampling the berries is possible by fastening wooden platforms with short pegs to the soles of boots.

Fill up on cranberry confections at **Cranberry Sweets** (280 1st St. SE Bandon, 541/347-9475 or 800/527-5748, 9am-5:30pm daily). For sale are confections ranging from cranberry fudge to cranberry truffles. Look here and at other shops in town for **Vincent Family** dried cranberries or cranberry juice. Three generations of Vincents have been tending cranberry bogs; they're committed to making the business sustainable and are working toward organic certification for their berries.

Books and Gallery (170 2nd St., 541/347-4111, www.winterriverbooks.com, 10am-6pm daily) has a wide-ranging assortment of travel titles, photo essays, and fiction that makes this the best bookstore on the south coast.

Close by, the **Bandon Driftwood Museum** (130 Baltimore Ave., 541/347-3719, 9am-5:30pm Mon.-Sat., 10am-5pm Sun., free) shows off an interesting collection of natural sculptures, from gnarly root balls to whole tree trunks. It's housed at the **Big Wheel General Store,** where you'll also find the Fudge Factory and 24 flavors of homemade ice cream and butter fudge.

◖ Bandon Historical Society Museum

The captivating **Bandon Historical Society Museum** (270 Fillmore St., 541/347-2164, http://bandonhistoricalmuseum.org,

10am-4pm Mon.-Sat., $3 adults, kids free), at the corner of U.S. 101 and Fillmore Street, in Bandon's former city hall, traces the history of the Coquille people and their forebears. The chronology continues with the steamers and the railroads that brought in white settlers. One room is devoted to Bandon's unofficial standing as the cranberry capital of Oregon. Black-and-white photos showing women stooping over in the bogs to harvest the ripe berries are captioned with such quips as this classic from an overseer: "I had 25 women picking for me, and I knew every one by her fanny." Color photos spanning five decades of Cranberry Festival princesses also adorn the walls.

Another room depicts Bandon's Resort Years, 1900-1931, when the town was called the "Playground of the Pacific." The most compelling exhibits in the museum deal with shipwrecks and the fires of 1914 and 1936.

The Face Rock Creamery renews a longtime dairy tradition in Bandon.

Face Rock Creamery

For over a century, Bandon was Oregon's "other" cheese-making center, and cheeses from the Bandon Cheddar Cheese Factory rivaled those of Tillamook until the operation closed in 2002. Cheese making returned to Bandon in 2013 with the opening of the **Face Rock Creamery** (680 2nd Street SE, just north of downtown Bandon on Hwy. 101, 541/329-0012, www.facerockcreamery.com, 10am-8pm Mon.-Sat., 10am-5pm Sun.). The factory and visitors center is small compared with Tillamook, but it's worth a stop to watch the production of cheddar and jack cheese (the creamery plans to expand to other types of cheeses soon), and to taste the local cheese made from local milk (the Coquille River valley east of Bandon is lined with dairies). The creamery also sells a large selection of cheeses from around the world—this is a good place to stock up for picnics—and offers freshly made ice cream as well.

Scenic Beach Loop

U.S. 101 follows an inland path for more than 50 miles between Coos Bay and Port Orford, but you can leave the highway in Bandon and take the four-mile Beach Loop for a lovely seaside detour south of town. Several access roads lead west from the highway to Beach Loop Drive (County Rd. 29), each about 0.25 mile from the others. Most people begin the drive by heading west from Old Town on 1st Street along the Coquille. Another popular approach is from 11th Street, which leads to Coquille Point. The south end of the drive runs through the northern portion of **Bandon State Natural Area,** providing parking, beach access, and picnic tables.

The once-bucolic drive along the Beach Loop has changed a bit—trophy homes form pretty much the only view you have for the first mile or two. Still, there are state park parking areas that let you put the McMansions to your back and allow a look at the gorgeous ocean views.

Along this fine stretch of beach are rock formations with such evocative names as Table Rock, Elephant Rock, Garden of the Gods, and Cat and Kittens Rocks. The whole grouping of sea stacks, included within the Oregon Islands National Wildlife Refuge, looks like a surrealist chess set cast upon the waters. The most eye-catching of all is **Face Rock,** Bandon's answer to New Hampshire's lately lamented Old Man of the Mountain. This basalt monolith resembles the face of a woman gazing skyward. An Indian legend says that she was a princess frozen by an evil sea spirit. Look for the Face Rock turnout 0.25 mile south of Coquille Point on the Beach Loop.

Despite their scenic and recreational attractions, the beaches south of town can be surprisingly deserted, perhaps because of the long, steep trails up from the water along some parts. In any case, this dearth of people can make for great beachcombing. Agates, driftwood, and tidepools full of starfish and anemones are commonly encountered, along with bird-watching opportunities galore. Elephant Rock has a reputation as the Parthenon of puffins,

© BILL MCRAE

the distinctive profile of Bandon's Face Rock

while murres, oystercatchers, and other species proliferate on the other offshore formations.

Bullards Beach State Park

Two miles north of Bandon, bordering the Coquille River estuary and more than four miles of beachfront, **Bullards Beach State Park** (541/347-2209 or 800/551-6949 information, www.oregonstateparks.org, $3 day-use fee) is a great place to fish, crab, bike, fly a kite, windsurf, picnic, or overnight in the large sheltered campground. The beach and lighthouse are reached via a scenic three-mile drive paralleling the Coquille River. Look for jasper and agates amid the heaps of driftwood on the shore. Equestrian trails and horse-camping facilities make this a popular destination for riders. The boat ramp gives anglers, kayakers, and canoeists access to the lower Coquille River and Bandon Marsh National Wildlife Refuge.

The riverside road going out to the Coquille's north jetty takes you through the dunes to the picturesque **Coquille River Lighthouse** (tours 11am-5pm daily early May-mid-Oct., free), a

squat tower with adjacent octagonal quarters. The last lighthouse built on the Oregon coast, it was completed in 1896 then abandoned in 1939 when the Coast Guard installed an automated light across the river. After years of neglect, the structure was restored in the late 1970s; its light is now solar-powered. Etchings of ships that made it across Bandon's treacherous bar—and some that didn't—greet you inside.

West Coast Game Park

Seven miles south of Bandon is the **West Coast Game Park** (46914 U.S. 101 S., 541/347-3106, www.gameparksafari.com, 9am-6pm daily mid-June-Labor Day, call for spring, fall, and winter hours, $17.50 adults, $16.50 seniors, $10 children ages 7-12, $7 ages 2-6), the self-proclaimed largest wild animal petting park in the country. There are 450 animals representing 75 different species, including tiger cubs, camels, zebras, monkeys, and snow leopards. Visitors may be surprised to see a lion and tiger caged together or a fox

Bandon has one of the most dramatic beachfronts in Oregon.

© BILL MCRAE

and a raccoon sharing the same nursery. The park tries raising different species together and often finds that animals can live harmoniously with their natural enemies. Free-roaming animals include deer, peacocks, pygmy goats, and llamas. An elk refuge is another popular area of the park. Even if you're not with a child, the opportunity to pet a pup, a cub, or a kit can bring out the kid in you. The park is open year-round, but call during winter because of restricted hours of operation.

SPORTS AND RECREATION

Bandon Beach Riding Stables (2640 Beach Loop Rd., 541/347-3423) is four miles south of Face Rock on the Beach Loop. Several beach rides are offered daily, plus sunset rides in the summer. Riders of all abilities are welcome, including those with disabilities. Prices range $40-60 for a 1- to 2-hour ride. Reservations are advised. Open year-round.

Kayak rentals are available on the waterfront; call 541/404-6566 or look for the sandwich board pointing to the marina just off 1st Street.

Golf

Duffers should head to the scenic seaside links two miles south of town at **Bandon Face Rock Golf Course** (3235 Beach Loop Rd., Bandon, 541/329-1927, www.bandonfacerockgolf-course.com), where greens fees are a mere $18 for nine holes (and jeans are permitted!). The course dates from 1927 and was recently renovated.

A couple of miles farther south, **Bandon Crossing Golf Course** (87530 Dew Valle Ln., 541/347-3232, www.bandoncrossings.com, $45-75 for 18 holes) is a forested, challenging, but fun course that's good for families, novices, and anyone looking for a less intense experience than at the Bandon Dunes Golf Resort.

◖ BANDON DUNES GOLF RESORT

Bandon Dunes Golf Resort (57744 Round Lake Dr., 541/347-4380 or 888/345-6008, www.bandondunesgolf.com, May-Oct. greens fees $235 for hotel guests, $285 for nonguests, off-season $75-165 for guests, $120-220 for nonguests) has drawn accolades from the golf press and is far and away the most spectacular place to golf in Oregon. The original Bandon Dunes course has 7 holes along the Pacific and unobstructed ocean views from all 18. Three other 18-hole courses, Pacific Dunes, Bandon Trails, and Old Macdonald (inspired by golf course architect C. B. Macdonald), give golfers a chance to stay for a few days and keep encountering new territory.

To preserve the natural surroundings along the ocean bluffs, this Scottish links course doesn't allow carts (the only amenity missing), so you'll have to hire a caddie or schlep your own bag (a practice that is frowned upon here). A luxurious resort with Pacific views and a fine restaurant are also available for those who come to worship in the south coast's Sistine Chapel of golf.

Golfers who have never played on the Oregon coast should come prepared for wind, especially in the afternoon. Oregon golfers may know about the wind, but we have a special piece of advice for you—dress up. This is a rather formal place, and you'll feel out of place in your baggy cargo shorts and faded polo shirt.

The resort is one mile north of the Coquille River. November through April, Oregonians are admitted at the guest rate. Caddies expect $80-100 per bag.

Fishing

The Coquille River runs 30 miles from its Siskiyou headwaters before meandering leisurely through Bandon. The north and south jetties are popular spots for perch and rockfish, while the city docks right in Old Town yield catches of perch and crab April-October and smelt July-September. The spring chinook run pales in comparison to those in the Rogue and Chetco Rivers to the south, but the fall runs of chinook (beginning Sept.-Oct.) and coho (Oct.-Nov.) are strong and productive. Steelhead usually arrive in November, and the run gathers steam January-February. A boat is necessary for the best steelhead and salmon water, but bank anglers can fish the mouth of Ferry Creek, just off Riverside Drive in Bandon. Fishing guides and gear can be

arranged through **Bandon Bait & Tackle** (110 1st St., 541/347-3905, 6am-5pm daily), across from the boat basin. The shop also rents crab rings and other gear and can point you to productive spots for catching Dungeness crab.

Just off the south end of Beach Loop Drive, 30-acre **Bradley Lake,** protected from ocean winds by high dunes, offers good trout fishing and a boat ramp. Each spring the lake is stocked with trophy rainbows, averaging five pounds, reared at the Bandon Fish Hatchery east of town.

Wildlife-Viewing

Bird-watchers flock to the tidal salt marsh and the elevated observation deck of the **Bandon Marsh National Wildlife Refuge** (541/347-1470, daily sunrise-sunset), especially in the fall, to take in what may be the prime birding site on the coast. The extensive mudflats attract flocks of shorebirds, including red phalaropes, black-bellied plovers, long-billed curlews, and dunlins, as well as such strays from Asia as Mongolian plovers.

Bandon Marsh lies a short paddle across the river from the Bullards Beach State Park, or via Riverside Drive, which runs from Bandon to U.S. 101 on the south side of the Coquille River bridge. The refuge protects more than 700 precious acres of the Coquille estuary's remaining salt-marsh habitat along the southeastern side of the river. Migrating waterfowl, bald eagles, California brown pelicans, and other birds feast on the rich food sources. From U.S. 101 just north of Bandon, turn west onto Riverside Drive and continue for about one mile, where you'll reach the refuge.

ENTERTAINMENT AND EVENTS

A barbecue, a parade, and a drift boat show are highlights of Bandon's **Fourth of July** celebration; at dusk, fireworks are launched across the Coquille to burst above the river.

The biggest weekend of the year for Bandonians comes the second weekend in September, when the **Cranberry Festival** (541/347-9616) brings everyone together in

Old Town for a parade, a crafts fair, tours of a cranberry farm, and the Bandon High Cranberry Bowl—in which the local footballers take on traditional rival Coquille High.

During the late November-early January holiday season, the merchants of Old Town and anglers deck their stores and boats with twinkling lights in the traditional **Festival of Lights.** Particularly striking is the Coquille River Lighthouse, lit up across the water like a Christmas tree.

ACCOMMODATIONS

For the best ocean views, often with nearby trails to the beach, look to the lodgings along the Beach Loop. If you want to be able to walk to dinner in Old Town, stay at one of the in-town locations. For the best of both worlds, bring a bike and cycle into town from a Beach Loop room. Bandon bills itself as America's storm-watching capital, and special packages are often available October-March.

$50-100

Right in the heart of Old Town, the **[Sea Star Guesthouse** (370 1st St., 541/347-9632, www.seastarbandon.com, $75-115) has just six rooms. Four rooms are spacious, charming, and uniquely decorated, with skylights, wood-beam ceilings, a verdant courtyard, and views onto the harbor. The other two rooms are less expensive and a bit less spacious, but are some of the best deals in town.

On a bluff at the top of Beach Loop Road, find an assortment of motel rooms and small cottages at **Table Rock Motel** (840 Beach Loop Dr., 541/347-2700 or 800/457-9141, www.tablerockmotel.com, $70-129). The least expensive rooms don't have ocean views, but all are a short, steep walk away from one of the coast's prettiest beaches.

Farther down the Beach Loop is **Sunset Lodging** (1865 Beach Loop Rd., 541/347-2453 or 800/842-2407, www.sunsetmotel. com, $75-290), a motel complex with a variety of lodging types. With some units built right into the cliff above a scenic beach, the view here is hard to beat. Whether you're looking for guest rooms with a kitchen, guest rooms that accommodate pets, or guest rooms with a fireplace, there's something here for you. A hot tub, an indoor pool, on-site laundry, and Lord Bennett's restaurant across the street also highlight this place. Nonetheless, the steep steps down the 80-foot-high bluff to the beach, the busy atmosphere, and the rusticity of the least expensive guest rooms might not be to everyone's liking.

$100-150

Set on a bluff overlooking Old Town, the **[Bandon Inn** (355 U.S. 101, 541/347-4417 or 800/526-0209, www.bandoninn.com, $124-165) has spectacular views, comfortable rooms all with balconies, and a path down to town. Pets are permitted in some rooms. This is a great spot to stay if you want the wining and dining of Old Town within walking distance.

A favorite place to stay on the Beach Loop is the older but refurbished **Windermere Motel** (3250 Beach Loop Rd., 541/347-3710, www.windermerebythesea.com, $135-198), where baby-boomers can relive their childhood beach getaways in cedar efficiencies or two-story condo-like units, situated on a bluff above a windswept beach. Housekeeping facilities and proximity to restaurants (Lord Bennett's) and the West Coast Game Park also make this an ideal family vacation spot.

$150-200

Another popular place is the **Best Western Inn at Face Rock** (3225 Beach Loop Rd., 541/347-9441 or 800/638-3092, www.innatfacerock. com, $169-219). Part of its popularity has to do with the motel's location—set back from the road near the end of the Beach Loop, across the street from Bandon's coastline, and near the Bandon Face Rock Golf Course. Many of the modern well-appointed guest rooms have magnificent ocean views. An indoor pool, a fitness room, a whirlpool, and a restaurant also make this an especially good choice for active travelers. Some suites have fireplaces, kitchenettes, and private patios. There is a short path to the beach.

Over $200

For avid golfers, the **Bandon Dunes Golf Resort** (57744 Round Lake Dr., 541/347-4380 or 888/345-6008, www.bandondunesgolf.com, $210-410 d) is the place to stay. Lodging is in several different locations around the resort and includes single lodge or inn rooms in various sizes, two- or four-bedroom suites, and multibedroom cottages. View options vary from golf course and ocean views to dune and surrounding woods. Bandon Dunes is five minutes from Bandon, a mile north of the Coquille, and 27 miles (30 minutes' drive) from the North Bend Airport, which is served by daily flights from Portland.

Vacation Rentals

Bandon is an easy place to spend a weekend, and there are several property management companies that can help you find a house to rent.

Coastal Vacation Rentals (541/347-3009 or 800/336-5693, www.coastalvacationrentals.com) has large houses that are good for family gatherings, including several places that accept pets. Many of the places offered by **Exclusive Property Management** (541/347-3790 or 800/527-5445, www.visitbandon.com) are large and quite upscale, with great locations and lovely interior design. It also rents a few more modest homes, so don't be afraid to call or check the website.

Bandon Beach Vacation Rentals (54515 Beach Loop Rd., 541/347-4801 or 888/441-8030, www.bandonbeachrentals.com) has several reasonably priced units available, including one place that'll sleep 10 people.

Camping

Bullards Beach State Park (541/347-2209 or 800/551-6949 information, 800/452-5687 reservations, www.oregonstateparks.org) is a wonderful state park in a great location between the Coquille River and four miles of beach. The park has 190 campsites ($24), 13 yurts ($26), eight horse-camping sites, and hiker-biker spaces. To get there, drive north of town on U.S. 101 for about one mile; just past

the bridge on the west side of the highway is the park entrance. The beach is reached via a scenic two-mile drive paralleling the Coquille River. Electricity, picnic tables, and grills are provided. You'll also find a store, a café, a laundry room, horse-riding/camping facilities, an inviting sandy beach, summer evening campfire talks Tuesday-Saturday, and hiking trails.

FOOD

Five miles south of Bandon, on the east side of U.S. 101, hit the brakes at **Misty Meadows Jams** roadside stand (48053 U.S. 101 S., 541/347-2575, 9am-5pm) for first-rate jams and jellies, including a variety of products incorporating Bandon cranberries. This family-owned and operated business has been making delicious concoctions from Oregon-grown fruits since 1970. In addition to preserves, the shop sells olives and fruit-based barbecue sauce, syrup, honey, and salsa. Look here and in other shops in town for Vincent Family dried cranberries or cranberry juice. Three generations of Vincents have been tending cranberry bogs, and they're committed to making the business sustainable and working toward organic certification for their berries.

American

If you're after a full breakfast, head to the **Minute Café** (145 2nd St., 541/347-2707, 5:30am-8pm daily, $8-14), where locals and tourists settle in with the morning paper, omelets, and pancakes. Later in the day, the menu features burgers, sandwiches, and chowder. For coffee, granola, and excellent pastries, head across the street to the **Bandon Baking Co. and Deli** (160 2nd St., 541/347-9440).

Italian

Although it's called a wine bar, **(Alloro Wine Bar** (375 2nd St., 541/347-1850, www.allorowinebar.com, 4pm-10pm Tues.-Sun., closed Jan.-Feb., dinner $12-27) is the top choice in town for an Italian dinner. But don't come looking for spaghetti—the food is much more upscale than that. Instead expect smoked steelhead

There's good food on the docks in Bandon's Old Town.

Alfredo or duck breast served with cranberry cherry salsa and polenta. The food here is excellent, and the pace is relaxed. The pasta is house-made, and most of the produce is local. If you don't want a full dinner, there's a small bar where you can taste a flight of wines and nibble on olives or Italian cheeses.

Pacific Northwest

From its second-floor perch above the harbor, **The Loft** (315 1st St. SE, 541/329-0535, www.theloftofbandon.com, 5pm-9pm Wed.-Sun., $18-38) serves some of the best dinners in town—definitely with the best views. Abundant use is made of local produce and there's always lots of good seafood on the menu along with steak, a high-end burger (topped with black truffle aioli), and chicken. The dining room is fairly small, so reservations are a good idea.

If you don't want to leave the Beach Loop for dinner, **Lord Bennett's** (1695 Beach Loop Dr., 541/347-3663, 5pm-9pm Mon.-Thurs., 11am-9pm Fri.-Sat., 10am-2pm and 5pm-9pm Sun.

$18-30) offers a dramatic ocean view. Lunch and dinner do justice to these surroundings with elegantly rendered pasta, steak, chicken, and seafood dishes. Jazz on selected evenings in the lounge adds a nice touch.

The **Bandon Dunes Golf Resort** (57744 Round Lake Dr., 541/347-4380 or 888/345-6008, www.bandondunesgolf.com) offers a number of dining options. In the main lodge is the **Gallery** (6am-9:30pm daily, $22-37), a good place to eat an excellent steak, and the many seasonal fish and seafood preparations are always noteworthy. If you're not staying at the resort, lunch is an interesting time to get a feel for the place and to enjoy the views out onto the Bandon Dunes course. If you're looking for a less formal atmosphere, check out the adjacent Tufted Puffin Lounge or the Bunker Bar downstairs, which has a gentlemen's club vibe; both serve snacks and light meals. Lunch (mostly soups, salads, and sandwiches) is also served at the **Trails End Clubhouse** (11am-5pm daily, $8-12), in the Bandon Trails Clubhouse. In the evening, a good spot for an informal meal is **McKee's Pub** (4pm-10pm, $9-37) which has a Scottish country pub atmosphere, plus a wide-ranging menu that includes individual pizzas, burgers, steaks, and hearty favorites like meatloaf and fish-and-chips. In addition to a good selection of regional microbrews, in good weather McKee's also offers a marvelous outdoor patio fronting onto the course. In the new Pacific Dunes Clubhouse is the **Pacific Grill** (8am-9:30pm daily, $9-39) for a dining-in-the-round experience with views of three courses. The menu ranges from burgers and sandwiches for lunch to Pacific seafood stew and pork with a honey-onion glaze for dinner.

Seafood

If you're looking for inexpensive street food, check along 1st Street near the Old Town Marina, where **Tony's Crab Shack** (155 1st St., 541/347-2875, dawn-dusk daily, $4-15) sells crab sandwiches, fish tacos, grilled salmon, steamer clams, and lots more. As the name implies, it's not really a sit-down place, though there are a few picnic tables on the dock.

Budget diners and smoked-fish connoisseurs will appreciate the **Bandon Fish Market** (249 1st St. SE, 541/347-4282, 11am-6pm Mon.-Thurs., 11am-7pm Fri.-Sat., 11am-4pm Sun., $10). Heartier appetites call for the market's excellent fish-and-chips (takeout only). A picnic table outside near the harbor is the place to enjoy it all, with a trip across the street to **Cranberry Sweets** (280 1st St. SE, 541/347-9475 or 800/527-5748, 9am-5:30pm daily) for dessert.

Chocolates and Dessert

You'll want to know about **Coastal Mist** (210 2nd Street SE, 541/347-3300, 11am-5:30pm Mon.-Thurs., 10am-7pm Fri., 10am-5pm Sat.-Sun., lunch $6-7), a chocolate boutique with house-made candies and desserts, plus lunchtime sandwiches and salads.

INFORMATION AND SERVICES

The **Bandon Chamber of Commerce** (300 W. 2nd St., Bandon, 541/347-9616, www.bandon.com) in Old Town distributes a comprehensive guide and a large annotated pictographic map of the town.

Southern Coos General Hospital (900 11th St. SE, 541/319-1031) features an ocean view that is in itself therapeutic, as well as an emergency room and facilities for coronary and respiratory care.

GETTING THERE AND AROUND

North- and southbound **Coastal Express** buses (800/921-2871, www.currypublictransit.org) run on weekdays between North Bend and Brookings.

Between Bandon and Coos Bay, you can escape the tedium of U.S. 101's inland route by taking **Seven Devils Road** about three miles north of Bandon. This route runs 13 miles to **Charleston,** a fishing village that sits closer to the ocean than its larger neighbors to the northeast, Coos Bay and North Bend. En route, beaches, state parks, and an estuarine preserve make the drive interesting, although the miles of heavily logged mountainsides may take you aback.

Port Orford and Vicinity

Port Orford marks the northernmost end of one of the most spectacular stretches of coastline in the United States. From Bandon, the highway runs inland; when it hits Port Orford, the road nearly runs into the Pacific. And what a splendid place to encounter the ocean: The beach is perfect for long treasure-hunting walks, and the bluffs just to the north are also fun to explore. A few miles north, blustery Cape Blanco is the westernmost point of the continental United States; a short distance south, Humbug Mountain rises almost directly from the ocean. All of these places are great for a quick ogle and a snapshot, but even better for hiking and exploring. Port Orford is a good base for all of that, with a wide range of accommodations and a few good places to eat.

In spite of its knockout views and great recreation, the area is not especially prosperous. Commercial fishing and cedar logging were once the leading revenue producers. In recent years, tourism and many eclectic cottage industries have sprung up to supplement the boom-bust resource-based economy. The outskirts of Port Orford host such diverse undertakings as llama and sheep ranches, a goat-milk dairy, and commercial berry growers, as well as plots of land devoted to Christmas trees and exotic herbs. Offshore, divers harvest kelp for use as a food supplement and sea urchins to supply the Japanese with a popular aphrodisiac and seafood delicacy. In town, the stunning scenery and relatively low rents have probably played a role in the development of a passel of galleries, evidence of a nascent artists' colony.

SIGHTS AND RECREATION

Port Orford has an ocean view from downtown that is arguably the most scenic of any town on the coast. A waterfront stroll lets you appreciate the cliffs and offshore sea stacks, as well as the unique sight of commercial fishing boats being hoisted by large cranes into and out of the harbor. With only a short jetty on its north side, Port Orford's harbor, the only open-water port in Oregon, is unprotected from southerly swells, so boats can't be safely moored on the water. When not in use, the

SOUTH COAST

PORT ORFORD INDIAN WARS

In 1850 the U.S. Congress passed the Oregon Donation Land Act, allowing white settlers to file claims on Native American land in western Oregon. This was news, of course, to the Native American nations of the region, who had not been consulted on the decision. William Tichenor, captain of the steamship *Gull,* hoping to exploit the new act, had ambitions to establish an outpost on the coast at what's now Port Orford. When Tichenor observed the hostility of the Quatomah band of the Tututni in the tidewater, he put nine men ashore on an immense rock promontory fronting the beach because of its suitability as a defensive position. The Native Americans besieged the rock for two weeks before the white men escaped under cover of night. Tichenor returned with a well-armed party of 70 men and succeeded in founding his settlement.

From this inauspicious beginning, "Awferd," as the locals call it, established itself as the first town site on the south coast. Shortly thereafter, the town became the site of the first fort established on the coast during the Rogue Indian Wars. This conflict started when gold miners and settlers came into Native American lands. As a result of the clashes, hundreds of local natives were rounded up and sent to the Siletz Reservation near Lincoln City in 1856.

SOUTH COAST

© BILL MCRAE

The coastline near Port Orford is particularly rugged.

fleet rests on wheeled trailer-like dollies near the foot of the pier.

A stroll or bike ride through town is a perfect way to visit Port Orford's galleries. These are, by and large, much different and far more interesting than the typical seaside-town collections of landscape paintings and sunset photos. Expect to find high-quality crafts, glass art, sculpture, and computer-generated art.

Battle Rock Park

As you come into town on U.S. 101, it's hard to ignore enormous Battle Rock on the shoreline, the site of the 1851 conflict between local Native Americans and the first landing party of white settlers. If you can make your way through the driftwood and blackberry bushes surrounding its base, you can climb the short trail to the top for a heightened perspective on the rockbound coast that parallels the town. You'll also notice the east-west orientation of the harbor. Once you get to the top of the rock, don't think that the battle is necessarily over. Bracing winds often chill you, and high tides

can sometimes render this coastal finger of land an island. The rock is also the focus of a **Fourth of July Jubilee Celebration,** which reenacts the historic battle.

Even if you're not up for a scramble on Battle Rock, do walk the short path down to the beach, which is relatively sheltered from the wind and a good place for a walk. It's also a good spot for beachcombing, with agates and fishing floats being the prize finds.

If you'd rather do your scavenging inland, try searching the nearby foothills for the lost Port Orford meteorite. The meteorite was found in the 1860s by a government geologist, who estimated its weight at 22,000 tons. Unfortunately, he was unable to locate the meteorite when he returned for another look.

Port Orford Heads State Park

Another shoreline scene worth taking in, featuring a striking panorama from north to south, is up West 9th Street at what the locals call the Heads, or **Port Orford Heads State Park** (www.oregonstateparks.org). If you go down the cement trail to the tip of the blustery headland, you look south to the mouth of Port Orford's harbor. To the north, many small rocks fill the water, along with boats trolling for salmon or checking crab pots. On clear days visibility extends from Cape Blanco to Humbug Mountain.

Also here is the historic **Port Orford Lifeboat Station** (541/332-0521, 10am-3:30pm Thurs.-Mon. Apr.-Oct., free), built by the Coast Guard in 1934 to provide rescue service to the southern Oregon coast. After it was decommissioned in 1970, the officers' quarters, the pleasingly proportioned crew barracks, and other outbuildings were converted into a museum depicting the work of the station. A trail leads down to Nellie's Cove, site of the former boathouse and launch ramp.

◖ Humbug Mountain

Some people will tell you that 1,756-foot-high Humbug Mountain, six miles south of Port Orford on U.S. 101, is the highest mountain rising directly off the Oregon shoreline. Because the criteria for such a distinction vary as much as the tides, let's just say it's a special place. There's more than one version of how the peak, formerly called Sugarloaf Mountain, got its name. According to one, gold miners who were drawn here in the 1850s by tales of gold in the black sands nearby soon discovered that the rumored riches proved to be "humbug."

Once the site of Native American vision quests, Humbug Mountain now casts its shadow upon an Eden-like state park campground surrounded by myrtles, alders, and maples. Just north is a breezy black-sand beach. A three-mile trail to the top of Humbug rewards hardy hikers with impressive vistas to the south of Nesika Beach and a chance to see wild rhododendrons 20-25 feet high. Rising above the rhodies and giant ferns are bigleaf maples, Port Orford cedars, and Douglas and grand firs. Access the trail from the campground or from a trailhead parking area off the highway near the south end of the park. In addition, the **Oregon Coast Trail,** which follows the beach south from Battle Rock, traverses the mountain

and leads down its south side to the beach at Rocky Point.

Prehistoric Gardens

What can we say about this unique roadside attraction, featuring a 25-foot-tall Formica-green *Tyrannosaurus rex* standing beside the parking lot? Is it kitsch, or is it educational? You decide. In any case, if you've got children in the car, unless they're sleeping or blindfolded, you're probably going to have to pull over. **Prehistoric Gardens** (36848 U.S. 101, 541/332-4463, www.prehistoricgardens.com, 9am-dusk daily spring-fall, call for winter hours, $8 adults, $7 seniors 65 and over and children ages 11-17, $6 children ages 3-10), about 10 miles south of Port Orford, is the creation of E. V. Nelson, a sculptor and self-taught paleontologist who began fabricating life-size dinosaurs here back in 1953 and placing them amid the lush rainforest on the back of Humbug Mountain. Paths lead through the ferns, trees, and undergrowth to a towering brontosaurus, triceratops, and 20 other ferroconcrete replicas, painted in a dazzling palette of Fiestaware colors.

◖ Cape Blanco State Park and Hughes House

Four miles north of Port Orford, west of U.S. 101, is **Cape Blanco,** whose remoteness gives you the feeling of being at the edge of the continent—as indeed you are, here at the westernmost point in Oregon. From the vantage of Cape Blanco, dark mountains rise behind you and the eaves of the forest overhang the tidewater. Below, driftwood and 100-foot-long bull kelp on slivers of black-sand beach fan out from both sides of this earthy red bluff. Somehow, the Spaniards who sailed past it in 1603 viewed the cape as having a *blanco* (white) color. It has been theorized that perhaps they were referring to the fossilized shells on the front of the cliff.

With its exposed location, Cape Blanco really takes it on the chin from Pacific storms. The vegetation along the five-mile state park road down to the beach attests to the severity of winter storms in the area. Gales of 100-mph winds (the record winds were clocked at 184 mph) and horizontal sheets of rain have given some of the usually massive Sitka spruces the appearance of bonsai trees. An understory of salmonberry and bracken fern help evoke the look of a southeast Alaskan forest.

Atop the weathered headland is Oregon's oldest, most westerly, and highest lighthouse in continuous use. Built in 1870, the beacon stands 256 feet above sea level and can be seen some 23 nautical miles out at sea. **Cape Blanco Lighthouse** (541/332-6774, 10am-3:30pm Tues.-Sun. Apr.-Oct., $2 adults, $1 children under 12) also holds the distinction of having had Oregon's first female lighthouse keeper, Mabel E. Bretherton, who assumed her duties in 1903. Tours of the facility include the chance to climb the 64 spiraling steps to the top. This is the only operational lighthouse in the state that allows visitors into the lantern room to view the working Fresnel lens.

Over the years, several shipwrecks have occurred on the reefs near Cape Blanco, including that of the *J. A. Chanslor,* an oil tanker that collided with the offshore rocks in 1919 with the loss of 36 lives.

Near Cape Blanco on a side road along the Sixes River is the **Hughes House** (541/332-0248, 10am-3:30pm Tues.-Sun. Apr.-Oct., free), a restored Victorian home built in 1898 for rancher and county commissioner Patrick Hughes. Owned and operated today by the state of Oregon, the house offers an intriguing glimpse of rural life on the coast over a century ago.

Grassy Knob Wilderness

The **Grassy Knob Wilderness** (Siskiyou National Forest, Powers Ranger District, 541/439-6200) encompasses 17,200 acres of steep rugged terrain and protects rare stands of Port Orford cedar. The wood of this majestic fragrant tree is light, strong, and durable. Its use in planes during World War II and in Japanese construction has made it highly valued, but a fatal root fungus spread by logging trucks accounts for its rarity and astronomically high price. (As you travel around the area, you may notice the dead or dying cedars.) During World War II, Japanese submarines used Cape Blanco Lighthouse as an orientation mark to aim planes loaded with incendiary bombs at the Coast Range. The Japanese hoped to ignite forest fires that would destroy the region's Port Orford cedar trees, which were used to construct airplanes. Because of the perennial dampness, the results were negligible. A short (0.8-mile) but moderately difficult trail leads to the summit of Grassy Knob. To get here, follow U.S. 101 north of Port Orford about four miles, then go east on County Road 196 to Forest Service Road 5105, which ends at the trailhead.

Fishing

The **Elk River,** which empties on the south side of Cape Blanco, and the **Sixes River,** which meets the sea north of the cape, are two popular streams for salmon and steelhead fishing. Chinook and steelhead begin to enter both rivers after the first good rains of fall arrive, usually in November. Private lands limit bank

The Cape Blanco Lighthouse sits at the westernmost point in Oregon.

© BILL MCRAE

SOUTH COAST

The boats at Port Orford are lifted out of the water when they are done sailing.

© BILL MCRAE

access, with the exception of a good stretch of the Sixes that runs through Cape Blanco State Park. The salmon season runs to the end of the year, and steelhead through the following March. **Lamm's Guide Service** (541/784-5145, www.umpquafishingguide.com) leads trips on both rivers.

Boating and Waterskiing
In the northwest of town, drive west of the highway on 14th or 18th Streets to 90-acre **Garrison Lake** for boating, waterskiing, and fishing for stocked rainbow and cutthroat trout. **Buffington Memorial City Park,** at the end of 14th Street, has a dock for fishing or swimming, plus playing fields, tennis courts, picnic areas, hiking trails, and a horse arena. Half a mile north of the lake, look for agates on **Paradise Point Beach.**

Surfing
The south-facing beach at **Battle Rock Beach,** in downtown Port Orford, can be okay for surfing during the winter, when northwesterly winds blow in. Otherwise, surfers tend to go about a mile south of town to the beach at **Hubbard Creek** (best in the spring). What these spots may lack in intensity, they make up for in scenery.

Windsurfing and Kiteboarding
Between Port Orford and Bandon (just south of Langlois) is **Floras Lake,** one of the southern Oregon coast's two great windsurfing and kiteboarding spots (the other is south of Gold Beach at Pistol River). The lake, just barely inland from the beach, catches incredible breezes. **Floras Lake Windsurfing School** (541/348-9912, www.floraslake.com) offers windsurfing and kiteboarding lessons and rentals; the proprietors also have a very nice B&B just above the lake. It's 11 miles north of Port Orford, about four miles west of the highway on Floras Lake Loop Road. On the lake is **Boice Cope County Park,** which has basic tent and RV sites and a boat ramp. When the wind's not blowing (fat chance of that!), explore the hiking trails from the campground to the beach. From Floras Lake north to Bandon is the most isolated beachfront on the Oregon coast—ideal for beachcombing. Grasses, dunes, and shore pines usher you the 25 miles back to Bandon, and chances are good you won't see a soul.

ACCOMMODATIONS
With one notable exception, Port Orford is the kind of place where a room with a view will not break your budget.

$50-100
The **Shoreline Motel** (206 6th St., 541/332-2903, $55-70), is right downtown, across the highway from Battle Rock. While not fancy, it's convenient and perfectly adequate for a basic night's stay.

Just south of town, the **Seacrest Motel** (44 U.S. 101 S., 541/332-3040, www.seacrestoregon.com, $65-85) features views of coastal cliffs and a garden from a quiet hillside on the east side of the highway. Pets are welcome at this older motel.

SOUTH COAST

◖ **Castaway-by-the-Sea** (545 W. 5th St., 541/332-4502, www.castawaybythesea.com, $85-165) features ocean and harbor views from high on a bluff, fireplaces, and housekeeping units, and it allows pets. In addition to the motel rooms, the Castaway has a two-bedroom lodge that'll sleep up to 10 (from $185). The rates on the upper-end lodgings go down significantly in the off-season. It's said that Jack London once stayed in an earlier incarnation of this place.

$150-200

North of Port Orford, the **Floras Lake House B&B** (92870 Boice Cope Rd., Langlois, 541/348-2573, www.floraslake.com, $150-180, includes breakfast) is perfectly suited for windsurfers or others who want to explore the beaches in this unpopulated area. The spacious light-filled house looks out onto Floras Lake and the ocean, and the proprietors also offer windsurfing and kiteboarding lessons.

Over $200

Port Orford's serene luxury resort is ◖ **Wildspring Guest Habitat** (92978 Cemetery Loop, www.wildspring.com, $278-308 d, including continental breakfast). The small (five-cabin) resort is in a forested setting on a bluff above the highway (but totally secluded from it), with views of the ocean from the main lodge and hot tub. The cabins are beautifully and meticulously designed and furnished (including a refrigerator, a massage table, and Wi-Fi access in each cabin, but no telephones or TVs) and are as comfortable as they are perfect-looking. The main guest hall has a kitchen that's available to guests as long as it's not being used to prepare breakfast. The well-tended grounds include a labyrinth and several meditation nooks, but perhaps the best place to hang out is the slate-lined hot tub, which looks out over treetops to the ocean. It's a good idea to take binoculars, as Wildspring is a stop along the Oregon Coast Birding Trail. Bikes, backpacks, and hiking trail maps are available to all guests. Guided meditation, drumming, and tai chi are all offered one or two times a month (check the

website or call to inquire). This is a good place for a romantic retreat or a solo contemplative getaway.

Camping

Humbug Mountain State Park (541/332-6774), six miles south of Port Orford on U.S. 101, features 62 tent sites ($17) and 32 sites for trailers and motor homes ($20), and wind-protected sites reserved for hikers and bikers ($5). Flush toilets, showers, picnic tables, water, and firewood are available.

Cape Blanco State Park (39745 U.S. 101 S., 541/332-6774 information, 800/452-5687 cabin reservations, $5-39) can be reached by driving four miles north of Port Orford on U.S. 101, then heading northwest on the park road that continues five miles beyond to the campground. It features 54 tent sites ($20), four cabins ($39), trailer and motor home sites ($20), a horse camp ($17), and hiker-biker sites ($5); picnic tables, water, and showers are available. For horseback riders, there's a seven-mile trail and a huge open riding area; horses are also allowed on the beach. Regular sites are first-come, first-served.

FOOD

Port Orford doesn't have a lot of restaurants, but there are a few good places to eat.

The spot for a hearty breakfast is the **Paradise Cafe** (1825 Oregon St., 541/332-8104, 6am-2pm daily, $8-12), where the locals go for stacks of pancakes in the morning and burgers for lunch.

If you're planning to visit Port Orford's docks, stop by **Griff's on the Dock** (303 Dock Rd., 541/332-8985, 11am-8pm daily), a weathered shack amid the boats and tackle shops. The fish here is as fresh as it gets, and the atmosphere, with crusty old anglers eating hot dogs and talking crabbing, is not a cookie-cutter idea of a fish-and-chips place.

More sophisticated fare can be had across the street from Battle Rock at **Paula's Bistro** (236 6th St., 541/332-9378, 5pm-9pm Tues.-Sat., $20-29), with a menu centered on local fish and seafood, although pasta, lamb, and steaks are also available. The atmosphere is casual and friendly, and the dining room doubles as an art gallery.

The best views and classiest food are at **C Redfish** (517 Jefferson St., 541/366-2200, www.redfishportorford.com, 9am-3pm and 5pm-9pm Mon.-Fri., 11am-3pm and 5pm-9pm Sat.-Sun., $10-29), where the Pacific Northwest coastal cuisine has a French twist. The local rockfish is pan-seared and served with buckwheat crepes, smoked salmon and cucumber relish, and red-onion crème fraîche. Adjoining the restaurant is an upscale gallery.

Chow down on vegetarian soup and sandwiches at **Seaweed Natural Food and Grocery** (832 Oregon St., 541/332-3640).

INFORMATION AND SERVICES

Begin your travels at **Battle Rock Information Center** (Battle Rock Wayside, 541/332-4106, www.discoverportorford.com, 10am-3pm daily), on the west side of U.S. 101. The people here are especially friendly and helpful. The **library** (555 W. 20th St.) is open weekdays 10am-5pm.

GETTING THERE

Curry County's **Coastal Express** buses (800/921-2871, www.currypublictransit.org) run up and down the south coast weekdays only between North Bend and the California border, including local service in Port Orford.

Gold Beach and Vicinity

This town is one part of the coast where the action is definitely away from the ocean. To lure people from Oregon's superlative ocean shores, the Rogue estuary has been bestowed with many blessings. First, the gold-laden black sands were mined in the 1850s and 1860s. While this short-lived boom era gave Gold Beach its name, the arrival of Robert Hume, later known as the Salmon King of the Rogue, had greater historical significance. By the turn of the 20th century, Hume's canneries were shipping out some 16,000 cases of salmon per year and established the river's image as a leading salmon and steelhead stream. This reputation was later enhanced by outdoorsman and novelist Zane Grey in his *Rogue River Feud* and other writings. Over the years, Herbert Hoover, Winston Churchill, Ginger Rogers (who had a home on the Rogue), Clark Gable, Jack London, George H. W. Bush, and Jimmy Carter, among other notables, have come here to try their luck. During the last several decades, boat tours focusing on the abundant wildlife, scenic beauty, and fascinating lore of the region have hooked other sectors of the traveling public.

Today, Gold Beach is a town of about 2,000 and the Curry County seat. Gold Beach serves as the south coast tourism hub, but a pulp mill and commercial ocean fishing industry round out the local economy. The seasonal nature of many local businesses creates serious wintertime unemployment. This fact, combined with torrential rains, drastically reduces the population of Gold Beach from Thanksgiving until spring. Thereafter, the wildflowers and warm weather transform this town into a vacation mecca.

At the north end of town, just before the road gives way to Conde McCullough's elegant Patterson Bridge, the harbor comes into view on the left, full of salmon trawlers, jet boats, pelicans, and seals bobbing up and down. Across the bridge is **Wedderburn,** a baby sister to Gold Beach named for the Scottish birthplace of Robert Hume.

SIGHTS
Beaches

The driftwood-strewn strand of **South Beach,** just south of Gold Beach's harbor, is convenient but only so-so. You'll find more exciting stretches both north and south of town. Tidepoolers might want to stop at the visitors

SOUTH COAST

© BILL MCRAE

The Gold Beach Bridge spans the Rogue River.

center before heading out to ask for the *Tide Pools Are Alive* brochure, with tips and species descriptions. Two miles south, there's easy access to a nice beach and some tidepooling at tiny **Buena Vista State Park,** at the mouth of Hunter Creek. Seven miles south of Gold Beach, there's more tidepooling amid the camera-friendly basalt sea stacks at beautiful **Myers Creek Beach,** part of Pistol River State Park south of Cape Sebastian. The south side of Cape Sebastian and **Pistol River State Park,** a couple of miles farther south, are the best places on the Oregon coast for windsurfers to enjoy wave sailing. The beaches around Pistol River are also great places to find razor clams.

Bailey Beach, north of town between the Rogue River jetty and Otter Point, is another popular spot for razor clamming, and **Nesika Beach,** seven miles north of Gold Beach, is another good tidepooling destination.

◖ Cape Sebastian

Seven miles south of Gold Beach is **Cape Sebastian.** This spectacular windswept headland was named by Sebastián Vizcaíno, who plied offshore waters here for Spain in 1602 along with Manuel d'Alguilar. At 720 feet above the sea, Cape Sebastian is the highest south coast overlook reachable by a paved public road. On a clear day, visibility extends 43 miles north to Humbug Mountain and 50 miles south to California. This is one of the best perches along the south coast for whale-watching. A trail zigzags through beautiful springtime wildflowers down the south side of the cape for about two miles until it reaches the sea. In April and May, Pacific paintbrushes, Douglas irises, orchids, and snow queens usher you along. In addition, Cape Sebastian supports a population of large-headed goldfields, a summer-blooming yellow daisy-like flower found only in coastal Curry County.

In 1942, a caretaker heard Japanese voices drifting across the water through the fog. When the mist lifted, he looked down from Cape Sebastian trail to see a surfaced submarine. This sighting, together with the Japanese bombing at Brookings and the incendiary balloon spotted over Cape Blanco, sent shock waves up the south coast. But the potential threat remained just that, and local anxiety eventually subsided.

Museums

At the **Curry County Historical Museum** (29419 S. Ellensburg Ave., 541/247-9396, www.curryhistory.com, 10am-4pm Tues.-Sat., closed Jan., $2), the local historical society has assembled a small collection of exhibits on Indian and pioneer life, mining in the region's golden age, logging, fishing, and agriculture. It's located at the county fairgrounds at the south edge of town. Particularly interesting are a realistic reconstruction of a miner's cabin, vintage photos, and Indian petroglyphs.

In the harbor area on the west side of U.S. 101, Jerry's Jetboats has assembled the best regional museum on the south coast, the **Rogue River Museum** (29980 Harbor Way, 541/247-4571, 8am-9pm summer, 8am-6pm fall-spring, free). Centuries of natural and human history are depicted. In addition to geologic history, the museum contains photos of pioneer families, arrowheads and other native artifacts, and a taxidermy collage of local critters to round out your introduction to the Rogue Valley. Jerry's river tour clientele will find that perspectives from the museum on the local salmon industry in the 1920s and on early river travel are expanded upon in their jet-boat guide's commentary. Museum photos of early river runs—hauling freight, passengers, and mail—can impart a sense of history to your trip upriver or up the road.

Scenic Drives

From U.S. 101, two miles south of town, you can pick up **Hunter's Creek Road,** which loops north through the forest, finally following the course of the Rogue back into Gold Beach along Jerry's Flat Road. The three-hour drive follows Hunter's Creek inland for several miles, passing several picnic areas and campgrounds.

Other roads less traveled include the old **Coast Highway,** which you can pick up near Pistol River and Brookings; the **Shasta Costa**

Road paralleling the Rogue from Gold Beach to Galice; and an unpaved summer-only road into the **Rogue Wilderness** from Agness (a town upriver on the Rogue) to Powers. Despite most of these routes being paved (except the last one), they are all narrow, winding, and not suitable for trailers or motor homes. Maps and directions to these back roads can be obtained from the **Gold Beach Ranger Station** (29279 Ellensburg Ave., 541/247-3600, 8am-5pm Mon.-Fri.).

SPORTS AND RECREATION
◖ Rogue River Jet-Boat Ride

The most popular way to take in the mighty Rogue is on a jet-boat ride from Gold Beach. It's an exciting and interesting look at the varied flora and fauna along the estuary as well as the changing moods of the river. Three different lengths of river tours are available. Most of the estimated 50,000 people per year who "do" the Rogue in this way take the 64-mile round-trip cruise. An 80-mile trip goes farther up the Rogue, and the most adventurous trip is the 104-mile excursion that enters the Rogue River canyon. Meals are not included in the cost of the cruise, and you can either bring your own food or have a meal at one of the secluded fishing lodges upriver, where the tours stop for meal breaks. The pilot-commentators are often folks who have grown up on the river, and their evocations of the diverse ecosystems and Native American and gold-mining history can greatly enhance your enjoyment. Bears, otters, seals, and beavers may be sighted en route, and anglers may hold up a big keeper to show off. Ospreys, snowy egrets, eagles, mergansers, and kingfishers are also seen with regularity in this stopover for migratory waterfowl.

In the first part of the journey, idyllic riverside retreats dot the hillsides, breaking up stands of fir and hemlock. Myrtle, madrona, and impressive springtime wildflower groupings also vary the landscape. All of the jet-boat trips out of Gold Beach focus on the section of the Rogue protected by the government as a Wild and Scenic River. Only the longer trips take you into the pristine Rogue Wilderness, an area that motor launches from Grants Pass do not reach. The 13 miles of this wilderness you see from the boat have canyon walls rising 1,500 feet above you. Geologists say this part of the Klamath Mountains is composed of ancient islands and seafloor that collided with North America. To deal with the rapids upstream, smaller and faster boats are used to skim over the boulders with just six inches of water between hull and the rock surface.

The season runs May-October 15. Remember that chill and fog near the mouth of the estuary usually give way to much warmer conditions upstream. These tour outfits have wool blankets available on cold days as well as complimentary hot beverages. Also keep in mind that the upriver lodges can be booked for overnight stays, and your trip may be resumed the following day.

Just south of the Rogue River Bridge, west of U.S. 101 on Harbor Way, is **Jerry's Rogue River Jetboats** (29985 Harbor Way, 541/247-4571 or 800/451-3645, www.rogue-jets.com). Jerry's offers 64-mile ($50 adult, $25 children 4-11), 80-mile ($80 adult, $35 children), and 104-mile ($95 adults, $45 children) trips. There are usually two departures for each trip daily: one in the morning, one near midday. This heavily patronized company is noted for personable well-informed guides. If you forgot a hat to buffer the winds at the mouth of the Rogue, stop in at Jerry's gift shop.

Fishing

Fishing is a mighty big deal in Gold Beach, which has one of the highest concentrations of professional guides in the state. There's something to fish for just about year-round, but salmon and steelhead are the top quarry. When the spring chinook pour in (Apr.-June), anglers will need to book guided trips well in advance to get a shot at them. Catches peak in May. Summer steelhead and fall-run chinook usually arrive July-September, then it's hatchery coho September-November (sometimes as early as August). In December, the first of the winter

© BILL MCRAE

The Rogue River is famous for salmon fishing.

steelhead make their appearance and continue into March.

The **Rogue Outdoor Store** (29865 Ellensburg Ave., 541/247-7142, 8am-5:30pm Mon.-Sat., 9am-3pm Sun.) is well stocked with fishing, camping, and other gear, and its staff can advise on where, when, and what to fish.

Typical rates for guided salmon trips are $250-400 per person depending on the size of your group. Contact the **Gold Beach Visitor Center** (541/247-7526 or 800/525-2334, www.goldbeach.org) or the **Curry Guide Association** (800/775-0886) for a list of over two dozen licensed guides.

Some well-established **guides** include: **Steve Beyerlin** (541/247-4138, www.fish-oregon.com), for both conventional and fly-fishing; **Shaun Carpenter** (541/247-2049, www.endoftherogue.com), conventional and fly-fishing; and **Ron Smith** (541/247-6046, www.sportfishingoregon.com) for salmon and steelhead fishing trips on a number of southern Oregon rivers.

Golf

The nine-hole **Cedar Bend Golf Course** (34391 Cedar Valley Rd., 541/247-6911, http://cedarbendgolf.com, $20 for 9 holes, $28 for 18) is in nearby Ophir. Eleven miles north of Gold Beach, pick up Ophir Road off U.S. 101. Follow it to Squaw Valley Road, turn right at the Old Ophir Store, and continue until you see the links. Woods line the fairways, and a winding creek offers a challenge on nine holes.

Hiking

The 40-mile **Rogue River Trail** (www.blm.gov) offers lodge-to-lodge hiking, which means you need little more in your pack than the essentials. The lodges here are comfortably rustic, serve home-style food in copious portions, and run $150-200 for a double room. They are also comfortably spaced, so extended hiking is seldom a necessity.

Before you go, check with the **Gold Beach Ranger Station** (29279 Ellensburg Ave., 541/247-3600, 8am-5pm Mon.-Fri.) on trail conditions and specific directions to the trailhead. Pick up the western end of the trail 35 miles east of Gold Beach, about 0.5 mile from Foster Bar, a popular boat landing. Park there and walk east and north on the paved road until you see signs on the left marking the Rogue River Trail. Go in spring before the hot weather and enjoy yellow Siskiyou irises and fragrant wild azaleas. The trail ends at Grave Creek, 27 miles northwest of Grants Pass. Be careful of rattlesnakes on the trail.

Windsurfing

Although beginners may want to hone their skills up north at Floras Lake, experienced windsurfers head out into the ocean near the debouchment of the **Pistol River.**

ENTERTAINMENT AND EVENTS

The **Wild Rivers Coast Seafood, Art, and Wine Festival** is a two-day event that celebrates wine, fine dining, and arts and crafts of the southern Oregon coast in mid-May at the **Event Center on the Beach** (29392 Ellensburg Ave., 541/247-4541, admission fees vary).

The **Pistol River Wave Bash National Windsurfing Competition** brings four days of competitive riding to Pistol River State Park each June. For details, contact the **Gold Beach Visitor Center** (541/247-7526 or 800/525-2334, www.goldbeach.org, admission fees vary).

The **Curry County Fair** takes place at the **Event Center on the Beach** (29392 Ellensburg Ave., 541/247-4541, admission fees vary) over the Fourth of July weekend. Highlights include Oregon's largest flower show and a lamb barbecue.

Since 1982, the **Pistol River Concert Association** (541/247-2848, www.pistolriver. com, $15 adults) has produced a top-notch **concert series,** encompassing bluegrass, folk, jazz, classical, and blues at the Pistol River Friendship Hall. Concerts are held roughly once a month throughout the year, and it's well worth fussing with your schedule in order to catch one. Past and present performers are a *Who's Who* of acoustic music, including Greg Brown, Mike Seeger, Peggy Seeger, Kevin Burke, Norman and Nancy Blake, Peter Rowan, and Tony Rice, to name a few. To get there from Gold Beach, take U.S. 101 for 10 miles south, to the second Pistol River exit (Pistol River/Carpenterville) and take the first right. The Pistol River Friendship Hall is 0.5 mile ahead on the right.

ACCOMMODATIONS

As in most coastal towns, there is no shortage of places to stay along the main drag, Ellensburg Avenue (a.k.a. U.S. 101). In fact, Gold Beach offers the largest number and widest range of accommodations on the south coast, with intimate lodges overlooking the Rogue as popular as the oceanfront motels. A discount of 20 percent or more on rooms is usually available during winter, when 80-90 inches of rain can fall.

$50-100

The best bet for a clean, inexpensive room is the **Wild Chinook Inn** (94200 Harlow St.,

541/247-6675, http://chinookinn.com, $60-75), where you get no-frills accommodations across from the fairgrounds. Rooms have Wi-Fi, a fridge, and a microwave; some full-kitchen units are available.

Don't turn up your nose at the **Motel 6** (1010 Jerry's Flat Rd., 541/247-4533 or 800/759-4533, $65-86); the location—perched above the Rogue River—is great, and the rooms are modern and comfy. Pets are permitted.

If you're looking for a simple place to spend a night or two and don't care about frills, the **Azalea Lodge** (29481 Ellensburg Ave., 541/247-6635 or 866/381-6635, www.azalealodge.biz, $85-105) is a good bet, with friendly owners and clean rooms. No pets are allowed; all guest rooms are nonsmoking and have refrigerators.

$100-150

Though it's true that ◖ **Ireland's Rustic Lodges** (29330 Ellensburg Ave., office 29346 Ellensburg Ave., 541/247-7718, www.irelandsrusticlodges.com, cabins $119-144, lodge rooms $104-149) include charming vintage cabins, it also offers more modern lodge rooms, condos, and beach houses. Many of the guest rooms have fireplaces, knotty-pine interiors, and distinctive decor. Best of all, the parklike grounds are lovingly landscaped with pine trees, flowers, and ocean views. A sandy beach is a short stroll to the west. There are 33 lodge units (some with kitchens), seven vintage but well-kept log cabins (recommended) that sleep up to five, and houses that sleep as many as 11. Immediately next door, and with the same owners, is the **Gold Beach Inn** (29346 Ellensburg Ave., 541/247-7091 or 888/663-0608, www.goldbeachinn.com, non-oceanview rooms $84, oceanview rooms $114-139), a modern hotel with oceanfront guest rooms, many with balconies. These two establishments share many facilities, including private beach paths and a series of outdoor hot tubs in the midst of an 11-acre property.

On the Rogue River's north bank, the immense **Jot's Resort** (94360 Wedderburn Loop, Wedderburn, 541/247-6676 or 800/367-5687, www.jotsresort.com, $135-180) can host a full vacation in one compound, featuring a pool and spa, a sports shop, a private dock, rental boats, and a restaurant across the street. The guest rooms are at a premium in summer, when the motor coach tours come through, leaving other travelers with the less desirable rooms. There are numerous room styles—from standard-view rooms to riverfront condos big enough for six people—and a wide range of prices, so it's best to call for current rates and specials. The Rod 'n' Reel Club across the street features evening entertainment with low-stakes blackjack, country music bands, and a big-band dance on weekends.

Another excellent option for beachside lodging is the **Inn of the Beachcomber** (29266 Ellensburg Ave., 541/247-6691 or 888/690-2378, www.innofthebeachcomber.com, $109-179), an older hotel complex that has recently been lovingly remodeled and updated. Most guest rooms are oceanview with private balconies or decks, and some have hot tubs. The rooms are furnished with Mission-style furniture and fittings, and there's even a wine store on the premises. A few nonview rooms are available starting at $89.

$150-200

For a more traditional oceanfront hotel, the **Gold Beach Resort** (29232 Ellensburg Ave., 541/247-7066 or 800/541-0947, www.gbresort.com, $155-185) offers nicely furnished oceanview rooms, all with balconies. Also part of this large complex, with easy beach access, are one- and two-bedroom condos, all with fireplaces. Facilities include an indoor pool and a fitness center; a complimentary continental breakfast is available.

Over $200

◖ **Tu Tu'Tun Resort** (96550 N. Bank Rogue River Rd., 541/247-6664 or 800/864-6357, www.tututun.com, rooms $290-375, suites $395-420) is the most luxurious place to stay on the southern Oregon coast, where lucky guests take in river views through the floor-to-ceiling windows, enjoy a good book from the lodge's library in front of the massive river-rock fireplace, and savor delicious Pacific Northwest cuisine. As you sit on your patio overlooking the water along with the resident bald eagles, only the sounds of an occasional passing boat may intrude upon your Rogue River reverie. Rooms are graciously furnished, but not overly fussy—why interfere with the stunning views? The lodge is seven miles up the Rogue River from Gold Beach.

This acclaimed retreat also offers a heated pool and other recreational facilities. Meals are available on an inclusive Modified American Plan ($68 per person), which includes hors d'oeuvres, a gourmet four-course dinner, and a bountiful breakfast buffet. Nonguests are welcome to dinner with reservations. The dining room is only open May-October. In the off-season, guests are served a continental breakfast only. Tu Tu Tun is not a secret, so reservations are required well in advance of your stay.

Upriver Lodges

Several lodges on the Rogue, some accessible only by boat or via hiking trails, lure visitors deep into the Rogue interior. Jet-boat trips can drop you off for an overnight or longer stay. Advance reservations are essential.

Also accessible by road and boat, the authentically rustic **Lucas Lodge** (3904 Cougar Ln., 541/247-7443, www.lucaslodgeoregon.com, $45-95) is 32 miles east of Gold Beach. Some cabins here come equipped with kitchen options. Lunch and dinner are served daily in the lodge—chicken, biscuits, and garden vegetables are standard fare. Reservations are required.

Accessible only by helicopter, boat, or on foot, the **Paradise Lodge** (541/247-6504 or 888/667-6483, www.paradise-lodge.com, $150-160 per person, $85 children, includes two or three meals) attracts nature enthusiasts interested in the "wildest" experience. Only the meals are scheduled, and you can take an eco-tour, enjoy a sauna, raft or jet-boat the rapids, or check out some of the old mining sites in the vicinity. A huge on-site garden provides ingredients for home-cooked meals.

Another backcountry lodge, the **Clay Hill Lodge** (541/859-3772, www.clayhilllodge.com, $150, $100 per child, includes three meals), is accessible via raft (from upstream), jet boat, or foot. By foot, it's about three hours (six miles) up from the trailhead near Foster Bar, east of Gold Beach.

Camping

There are no public campgrounds along the coast between Humbug Mountain, just south of Port Orford, and Harris Beach, at the northern entrance to Brookings. But campsites east of town up the Rogue River provide wonderful spots to bed down for the night. Those taking the road along the Rogue should be alert for oncoming log trucks, raft transport vehicles, and other wide-body vehicles. In addition to the public campgrounds listed, there are *many* private RV resorts up the north bank of the Rogue.

Foster Bar Campground (Siskiyou National Forest, Gold Beach Ranger Station, 1225 S. Ellensburg Ave., 541/247-6651, www.fs.fed.us, open year-round, flush toilets available May-Oct., $10) is 30 miles east of Gold Beach on the south bank of the Rogue. Take Jerry's Flat Road east for 30 miles to the turnoff for Agness. Turn right on Illahe Agness Road and drive three miles to camp. Campsites here come equipped with drinking water, toilets, ADA-compliant facilities, picnic tables, fire rings, and a boat ramp. Sites are available on a first-come, first-served basis only. This is a popular spot from which to embark on an eight-mile inner-tube ride to Agness. It's also where rafters pull out, so the parking lot may be jam-packed. The rapids are dangerous—wear a life jacket. You are also within walking distance of the trailhead of the Rogue River Trail.

Lobster Creek Campground (541/247-3600, www.fs.fed.us, $10) is nine miles east of Gold Beach via Forest Service Road 33. This campground is open year-round and has three tent sites, three trailer sites, one group site, picnic tables, fishing, and flush toilets—but no drinking water. Ask the Forest Service for directions to the Schrader old-growth trail nearby. It is a gentle one-mile walk through a rare and majestic ecosystem that is under siege in other forests throughout the state. Also nearby is the world's largest myrtle tree.

Honeybear Campground and RV Resort (34161 Ophir Rd., Ophir, 541/247-2765 or 800/822-4444, www.honeybearrv.com, open year-round, $18-35) is not up the Rogue; it's nine miles north of Gold Beach on U.S. 101, then two miles north on Ophir Road—but it could just as well be in the Black Forest. The owners have built a large rathskeller with a dance floor. Six nights a week during the summer, there are dances here with traditional German music. Check out their version of Oktoberfest, a traditional fall festival held two weekends in late September. Locals praise the Honeybear's on-site delicatessen for its homemade German sausage. There are 20 tent ($18) and RV ($30-35) sites, picnic tables, flush toilets, hot showers, firewood, laundry facilities, and ocean views.

FOOD
American
Stop by **Biscuits Café** (29707 Ellensburg Ave., 541/247-2495, 7am-7pm daily) inside Gold Beach Books for coffee and pastries. Be sure to take a look in the rare book room of this very good bookstore after you finish eating. **Indian Creek Café** (94682 Jerry's Flat Rd., 541/247-0680, 5:30am-2pm daily, $8-12) is a great spot for breakfast. Just a mile east of the Rogue River Bridge, the café is on the south shore of the Rogue, where Indian Creek joins the river. In good weather, there's seating on a deck overlooking the creek. Omelets, pancakes, and other traditional breakfast items are well prepared; lunch is mostly burgers and sandwiches.

Locals recommend the **Port Hole Café** (29975 Harbor Way, 541/247-7411, 11am-9pm daily, $4-20), in the Cannery building at the port, with bay and river views, for hearty portions of fish-and-chips, chowder, and homemade pies at decent prices.

Barnacle Bistro (29805 Ellensburg Ave., 541/247-7799, 11am-8pm Mon.-Thurs.,

11am-9pm Fri.-Sat., 11am-6pm Sun., $8-15) is a lively spot for light meals, offering a selection of sandwiches, soups, salads, pizzas, and fish-and-chips. The salad greens are local and organically grown, and all the sauces and dressings are made in-house.

Perched on a hill above the highway, the **Cape Cafe** (29251 Ellensburg Ave., 541/247-6114, 4:30pm-9:30pm weekdays and Sat.-Sun. mornings, $9-25) is a good bet for tasty but healthy meals, with lots of vegetarian options. Though basically a dinner house, they're open for coffee and pastries on weekend mornings.

Italian
Mangia Buff Café (29692 Ellensburg Ave., 541/247-4606, 10:30am-8pm Mon.-Sat., $11-25) is a small, art-filled dining room with excellent Italian cooking, not a cuisine you find often on the Oregon coast. At lunch, expect salads, meatball sandwiches and sausages, while in the evening the menu features fresh pasta (clam sauce ravioli) and meat dishes such as chicken Marsala and grilled Tuscan rib eye steak. This is a chef-owned operation, and the attention to detail shows on every plate.

Steak and Seafood
The Nor'Wester (10 Harbor Way, 541/247-2333, 5pm-9pm nightly, $12-28) is in an upstairs location at the port of Gold Beach, so sometimes you get to watch boats unloading your dinner. Not surprisingly, the menu is dominated by old-fashioned seafood preparations, although the waitstaff also recommends the New York strip steaks and the chinook salmon grilled with a glaze of sake, cayenne, ginger, and soy.

A very good dinner house is ● **Spinner's Seafood, Steak and Chophouse** (29430 Ellensburg Ave., 541/247-5160, 4:30pm-10pm nightly, $15-32). The menu is wide-ranging, and the dining room extremely pleasant. Look for fresh, well-prepared seafood, pasta, prime rib, and a choice beef and chops. A children's menu is available.

Pick up some fresh seafood or the best canned tuna you'll ever taste at **Fishermen**

Direct Seafoods (29975 Harbor Way, 541/247-9494, 9am-5:30pm Mon.-Sat., 9am-2pm Sun.).

Wine Bars

€ **Anna's By the Sea** (29672 Stewart St., 541/247-2100, 11:30am-2:30pm Wed.-Fri., 11:30am-2:30pm and 5pm-9pm Sat., $9-12), tucked into a residential neighborhood a couple of blocks east of busy Ellensburg Avenue, is that rare thing on the southern Oregon coast—a chic little wine bar with excellent appetizers and unpretentious but delicious light entrées. Prices are very modest for the quality of the food—enjoy an assortment of artisan cheeses or shrimp with black truffle oil served over an oven-baked potato pancake. Anna's is a tiny place—just 15 seats—so come early if you don't want to wait (in summer, there's more seating on the deck).

INFORMATION AND SERVICES

The **Gold Beach Visitor Center** (94080 Shirley Ln., 541/247-7526 or 800/525-2334, www.

goldbeach.org) is open 9am-5pm Monday-Friday and 10am-4pm Saturday-Sunday. Its website is excellent and informative, and staff will send you a good comprehensive information folder upon request. The **Gold Beach Ranger District** (29279 Ellensburg Ave., Gold Beach, 541/247-3600, 7:30am-5pm Mon.-Fri.) can provide information on camping and recreation in the district.

The **post office** (541/247-7610) is at the port on Harbor Way. A modern building houses the **public library** (94341 3rd St., 541/247-7246, 10am-8pm Mon.-Thurs., 10am-5pm Fri.-Sat.), one block east of the highway in the north end of town. **Curry General Hospital** (94220 4th St., Gold Beach, 541/247-6621) is the only hospital in the county.

GETTING THERE

Curry County's **Coastal Express** buses (800/921-2871, www.currypublictransit.org) run up and down the south coast weekdays only between North Bend and the California border, including local service in Gold Beach.

Brookings-Harbor and Vicinity

There are people who don't like Brookings, and if you form your judgment by simply driving down U.S. 101, it's easy to join that crowd. But something as simple as turning off into Harris Beach State Park can begin to change your view. To really fall for the area, it may take a drive up the Chetco River. A couple of miles inland, the fog that frequently drenches the coastline during the summer months burns away. There are ample hiking opportunities upriver, especially in the Kalmiopsis Wilderness Area.

During winter Brookings (pop. 6,000) and its neighbor, Harbor (pop. 2,600), enjoy mild temperatures. Enough 60-70°F days occur during January and February in this south coast "banana belt" town that more than 50 species of flowering plants thrive—along with retirees, outdoor-sports lovers, and beachcombers. With two gorgeous state parks virtually part of the

city and world-class salmon and steelhead fishing nearby, only the lavish winter rainfall, averaging over 73 inches a year, can cool the ardor of local outdoor enthusiasts. In the springtime, the area south of town is lush with lilies—it's the Easter lily capital of the world.

Brookings and Harbor sit on a coastal plain overlooking the Pacific six miles north of the California border, split by U.S. 101 (Chetco Ave.) and the Chetco River. Flowing out of the Klamath Mountains east of town, the Chetco drains part of the nearby Siskiyou National Forest and the Kalmiopsis Wilderness, extensive tracts encompassing some of the wildest country in the Lower 48 and renowned for their rare flowers and trees. This area enjoys strict federal protection, safeguarding the northernmost stand of giant redwoods as well as the coveted Port Orford cedar (whose

SOUTH COAST

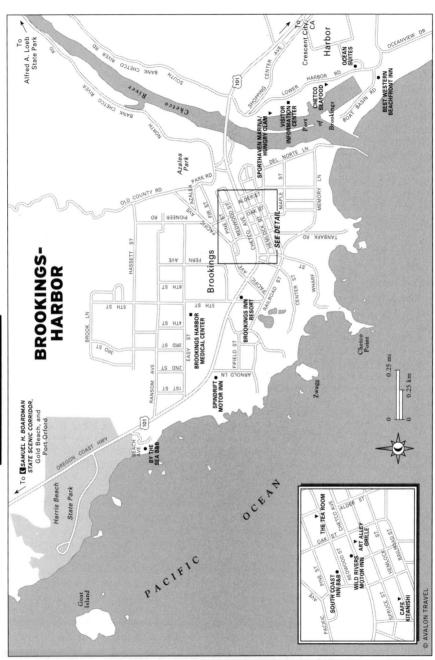

BROOKINGS-HARBOR

To Alfred A. Loeb State Park

Chetco River

NORTH BANK CHETCO RIVER RD

SOUTH BANK CHETCO RIVER RD

Azalea Park

OLD COUNTY RD

AZALEA PARK RD

PIONEER RD

HASSETT ST

BROOK LN

3RD ST

2ND ST

1ST ST

RANSOM AVE

FERN AVE

PACIFIC AVE

FIR ST

PINE ST

REDWOOD ST

CHETCO AVE

OAK ST

HEMLOCK ST

ALDER ST

Brookings

5TH ST

5TH ST

4TH ST

3RD ST

EASY ST

FIFIELD ST

RAILROAD ST

CENTER ST

WHARF ST

MAPLE ST

MEMORY LN

TANBARK RD

DEL NORTE LN

SEE DETAIL

SHOPPING CENTER AVE

LOWER HARBOR RD

Port of Brookings

SPORTHAVEN MARINA/ HUNGRY CLAM ▶

▶ **VISITOR INFORMATION CENTER**

CHETCO SEAFOOD ■

OCEAN SUITES ●

BEST WESTERN BEACHFRONT INN ●

BOAT BASIN RD

OCEANVIEW DR

To Crescent City CA

Harbor

Ocean

101

BROOKINGS HARBOR MEDICAL CENTER ■

BROOKINGS INN RESORT ●

ARNOLD LN

SPINDRIFT MOTOR INN ●

Chetco Point

Zwagg

0.25 mi
0.25 km

To ◀ **SAMUEL H. BOARDMAN STATE SCENIC CORRIDOR,** Gold Beach, and Port Orford

OREGON COAST HWY

BEACH AVE

BY THE SEA B&B ●

Harris Beach State Park

101

Goat Island

PACIFIC OCEAN

PINE ST

PACIFIC AVE

OAK ST

CHETCO AVE

ALDER ST

▶ **THE TEA ROOM**

REDWOOD ST

HEMLOCK ST

RAILROAD ST

SPRUCE ST

▶ **ART ALLEY GRILLE**

● **WILD RIVERS MOTOR INN**

SOUTH COAST INN B&B ●

▶ **CAFE KITANISHI**

© AVALON TRAVEL

BROOKINGS: FROM BOX FACTORY TO RETIREMENT HAVEN

What is now the shopping hub of rural Curry County started out as a factory town for the Brookings Box Company in 1913. Owner J. L. Brookings hired the architect Bernard Maybeck (famous for designing the Palace of Fine Arts in San Francisco) to lay out the streets and design housing and community buildings for his mill workers. Maybeck drew up extensive plans for a model company town, but most of them were never realized; his central vision was eventually gutted when the state highway was laid through, rather than around, the town. Examples of Maybeck's craftsmanship can still be seen around Brookings, notably in the 1917 Craftsman-style residence (now the South Coast Inn B&B) he designed for lumber baron William Ward.

In the years that followed, the lumber industry was augmented with fishing, horticulture, and tourism. Omitting for the moment the possibility that the offshore waters here were visited by Juan Cabrillo (in 1542) and the English explorer Sir Francis Drake (in 1579), the local event with the greatest historical significance was a Japanese aerial bombing on September 9, 1942. On that day, a Japanese incendiary bomb scorched the treetops of Mount Emily, southeast of town, in one of only two documented wartime air bombing missions against the U.S. mainland (the other occurred three weeks later near Port Orford). The resulting fires were quickly doused by the damp conditions, and no significant harm was done.

Twenty years after the bomb attack, the Japanese pilot, Nobuo Fujita, accepted an invitation to return to Brookings during the town's Azalea Festival. He brought with him the 400-year-old samurai sword he had carried on his missions during the war and presented it to the people of Brookings as a token of reconciliation. It still hangs on display in the Brookings city library. Fujita returned again in 1992 as the guest of honor for the opening of a new Forest Service trail to the bombsite, on the 50th anniversary of the attack. At age 80, he hiked the new trail and planted a redwood seedling in the bomb crater as a token of peace.

Since the late 1980s, Brookings's greatest growth industry has been as a haven for retirees, and that population has been booming in recent years.

strong but pliable lumber can fetch over $10,000 for a single tree). The Kalmiopsis Wilderness is named for a unique shrub, the *Kalmiopsis leachiana,* one of the oldest members of the heath family (Ericaceae) that grows nowhere else on earth.

But you don't have to trek miles into the backcountry to enjoy the natural beauty of Brookings and its vicinity. Just make your way past the somewhat drab main drag to Samuel Boardman State Park north of town, where 11 of the most scenic miles of the Oregon coast await you. Or head down to the harbor to embark on a boating expedition, with some of the safest offshore navigation conditions in the region. Although the harbor was battered by the tsunami that followed the Japanese earthquake in March 2011, few signs of damage remain. In short, Brookings is the perfect place to launch an adventure by land or by sea.

SIGHTS

In Brookings, camellias bloom at Christmas, and the flowering plums add color the next month. Daffodils, grown commercially on the coastal plain south of Brookings, bloom in late January and into February. Magnolia shrubs, some early azaleas, and rhododendrons bloom in late winter. The area also produces 90 percent of the world's Easter lily crop.

Harris Beach State Park

At the northern limits of Brookings, across from the State Information Center on U.S. 101, **Harris Beach State Park** makes up for all the ugly architecture you'll find on Chetco Avenue.

One look at the 24 miles of rock and tide visible from the parking lot promontory should quell any misgivings.

Harris Beach was named after the Scottish pioneer George Harris, who settled here in the late 1880s to raise sheep and cattle. Besides stunning views, this state park offers many incoming travelers from California their first chance to actually walk on the beach in Oregon. You can begin directly west of the park's campground, where a sandy beach strewn with boulders often becomes flooded with intertidal life and driftwood. The early morning hours, as the waves crash through a small tunnel in a massive rock onto the shoreline, are the best time to look for sponges, umbrella crabs, solitary corals, and sea stars.

Offshore, **Bird Island** (also called Goat Island) is the largest island along the Oregon coast and the state's largest seabird rookery. This outpost of Oregon Islands National Wildlife Refuge dispatches squadrons of cormorants, pelicans, tufted puffins, and other waterfowl, which dive-bomb the incoming waves for food.

In addition to beachcombing, you can picnic at tables above the parking lot, loll about in the shallow waters of nearby Harris Creek, or cast in the surf for perch.

Mill Beach is the southernmost part of the Harris Beach area. Locals prefer the beach access from downtown, which is easy to miss. To get there, drive toward the ocean on Center Street in downtown Brookings, make a right at the plywood mill, and stop next to a small ballpark. An unimproved road leads to a hillock from which trails take you down to a beach full of driftwood. Residents say that Japanese fishing floats occasionally roll up onto the beach after a storm.

Chetco Valley Historical Society Museum

The **Chetco Valley Historical Society Museum** (5461 Museum Rd., Brookings, 541/469-6651, www.chetcomuseum.com, noon-4pm Sat.-Sun. Memorial Day-Labor Day, $3 donation suggested), in the red-and-white Blake House, sits on a hill overlooking U.S. 101 two miles south of the Chetco River. The structure dates to 1857 and was used as a stagecoach way station and trading post before Abraham Lincoln was president.

Even if you are not one for museums, several exhibits here stand apart from the traditional collections of pioneer wedding dresses, Native American baskets, and spinning wheels. These include a small trunk that came around Cape Horn in 1706 and a Native American dugout canoe. Should these fail to inspire, a mysterious iron casting of a woman's face might do the trick, especially in light of the speculation that this relic was left by an early undocumented landing on the Oregon coast, perhaps by Sir Francis Drake. Drake has been commonly suggested because of the mask's likeness to Elizabeth I.

Oregon's largest Monterey cypress tree is located on the hill near the museum. The 99-foot-tall tree has a trunk circumference of more than 27 feet and has been home to a pair of owls for years.

◖ Samuel H. Boardman State Scenic Corridor

The stretch of highway from Brookings to Port Orford is known as the "fabulous 50 miles." Some consider the section of coastline just north of Brookings to be the most scenic in Oregon—and one of the most dramatic meetings of rock and tide in the world. The offshore rock formations and winding roadbed hundreds of feet above the surf invite comparison to Europe's Amalfi Drive. The "fabulous 50" sobriquet is perhaps most apt in the dozen miles directly north of Brookings, encompassed by **Samuel H. Boardman State Scenic Corridor.** You'll want to have a camera close at hand and a loose schedule when you make this drive, because you'll find it hard not to pull over again and again, as each photo opportunity seems to outdazzle the last. Of the 11 named viewpoints that have been cut into the highway's shoulder, the following are especially

Samuel H. Boardman State Scenic Corridor offers miles of dramatic coastline.

recommended (all viewpoints are marked by signs on the west side of U.S. 101 and are listed here from north to south).

Near the north end of Boardman State Park, a short walk down the hillside trail leads you to the **Arch Rocks** viewpoint, where an immense boomerang-shaped basalt archway juts out of the water about a quarter mile offshore. This site has picnic tables within view of the monolith.

A few miles south, the sign for **Natural Bridges Cove** seems to front just a forested parking lot. However, the paved walkway at the south end of the lot leads to a spectacular overlook. Below, several rock archways frame an azure cove. This feature was created by the collapse of the entrance and exit of a sea cave. A steep, winding trail through giant ferns and towering Sitka spruce and Douglas fir takes you down for a closer look. Thimbleberry (a sweet but seedy raspberry) is plentiful in late spring. As in similar forests on the south coast, it's important to stay on the trail. The rainforest-like biome is exceptionally fragile, and the

soil erodes easily when the delicate vegetation is damaged.

Thomas Creek Bridge, the highest bridge in Oregon (345 feet above the water) as well as the highest north of San Francisco, has been used as a silent star in many TV commercials. A parking lot at the south end of the bridge marks a trailhead down. Do not take the path you see closest to the bridge; it's too steep. At the south end of the lot, the true trail eventually leads down to a view of the bridge on one side and miles of coast on the other. The offshore rock formations are especially interesting. From here hikers can access the Indian Sands Trail, ending up in pine-rimmed dunes and a sandstone bluff high above the sea.

House Rock was the site of a World War II air-raid sentry tower that sits hundreds of feet above whitecaps pounding the rock-strewn beaches. To the north, you'll see one of the highest cliffs on the coast, Cape Sebastian. A steep circuitous trail lined with salal goes down to the water. The path begins behind the Samuel Boardman monument on the west end of the parking lot. The sign to the highest viewpoint in Boardman State Park is easy to miss, but look for the turnout that precedes House Rock, called Cape Ferrelo (for Juan Cabrillo's navigator, who sailed up much of the West Coast in 1543).

Carpenterville Road

The current roadbed of U.S. 101 was laid in southern Oregon in 1961. The previous coastal route still exists along **Carpenterville Road,** which can be picked up near Harris Beach. It comes out near the Pistol River, where it descends in a series of switchbacks. Its highest point is 1,700 feet above sea level at Burnt Hill. Views of the Siskiyous to the east and the Pacific panoramas to the west make the sometimes-rough road worth the effort. In very clear weather, it's possible to look back toward the southeast at Mount Shasta between the ridgelines. This route is best appreciated going south, and it makes a great 20-mile bike ride, with a long climb to 1,700 feet above sea level.

Alfred A. Loeb State Park

Eight miles northeast of Brookings on North Bank Chetco River Road along the Chetco River, the **Alfred A. Loeb State Park** preserves 320 acres of old-growth myrtlewood, the state's largest grove. Many of these aromatic trees are much older than 200 years.

The 0.25-mile Riverview Trail passes numerous big trees to connect Loeb Park with the **Redwood Nature Trail.** This trail winds 1.2 miles through the northernmost stands of naturally occurring *Sequoia sempervirens*. This is Oregon's largest redwood grove and contains the state's largest specimens. Within the grove are several trees more than 500 years old, measuring 5-8 feet in diameter, towering more than 300 feet above the forest floor. One tree has a 33-foot girth and is estimated to exceed 800 years in age. When the south coast is foggy and cold on summer mornings, it's often warm and dry in upriver locations such as this one, inviting the possibility of swimming in the Chetco River.

Kalmiopsis Wilderness

The lure of untrammeled wilderness attracts intrepid hikers to the **Kalmiopsis Wilderness,** despite the summer's blazing heat and winter's torrential rains. In addition to enjoying the isolation of the wilderness, they come to take in the pink rhododendron-like blooms of *Kalmiopsis leachiana* (in June) and other rare flowers. The area is also home to such economically valued species as Port Orford cedar and *Cannabis sativa*. The illicit weed is a leading cash crop in this part of the state, and its vigilant protection by growers should inspire extra care for those hiking during the late fall harvest season. The potential for violence associated with the lucrative mushroom harvest also mandates a measure of caution.

In any case, the Forest Service prohibits plant collection *of any kind* to preserve the region's special botanical populations. These include the insect-eating darlingtonia plant and the Brewer's weeping spruce. The forest canopy is composed largely of the more common Douglas fir, canyon live oak, madrona, and chinquapin. Stark peaks top this red-rock forest, whose understory is choked with blueberry, manzanita, and dense chaparral.

Many of this wilderness's rare species survived the glacial epoch because the glaciers from that era left the area untouched. This, combined with the fact that the area was once an offshore island, has enabled the region's singular ecosystem to maintain its integrity through the millennia. You'd think that federal protection, remoteness, and climatic extremes would ensure a sanguine outlook for this ice-age forest, but an active debate still rages over the validity of some logging claims.

In summer 2002, the so-called **Biscuit Fire** raged out of control for weeks, ravaging nearly half a million acres of southwestern Oregon, engulfing most of the Siskiyou National Forest and virtually all of the Kalmiopsis Wilderness. This inferno, the nation's largest wildfire of 2002 and the biggest in Oregon for more than a century, destroyed extensive habitat of the endangered northern spotted owl. The good news, however, is that flora of the region is well adapted to periodic fires; many of the old-growth trees survived the blaze, and within a few months green sprouts and new growth of many species were reappearing amid the ashes.

In the years since the fire, a young new forest has taken hold. Certain tree species, including rare Brewer spruce and knob cone pine, are growing back abundantly, as their seed cones require fire for germination. With the once-thick overstory vegetation mostly dead, lower-growing plants such as ferns, huckleberries, and bear grass are thriving in the sun. Soils are moister, too, since massive adult trees aren't sucking up the groundwater. Forest scientists estimate that it will take a century for trees of the mature forest, including stands of Douglas fir and sugar pine, to return and erase the evidence of the 2002 fire. Meanwhile the charred snags of the former primary forest stand above the lush growth of quickly rejuvenating woodlands.

Even if you don't have the slightest intention of hiking the Kalmiopsis, the scenic drive through the **Chetco Valley** is worth it. From Brookings, turn off U.S. 101 at the north end of the Chetco River Bridge, follow this paved road upriver past Loeb State Park, and continue along the river on County Roads 784 and 1376 until a narrow bridge crosses the Chetco. From here, turn right for 18 miles along national forest roads 1909, 160, and 1917 to reach the Upper Chetco Trailhead (just past the Quail Prairie Lookout). The driving distance from Brookings is 31 miles. If you're not hiking into the wilderness, you can continue west on national forest road 1917 (portions are not paved), which will return you to the above-mentioned narrow bridge over the Chetco.

Bombsite Trail

Brookings takes a peculiar pride in having been bombed by the Japanese during World War II. In 1942, two incendiary bombs were dropped about 16 miles east of town on the slopes of Mount Emily. Although they were intended to

start a fire, conditions were wet, and the small fire that resulted was easily controlled. A sort of mutual respect eventually developed between the Japanese pilot who dropped the bomb and the town of Brookings. The pilot was a guest of honor at one Azalea Festival, and his family later presented the town with his samurai sword, which he wore during the bombing and throughout the war. The sword is now on exhibit at the local library (420 Alder St.).

The Mount Emily **Bombsite Trail** commemorates the bombing. It's a two-mile stretch with redwoods near the beginning and fire-dependent species such as knobcone pine and manzanita along the way. To reach the trail, head eight miles east up South Bank Road and turn right onto Mount Emily Road. At the fork, turn onto Wheeler Creek Road and follow the signs.

Crissey Field State Recreation Area

Crissey Field State Recreation Area lies south of Brookings, almost to the California border, and is set along the Winchuck River. The park, which was added to the state park system in 2008, is great place to watch birds, harbor seals, California sea lions, and other wildlife. A trail leads through a huge pile of driftwood logs to dunes that shelter native plants, tiny wetlands, and old-growth Sitka spruce trees. Incidentally, the park's name has nothing to do with the San Francisco park (that's Crissy); it's in the heart of the lily-growing area and is named for a lily bulb grower.

SPORTS AND RECREATION

For some more mellow fun in the sun, cruise down Easy Street, east off U.S. 101, to **Bud Cross City Park** for some tennis, a dip in the outdoor pool, or a visit to the skate park.

Fishing

Fishing on the Chetco was once one of southern Oregon's best-kept secrets, but word has gotten out about the river's October run of huge chinook and its superlative influx of winter steelhead. If river traffic becomes too

© BILL MCRAE

The Brookings marina is at the mouth of the Chetco River.

heavy, the late-summer ocean salmon season out of Brookings may be the best in the Pacific Northwest. Boatless anglers can try their luck at the public fishing pier at the harbor and on the south jetty at the mouth of the Chetco. Chinook season generally runs mid-May–mid-September, but that's subject to change, so check the regulations.

Various fishing trips for salmon, tuna, and bottom fish can be arranged through **Sporthaven Marina** (16374 Lower Harbor Rd., Brookings, 541/469-3301). In addition to fishing charters, **Tidewind Sportfishing** (16368 Lower Harbor Rd., 541/469-0337, www.tide-windsportfishing.com) offers whale-watching excursions in season.

In the fall and winter, look upriver. Pick up literature on fishing and a Siskiyou National Forest map at the ranger station in town. In addition to offering printed matter about Siskiyou and Kalmiopsis trails for hikers, the rangers can tell you where to find some good fishing holes on the nearby Chetco River, noted for its good fall salmon runs and winter steelhead.

Golf

All the press about Bandon Dunes has obscured the development of another great course, **Salmon Run Golf Course** (99040 South Bank Chetco River Rd., 541/469-4888, www.salmonrun.net, greens fees $30 for 9 holes, $55 for 18 holes, includes cart). This beautiful 18-hole public links—not far from the Kalmiopsis Wilderness—was designed with environmentally sensitive imperatives, so numerous wildlife sightings may be enjoyed here long into the future. Whether it's the chance to see salmon (usually after the first rains in November) and steelhead spawning (January), black bears, elk, and wild turkeys, or just the opportunity to play a first-rate course, golfers shouldn't overlook this one. Beginner and intermediate players may find the executive nine-hole course ideal. This par-34 course within a course is located on the back nine holes and measures 1,310 yards. Your Oregon coastal golf pilgrimage can begin here, then hit Bandon Dunes, Sandpines (Florence), and Salishan (near Lincoln City).

Hiking

A good introduction to the Kalmiopsis Wilderness is along the one-mile trail to **Vulcan Lake** at the foot of Vulcan Peak, which is the major jumping-off point for trails into the wilderness. The trail begins at Forest Road 1909 and takes off up the mountains past Pollywog Butte and Red Mountain Prairie. The open patches in the Douglas firs reveal a kaleidoscope of Pacific Ocean views and panoramas of the Chetco Valley and the Big Craggies. For the botanist in search of rare plants, however, the real show is on the trail. No matter how expert you might consider yourself, bring along a good plant guide to help you identify the many exotic species. On the final leg of the hike, Sadler oak, manzanita, Jeffrey pine, white pine, and azalea precede the sharp descent to the lake. Despite steep spots, the walk from County Road 1909 to Vulcan Lake is not difficult.

If you backtrack from the lake to Spur 260 on the trail, you can make the steep ascent over talus slopes and brush to Vulcan Peak. At the top, from an old lookout, a view of Kalmiopsis treetops and the coast awaits. Before going, check with the Forest Service in Brookings to see if the road to the Vulcan Lake trailhead is open, because weather-related closures occasionally occur.

To reach the trailhead from Brookings, turn east off U.S. 101 at the north end of the Chetco River Bridge, follow North Bank Road (County Rd. 784) and Forest Road 1376 along the Chetco River for six miles, and then turn right and follow Forest Road 1909 to its bumpy end. Driving distance from Brookings is 31 miles. Hikers should watch out for the three shiny leaves of poison oak, as well as for rattlesnakes, which are numerous. Black bears also populate the area, but their lack of contact with humans makes them shier than their Cascade counterparts.

Surfing and Boogie Boarding

The best surfing is usually found at **Sporthaven Beach,** at the north end of the jetty in Harbor. Reach it by driving to the end of Boat Basin Road to the RV park. There's plenty of parking at the very end of the road. Even if the surf is not spectacular (it's usually best in the winter), it's a pretty mellow place for beginners, and as a fringe benefit, it can be a good spot to see whales during their springtime or December migrations.

Boogie boarders tend to favor **Harris Beach State Park.** From fall to spring, the waves are big and dangerous, and the water is cold. If you know what you're doing, come on in.

Rent gear for surfing or boogie boarding from the friendly folks at **Escape Hatch Sports** (649 Railroad St., 541/469-2914, 10am-5:30pm Mon.-Fri., 10am-5pm Sat.).

ENTERTAINMENT AND EVENTS

The **Beachcomber's Festival** (800/535-9469), held in late March at the **Azalea Middle School** (505 Pacific Ave.), features exhibits, demonstrations, and slide shows as well as an art competition for the best works wrought from indigenous materials such as driftwood, agates, and other beachcomber treasures. To get there, follow Pacific Avenue east of the highway.

Brookings's big event is the **Azalea Festival** (541/469-3181 or 800/535-9469), an unforgettable floral fantasia that takes place each Memorial Day weekend. Among the activities are a parade, a flower display, a crafts fair, a 5K run, a seafood luncheon, and a beef barbecue. Much of the activity revolves around Azalea Park. This Works Progress Administration-built enclave features 20-foot-high azaleas (which are several hundred years old) and hand-hewn myrtlewood picnic tables. Wild cherry and crab apple blooms, wild strawberry blossoms, and purple and red violets round out the bouquet. Butterflies, bees, and birds all seem to concur with locals that this array smells sweetest around graduation time in mid-June. To get there, take Pacific Avenue east of the highway, and turn onto Azalea Park Road.

Like several other Oregon coast towns, Brookings puts its windy weather to good use with its annual **Southern Oregon Kite Festival** (541/412-2941, www.southernoregonkitefestival.com), held over two days in mid-July.

SOUTH COAST

Individuals and teams display their aerial skills at the port of Brookings-Harbor.

Azalea Park is also home to **Nature's Coastal Holiday Light Show** in December, with more than 75,000 lights. The city park is on the south end of town. The Brookings-Harbor Garden Club and Chamber of Commerce (541/469-3181) offer garden tours of this park and other gardens. Call the chamber for more information on tours and garden-related events.

ACCOMMODATIONS

Rooms in Brookings are generally rather expensive; there are more budget accommodations 29 miles north in Gold Beach. It's also harder to find pet-friendly lodgings here than in most other coast towns.

Coastal Country Rentals (541/469-9568, www.coastalcountryrentals.com) can provide a list of available vacation rental homes.

$50-100

Just north of the Chetco River Bridge, **Wild Rivers Motorlodge** (437 Chetco Ave., 541/469-5361, www.wildriversmotorlodge.com, $80-100) is the most attractive roadside budget motel in town. Rooms come with refrigerators and microwaves.

The **Spindrift Motor Inn** (1215 Chetco Ave., 541/469-5345 or 800/292-1171, www.spindriftbrookings.com, $79-95) is a well-managed property and a decent value. However, its ambience is strictly roadside-budget, and it is a bit of a walk to the beach.

At the southern edge of the Brookings-Harbor stretch of U.S. 101, the **Harbor Inn Motel** (15991 U.S. 101 S., 541/469-3194 or 800/469-8444, www.harborinnmotel.com, $70-90) is not a bad place to land. It's nothing fancy, but it's pretty quiet and permits pets; all rooms have a fridge, a microwave, and Wi-Fi. If you head west from the stoplight at the motel, it's about a mile to the port of Harbor.

For a more full-service lodging choice, the highway-side **Brookings Inn Resort** (1143 Chetco Ave., 541/469-2173 or 800/822-9087, www.brookingsinnresort.com, $85-95) is about

a mile from the ocean, but it's family-friendly, with a pool and whirlpool tub, a comfy myrtlewood-paneled lounge, and a decent on-site restaurant.

$100-150

The nicest places to stay in the Brookings area are bed-and-breakfast inns, and they aren't that much more expensive than the local run-of-the-mill motel rooms.

A coastal gem one block north of the highway, the **(South Coast Inn B&B** (516 Redwood St., Brookings, 541/469-5557 or 800/525-9273, www.southcoastinn.com, $119-159) is a 1917 Craftsman building and was once the home of lumber baron William Ward. Designed by famed architect Bernard Maybeck and situated in the heart of old Brookings just blocks away from the beach and shopping, this 4,000-square-foot B&B offers four guest rooms, a guest cottage, and an apartment. All rooms have TVs with VCR (and access to the inn's video library), private bathrooms, and other amenities. An indoor spa with a sauna and a hot tub and an included breakfast featuring a health-conscious menu are additional enticements to book space early. Ask the friendly innkeepers about other Maybeck structures in town.

For a B&B that's close to the ocean, **By the Sea B&B** (1545 Beach Ave., 541/469-4692 or 877/469-4692, www.brookingsbythesea.com, $150) offers a choice of two theme-decorated guest rooms and a cottage. Enjoy breakfast and breathtaking ocean views from the stained-glass-topped windows. On the upper veranda, a spa and a wood-burning fire pot are available for guest use.

Perhaps the best value in Brookings lodgings is **(Ocean Suites** (16045 Lower Harbor Rd., 541/469-4004, www.oceansuitesmotel.com, $109-119), at the Harbor end of town. These really are suites—each has a full kitchen and a living room. No pets are allowed.

Another option is to rent a cottage at **Whaleshead Beach Resort** (19921 Whaleshead Rd., 541/469-7446 or 800/943-4325, www.whalesheadresort.com, $110-165) by the night or by the week. This sprawling development is on a bluff about eight miles north of Brookings, just across the highway from Whaleshead Beach, a beautiful spot in Boardman State Park. The little cabins are fully furnished, and facilities include a restaurant and a 700-foot-long tunnel under the highway to the beach.

$150-200
The best conventional hotels are south of the Chetco River in Harbor. The ◖ **Best Western Beachfront Inn** (16008 Boat Basin Rd., Harbor, 541/469-7779, $179-250) sits on the beach at the mouth of the Chetco River, just past the port and marina. All units feature private decks, microwaves, and refrigerators. Kitchenettes as well as suites with ocean-view hot tubs and an indoor pool are available. Pets are permitted on a very limited basis; call the hotel directly to plead your case.

Camping
Harris Beach State Park (1655 U.S. 101, 541/469-2021 or 800/452-5687, www.reserveamerica.com, $20-26), two miles north of town, is open all year, but reservations are definitely necessary Memorial Day-Labor Day. With a total of 155 spaces, there are 149 paved sites (50 electricity only, 36 full), some with shade; six yurts; and a special camping area for hikers and bicyclists. Picnic tables and grills are provided. Flush toilets, electricity, piped-in water, sewer hookups, sanitary service, showers, firewood, laundry, and a playground are available. Whale-watching is particularly good here in January and May, and the birding is good year-round.

The 320-acre **Alfred A. Loeb State Park** (541/469-2021, sites $16-20 depending on season, cabins $39 year-round) is nine miles northeast of Brookings on North Bank Chetco River Road. There are 53 sites with electrical hookups for trailers/motor homes (50 feet maximum), a special campground for bicyclists and hikers, and some cabins. Electricity, piped water, and picnic tables are provided; flush toilets and firewood are available. The campground is in

a fragrant and secluded myrtlewood grove on the east bank of the Chetco River. From here, the Riverview Trail takes hikers to the Siskiyou National Forest's Redwood Nature Trail, where nature lovers will marvel at 800-year-old redwood beauties. Although cabins can be reserved (800/452-5687), campsites are all first come, first served.

Beyond Loeb State Park is the more primitive **Little Redwood Campground** (contact Chetco Ranger District, 539 Chetco Ave., 541/412-6000, www.fs.us, campground open mid-May-Sept., no water, free). To get there, go 0.5 mile south of Brookings on U.S. 101 to County Road 784, then go northeast for seven miles. At Forest Service Road 376, turn northeast and drive six miles to the campground. Little Redwood is on the main access route to the Kalmiopsis Wilderness, 20 miles away, and is a good spot for fishing during the winter steelhead run.

The Forest Service rents several cabins and fire lookouts ($40-50/night); advance booking is required. Contact the **Chetco Ranger District** (539 Chetco Ave., 541/412-6000, www.fs.fed.us) for information about renting Packer's Cabin, Ludlum House, or the Quail Prairie Lookout.

FOOD
Brookings has a profusion of family-friendly, though unexciting, restaurants that serve large portions at a good value—this is not a fine-dining capital. For slightly more distinctive fare than the usual fast food and family-dining joints, check out the following places.

American
Ask a local where to eat breakfast, and invariably you'll hear the name of **Mattie's Pancake House** (15975 U.S. 101 S., 541/469-7311, 6am-1:45pm Mon.-Sat., $5-13), a family-friendly operation that serves good pancakes, omelets, and biscuits and gravy. The lunch menu offers burgers and sandwiches.

For lighter fare, try **The Tea Room** (434 Redwood St., No. 4, 541/469-7240, 7am-2pm Mon.-Fri.) for sandwiches, soups, salads, and baked goods; fill your to-go mugs with a nice cup of the hot stuff. This place is worth seeing just for its enormous collection of teapots.

Pacific Northwest

Brookings's only real fine dining is at the quirky and charming **◖ Art Alley Grille** (515 Chetco Ave., 541/469-0800, 11am-2:30pm Tues., 11am-2:30pm and 5pm-8:30pm Wed.-Sat., $19-27), a basement spot tucked downstairs from an art gallery. The menu is fairly wide ranging, with items such as roasted lamb with a marionberry-hazelnut crust and grilled, bacon-wrapped albacore tuna loin offering a real Oregon touch. At lunchtime, head upstairs from the gallery for sandwiches and soup.

Seafood

A coastal town is certainly a safe place to eat sushi. In Brookings, find it at **Cafe Kitanishi** (632 Hemlock St., 541/469-7864, www.cafekitanishi.com, 11am-3pm Tues.-Wed., 11am-3pm and 5pm-9pm Thurs.-Fri., 5pm-9pm Sat., $5-27), which also serves bento boxes to go and has an espresso bar with Internet access.

Down in the harbor area, you'll find a number of seafood shops. For fresh, traditional fish-and-chips, you can't miss at **Sporthaven Marina** (16374 Lower Harbor Rd., 541/469-3301, 11am-6pm Mon.-Sat., 11am-5pm Sun., $6-15) with good clam chowder and fried seafood done up in traditional Oregon style. Yet more fresh fried seafood is ready for you at the adjacent **Hungry Clam** (16350 Lower Harbor Rd., 541/469-2526, $8-15), with crab cake sliders, fresh tuna melts, crab cocktails, and a host of fried fish with slaw and chips.

Brewpub

Wild River Pizza (16279 U.S. 101 S., Harbor, 541/469-7454, 11am-10pm Sun.-Thurs., 11am-11pm Fri.-Sat., medium pizza $13-18) is part of the Wild River Brewing family, with pizza-brewpubs in Cave Junction, Medford, and Grants Pass. The crispy crust pizza is the best you'll find in the area. While the food is good and inexpensive, this large restaurant tends to fill up with families enjoying the video games and pool tables on weekends. In other words, go elsewhere for an intimate Saturday night dinner. Look for it on the east side of the highway about a mile south of the Brookings-Harbor Bridge at the four-way stoplight.

INFORMATION

Pull off the highway and talk to the friendly folks at the **Crissey Field Welcome Center** (16633 Hwy. 101 S., 541/469-4117, 8am-5pm daily Apr.-Oct., 8:30am-4:30pm Mon.-Fri. Nov.-Mar.), where you can gather information and brochures about the coast and the rest of the state. For additional information pertinent to Brookings and environs, the **Brookings-Harbor Chamber of Commerce** (16330 Lower Harbor Rd., Brookings, 541/469-3181, www.brookingsharborchamber.com) is down at the harbor.

GETTING THERE

It takes determination to get to Brookings using public transportation. Curry County's **Coastal Express buses** (800/921-2871, www.currypublictransit.org) run up and down the south coast weekdays only between North Bend and the California border, including local service in Brookings. **Porter Stage Lines** (541/269-7183, www.porterstageline.com) has a run that links North Bend with points north to Florence, then turns inland at Florence and goes to Eugene, Bend, and Ontario.

BACKGROUND

The Land

The Oregon coast we know today encompasses nearly 400 miles of beaches, rainforest, dunes, high-rise headlands, rocky sea stacks and islands, and tidal pools showcasing marine worlds in miniature. The narrow coastal plateau is hemmed in by the Klamath Mountains in the state's southern quarter and by the Coast Range beginning near Coos Bay in the north, which together form a palisade between the sea and the state's interior. Neither range is particularly high; the tallest peaks in each of these cordilleras barely top 4,000 feet. More than a dozen major rivers and scores of smaller streams cut through these mountain barriers to the sea.

The valleys that the rivers follow through the mountains are the same routes traversed now by the east-west highways that link the coast with the rest of the state.

Tectonics

Timeless as it may appear to the modern observer, the Oregon coast hasn't always been where or as we see it today. Titanic forces shaped—and continue to affect—this coastal region and indeed the entire Pacific Northwest. The giant tectonic plates that make up the earth's crust slide under one another as they collide. In Pacific Northwest coastal regions,

this takes place when the Juan de Fuca plate's marine layer is subducted, or pushed under, the continental North American plate. The stress of this collision heaved up the Klamath Mountains some 225 million years ago and created the Coast Range 20-50 million years ago. This subduction is ongoing, and the resulting geologic pressure that builds from it is released periodically in earthquakes, large and small.

With virtually every part of the coastline possessing seismic potential that hasn't been released in many years, the pressure along the fault lines is increasing. Scientists have unearthed discontinuities in rock strata and tree rings on the north Oregon coast that indicate that Tillamook County has experienced major tremors every few hundred years. They estimate that the next one could come within our lifetime and be of significant magnitude. In coastal areas, one of the greatest dangers associated with earthquakes is the possibility of tsunamis.

The ocean waves produced by seismic activity can be enormous and devastating. Ever since a tsunami unleashed by Alaska's Good Friday quake in 1964 (measured at 14.2 feet high at the mouth of the Umpqua River) resulted in four casualties in Beverly Beach and more than $1 million in damage, local authorities have made seismic preparedness a priority.

Along the coast today, warning sirens stand ready. Visitors will also see blue evacuation signs pointing the way to higher ground and escape routes, acknowledging the imminent danger of a 30-foot wave that could strike within minutes of an offshore temblor. When a tsunami warning was issued following the Japanese earthquake of 2011, coastal residents and visitors hurried to higher ground; the resulting waves were fairly small along most of the coast, but did cause serious damage to the harbor in Brookings. Debris from that event continues to wash up on the Oregon coast; the most significant was a 180-ton dock that landed on Newport's Agate Beach in 2012. (It was removed.)

Ice and Fire

At the height of the most recent major glaciation, sea level of the world's oceans was some 300-500 feet lower than it is now. North America and Asia were connected by a land bridge across the Bering Strait. The Oregon seashore lay miles west of where it is now, and the Columbia Gorge extended out past present-day Astoria.

As the glaciers melted, the sea rose. When that glacial epoch's final meltdown 12,000 years ago unleashed water dammed up by thick ice, great rivers were spawned and existing channels enlarged. A particularly large inundation was the Missoula Floods, which began with an ice dam breaking up in present-day Montana. Before it subsided, it carved out the contours of what are now the Columbia River Gorge and the Willamette Valley. Other glacial floodwaters found their outlet westward to the sea, flushing out silt-ridden estuaries in the process. Pacific wave action eventually washed this debris back up onto the land, creating beaches and sand dunes.

Like the rest of the state, the Oregon coast also shows off distinct remnants of Oregon's volcanic past. The offshore waters are scattered with 1,477 volcanic islets. These rocky outcrops, as well as many of the headlands that separate the beaches, are made of erosion-resistant basalt, an extremely durable igneous material that has endured long after wind and waves have eroded the softer surrounding earth.

The Beach: Contours and Character

Most Oregon visitors who travel west of the Coast Range head straight to the beach. Despite Pacific temperatures cold enough to render swimming an at-your-own-risk activity, the cliff-side ocean vistas, wildlife, beachcombing, and other attractions make the coast the state's number-one regional destination.

With rare exceptions, all beaches in Oregon below mean high tide are owned by the public. This is thanks largely to Governor Oswald West, who in 1913 pushed through legislation defining Oregon's ocean beaches as public highways (which in fact they were before real roads were built) and thus off-limits to private encroachment. Later, Oregon's Beach

© JUDY JEWELL

Ancient lava flows extend into the surf near Cape Perpetua.

Bills of 1967 and 1972 were written to further guarantee public access to the state's gem of a coastline. In recent years, however, certain sections of this publicly owned paradise have increasingly become exclusive bailiwicks of the wealthy, with gated communities cutting off easy access to a few beaches.

Black sand, high in iron and other metals, is common on the coast, particularly south of Coos Bay. There was also enough gold in the black sands to spur a flurry of gold-mining activity on the south coast in the 1850s and 1860s. Scientists have known for decades of the placer deposits of heavy minerals washed ashore on prehistoric beaches thousands of years ago when ocean levels were much lower. These beach sands now lie submerged. These days, mining companies are eyeing the continental shelf off the south coast for possible exploitation of ilmenite, magnetite, chromite, zircon, garnet, gold, and platinum. Despite a study indicating a significant presence of precious metals in the sands offshore from the Rogue River and Cape Blanco, incipient prospecting ventures were abandoned.

Speaking of sand, the central Oregon coast has about 32,000 acres of shimmering white dunes, the largest oceanfront collection in North America and the highest in the world. Some hills top out at more than 500 feet high. Oregon's Sahara is located along a 40-mile stretch between Coos Bay and Florence. Buffeted by winds, the dunes are continually on the move; in some places, roads are in danger of being engulfed by the shifting sands.

CLIMATE

Oregon's location equidistant from the equator and the North Pole subjects the state to weather from both tropical and polar airflows. This makes for a pattern of changeability in which calm often alternates with storm. Although it's difficult to predict daily weather patterns in western Oregon, there are definite seasonal climatic shifts. In winter, arctic and tropical air masses collide over the Pacific, producing much of the state's rain. During summer, the clashes are much less frequent. At that time, Oregon weather is most affected by Pacific

SUMMER FOG

Mark Twain reportedly once quipped that "the coldest winter I ever spent was summer in San Francisco." That's because he never spent time on the Oregon coast, where summer fogs can really put the chill into your summer vacation.

When the Willamette and other inland valleys are hot and sunny, and you're dreaming of perfect sun-drenched weather at the beach, it's often the case that the Oregon coast is encased in bone-chilling fog. High pressure inland pulls low-pressure marine mists in off the ocean, wrapping beaches and startled tourists in thick fog and 50°F temperatures. This can be very annoying to photographers, who find lighthouse and sea stack vistas completely obscured by pea-soup conditions. Often the fog bank extends only half a mile inland, and it tends to burn off as the day proceeds, but the hotter the temperatures inland, the thicker and longer-lasting the fog.

There's not much you can do about it, except to remember to bring a jacket and long pants, *particularly* at the height of summer. When planning a summer trip, have a fall-back plan for a cold and foggy day. For instance, when fog obscures the beach, plan a hike in the Coast Range—chances are that you'll leave the fog behind you as you drive inland.

Ocean temperatures and air pressure differences between inland and coastal areas.

Oregon's coastal weather can best be summed up as wet and mild. The coast as a whole receives roughly 70 inches of rain yearly on average. Most of that falls from late fall to mid-spring, whereas May-September is generally fairly dry.

Lincoln City and vicinity tend to record the highest amounts of rain, with nearly 100 inches per year, while towns both north and south are generally less wet by comparison. Coast-bound travelers should bear in mind that inland from the coastal plateau, the Coast and Klamath Ranges receive substantially more precipitation because as moisture-laden westerlies blow in from the Pacific, they slam into the mountain slopes and are pushed upward. As the clouds climb higher, they drop their moisture in the form of rain or snow because rising air cools, and cooler air can't hold as much moisture as warm air. As a consequence, precipitation averages 150 inches per year over the coastal mountains. Anyone driving through the Coast Range sees evidence of the siege mentality that sets in with each winter monsoon season. Giant satellite-TV dishes and stacks of firewood covered in blue plastic tarps are common lawn ornaments here in the rainiest part of the state.

The moderating influence of the Pacific Ocean gives the coastal region an unusually mild climate for a state so far north. Coastal temperatures are fairly constant throughout the year, and extremes are rare. With infrequent freezes and rarely recorded snowfall, Old Man Winter definitely pulls his punches. In fact, Coos Bay, for example, is often touted as having one of the mildest (in terms of absence of extremes) year-round climates in the United States. Even in winter, daytime highs along the coast tend to reach the mid-50s Fahrenheit, and nighttime lows generally drop into the 40s. Spring, summer, and fall see highs in the 60s and into the 70s, with overnight lows staying in the mid-40s to mid-50s. Summer highs above 90°F are unusual, although the mercury in south coast locations such as Brookings and Bandon has topped 100°F on rare occasions. Midwinter and spring dry spells with 60°F-plus temperatures commonly occur.

Any time of year, the coast can be very windy; particularly in winter and spring, you may encounter proper gales scouring the beach. Although that can make for terrific kite-flying, picnics aren't quite so much fun at those times. In winter, the winds typically blow from the south and southwest, whereas the gentler summer winds usually come from the northeast.

Flora and Fauna

FLORA

Although giant conifers and a profuse understory of greenery are the most noticeable traits of coastal Oregon's flora, this ecosystem represents only the most visible part of the region's bountiful botany. In addition to Brookings's Azalea Festival and Florence's Rhododendron Festival, coast-bound travelers come to take in such horticultural highlights as the insect-eating darlingtonia plant, Oregon myrtle trees, and some remaining stands of ancient old-growth forest. Serious botanists might search out the pine mushroom (a.k.a. matsutake), found in the Oregon dunes and a few other places across the state, or probe the Kalmiopsis Wilderness near the south coast, habitat to many rare plants.

Coos Bay marks the boundary between the Mediterranean beach flora found south into California and the subarctic species growing north from there into Washington and British Columbia.

Trees

Sandwiched between the mountains and the sea, the mixed-conifer ecosystem of western Oregon's wet lowlands, comprising primarily fir, western hemlock, Sitka spruce, and cedar, is the most productive belt of evergreens in the world. The conifers are broken up by pockets of alder, oak, vine maple, bigleaf maple, and myrtle trees. With its dense understory of rhododendron, thimbleberry, salmonberry, blackberry, and salal interspersed among the ferns and mosses that carpet the forest floor, this woodland carries up to 1,000 tons of plant matter per hectare and sometimes more. Because of the construction industry's penchant for Douglas fir (*Pseudotsuga menziesii*), which is replanted assiduously, this tree predominates.

Oregon schoolchildren learn to distinguish between fir, spruce, and hemlock by a mnemonic device: The needles of a fir are flat, flexible, and friendly. Spruce needles are square, stiff, and will stick you. Hemlock needles have a hammock-like configuration, and the crown of the tree is curved like it's tipping its hat. *Trees to Know in Oregon,* published by the Oregon State University Extension Service in Corvallis, is an excellent aid to tree identification, as well as a compendium of useful facts.

The Oregon myrtle, *Umbellularia californica,* the only tree in its genus, is native only to the Holy Land, southern Oregon, and northern California (where it's more commonly known as California laurel or California bay). The hard yellowish wood of the aromatic myrtle tree is so dense that when it's green it sinks in water. It is prized by woodworkers and especially wood turners for its distinctive coloring and grain. The value of myrtlewood, in fact, reached a peak during the Depression, when North Bend issued myrtlewood scrip in the

Coastal trails often lead through old-growth temperate rain forests.

© BILL MCRAE

form of coins valued $0.50-10, after the only bank in town failed.

Among these coastal forests, several extraordinary individual trees have managed to survive the ax and chainsaw, and the region boasts such record specimens as the 326-foot-high 11.5-foot-diameter Doerner fir in the Coast Range near Coquille, rated the nation's largest Douglas fir by the American Forestry Association based on height, diameter, and crown size. An exceptionally large Sitka spruce grows at Cape Meares, and the state's largest Monterey cypress is found in Brookings.

Dunes, Beaches, and Bogs

Apart from the spectacular springtime fireworks of rhododendron and azalea blossoms, the Oregon coast doesn't show off its wildflowers as boldly as other parts of the state, such as Steens Mountain, the Cascades, and the Wallowas. The flowering plants of beach, dunes, and headlands tend to be subtler but are nevertheless varied and worth seeking out. Among some of the species found only along the Oregon coast are beach bursage, yellow sand verbena, beach evening primrose, seashore bluegrass, dune tansy, and silvery phacelia. The best time for wildflowers is usually June and July. An excellent guide for those interested in coastal wildflowers is *Introduction to Shore Wildflowers of California, Oregon, and Washington,* published by the University of California Press.

Many coastal travelers will notice **European beachgrass** (*Ammophila arenaria*) covering the sand wherever they go. Originally planted in the 1930s to inhibit dune growth, the thick, rapidly spreading grass worked too well, solidifying into a ridge behind the shoreline, blocking the windblown sand from replenishing the rest of the beach and suppressing native plants. Populations of formerly common natives such as beach morning glory, yellow abronia, gray beach pea, and American dune-grass are now much diminished. The endangered pink sand verbena—once abundant along the coast from British Columbia to northern California—is now restricted to a few locations along the

The Oregon Dunes are not just for hikers.

© BILL MCRAE

central and southern Oregon coast. Herbicides, burning, and tilling have been employed in recent years to remove European beachgrass and restore the dune ecosystem to a more natural state, but progress against the pernicious weed is slow and difficult.

Freshwater wetlands and bogs, created where water is trapped by the sprawling sand dunes along the central coast, provide habitats for some unusual species. Best known among these is the cobra lily (*Darlingtonia californica*), which can be viewed up close at Darlingtonia State Natural Site or Darlingtonia Botanical Gardens just north of Florence. Also called darlingtonia or pitcher plant, this carnivorous bog dweller survives on hapless insects lured into its specialized chamber. **Coastal salt marshes,** occurring in the upper intertidal zones of coastal bays and estuaries, have been dramatically reduced because of land reclamation projects such as drainage, diking, and other human disturbances. The halophytes (salt-loving plants) that thrive in this specialized environment include pickleweed, saltgrass, fleshy jaumea, salt marsh dodder, arrow-grass, sand spurrey, and seaside plantain. For an excellent introduction to this complex ecosystem, visit the South Slough National Estuarine Research Reserve, south of Coos Bay. Bandon Marsh National Wildlife Refuge protects the largest remaining tract of salt marsh within the Coquille River estuary. Major habitats include undisturbed salt marsh, mudflat, and Sitka spruce and alder riparian communities, which provide resting and feeding areas for migratory waterfowl, shore and wading birds, and raptors.

Mushrooms

Autumn, particularly from the first rains until the onset of frosts, is the season for those who covet chanterelle, matsutake, and morel mushrooms. The Coast Range is the prime picking area September-November for chanterelles—a fluted orange or yellow mushroom in the tall second-growth Douglas fir forests. If you plan to sell what you find or gather more than a gallon of mushrooms, you need to purchase a permit from the Forest Service. Of course, you should be absolutely certain of any wild mushroom's identity before you eat it.

In recent years, fungus fever reached epidemic proportions, largely because of a matsutake mushroom shortage in Japan, where it is prized for medicinal and spiritual qualities and enjoyed as a soup garnish. In the mid-1990s, for example, matsutakes fetched up to $500 per pound in Japan, a price that precipitated violence in northern Klamath County forests and other areas saturated with pickers during the fall harvest. This mycological harvest, along with the cutting of ferns (maidenhair ferns command an especially high price from florists), beargrass, and other ornamental greenery, helps many residents of forest communities make ends meet.

FAUNA

The animal kingdom is well represented by a great diversity and abundance of creatures along the coast, in the air, on the land, under the water, and in between. Opportunities for wildlife viewing abound all along the coast, but standout areas include the state's six coastal national wildlife refuges: Oregon Islands, Cape Meares, and Three Arch Rocks protect important habitat for seabirds, seals, and sea lions among coastal rocks, reefs, islands, and several headland areas, while Nestucca Bay, Siletz Bay, and Bandon Marsh National Wildlife Refuges preserve estuarine habitats of salt marsh, wetlands, and woods rich in waterfowl, raptors, fish, and other fauna. *The Audubon Guide to the National Wildlife Refuges: Alaska and the Northwest* is an excellent reference book to have along on your explorations.

Tidepools

For most visitors, the most fascinating coastal ecosystems in Oregon are the rocky tidepools. These Technicolor windows offer an up close look at one of the richest—and harshest—environments, the intertidal zone, where pummeling surf, unflinching sun, and the cycle of tides demand tenacity and special adaptation of its inhabitants.

Marine biologists subdivide this natural

blender where surf meets bedrock into three main habitat layers, based on their position relative to tide levels. The **high intertidal zone,** inundated only during the highest tides, is home to creatures that can move, such as crabs, or are well adapted to tolerate daily desiccation, such as acorn barnacles, finger limpets, chitons, and green algae. The turbulent **mid-intertidal zone** is covered and uncovered by the tides, usually twice each day. In the upper portion of this zone, California mussels and goose barnacles may thickly blanket the rocks, while ochre sea stars and green sea anemones are common lower down, along with sea lettuce, sea palms, snails, sponges, and whelks. Below that, the **low intertidal zone** is only exposed during the lowest tides. Because it is covered by water most of the time, this zone has the greatest diversity of organisms in the tidal area. Residents include many of the organisms found in the higher zones, as well as sculpins, abalone, and purple sea urchins.

Standout destinations for exploring tidepools include Cape Arago, Cape Perpetua, the Marine Gardens at Devil's Punchbowl, and beaches south and north of Gold Beach—among many other spots. Tidepool explorers should be mindful that, although the plants and animals in the pools are well adapted to withstand the elements, they and their ecosystem are fragile, and they're sensitive to human interference. Avoid stepping on mussels, anemones, and barnacles, and take nothing from the tidepools. In the Oregon Islands National Wildlife Refuge and other specially protected areas, removal or harassment of any living organism may be treated as a misdemeanor punishable by fines.

Birds

One of the most immediately noticeable forms of wildlife at the coast must be the birds of sea, shore, and estuary. The abundance and variety of species you may encounter are a large part of the reason that Oregon has a reputation as one of the best bird-watching states. Seasonal variance in populations is often dramatic, so timing is important. Check out the Oregon Coast Birding Trail (www.oregoncoastbirding.com) to learn about regional hot spots and events.

The **Oregon Islands National Wildlife Refuge,** which comprises all the 1,400-plus offshore islands, reefs, and rocks from Tillamook Head to the California border, is a haven for the largest concentration of nesting seabirds along the West Coast of the United States, thanks to the abundance of protected nesting habitat. During the April-August breeding season, seabirds that can be seen here include **common murres, pigeon guillemots, tufted puffins, Brandt's** and **pelagic cormorants,** and **black oystercatchers,** along with the ubiquitous **western gulls.** June-October you may spy **brown pelicans** skimming the waves. **Aleutian Canada geese** use Table and Haystack Rocks during March and early April.

In terms of sheer numbers and variety, the coast's mudflats at low tide and the tidal estuaries also make excellent bird-watching environments. Species to look for on the flats and shorelines include **Pacific golden plovers** as well as **pectoral** and **Baird's sandpipers.** The

oystercatcher atop a rock

California sea lions hanging out in Astoria

western snowy plover, listed as threatened under the Endangered Species Act, gets special protection at the state's nine nesting sites in Curry, Coos, Douglas, and Lane Counties. The small shorebird, which resembles a sandpiper, nests on open sandy beaches above the high-tide line and is sensitive to disturbance from human foot traffic, vehicles, and unleashed dogs. During the nesting season, mid-March to mid-September, coast visitors may encounter areas posted or roped off to protect snowy plover nests.

Resident and migratory birds commonly spotted on the estuaries and lakes of the coast include the common loon, western and horned grebes, great blue heron, American widgeon, greater scaup, common goldeneye, bufflehead, and red-breasted merganser.

Seals, Sea Lions, and Otters
Pacific harbor seals, California sea lions, and **Steller sea lions** are frequently sighted in Oregon waters. California sea lions are 1,000-pound mammals characterized by their large

size and small earflaps, which seals lack. Unlike seals, they can point their rear flippers forward to give them better mobility on land. Without the dense underfur that covers seals, sea lions tend to prefer warmer waters.

Steller sea lions can be seen at the Sea Lion Caves north of Florence. They also breed on reefs off Gold Beach and Port Orford. They are the largest sea lion species, with males sometimes weighing more than a ton. Their coats tend to be grayer than the black-coated California sea lion. They also differ from their California counterparts in that they are comfortable in colder water.

Look for Pacific harbor seals in bays and estuaries up and down the coast, sometimes miles inland. They're nonmigratory, have no earflaps, and can be distinguished from sea lions because they're much smaller (150-300 pounds) and have mottled fur that ranges in color from pale cream to rusty brown.

Another marine mammal that was once common on the Oregon coast, and along the entire Pacific coast from Japan to Mexico, is the **sea otter.** Two centuries of ruthless hunting by Russian, European, and American fur traders nearly eradicated the species. By the time Oregon's last known sea otter was killed in 1906, the otters had disappeared from British Columbia to central California. For many years, the only sea otters living in Oregon were those in the Oregon Zoo and the Oregon Coast Aquarium, but in the winter of 2009 an otter was spotted from the U.S. 101 bridge in Depoe Bay. An organization called the Elakha Alliance is working to restore wild otters to their natural habitat. You can learn about and support their work at www.ecotrust.org.

Gray Whales
Few sights along the Oregon coast (or any coast, for that matter) elicit more excitement than that of a surfacing whale. The most common large whale seen from shore along the West Coast of North America is the gray whale (*Eschrichtius robustus*). These behemoths can reach 45 feet in length and weigh 35 tons. The sight of a mammal as big as a Greyhound bus breaking water

© BILL MCRAE

Whale-watching trips leave from Depoe Bay and many other coastal communities.

early March-April. This annual journey from the rich feeding grounds of the Bering and Chukchi Seas of Alaska to the calving grounds of Mexico amounts to some 10,000 miles, the longest migration of any mammal.

Grays feed primarily on bottom-dwelling shrimp-like amphipods, scooping up huge mouthfuls from which they filter out water and sediment through the fringe of baleen inside their mouths. After fattening up in the rich waters of the arctic during the summer and fall, gray whales begin their migration south. In early December, pregnant females are the first to begin showing up along the Oregon coast, followed by mature adults of both sexes and then by juveniles. Their numbers peak usually during the first week of January, when as many as 30 per hour may pass a given point. By mid-February, most of the whales will have moved on toward their breeding and calving lagoons on the west coast of Baja California.

Early March-April, the juveniles, adult males, and females without calves begin returning northward past the Oregon coast. Mothers and their new calves are the last to leave Mexico and move more slowly, passing Oregon late April-June. During the spring migration, the whales may pass within just a few hundred yards of coastal headlands, making this a particularly exciting time for whale-watching from many vantage points along the coast. Researchers speculate that gray whales stay close to shore as a way to help them navigate.

Land Mammals

Many of the most frequently sighted animals in coastal Oregon are small scavengers, which are often encountered in woodsier campgrounds, parks, and picnic areas: **raccoons, skunks, Townsend's chipmunks, Douglas squirrels, and opossums.**

Black-tailed deer are commonly spotted in woods and meadows all along the coast, and a herd of their larger cousin, the majestic **Roosevelt elk,** can be seen at the Dean Creek Elk Viewing Area near Reedsport.

On streams and brooks, observant hikers

has a way of emptying the mind of mundane concerns. Wreathed in seaweed and sporting barnacles and other parasites on its back, a gray whale might look more like the hull of an old ship but for its expressive eyes.

After decades of hunting brought them to the brink of extinction, gray whales gained full protection in 1946 by the International Whaling Commission. In the ensuing years, the population has recovered dramatically. When the gray whale was delisted from the Endangered Species List in 1994, the population was estimated at 23,000, which is thought to be close to the pre-whaling population. Gray whales continue to enjoy protection worldwide, apart from a quota of 176 whales harvested each year along the Siberian coast.

Some gray whales are found off the Oregon coast all year, including an estimated 200-400 during summer, although they're most visible and numerous when migrating populations pass through Oregon waters on their way south December-February and northward may spot the handiwork of **beavers**—lodges and dams built of branches and twigs—if not the camera-shy builders themselves. The state's animal mascot is most commonly sighted in second-growth forests near marshes after sunset. Fall is a good time to spot beavers as they gather food for winter.

Although **black bears** proliferate in remote mountain forests of Oregon (the state's Department of Fish and Wildlife estimates that 14,000-19,000 black bears roam the western Cascades and the Coast Range), chances are slim that you'll sight one. Black bears shy away from people except when provoked by the scent of food, when cornered or surprised, or on human intrusion into territory near their cubs.

A little-known oddity of the coast, from southern British Columbia to northern California, is the **mountain beaver** (*Aplodontia rufa*), known locally as "boomers." This most primitive species of living rodents is not actually a beaver but resembles (and is roughly the size of) a grayish-brown guinea pig. Although the animal was first reported by Lewis and Clark, and it's still fairly prevalent, most people have never heard of the boomer, let alone seen one. They thrive in dense understory vegetation such as coniferous forests and coastal scrub. These herbivores eat all types of succulent vegetation, including plants that are inedible to other species such as nettle, bracken fern, and salal. Their predilection for Douglas fir seedlings has made them the scourge of the timber industry.

Another rodent common along the coast is the **nutria,** introduced to Oregon in the 1930s from South America to be farmed for its fur (and meat). After numerous escapes, this furry pest established a niche in the woodlands of the Coast Range. About two feet long and similar in appearance to a true beaver (minus the flat tail), voracious nutrias damage many crop plants in Oregon. Furthermore, they may cause erosion by digging into streambeds or the levees that protect lowlands from floods. Currently, a year-round open season encourages hunting and trapping of this varmint to reduce its numbers.

Other Land Creatures

You won't have to look for long in the coast woodlands or underbrush before you encounter Oregon's best-known invertebrates—**banana slugs**—and lots of them. In few places on earth do these snails-out-of-shells grow as large and in such numbers. The reason is western Oregon's climate: moister than mist but drier than drizzle. This balance and calcium-poor soil enable the native banana slug and the more common European black slug to thrive as the bane of Oregon gardeners. When these 3- to 10-inch squirts of slime are not eating plants, you'll see them moving along at a snail's pace on some sidewalk or forest trail. The sixteen or so species of nonnative slugs that have established themselves in the Pacific Northwest tend to prey on crops and gardens. Native species generally confine themselves to forests and eat indigenous plants.

Another distinctive but rarely sighted resident of coastal forests is the **Pacific giant salamander** (*Dicamptodon tenebrosus*), the largest terrestrial salamander found in the United States and Canada. This stout, mottled brown or blackish amphibian can reach lengths of 13-14 inches from nose to tail. They may be found around cold streams and mountain lakes in damp forests and around stagnant pools in the Kalmiopsis Wilderness. They have been known to climb in shrubs and small trees. Among the few salamanders capable of vocalizing, Pacific giants may produce a sharp, low-pitched, doglike yelp when agitated. Their powerful jaws can inflict a painful bite and make them a formidable predator of just about anything they can catch, including insects, slugs, snails, frogs, snakes, and rodents.

Salmon and Steelhead

In recent decades, dwindling Pacific salmon and steelhead stocks have prompted restrictions on commercial and recreational fishing in order to restore threatened and endangered species throughout the Pacific Northwest. For more information about fish populations and fishing restrictions, visit the Oregon Department of Fish and Wildlife's website (www.dfw.state.or.us).

The salmon's life cycle begins and ends in a freshwater stream. After an upriver journey from the sea of sometimes hundreds of miles, the spawning female deposits 3,000-7,000 eggs in hollows (called redds) she has scooped out of the coarse sand or gravel, where the male fertilizes them. These adult salmon die soon after mating, and their bodies then deteriorate to become part of the food source for young fish.

Within three to four months, the eggs hatch into alevins, tiny immature fish with their yolk sacs still attached. As the alevin exhausts the nutrients in its yolk sac, it enters the fry stage and begins to resemble a very small salmon. The length of time they remain as fry differs among various species. Chinook fry, for example, immediately start heading for saltwater, whereas coho or silver salmon will remain in their home stream for 1-3 years before moving downstream.

The salmon are in the smolt stage when they start to enter saltwater. The 5- to 7-inch smolt will spend some time in the estuary area of the river or stream, while it feeds and adjusts to the saltwater.

When it finally enters the ocean, the salmon is considered an adult. Each species varies in the number of years it remains away from its natal stream, foraging sometimes thousands of miles throughout the Pacific. Chinook can spend as many as seven years away from their nesting (and ultimately their resting) place; most other species remain in the salt for 2-4 years. Theories about how the salmon's miraculous homing instinct works range from electromagnetic impulses in the earth to celestial objects, but one thing has been established with certainty—"the nose knows." When salmon's olfactory orifices were stuffed with cotton and petroleum jelly, they were unable to find their spawning streams. The current belief is that young salmon imprint the odor of their birth stream, enabling them to find their way home years later.

The salmon's traditional predators, such as the sea lion, northern pike minnow, harbor seal, black bear, Caspian tern, and herring gull, pale in comparison to the threats posed by modern civilization. Everything from pesticides to sewage to nuclear waste has polluted Oregon waters, and until mitigation efforts were enacted, dams and hydroelectric turbines threatened to block Oregon's all-important Columbia River spawning route.

History

THE FIRST PEOPLE

No one knows when the first inhabitants took up residence on the Oregon coast, but ongoing research periodically turns up ever-older evidence. In 2002 archaeologists began excavating a site at Indian Sands, in Samuel H. Boardman State Park north of Brookings, which yielded artifacts dating back more than 12,000 years, making it the oldest known site of human activity yet found on the coast. Prior to that discovery, the dig site at Tahkenitch Landing, in the Oregon Dunes near Gardiner, had been the earliest known coastal habitation, dated at 9000-8630 BC. It seems likely that further digs will uncover even older human artifacts, although scientists speculate that the oldest sites lie underwater, dating to a time when sea level was significantly lower.

A popular theory concerning the origins of Native Americans maintains that their ancestors came over from Asia on a land-ice bridge spanning what is now the Bering Strait. Along with archaeological evidence, shipwrecks of Asian craft on the Pacific Coast also support the theory that Native Americans had eastern hemisphere contact. This contention has been further substantiated by facial features and dental patterns common to both peoples, as well as isolated correspondences in ritual, music, and dialect.

Despite common ancestry, the Native Americans on the rain-soaked coast and in the Willamette Valley lived quite differently than those on the drier eastern flank of the Cascade Mountains. People west of the Cascades enjoyed abundant salmon, shellfish, berries, and game. Great broad rivers facilitated travel, and thick stands of the finest softwood timber in the world ensured that there was never a dearth of building materials. A mild climate with plentiful food and resources allowed the wet-siders the leisure time to evolve a startlingly complex culture. This was perhaps best evidenced in their artistic endeavors, theatrical pursuits, and ceremonial gatherings such as the traditional potlatch, where the divesting of one's material wealth was seen as a status symbol. Dentalium and abalone shells, woodpecker feathers, obsidian blades, and hides were especially coveted. Later on, Hudson's Bay blankets were added to this list.

After contact with traders, Chinook—a patois of Native American tongues with some French and English thrown in—became the common language among the diverse native groups that gathered in the Columbia Gorge during the summer solstice. At these powwows, the coast and valley dwellers came into contact with their poorer cousins east of the Cascades.

By the time the white explorers and settlers came, Native American culture was a patchwork of languages and cultural traits as diverse as the topography. Most native coastal communities typically included a dozen or more small bands linked by a common dialect. These bands or villages consisted of an extended family in one or two houses or a larger grouping under a headman. The linguistic and lifestyle divisions between native communities were reinforced by mountains, an ocean too rough for canoes, and other geographic barriers.

EARLY EXPLORERS

In 1542 the Spanish explorer Juan Rodríguez Cabrillo sailed into what are now southern Oregon waters. Although partisans in California may dispute it, there's tantalizingly compelling evidence that the English privateer Francis Drake spent the summer of 1579 at Whale Cove and named the land New Albion, claiming it in the name of Queen Elizabeth. Other voyagers of note included Spain's Sebastián Vizcaíno and Martin de Aguilar (1603) and Don Bruno de Heceta (1775), and England's James Cook and John Meares during the late 1770s, as well as George Vancouver (1792). Robert Gray's 1792 voyage 13 miles up the Columbia River estuary was the first American incursion into the area. A succession of Spanish, English, American, and Russian explorers followed in search of whales as well as sea otter and beaver pelts, and hides for the tallow trade.

A major impetus for exploring this coast was the quest for the Northwest Passage—a sea route connecting the Pacific with the Atlantic. Although the Northwest Passage turned out to be a myth, the fur trade became a basis of commerce and contention between European, Asian, and eventually American governments. The pattern was repeated inland when the English beaver brigades eventually moved down from Canada to set up headquarters on the Columbia near present-day Portland.

Dispatched by President Thomas Jefferson to explore the lands of the Louisiana Purchase and beyond, the first American overland excursion into Oregon was made by the Corps of Discovery, which crossed the continent 1804-1806. Led by Meriwether Lewis and William Clark, the expedition trekked to the mouth of the Columbia in the fall of 1805, spent a wet and miserable winter camped south of the river, and explored as far south as Cannon Beach. Lewis and Clark's trailblazing dramatically accelerated interest in the Oregon Territory, and by 1811 John Jacob Astor's Pacific Fur Company had established the settlement of Astoria, just north of the Corps of Discovery's campsite.

ROGUE RIVER WARS

In the 1850s, a short-lived gold-mining boom in the Rogue River Valley and south coast beaches drew settlers to southern Oregon. Another gold rush, however, had the greatest implications for development of the region. In 1849 the influx of prospectors into California's Sierra Nevada occasioned a housing boom in San Francisco, port of entry to the goldfields. The demand for Coast Range timber and food-stuffs from Oregon's inland agricultural valleys caused downriver Pacific ports such as Astoria and Newport to flourish. As a result, the coastline of California's friendly neighbor to the north was able to develop the necessary economic base for it to prosper and endure.

Like the tragic story played out all across the continent, however, the coming of white settlers to Oregon meant the usurpation of Native American homelands, exposure to European diseases such as smallpox and diphtheria, and the passing of a way of life. Violent conflicts ensued on a large scale with the influx of settlers and government land giveaways, and the mining activity in southern Oregon and on the coast incited the Rogue Indian Wars, when the native peoples along the south coast began to fight back. The conflict lasted for six years, during which more than 2,000 Native Americans died.

The hostilities compelled the federal government to send in troops and to eventually set up treaties with Oregon's first inhabitants. In the aftermath of the Rogue Indian Wars in the 1850s, the Chetco, Coquille, Coos, Umpqua, Siuslaw, Alsea, Yaquina, Nestucca, and Tillamook peoples were grouped together with the Rogue River peoples and forced to live on the 1.1-million-acre Siletz Reservation, which reached from Cape Lookout in Tillamook County to near the mouth of the Umpqua River. The culture and heritage of many indigenous peoples were lost forever. More tragic than the watering down of cultural distinctiveness was the huge mortality rate resulting from people being forcibly removed to the reservation. Of the approximately 3,240 Native Americans moved to the reservation in 1857, disease, starvation, and exposure would reduce their number to 1,015 in 1880; by 1900, only 430 coastal Native Americans survived on the reservation.

Over the years, whatever wealth the Siletz peoples had left was stripped as a result of the United States not honoring a multitude of treaties. The final indignity came in 1951 with the termination of the Siletz Reservation. The divestiture of tribal status meant the loss of health services, educational support, tax exemptions, and other benefits. Predictably, this last in a long line of forced transitions brought about alcoholism and despair for many native peoples. In 1977, Senator Mark Hatfield and Congressman Les AuCoin helped push a bill through Congress for restoration of the Siletz Reservation. This has resulted in the Siletz people getting the wherewithal to flourish economically in everything from logging and construction projects to gaming establishments. The casino endeavor has been accompanied by an interest in the old ways and a renewed sense of pride in Native American identity.

INDUSTRY, EXPLOITATION, AND DEVELOPMENT

The exploitation of Oregon's fishing resources has been an enduring aspect of life in the region for thousands of years. Salmon has always been the most valued species, from prehistory up to modern times. Native Americans on both sides of the Cascades depended on it, and commercial anglers have viewed it as a mainstay for more than a century. Canning technology and fishing methods first perfected in Alaska made their way to Oregon in the 1860s, in time to meet the demands of emerging domestic and foreign markets. Canneries crowded the shores of the Columbia at Astoria and all of the other major rivers down the coast and exported thousands of tons of fish yearly until the dwindling supplies finally closed them down.

Intensive logging of coastal and inland forests supplied sawmills with timber, providing jobs at nearly every port and feeding the building booms of the Pacific Northwest and beyond. A brisk coastal trade developed, as steamships plied Oregon ports on busy routes between San Francisco and Seattle. Before roads were built through the coastal ranges, transportation between coastal communities and the inland valleys was by river, and sternwheelers moved goods and passengers up and down the Siletz, Yaquina, Umpqua, and other navigable rivers. Popular tourist areas developed in Newport, Seaside, and other towns.

In the latter half of the 19th century, rail lines began to connect the coast to the interior, but it took the development of reliable roads to bring the coast out of its isolation. In 1919, Oregon voters approved construction of a north-south coastal route, first called the Roosevelt Military Highway and later the Oregon Coast Highway. The road was completed in 1932, and the last of a dozen magnificent bridges, designed by Oregon's master bridge builder Conde McCullough, was finished in 1936, finally opening up the entire coast to auto travel.

ESSENTIALS

Getting There and Around

BY AIR

North Bend's Southwest Oregon Regional Airport has regularly scheduled commercial service through **SeaPort Airlines** (www.seaportair.com), which flies from North Bend to Portland and Pendleton.

BY BUS

Greyhound has largely abandoned its coastal routes, some of which have been picked up by regional carriers, making for a patchwork quilt of mass-transit providers on the western edge of the state. Add a dearth of city buses and you can understand why it's especially difficult to see this area if you're not traveling by car. In most coastal towns, a local supermarket or convenience store usually acts as the bus stop.

For the north coast, **Northwest Point** (800/442-4106, www.northwest-point.com) buses run a twice-daily coastal loop: Astoria-Warrenton-Gearhart-Seaside-Cannon Beach-Portland's Union Station and back to Astoria.

To get to and from the central coast, **Valley Retriever** (541/265-2253) buses connect Newport with Corvallis, Portland, and Bend.

Porter Stage Lines (541/269-7183, http://porterstageline.com) runs along the southern Oregon coast between North Bend and

© PAUL LEVY

Florence, then turns inland at Florence and goes to Eugene.

Local north coast service in Clatsop County is provided by the Sunset Empire Transportation District, better known as **The Bus** (503/861-RIDE, 503/861-7433, www.ridethebus.org), which provides reasonably frequent transportation around Astoria and along the coast from Warrenton (including Fort Stevens State Park and Fort Clatsop) to Cannon Beach.

On weekdays, **Lincoln County Transit** (541/265-4900, www.co.lincoln.or.us/transit) runs buses several times daily between Lincoln City and Yachats, with numerous stops en route. On the south coast, **Coastal Express** buses (800/921/2871, www.currypublictransit.org) run between North Bend and Brookings, weekdays only.

BY CAR

Ever since the "Daddy Train" linking Portland to Seaside shut down in the 1930s, the automobile has been the vehicle of choice for getting to and around the coast.

Car Rentals

Car rental agencies are not unheard of on the coast, but most visitors drive their own vehicles or rent cars at a big-city airport. Renting a car is pain-free, as long as you plan ahead and have a credit card. The rental chains (Avis, Alamo, Budget, Dollar, Enterprise, National, and Thrifty) have outlets in the main population centers and airports (such as Portland, Medford, and Eugene). Astoria has the most car rental agencies on the coast but still offers far fewer than in larger cities elsewhere. For other locations, check www.american-car.net/car-rental/OR for a statewide directory of car rental agencies.

You can try to save some bucks with an independent operator, but consider that the larger chains have more service centers set up to assist you in case you break down in a backwater. Members of AAA can call 503/222-6734 to receive tow, repair, and insurance services applicable to car rental.

Fuel

Gas is readily available on the Coast Highway, but motorists heading to the coast via some of the 10 main routes through the coast ranges should be aware that there are long stretches without a drop, so be sure to fill up beforehand. Out-of-state visitors will soon learn that Oregon is one of the few states that does not allow motorists to pump their own gas. This, combined with the gas tax levied to help pay for Oregon's roads, helps give the state some of the highest gas prices in the country; however, the state's least expensive gas is often in Coos Bay or Reedsport.

Routes to the Coast

From the I-5 corridor, where most of the state's population is concentrated, 10 main routes will get you to the coast. All are two-lane highways for all or part of the journey through rural hinterlands and the coastal mountains. In addition to the routes described here, there are a number of remote back roads involving at least some travel on gravel roads. These are not necessarily open year-round; winter travelers should use great caution and check road conditions with the **Oregon Department of Transportation** (800/977-ODOT or 800/977-6368 in Oregon, 503/588-2941 out of state, www.tripcheck.com) or by asking in nearby towns.

From Portland, **U.S. 30** runs north through St. Helens and follows the bottomlands along the south bank of the Columbia River to Astoria, 98 miles (about two hours) to the northwest. If you're coming down from the north on I-5, cross the Columbia from Longview, Washington, to Rainier, Oregon, and continue west on U.S. 30 from there.

Busy **U.S. 26** runs west, then angles northwest, from Portland, through agricultural Washington County and then into the woods of the Clatsop State Forest before joining U.S. 101 between Cannon Beach and Seaside (80 miles, 90 minutes). About 25 miles west of Portland, **Highway 6** branches off from U.S. 26 and follows a roller-coaster course alongside the Wilson River to Tillamook (73 miles, about 90 minutes).

A third route from Portland starts with **Highway 99W** and a dozen maddening stop-and-go miles through the strip development of Tigard. Past Newburg you emerge into a lovely countryside of vineyards and hazelnut orchards around Dundee. Pick up **Highway 18** for the second half of the trip, which runs past Oregon's number-one attraction, the Spirit Mountain Casino in Grand Ronde, before you hit the Coast Highway just north of Lincoln City and another Native American-owned casino, Chinook Winds. Note that the casinos attract more than 3 million visitors per year, which helps make Highway 18 one of the most dangerous roads to drive in the state. The 89 miles from Portland to Lincoln City usually take a little over two hours to drive (much longer during rush hours).

From Salem, **Highway 22** runs 26 miles to the west and connects with Highway 18 about midway to the coast (about 1.25 hours).

Farther south, **U.S. 20** curves down from Albany through Corvallis and on to Philomath. From there you can continue 46 miles to Newport (1.5 hours from Albany) or veer southwest on **Highway 34** for a winding 59 miles through a remote section of the Siuslaw National Forest to Waldport (a very pretty two-hour drive from Albany).

Highway 126, from Eugene to Florence, is one of the more direct routes, but after zipping through the flatlands and foothills, curves toward the coast slow this 61-mile trip through Mapleton and alongside the Siuslaw River to a nearly 90-minute drive.

Near Curtin, south of Cottage Grove, leave I-5 for a brief detour on Highway 99 before catching **Highway 38**. This scenic two-lane road—Oregon's "foremost motorcycle road," according to Harley-Davidson—follows the valley of the mighty Umpqua River to Reedsport; allow over an hour for this 57-mile trip. If you're coming from the south on I-5, cut off onto **Highway 138** at Sutherlin to save some miles on this route.

Highway 42 shadows the Coquille River through farm country for much of its course from Roseburg to Coos Bay. Although it is possible to get there in less than two hours, it's a longish 87 miles. Motorists should be aware that this thoroughfare carries more truck traffic than any other interior-to-coast road in Oregon. But weekenders will encounter few trucks and light traffic to impede the enjoyment of the waysides, wineries, and historic buildings. If the southern coast is your destination, branch off on **Highway 42S** at Coquille; from there it's 17 miles to Bandon.

South of Roseburg, if you're partial to pavement (which you definitely should be, except during perfect summer weather), there's no good direct route to the coast. The only option is **U.S. 199** from Grants Pass, skirting the remote eastern edge of the Kalmiopsis Wilderness before dropping into northern California's Smith River Canyon. The highway runs through the awesome giants of Redwoods National Park before hitting the Coast Highway near Crescent City, California. From there, it's 22 miles north up to Brookings. All told, count on about two hours to travel this roundabout, albeit beautiful, 100-mile route.

Driving the Oregon Coast Highway (U.S. 101)

The Main Street of the Oregon coast, this 363-mile National Scenic Byway has been designated an "All-American Road," one of 20 in the country selected for their archaeological, cultural, historic, natural, recreational, and scenic importance.

As such, it's a route to be savored, not hurried through—and that's just as well, because sustained high-speed travel is not among the highway's many qualities. The maximum posted speed on U.S. 101 is 55 miles per hour; the actual average speed is usually 50 mph or less. Along the way, several beach loops and inland routes are often less traveled and offer some outstanding scenery in their own right.

U.S. 101 is a two-lane road most of the way, with occasional passing lanes and four lanes along the main drags of the larger coastal cities. You can count on heavy traffic during summer and holidays, and chances are you'll spend at least a little time getting to know the rear end of a slow-moving log truck or a lumbering Winnebago. Relax. Be prepared to modify your schedule to accommodate inevitable slowdowns, and enjoy the breathtaking scenery surrounding the road.

The automobile may be the first transportation choice for most visitors to the coast, but it's not the only vehicle on the road. Especially in summer, be mindful of bicyclists sharing the shoulder. Hills and dips, tight turns, and foliage can often obscure them from view until the last moment. And always beware of cars whose drivers are paying more attention to the view than to the road.

In winter, heavy rain and wind are possible dangers, and you may encounter thick fog just about any time of year.

The **Oregon Department of Transportation** (800/977-ODOT or 800/977-6368 in Oregon, 503/588-2941 out of state) advises on road conditions by phone and via its excellent and comprehensive **TripCheck website** (www.tripcheck.com).

Sports and Recreation

The outdoor appeal of the Oregon coast is unmatched, and the beaches are only the beginning. Hikes through ancient rainforests, excellent fishing for salmon and steelhead, crabbing and clamming in bays and estuaries, white-water jet-boat rides, hiking, cycle-touring, surfing, whale-watching, and birding are all on the agenda. Following is an overview of recreational opportunities along the coast.

PARK FEES AND PASSES

Many state and federal parks, national recreation areas, trails, picnic areas, and other facilities charge day-use fees, which are separate from overnight camping fees (the exception to this is camping at rustic campsites in national forests, which is covered by the Northwest Forest Pass). At sites that charge fees, the day-use fee is $5 per vehicle at both state parks and federal sites. Visitors can pay for day use at individual sites, or, if you're planning to visit several coastal parks or hike the trails on federal lands, you can save money by purchasing one of the passes described here.

Oregon Pacific Coast Passport

The best deal if you plan to visit many state and federal sites, this pass covers entrance, day-use, and vehicle parking fees at all state and federal fee sites along the entire Oregon portion of U.S. 101. It does not cover the cost of camping at state parks, which is a separate fee. This pass was created to alleviate some of the confusion caused by having to buy different passes at the various federal (Forest Service, National Park Service, Bureau of Land Management or BLM) and state (Oregon Parks and Recreation Department) fee sites along the U.S. 101 corridor.

Sixteen coastal sites managed by the National Park Service, U.S. Forest Service, BLM, and Oregon state parks are covered by the passport, including Fort Stevens State Park, Ecola State Park, Nehalem Bay State Park, Cape Lookout State Park, Fogarty Creek State Recreation Area, Heceta Head Lighthouse Viewpoint, Honeyman State Park, Shore Acres State Park, Fort Clatsop National Memorial, Oregon Dunes National Recreation Area, Sutton Recreation Area, Cape Perpetua Scenic Area, Sand Lake Recreation Area, Drift Creek Falls Trail, Yaquina Head Outstanding Natural Area, and Hebo Lake.

Two basic passports are available, depending on your needs and preferences. An annual passport, valid for the calendar year, is $35. A five-day passport is $10. Passports may be purchased at welcome centers, ranger stations, national forest headquarters, national memorials, and state park offices. Call 800/551-6949 to purchase by credit card or for directions to a convenient location.

State Park Passes

Another option, valid only at Oregon state parks, is to buy a one-year ($30) or two-year ($50) pass. They're available from state park offices, by phone (800/551-6949), and from some sporting goods stores and other vendors. See the **Oregon State Parks website** (www. oregonstateparks.org) for more details and a complete list of vendors.

Northwest Forest Pass

In response to major reductions in timber harvests and cutbacks in federal money, revenue shortfalls have made it hard to keep up trails and campgrounds at a time when the region's population has put more demand on these facilities. The **Northwest Forest Pass** ($5 for one day, $30 one year) is a vehicle-parking pass for the use of many improved trailheads, picnic areas, boat launches, and interpretive sites in the national forests of Oregon and Washington. Funds generated from pass sales go directly to maintaining and improving the trails, land, and facilities. You will see "Northwest Forest Pass Required" signs posted at participating sites. Passes are available at trailhead kiosks or at many local vendors, as well as by phone (800/270-7504).

The Northwest Forest Pass is good all over the Pacific Northwest, eliminating the need to purchase a separate pass with each entrance to another national forest. This pass covers most national park and forest service sites in Oregon and Washington but is not valid for campground fees (with the exception of rustic campsites), concessionaire-operated sites, and Sno-Parks.

National Parks and Federal Recreational Lands Annual Pass

This pass is honored at all U.S. Forest Service, National Park Service, Bureau of Land Management, Bureau of Reclamation, U.S. Fish and Wildlife Service, and U.S. Army Corps of Engineers sites charging entrance or day use fees. Anybody can buy one, and a pass is good for the pass holder and passengers in a noncommercial vehicle at per-vehicle fee areas; and the pass holder plus 3 adults, not to exceed 4 adults, at per-person fee areas. Children under 16 are admitted free. Get additional details or purchase these $80 passes from 888/ASK-USGS (888/275-8747), ext. 1, or http://store.usgs.gov/pass.

BEACHCOMBING

Among the first things a newcomer to the Oregon coast notices are the huge piles of driftwood on the beach. Closer inspection usually reveals other treasures. Beachcombers particularly value agates and Japanese glass fishing floats. The volume and variety of flotsam and jetsam here come courtesy of the region's unique geography. Much of the driftwood, for instance, originates from logging operations located upriver on the many waterways that empty into the Pacific. In addition, storms, floods, rock slides, and erosion uproot many trees that eventually wash up on shore. In addition to driftwood and floats, shells, coral, sand dollars, sea stars, and other seaborne trophies can be best culled from the intertidal zone on south coast beaches. Although you may not always come across a perfectly polished agate or a message in a bottle, you'll probably find beachcombing on the Oregon coast its own reward.

Japanese fishing floats are swept into Oregon waters when the Kuroshio current crosses the Pacific and takes a southerly turn. These balls of green and blue glass sometimes require more than a decade to reach the Oregon coast after breaking free from fishing nets thousands of miles across the sea. Although glass floats are quite rare these days, having largely been replaced by plastic and foam, March is the best time to look for them, especially after two-day storms from the northwest, west-southwest, or due west. In Lincoln City, hand-blown glass floats are planted on the beaches October-May; if you find one of these beauties, it's yours to keep! December-April is the best season to find agates, jaspers, petrified wood, and a variety of fossils. At that time, the gravel bars covered by sand in summer are exposed.

On the southern coast, the Coos Bay sand spit, Bandon's beachfront, the beaches on the western side of Humbug Mountain, and the isolated shorelines of Boardman State Park are choice treasure-hunting spots. Tenmile Creek south of Yachats and Agate Beach north of Newport are the central coast's best places to look. The more settled and accessible north coast has slimmer pickings because of the larger population of resident beachcombers and the higher visitor influx; the best beachcombing is on the Nehalem, Netarts, and Nestucca sand spits.

Even in remote locations, beachcombers may be surprised at the amount of plastic and other debris that washes up. Join with the environmental stewards at SOLV (www.solv.org) and help out with the annual springtime beach cleanup. It's a huge community effort, usually drawing well over 3,000 volunteers to beaches along the Oregon coast.

Consult a **tide chart** anytime you anticipate an extended beachcombing excursion (or any other activity on or near the sea). Half a dozen people perish yearly from being washed off a beach, jetty, or outcropping. Local newspapers usually include tide predictions, and tide charts are available from visitors centers, chambers of commerce, and shops. Online, you can get free tide charts for over 40 coastal locations at www.saltwatertides.com. It's also wise to anticipate weather changes, so bring layers.

BICYCLING

In the wake of the oil shocks of the 1970s, the Oregon legislature allocated 1 percent of the state highway's budget to encourage energy-saving bicycling by developing bike lanes and special parks and campgrounds with bicycle and foot access specifically in mind.

Although not for everybody, biking part or all of the Oregon coast is the surest way to get on intimate terms with this spectacular region. Before going, get a free copy of the extremely useful **The Oregon Coast Bike Route** map from the **Department of Transportation** (1158 Chemeketa St. NE, Salem, OR, 97310, www. oregon.gov) or from coastal information centers and chambers of commerce. This brochure features strip maps of the route, noting services

from Astoria to the California border. With information on campsites, hostels, bike-repair facilities, elevation changes, temperatures, and wind speed, this pamphlet does everything but map the ruts in the road. Because the prevailing winds in summer are from the northwest, most people cycle south on U.S. 101 to take advantage of a steady tailwind. You'll also be riding on the ocean side of the road with better views, easier access to turnouts, and generally wider bike lanes and shoulders. The entire 370-mile (or 380 miles, including the optional Three Capes Scenic Loop) trip involves nearly 16,000 feet of elevation change. Most cyclists cover the distance in 6-8 days, pedaling an average of 50-65 miles daily.

If you want to cycle the full length of the coast, fly into Portland and ride to Astoria. (Unpack your bike and take it on the MAX train if you don't want to ride from the airport into town.) It's a little harder to figure out how to end your trip, as public transportation is rather limited on the southern Oregon coast. Consider riding about 25 miles into California, where you'll find Greyhound service in Crescent City.

On Oregon's roads and highways, bicyclists have the right of way, which means that cars and trucks are not supposed to run you off the road. Most drivers will give you a wide berth and slow down if necessary in tight spots, but remember that there are also motorists whose concepts of etiquette vis-à-vis cyclists were formulated elsewhere. Play it safe: Always wear a helmet and bright or reflective clothing, keep as close to the shoulder of the road as you safely can, and use a light if you must ride at night.

Cycle Tours

Several companies offer preplanned group bicycle trips, with everything from the bicycle to the meals and lodging included. **Bicycle Adventures** (206/786-0989 or 800/443-6060, www.bicycleadventures.com, $2,745 for a six-day trip with hotel accommodations). The **Adventure Cycling Association** (800/755-2453, www.adventurecycling.org, $1,150) runs a week-long tour starting in Eugene and cutting over through Corvallis to Lincoln City, traveling down the coast to Florence, and then riding back to Eugene; accommodations are in campgrounds, but the tour is fully supported, with gear hauled in a van.

CAMPING

Oregon lodging prices are, for the most part, lower than those of neighboring California and Washington. Nonetheless, coastal resort areas can put a strain on the pocketbook. Fortunately, state park and national forest campgrounds proliferate in these areas, offering low-cost overnight lodgings in attractive settings. As if by design, the highest percentage of Oregon's 200 state parks surround the high-ticket areas, with sites usually priced around $20 per night. Most of these have restrooms, showers, fire rings, piped water, and other basic amenities. National Forest campgrounds often cost less but offer more primitive facilities; many of them are chosen for their proximity to swimming holes or scenic appeal.

If creature comforts are a priority, privately owned RV parks and campgrounds are often equipped with every amenity you can ask for, from laundry facilities to game rooms to cable hookups.

State Parks

Despite charging the highest camping fees in the West, the coast's state parks are still the most heavily used (per state park acre) in the country—a tribute to their excellence.

Prices for camping at state parks May 1-September 30 average the following rates: electrical hookup sites $20-28; tent sites $17-20; hiker-biker sites $5-6; yurts $36-41. During the discounted Discovery Season, October 1-April 30, prices drop by a few dollars. The extra vehicle charge during any season is $5-7.

Yurts are available for rent at most state park campgrounds. Yurts are canvas-walled, wood-floored, and equipped with fold-up beds, heaters, and lamps but no bathrooms; they sleep five people. Pets are permitted at some locations.

Most of Oregon's coastal state park

Camping is an affordable option along Oregon's coast.

© PAUL LEVY

campgrounds accept campsite reservations, but a few are first-come, first-served. The state has a central information line, 800/551-6949, and a reservation line, 800/452-5687. Go to www. oregonstateparks.org to look up specific rates or to get information. You can also make reservations for any of these options online with a Visa or MasterCard through **ReserveAmerica** (800/452-5687, www.reserveamerica.com). Reservations may be made from two days up to nine months in advance. In addition to the campsite fee, an $8 reservation fee is charged. Telephone hours are 8am-7pm Monday-Friday.

If you need to cancel your reservation three days or more before your scheduled arrival, call **Reservations Northwest** (800/452-5687 statewide, 503/731-3411 in Portland). Two or fewer days before your trip, call the park directly to cancel your reservation. Phone numbers for all parks are found on each individual park's website (www.oregonstateparks.org). Cancellation service fees and requirements for special facilities, such as yurts and cabins, may vary. Your $8 reservation fee is nonrefundable, and the first night's camping fee will be charged if you cancel in the last two days. If you reserve through ReserveAmerica, the cancellation policy differs; see its website for details.

National Forests

The U.S. Forest Service maintains campsites, trails, and day-use areas in both the Siuslaw and Siskiyou National Forests. The Siuslaw National Forest encompasses more than 630,000 acres and is situated within the Oregon Coast Range. It's one of only two national forests in the Lower 48 that include beachfront area. The Siskiyou National Forest is located in the Klamath Mountains and the coast ranges of southwestern Oregon, with a small segment of the forest extending into northern California and the Siskiyous. It includes 1,163,484 acres within its boundaries, 69,234 acres of which are owned or privately managed by other agencies. Within the boundaries of these two national forests, there are hundreds of choices. Refer to the **Forest Service** website (www.fs.fed.us.gov/recreation) for listings.

Campsites generally include a table, a fire grate, and a tent or trailer space. Electric hookups are not available, although most campgrounds have water and vault or flush toilets. Most overnight sites require a user fee. You may camp in the forest a maximum of 14 days out of every 30. Fees are $10-20 for campsites and $5-7 for an extra vehicle. Campsites can be reserved online with a Visa or MasterCard through www.recreation.gov or 800/452-5687.

It's important to note that National Forest passholders who plan to use specialized facilities (such as camping, trailhead, parking, boat launch, ramps, swimming sites, etc.) in the national forest still have to pay for an overnight campsite.

RVs

The Oregon coast is a summer haven for RVers, with activities in each coastal town designed to appeal to this perennial visitor. RV sites in private parks and state parks are abundant but can fill up as early as April with travelers fleeing the hot winds of the California desert for the balmy climes of the coast. Many RV grounds are open year-round, but some are seasonal, responding to the number of visitors.

Along the coast, many service stations, truck stops, campgrounds, and RV parks provide RV sanitary dump stations. Local chambers of commerce and visitors centers can provide information on activities for seniors, RV-friendly sites, and other services.

FISHING

Since the first people arrived on these shores 12,000 or more years ago, Oregon's rich coastal waters have provided sustenance and sport. The king of fish, in terms of economic impact as well as recreational activity, is the salmon. The once-abundant fish was a self-replenishing gold mine that enriched the state and fueled the development of coastal towns like Astoria and Gold Beach.

In the modern era, Oregon salmon fisheries grew into a megabusiness, until stocks dramatically declined in the 1990s. The many factors that caused the decline are complex and fraught with political tension. In the early days, fish wheels and nets depleted rivers once so choked with spawning fish that a pioneer pitchfork stuck haphazardly into the water would often yield a salmon. Dam construction and pollution joined overfishing to further reduce the catch. Watersheds have been compromised by clear-cuts, which increase erosion that clogs spawning streams with silt and mud and reduces shaded riparian environments for the cold-water-loving salmon. Cattle grazing has also affected spawning areas with collapsed stream banks and polluted water.

Despite the habitat degradation and other pressures, there have recently been several good salmon years as well as poor ones. The numbers of returning salmon can vary greatly from year to year, and according to seasonal runs (the spring run of chinook may be healthy, while the fall run is not). In addition, each coastal river has its own unique run of salmon, and due to a great many factors, different rivers often have salmon runs of varying strength.

If salmon fishing is a crucial element of your trip to the Oregon coast, it's a good idea to contact a local outfitter to find out what the salmon run will be like during your visit, and which waters will be open for sportfishing.

Runs of spring and fall chinook, coho, and steelhead draw thousands of anglers to the coast each year. Fleets of charter boats operate out of all the navigable ports on the coast, and there are countless opportunities for do-it-yourselfers from boats, banks, jetties, and piers.

Past salmon shortfalls have spawned alternative ocean fisheries. Bottom fishing for black lingcod and rockfish, together with the harvest of such long-ignored species as hake, whiting, and pollock, have increased in proportion to the decline of salmon, flounder, albacore tuna, smelt, and halibut. Growing out of the pollock fishery has been the development of a successful *surimi* (artificial crab) industry, supplying Asian and U.S. markets. Be that as it may, the aggressive harvest of the 55 species of rockfish that are marketed as red snapper brought about catch limits in 2000, giving another signal that fisheries are in transition.

Where and When to Go

Salmon are targeted offshore as well as in freshwater. For up-to-date information on exactly where, when, and how you can fish—which is subject to frequent change—get a copy of the **Oregon Department of Fish and Wildlife**'s regulations (2501 SW 1st Ave., Portland, 503/872-5268, www.dfw.state.or.us), available at sporting goods stores and many other outlets; better yet, check the website for the most current information.

In addition to chinook and coho salmon and steelhead in scores of coastal rivers, the Kilchis and Miami Rivers near Tillamook see Oregon's only runs of chum salmon, in the fall; this is a catch-and-release fishery only. Another catch-and-release-only species is wild sea-run cutthroat trout, which return to the Alsea River and Yaquina Bay, among other waterways, in summer. Sturgeon is a popular game fish (weighing into the hundreds of pounds) in the larger rivers, particularly the Columbia and the Umpqua.

Bottom fishing for rockfish and other species is pretty much a year-round activity—depending on the weather. Warm ocean currents bring albacore tuna in August and September, and halibut are usually available in summer, although the season is variable and is set yearly by the Pacific Fishery Management Council.

Charters and Guides

Major charter-fishing centers on the coast include Astoria, Hammond, Warrenton, Garibaldi, Depoe Bay, Newport, Winchester Bay, Charleston, Gold Beach, Bandon, and Brookings. Charter rates vary a bit, but typical prices up and down the coast are $100 for a half day (5-6 hours) of bottom fishing; $175 for a full eight-hour day of salmon or bottom fishing; $225 for 12 hours of tuna fishing; and $185 for a 10-hour halibut charter. Chambers of commerce in each town can also provide extensive listings.

Crabbing and Clamming

Egalitarian ventures that require a minimum of gear, crabbing and clamming are popular ways to land a delicious meal. The Oregon Department of Fish and Wildlife's *Sport Fishing Regulations* booklet has details, or check its website (www.dfw.state.or.us) for more information. Crabbing requires a **shellfish license** ($7 resident, $11.50 for a 3-day nonresident license) that's available just about anyplace that rents traps or sells fishing gear.

Crabbing just requires a trap, ring, or pot and some bait (veteran crabbers recommend rotting raw poultry—chicken or turkey backs and necks). Opinions vary about the best time to crab, but many agree that an incoming tide yields the best catches. Just drop your trap in a likely spot, with a tethered float marking the spot, and haul it up 15-30 minutes later—hopefully full of legal-size male Dungeness crabs. A handy item to have is a crab caliper, a gauge that measures the minimum-size crabs you can keep. Bait shops and marinas can instruct you on how to catch dinner. Boats and crab pots are usually available to rent at these places. If boats are unavailable, many harbors have public piers. Some of the best crabbing spots are the estuaries of the Coos, Siuslaw, Yaquina, Tillamook, Netarts, and Nehalem Rivers. Bays and estuaries are open for Dungeness crab year-round; the ocean is open year-round except August 15-November 30.

A spade or small pitchfork—and a bucket to carry away your take—are all you need to dig clams on beaches and mudflats. Large gaper clams, cockles, soft-shells, and littlenecks are the most common clams found in tidewater areas, while prized razor clams are found on north coast beaches. With the exception of the summer closure for razor clams north of Tillamook Head, the season on shellfish is year-round in Oregon. Low tides, particularly morning minus tides during spring and summer, are the best times for clamming. Mussels are also available for harvest from rocky intertidal areas. Note that all oyster beds are privately owned. Check the *Sport Fishing Regulations* for catch limits, and before harvesting always inquire locally or contact the **Recreational Shellfish Hot Line** (503/986-4728 or 800/448-2474) to get current information on shellfish toxins and quarantines.

HIKING

Opportunities for hiking abound on the coast, from short loops suitable for just about anyone to the magnificent Coast Trail running the entire length of the coast, and a myriad of choices in between. Wherever you choose your outing, here are some suggestions to help keep the environment as natural as possible:

- Stay on the trails so you do not increase the rate of erosion or destroy such fragile vegetation as dune and wetland wildflowers.

- Use established campsites, and avoid digging tent trenches or cutting vegetation.

- In wilderness areas, camp several hundred feet from water sources. Bring a tool to dig a latrine, and make it at least six inches deep.

- If you pack it in, pack it out. Leave nothing but footprints.

- Avoid feeding wild animals so you don't inhibit their natural instinct to fend for themselves.

The Oregon Coast Trail

For 362 miles, from the Columbia River to the California border, the **Oregon Coast Trail** hugs the beaches and headlands, leading hikers into intimate contact with some of the most beautiful landscapes anywhere. Most of the trail runs through public lands, although some portions traverse easements on private parcels, and the trail follows the highway and city streets in several places. The only coastal long-distance treks separated from U.S. 101 are the 30 miles between Seaside and Manzanita and between Bandon and Port Orford. A free trail map and directory are available from the **Oregon state parks information center** (800/551-6949, www.oregonstateparks.org). This pamphlet makes it clear where the trail crosses open beaches, forested headlands, the shoulder of the

Coast Highway, and even city streets in some towns. Be sure to bring water, particularly on northerly sections of the trail, because much of the trek is on beachfront away from a potable water supply.

WHALE-WATCHING

Whale-watching charters of various kinds are offered along the coast from December into the spring. By land or by sea, early morning hours are best because winds can whip up whitecaps later in the day, obscuring the signs of surfacing whales. Remember to bring your binoculars and sunglasses. If you go by boat, dress warmly, take precautions against seasickness, and expect to get wet if you go out on deck.

You don't need to be on a boat or plane to successfully spot whales, however. Coastal headlands and beaches provide excellent vantage points from which to spy the gray whales on their 10,000-mile round-trip between Baja and the arctic, the longest migratory movement by land or sea of any mammal. It's possible to spot whales here year-round because several hundred have taken up permanent or semipermanent residence in Oregon waters, but whales are far more numerous (and your chances of sighting them far better) during their twice-yearly migrations. The southward migration along the Oregon coast lasts until early February, although their numbers usually peak around the last week in December. Whales migrating northward can be sighted off Oregon March-May, with numbers usually peaking in late March. Recently, changing weather and current patterns seem to have induced a growing number of whales to remain off Oregon throughout the summer, June-October, but the peak times are August, September, and October.

By Land

Just about any coastal location with a view of the sea holds the potential for a whale sighting, but some spots are definitely better than others. Offshore reefs supporting the proliferation of amphipods, the food of the gray whale, are conducive to sightings. Combine the latter with a promontory such as Cape Perpetua or Yaquina Head and you increase your chances even more.

Whale Watching Spoken Here (www.oregonstateparks.org) is an organization of enthusiastic trained volunteers who staff 28 prime whale-watching sites in Oregon during key weeks of the gray whale migrations. In coordination with the Oregon Parks and Recreation Department, these folks provide information and assist in spotting whales 10am-1pm December 26-January 2 and through the week of spring break in late March. Get more information from the website.

These sites, marked by "Whale Watching Spoken Here" signs during Whale Watch Weeks, are among the best vantage points any time of year. From north to south, with their nearest town, they are:

- Ecola State Park (Cannon Beach)

- Neahkahnie Mountain Historic Marker Turnout (Manzanita)

- Cape Meares State Scenic Viewpoint (Three Capes Scenic Loop)

- Cape Lookout State Park (Three Capes Scenic Loop)

- Inn at Spanish Head (Lincoln City)

- Boiler Bay State Scenic Viewpoint (Depoe Bay)

- Depoe Bay Sea Wall (Depoe Bay)

- The Whale Watching Center (Depoe Bay)

- Rocky Creek State Scenic Viewpoint (Depoe Bay)

- Cape Foulweather (Depoe Bay)

- Devil's Punchbowl State Natural Area (Otter Rock)

- Yaquina Head Lighthouse (Newport)

- Don A. Davis City Kiosk (Nye Beach, Newport)

- Yaquina Bay State Recreation Site (Newport)

- Devil's Churn Viewpoint (Yachats)

- Cape Perpetua Overlook (Yachats)

- Cape Perpetua Interpretive Center (Yachats)

- Cook's Chasm Turnout (Yachats)

- Sea Lion Caves Turnout (north of Florence)

- Umpqua Lighthouse (Winchester Bay)

- Shore Acres State Park (Charleston)

- Face Rock Wayside State Scenic Viewpoint (Bandon)

- Cape Blanco Lighthouse (Port Orford)

- Battle Rock Wayfinding Point (Port Orford)

- Cape Sebastian (Gold Beach)

- Cape Ferrelo (Brookings)

- Harris Beach State Park (Brookings)

By Sea

Depoe Bay and Newport are the centers for whale-watching, attracting the majority of the state's whale-watching visitors. Other major ports are Charleston, Winchester Bay, and Garibaldi, but you'll find whale-watching charters operating out of just about all the ports along the coast. Rates range $25-75 per person for a 2-3-hour tour. See each destination for specific charter companies and details.

Accommodations and Food

ACCOMMODATIONS

Coastal accommodations run the gamut from campgrounds and humble fishing lodges to bona fide five-star resorts. In between you will find a kaleidoscopic range that include condominiums rented as guest rooms, bed-and-breakfasts, vacation rentals, a lighthouse keeper's quarters, yurts, a paddle-wheeler, and a plethora of conventional motels.

Regardless of the lodging, you'll generally pay more for direct access to the beach or for an ocean view. If you're willing to walk a block or two, or settle for a view of mountains or forests, you'll probably save a few dollars.

Finally, keep in mind that a hotel reservation at many lodgings *does not* guarantee exactly what you reserved. Regardless of how far in advance you reserve or even if you give your credit card number, all you are really guaranteed is a room. Especially during peak season, this may translate to the whole family piling onto a king-size bed for a dubious night's rest,

sleeping in a foul-smelling smokers' den, or perhaps bedding down in a dingy closet-size cell instead of the suite you requested. Nonsmoking rooms, bed configurations, and preferred room styles are often given out to confirmed-reservation guests on a first-come, first-served basis. To avoid problems, clarify your room type and the check-in time when you make the reservation, and schedule an early check-in time (most hotels have mid-afternoon vacancies available) that may be followed up by an afternoon activity.

In our descriptions of lodgings, the price that we quote is for the lowest-priced double room during high season (summer). Although there's no sales tax in Oregon, note that you will find local lodging taxes—ranging 8-12 percent, depending on the locale—added to your bill.

Cutting Costs

Prices along the coast peak during summer, a flexible term that generally means Memorial

Day to Labor Day. In summer, as well as during spring break, many destinations fill up, and you'll need to reserve well in advance if you don't want to sleep in your car. Many lodgings drop their rates a bit during spring and fall shoulder seasons. In winter, euphemistically called the storm-watching season, room rates can drop still further, sometimes approaching 50 percent less, with special weekend-getaway packages being quite common. This can be a wonderful time for a stay at the coast, when the crowds are long gone and the sea and sky are at their most dramatic. When making a reservation, it pays to ask (or check the lodging's website) about specials and discounts.

The cost-conscious traveler should also keep in mind that there is no shortage of large condos and vacation homes that rent out to large parties who can split costs.

Paying More

As noted, lodging prices along the coast peak in the summer, when rather unexceptional motel rooms go for close to $100. If your budget can tolerate it, this is a good time to investigate some of the slightly more expensive B&Bs and lodges. The difference in quality between a $95 highway-side motel and a $130 B&B room can be astounding and can make for a far more memorable and enjoyable trip.

Vacation Rentals

B&Bs can add to a romantic weekend on the coast, but these establishments don't make sense all the time for everyone. This book also lists property rental agencies and realty companies in certain locations whose properties afford more privacy. Deals are plentiful, thanks to the volume of vacation homes that often sit idle or can accommodate large enough parties to offset a high nightly rate.

FOOD AND DRINK

Visiting gourmets can tell you why many people will happily drive two hours from Portland for a meal at any number of coastal restaurants: Inventive chefs who fully exploit the freshest regional ingredients—wild chanterelles, fiddlehead ferns, marionberries, locally made cheeses, Oregon wines, and, of course, seafood—mean that limited notions of clam chowder and greasy fish-and-chips are long out of date. Not that there aren't plenty of eateries along the coast where everything but your salad—if you can get one—has been battered and deep-fried; it's just that now there are plenty of exciting alternatives. The coast seems to attract restaurateurs who want to dispel the old myths about the region being a culinary backwater, and here they can start with unbeatable raw materials to work their craft on, especially when it comes to seafood. The fish, oysters, crab, and clams here are as fresh as they can be. At many restaurants, it's a very short trip from the boat to the plate, with a short detour through the kitchen.

Not so long ago, coffee on the coast meant a thin, vengeful, and bitter brew that tasted like bilgewater. How things have changed! Now, it seems as if every bait shop and gas station has a neon "Espresso" sign glowing warmly in its window, and latte addicts no longer have to suffer through withdrawals as they drive U.S. 101.

Tipping

Tipping for food service is customary but discretionary. As elsewhere in Oregon, the suggested rate of recompense for acceptable service is 15-20 percent. Diners in larger parties (usually six or more) may find that a restaurant enforces a mandatory tipping policy as part of the bill.

Coastal Cuisine

What will newcomers to the Oregon coast notice most on their plates? The coast boasts such delicacies as Dungeness crab, razor clams, Yaquina Bay oysters, and bay shrimp, as well as world-famous salmon.

Let's start with the bay shrimp as an appetizer. Although a hasty visual appraisal of an Oregon shrimp cocktail might prompt an unfavorable comparison to the larger gulf prawns, these savory morsels prove that good things come in small packages. Expect them to be in season during August. Another

I.C.M.
Biggest Selection of Wild Caught
SeaFood on the Oregon coast

Shell Fish

Lobster Tail
Manila Clams
Mussels
Mexican Prawns
Razor Clams
Dungeness Crab
Calamari
Octopus
Oysters

I.C.M.
Biggest Selection of
SeaFood on the Oregon coast

ALL YOU CAN EAT CRAB EVERYDAY!

I.C.M.
Biggest Selection of Wild Caught
SeaFood on the Oregon coast

Fish Choices

Salmon
Halibut
Alaskan Cod
Albacore Tuna
Mahi Mahi
Yellow Fin Tuna
Fillet of Sole
Pacific Snapper
Sea Bass

© BILL MCRAE

Coastal restaurants offer a variety of freshly caught seafood.

coveted crustacean is the Dungeness crab. Few West Coast chefs have mastered the succulence of Maryland-style crab cakes, but the Dungeness tastes richer in a cocktail than the less meaty Atlantic blue crab. The firm texture of Dungeness in its wintertime peak season has been compared to that of Maine lobster.

Speaking of which, those used to *Homarus americanus* from the East Coast will be disappointed by the oversize crayfish passed off as lobster on some menus. Freshwater crawdads here are another distant cousin. Among mollusks, Oregon's Yaquina Bay oysters are considered gourmet fare. If you want them fresh, avoid the summer months and wait until the weather is cooler. Razor clams are another indigenous shellfish—an acquired taste for some. Once you get past their rubbery consistency, however, you might enjoy this local favorite. Local mussels and albacore tuna near the end of July are also worth a try.

When it comes to fresh fish, you'll notice a variance in price based on how the salmon was caught. Troll-caught salmon (usually chinook and coho in Oregon) are landed in the ocean by hook and line, one at a time. This method permits better handling than netted salmon, which are caught in large groups as they come upriver from the ocean to spawn. Thus you'll pay more for troll-caught salmon, but you can taste the difference. Currently, as efforts are undertaken to restore the species in the Pacific Northwest, most grocery-store and some restaurant salmon come from Alaska or fish farms in Canada. There are limited stocks of Oregon-caught salmon available, however, and it pays to be sensitive to nuances of how they are harvested as well as preparation.

Spring chinook salmon (Apr.-May) from the Rogue River is a can't-miss item for almost everyone. Although red snapper would normally also merit such an assessment, this is not always the situation in Oregon, largely because of a case of mistaken identity. In contrast to the red snapper found on southern and eastern U.S. menus, this Pacific version is a bottom fish. The brown widow rockfish and dozens of other bottom fish species that receive the "red

THE COAST'S BEST BAKERIES

There's nothing like a ginger scone after a morning of beachcombing . . . unless it's a still-warm cinnamon roll. The following bakeries are the real deal—no doughy white bread that ends up as gull food.

- **Astoria—Blue Scorcher.** Come for a cardamom almond roll, and then return for lunch. They make great vegetarian sandwiches, and the people-watching is first rate. Fridays feature a range of gluten-free pastries and sandwiches.

- **Gearhart—Pacific Way Bakery and Cafe.** The café next door is locally famous; forget the struggle to get a table there and settle in with a pastry from the bakery.

- **Cannon Beach—Waves of Grain.** Head south of downtown for the Tillamook cheese biscuits and marionberry scones.

- **Pacific City—Grateful Bread.** French toast made from challah bread, gingerbread pancakes, and the town's best pizza make this airy café a place to spend some time.

- **Newport—Panini Bakery.** Who needs the beach when you've got a cup of coffee and a chocolate panini?

- **Yachats—Green Salmon.** After a morning at the Green Salmon, you'll be checking the real estate ads for your own little Yachats bungalow.

- **Florence—The Shed.** Stop by for a muffin and a chat with the friendly baker.

snapper" designation out here have a similar consistency but a fishier taste than their East Coast counterpart.

Despite the many delicacies available on the Oregon coast, it *is* still possible to have a bad meal in the region. In fact, the quality of the cuisine in some smaller towns is a source of self-deprecating humor for the locals. As many Yankees will tell you, there is no shortage of bland New England-style clam chowder on the Oregon coast. And some of the freshest fish can be had at even the most basic chowder house along the coast, although it may be fried to a crisp.

Still, it's easy to dine well at an affordable price; the region abounds in places with genuine ambience and home cooking at a good value.

Alcohol

As more and more wineries and wine outlets pop up throughout Oregon, it's exciting to match Oregon wines with locally grown produce and freshly caught fish and seafood. Particularly notable for coastal travelers focused on fish and seafood are Oregon wines made from Pinot gris and Chardonnay grapes. Pinot gris grows well in the cool valleys of western Oregon and makes a light-bodied off-dry wine that's a perfect complement to most seafood meals. Oregon's version of chardonnay is light and citrusy without the cloying butteriness that typifies many California chardonnays. It makes a great addition to a meal of fresh oysters.

Please note Oregon's liquor laws: Liquor is sold by the bottle in state liquor stores, which are open Monday-Saturday; many now offer limited Sunday hours as well. Beer and wine are sold in grocery stores and retail outlets any day of the week. Liquor is sold by the drink in licensed establishments 7am-2:30am. The minimum drinking age throughout the state is 21.

Health and Safety

EMERGENCY SERVICES

Throughout Oregon, dial **911** for medical, police, or fire emergencies. There are hospital facilities in Gold Beach, Bandon, Coos Bay, Florence, Newport, Seaside, and Astoria with 24-hour emergency rooms. Medical costs are high here, as in the rest of the United States. Emergency room care is the most expensive.

COASTAL HAZARDS

Whether you're merely admiring its natural beauty or braving its waves, the Oregon coast holds potential dangers. Children are especially at risk because they can be easily distracted by tidepools and sand castle construction, and they may not be aware of tidal changes, shifts in weather, or other natural dangers. For both adults and children, a little common sense goes a long way.

Hypothermia

The cold temperatures of Oregon's coastal waters (as low as 40-45°F) make swimming and other water sports potentially dangerous any time of year. Even in the hottest days of summer, sea temperature doesn't exceed 62°F. Hypothermia—a condition that sets in when the core temperature of the body drops to 95°F or below—is a danger visitors should be aware of. Hikers and others engaging in outdoor activities away from the water can be at risk as well, particularly when the weather is cool and windy.

One of the first signs of hypothermia is a diminished ability to think and act rationally. Speech can become slurred, and uncontrollable shivering usually takes place. Stumbling, memory lapses, and drowsiness also tend to characterize those afflicted. Unless the body temperature can be raised several degrees by a knowledgeable helper, cardiac arrhythmia or arrest may occur. A wet human body loses heat 23 times faster than a dry one, so getting out of the water and being sheltered from the wind

and rain in a dry warm environment are essential for survival. This might mean placing the victim into a prewarmed sleeping bag, which can be prepared by having another person strip and climb into the bag with the endangered person. Ideally, a ground cloth should be used to insulate the sleeping bag from cold surface temperatures. Internal heat can be generated by feeding the victim high-carbohydrate snacks and hot liquids. Placing wrapped heated objects against the victim's body is also a good way to restore body heat. Be careful, however, not to raise body heat too quickly, which could also cause cardiac problems. If body temperature doesn't drop below 90°F, chances for complete recovery are good; with body temperatures between 80-90°F, victims are more likely to suffer lasting damage. Most victims won't survive a body temperature below 80°F.

Measures you can take to prevent hypothermia include avoiding the cold water of the Pacific, eating a nutritious diet, avoiding overexertion followed by exposure to wet and cold, and dressing warmly in layers of wool and polypropylene. Wool insulates even when wet, and because polypro wicks moisture away from your skin, it makes a good first layer. Gore-Tex and its counterparts make for more comfortable rain gear than nylon because they don't become cumbersome and hot. Finally, wear a hat to avoid heat loss through your head.

Swimming Hazards

Hypothermia aside, casual waders and swimmers alike are at risk of being swept off by riptides or undertows, which occur when one layer of water flows against the direction of the surface water. These powerful, usually localized, currents can be found just about anyplace along the coast and would be a challenge even to swimmers of Olympic ability. What every swimmer must know is that when caught in a riptide, one should swim with or across the current, not against it, which will only exhaust you; rather, try to swim parallel to shore, edging closer and closer to shore until it's possible to come in or call for help.

Floating debris is another concern for swimmers and waders. Storms can churn up inland riverbanks, yielding huge floating logs, which are then carried in to shore along the backs of waves. These heavy objects can slam into swimmers or pin them down, so give these potential killers a wide berth.

Sharks

"No, dude, that's a porpoise." That's what one Oregon coast surfer said a moment before the great white shark bit his foot. Although shark attacks are rare in Oregon, they do occasionally occur.

The most common areas for an attack are places where rivers enter the ocean. Some of these places, such as Florence's South Jetty, are also popular surfing spots. Anyone who goes into the ocean should seriously consider taking some precautions.

Because sharks can detect minute amounts of blood, don't go into the water if you're bleeding—this includes menstruating. Stay near other surfers, and don't go too far out from shore. Avoid areas where anglers have been using bait, or where birds are circling. Also, know that sharks are most active at twilight and after dark, and that they tend to hang out near steep drop-offs. Some experts note that shiny jewelry could resemble fish scales to a shark and that they could be attracted to brightly colored clothing (your rental wetsuit will almost certainly be black, making you resemble, above all else, a seal).

If you see a shark, or something you can't quite identify, swim quickly and calmly to shore. If you are attacked by a shark, fight. Try to punch it on the nose, eye, or gills, using your board if possible. Do not play dead! Alert other surfers if they don't hear your screams, and as soon as it lets go, swim to shore immediately.

Boating

Life jackets or vests are strongly advised for anyone aboard a watercraft. In 2003, a tragic fishing accident on Tillamook Bay yielded stark proof that life vests save lives. A 35-foot charter boat capsized while crossing the bar in rough conditions. Eleven people—none wearing life vests—were lost. In addition to keeping a person afloat and face-up, whether or not he or she can swim, the vests provide some insulation from the frigid water, decreasing the risk of hypothermia and injury.

State law requires that all children ages 12 and younger must wear a Coast Guard-approved personal flotation device (PFD)/life vest while on an open deck or cockpit of sailboats or motorized and nonmotorized vessels (such as canoes, kayaks, and rafts). Life vests are a smart idea for small children any time they're near the water.

Dangerous Terrain

Part of the appeal of the coast is its rugged terrain and raw natural state—two features that can also make it a dangerous place to explore. High cliffs, undesignated trails, rocky outcroppings, tidepools, and pocket beaches often lure intrepid hikers bent on getting that perfect view or photo opportunity. These are the same folks who are rescued from cliff tops, stranded by a changing tide, or worse. In other words, stay on designated paths, avoid unfenced cliff edges, check your tide tables, and follow signage. The worst damage is often done to the environment, when hikers trample a native species habitat or disturb organisms living in tidal areas. Please stay on paths and avoid climbing on rocks that may be home to living things.

Sneaker Waves

Many a visitor to Oregon's coast has been the victim of the potentially deadly "sneaker wave." Not as uncommon as one might imagine, these treacherous out-of-nowhere waves have a habit of cropping up when you least expect them. Most prevalent during the stormiest times of the year, sneaker waves are powerful enough to knock an angler from his or her perch or sweep an unsuspecting beachcomber out to sea. Unfortunately, small children are most vulnerable, so constant supervision is a must.

Tsunamis

A tsunami is not just one wave; it is a series of waves that are the direct result of seismic activity, such as earthquakes or marine quakes. A tsunami may begin in the middle of the ocean as a two-foot wave heading for shore at several hundred miles per hour—by this definition, it may sound like a great opportunity to put your surfing skills to the test—but once it reaches land or a harbor, it can strike with devastating force.

As a tsunami draws closer to the shore, driven by the force of the quake, it takes in preceding waters and builds into a series of waves traveling as fast as 500 miles per hour and reaching as high as 100 feet. Waves of this size would submerge whole towns; smaller ones would cause major property damage and threaten the lives of those in its path.

Along the coast, you will see blue-and-white tsunami evacuation signs, which warn locals and visitors of impending danger and direct them to higher, safer ground. Visitors should also be aware of the global alarm system, which sounds off when tsunami danger is high. To be fully prepared, one must be attuned to any news of seismic activity in the area or in the Pacific Rim. Also note that any dramatic change in water levels that are not part of the normal tidal activity may be nature's own early warning that a tsunami may be minutes away.

© BILL MCRAE

Signs along the coast point the way to safer ground in the event of a tsunami warning.

Even the unexpected large breaker can have the same effect as the rogue wave. So, be mindful of the everyday risks of strolling the beach or admiring the vista. Pocket beaches rimmed with cliffs are especially hazardous, as are rocky areas. A flat, gradually sloping sand beach is usually safer, but not without some risk.

Information and Services

TIPS FOR TRAVELERS
Access for Travelers with Disabilities

The **Access Pass,** which allows free entry to designated federal recreation areas such as national parks and monuments, Bureau of Land Management lands, and U.S. Fish and Wildlife sites, is available to those who are blind or permanently disabled. The pass is free to qualified applicants ($10 processing fee); get details from the **U.S. Geological Survey** (http://store.usgs.gov).

The **Oregon Department of Fish and Wildlife** (503/872-5263, www.dfw.state.or.us) puts out a really good guide called *Access Oregon*, which lists accessible recreation areas.

FESTIVALS AND EVENTS

It seems there's some kind of festival or other event happening just about every week somewhere on the coast. Celebrations revolving around cultural or historical heritage, food and wine, crafts, kites, sand castles, windsurfing, the arts—you name it, and there's probably a festival dedicated to it—and more sprout up every year. Most are concentrated during summer, when the choices can be overwhelming.

SHOPPING

Visitors can revel in the shopping opportunities on the coast, which include a profusion of shops selling local art, collectibles and antiques, handmade items, as well as the requisite T-shirts and trinkets.

If it's mall-type shopping you live for, the **Seaside Factory Outlets Center** (1111 N. Roosevelt Dr., 503/717-1603, www.seaside-outlets.com) has 30 big-name manufacturers with designer labels and national brands. With products (of all quality levels) at about 20-50 percent below regular retail price, the center is also home to one of the best wine shops on the Oregon Coast, featuring more than 850 labels, plus 309 imported and domestic beers. Lincoln City is home to another outlet mall, **Tanger Outlets** (1500 SE East Devils Lake Rd., 541/996-5000), with similar offerings.

For unique arts and crafts, the coastal resort areas are overflowing with the work of local and nationally known potters, woodworkers, painters, jewelers, and glass artisans. While these arts cottage industries don't have the bottom line of timber and agriculture, they are one of the more visible and appreciated forms of economic activity on the coast.

Seasonally, farm stands, farmers markets, and you-pick options dot the routes to the coast. Oregon berries (so quick to ripen that their unparalleled sweetness is more likely to be appreciated in jams and ice cream than in the supermarket) and other indigenous treats can be bought direct from the farmer. Oregon coast stores also purvey locally made food products, which make excellent gifts. You'll come across Oregon jams, smoked fish, hazelnuts, wines, cheese, sweets, and similar products.

MONEY

Oregon has no state sales tax, which makes purchases at the coast all the more attractive, particularly to out-of-state visitors. Major credit cards are widely accepted at shops, lodgings, restaurants, and other establishments, but not everywhere. Acceptability of personal checks varies; it's best to ask beforehand. Traveler's checks in U.S. currency, issued by major firms such as American Express, are generally accepted with an official photo ID.

Nearly all the towns covered in this guide have numerous banks or other businesses with an ATM, which makes getting cash easy. In addition, large grocery stores, such as Fred Meyer, Safeway, Ray's, and Clark's, all with numerous coastal locations, usually have an ATM or offer cash back with a debit-card purchase.

COMMUNICATIONS AND MEDIA

For major newspapers, either the Portland *Oregonian* or the *Eugene Register Guard* is normally available on the coast.

Even though regional monthlies such as *Northwest Travel* and *Sunset* magazines do not have a strictly Oregon focus, there are usually several destination pieces about the state in each edition. Sold throughout the state, *Oregon Coast* magazine is an excellent bimonthly about life on Oregon's western edge.

The alternative newspaper *Hipfish,* published in Astoria, is one of the liveliest community-based monthlies in the state. Frequent coverage of environmental issues is interspersed with cultural listings, reviews, and commentary. It's distributed free at selected locales on the coast.

Mail

Most post offices open around 9am and close around 5pm. Sometimes drugstores or card shops have a postal substation open on weekends and holidays when the government operations are closed. If it happens to be Sunday and the post office is closed, you can also get stamps from grocery stores and hotels, with little or no markup. Oregon also has many FedEx, UPS, and other private shipping companies operating across the state to complement government services.

Telephone

Coastal Oregon has two area codes: **503** for Astoria to Neskowin and **541** for the rest of the coast. Note that you must dial the area code, even for local calls. **Cell phone** users should be aware that service in some coastal areas and in the coast ranges can be spotty, particularly along the south coast.

Internet Access

Wireless Internet service is widely available along the Oregon coast; it's relatively easy to find a hotel or coffee shop where you can fire up your laptop and check your email.

MAPS AND TOURIST INFORMATION

The **Oregon Coast Visitors Association** (137 NE 1st St., Newport, 541/574-2679 or 888/628-2101, http://visittheoregoncoast.com) is a good clearinghouse of information for the entire coast, including events listings, weather, and links to all coastal chambers of commerce. The best sources of detailed current information for the coast are the individual chambers of commerce in each town. Most do an excellent job of helping travelers with their questions, and all have websites.

The state tourist bureau, **Travel Oregon** (800/547-7842, www.traveloregon.com), is another good resource, producing several useful free maps and pamphlets about the coast and offering extensive listings of lodgings and activities throughout the state.

Other useful contacts are the **Oregon Parks and Recreation Department** (503/378-6305 or 800/551-6949, www.oregonstateparks. org), the **U.S. Bureau of Land Management** (503/808-6002, www.blm.gov/or), and the **U.S. Forest Service** (503/808-2971, www. fs.usda.gov/r6). All offer free information and maps on the specific recreation areas and preserves under their respective auspices.

For members only, **AAA Oregon/Idaho** (600 SW Market St., Portland, 503/222-6734 or 800/452-1643, www.aaaorid.com) provides free, high-quality, detailed maps of each coastal county. Its *Oregon Coast Tour Map* is particularly good.

RESOURCES

Suggested Reading

HISTORY

Beckham, Steven Dow, and Robert M. Reynolds (photographer). *Lewis & Clark from the Rockies to the Pacific*. Portland, OR: Graphic Arts Center Publishing, 2002. Focusing on the second half of the expedition's outward-bound journey, this gorgeously illustrated and insightful book covers Lewis and Clark's trying months spent camped in the rainy woodlands of the north Oregon coast.

Gibbs, James A. *Shipwrecks of the Pacific Coast*. Portland, OR: Binford and Mort, 1989. Endlessly fascinating and frequently heartbreaking reading from a master of Pacific Northwest maritime lore. This book covers all known shipwrecks off the coasts of Oregon, Washington, and California.

Hadlow, Robert W. *Elegant Arches, Soaring Spans: C. B. McCullough, Oregon's Master Bridge Builder*. Corvallis, OR: Oregon State University Press, 2003. Driving U.S. 101 along the Oregon coast wouldn't be the same without the dozen beautiful bridges designed by McCullough between the two world wars—he called the bridges "jeweled clasps in a wonderful string of pearls."

NATURE

Alt, David, and Donald W. Hyndman. *Roadside Geology of Oregon*. Missoula, MT: Mountain Press Publishing, 2003. Part of the fine Roadside Geology Series, the coast chapters describe, in layman's language, the geologic forces that shaped the region.

Davis, James Luther. *The Northwest Nature Guide*. Portland, OR: Timber Press, 2009. Describes (with enthusiasm and wit) the best time and the best places to see wildlife.

Evanich, Joseph E., Jr. *Birder's Guide to Oregon*. Portland, OR: Audubon Society of Portland, 2003. A good all-around guide to the state's birdlife, with a useful breakdown of specific coastal locations and details on what species to watch for and when.

Paulson, Dennis. *Shorebirds of the Pacific Northwest*. Seattle: University of Washington Press, 2003. For the specialist rather than the generalist, there is no better book than this richly detailed guide for distinguishing an avocet from a stilt, a plover from a curlew, and identifying any of the dozens of other species found near the water's edge.

Pojar, Jim, and Andy MacKinnon, eds. *Plants of the Pacific Northwest Coast: Washington, Oregon, British Columbia, and Alaska*. Edmonton, Canada: Lone Pine Publishing, 2003. A highly regarded guide, illustrated with excellent photos, to the flora of the entire Pacific Northwest region.

Sept, J. Duane. *The Beachcomber's Guide to Seashore Life in the Pacific Northwest*. Vancouver,

Canada: Harbour Publishing, 2003. This ideal guide for the casual and curious observer aids in understanding the intertidal zone and in identifying more than 270 species encountered there, including crabs, clams, and other mollusks, seaweeds, sea stars, sea anemones, and more.

SPORTS AND RECREATION

Henderson, Bonnie. *Day Hiking Oregon Coast.* Seattle: Mountaineers Books, 2007. Covers all the standards as well as several lesser-known but rewarding hikes, and enriched with information on flora and fauna.

Ostertag, Rhonda, and George Ostertag. *75 Hikes in the Oregon's Coast Range and Siskiyous.* Seattle: Mountaineers Books, 2003. A well-chosen selection of hikes along the length of the coastal ranges covers a broad variety of terrain and difficulty levels. Detailed trail descriptions and maps make this guide particularly useful.

Stienstra, Tom. *Moon Oregon Camping.* Berkeley, CA: Avalon Travel Publishing, 2010. Details more than 700 campgrounds across the state, with an excellent selection on the coast. Rich with tips on gear, safety, and other topics.

Sullivan, William. *100 Hikes Travel Guide: Oregon Coast and Coast Range.* Eugene, OR: Navillus Press, 2002. Hikes and tips from Oregon's best chronicler of hiking trails.

TRAVEL

Nelson, Sharlene, and Ted Nelson (contributor). *Umbrella Guide to Oregon Lighthouses.* Kenmore, WA: Epicenter Press, 2003. Tells the stories of 11 Oregon coast lighthouses, as well as beacons on the Columbia and Willamette Rivers. A good reference for anyone curious about these romantic aids to navigation.

Oberrecht, Kenn. *Oregon Coastal Access Guide: A Mile-by-Mile Guide to Scenic and Recreational Attractions.* Corvallis, OR: Oregon State University Press, 2008. Meticulously researched and informative guide to major sights, natural features, and recreational opportunities. Contains no restaurant or lodging info, but is an eminently useful resource for travelers nonetheless.

Vaughn, Greg. *Photographing Oregon.* Rancho Cucamonga, CA: Graphie International, 2009. Advice on how, when, and where to take the best photos in Oregon, with lots of tips on capturing the best possible shots along the Oregon Coast.

Internet Resources

INFORMATION AND TRAVEL

Oregon Coast Visitors Association
www.visittheoregoncoast.com
A good clearinghouse of information for the entire coast, including events listings, weather, and links to all coastal chambers of commerce.

Travel Oregon
www.traveloregon.com
A good statewide resource for useful free maps and pamphlets and extensive listings of lodgings and activities.

PARKS AND PUBLIC LANDS

Oregon State Parks
www.oregonstateparks.org
Descriptions, maps, contact information, and more details on all Oregon state parks.

Recreation.gov
www.recreation.gov
Reserve sites in Forest Service campgrounds.

ReserveAmerica
www.reserveamerica.com

The central site for reserving campsites in state park and private campgrounds.

Rogue River-Siskiyou National Forest
www.fs.fed.us/r6/rogue-siskiyou/
Details on recreation, camping, and resources in the national forest.

Siuslaw National Forest
www.fs.fed.us/r6/siuslaw
Details on recreation, camping, and resources in the national forest and the Oregon Dunes National Recreation Area.

U.S. Bureau of Land Management
www.or.blm.gov
The BLM manages numerous recreational sites along the coast and the coastal mountains, including the Dean Creek Elk Viewing Area, Yaquina Head Outstanding Natural Area, and Cape Blanco Lighthouse.

RECREATION
Oregon Department of Fish and Wildlife
www.dfw.state.or.us
Complete details on fishing and hunting seasons, licenses, regulations, and more. Includes useful species-identification charts.

Oregon State Marine Board
www.oregon.gov/OSMB
Extensive information on boating safety, ramps and other facilities, bar conditions, and more.

Surf Forecasts
http://magicseaweed.com
User-driven surf forecasting service includes forecasts, graphs, and charts designed specifically for surfers.

Surfrider Foundation
www.surfrider.org
A nonprofit organization working to preserve oceans, waves, and beaches, including beach access.

Tide Predictions
www.saltwatertides.com
Current and future tide-prediction charts for coastal Oregon locations.

Whale Watching Spoken Here
http://whalespoken.org
Volunteer organization assists visitors with spotting whales at 29 sites from southern Washington to northern California.

REGIONAL INFORMATION
Astoria-Warrenton Area Chamber
www.oldoregon.com

Bandon Chamber of Commerce
www.bandon.com

Bay Area Chamber of Commerce
www.oregonsbayareachamber.com

Brookings/Harbor Chamber of Commerce
www.brookingsor.com

Cannon Beach Chamber of Commerce
www.cannonbeach.org

Depoe Bay Chamber of Commerce
www.depoebaychamber.org

Florence Area Chamber of Commerce
www.florencechamber.com

Gold Beach Promotion Committee
www.goldbeach.org

Lincoln City Visitor Center
www.oregoncoast.org

Nehalem Bay Area Chamber of Commerce
www.nehalembaychamber.com

Newport Oregon
www.discovernewport.com

Port Orford Chamber of Commerce
www.portorfordoregon.com

Reedsport/Winchester Bay Chamber of Commerce
www.reedsportcc.org

Rockaway Beach Chamber of Commerce
www.rockawaybeach.net

Seaside Visitors Bureau
www.seasideor.com

Tillamook Chamber of Commerce
www.tillamookchamber.org

Waldport Chamber of Commerce
www.waldport-chamber.com

Yachats Area Chamber of Commerce
www.yachats.org

TRANSPORTATION
Amtrak
www.amtrak.com
Operates bus service between Portland and Astoria.

Greyhound
www.greyhound.com
Operates a coast route between Eugene and Newport.

Oregon Department of Transportation Road Conditions
www.tripcheck.com
Displays current road conditions and advisories.

Ride Oregon
www.rideoregonride.com
Information on transporting your bike to and from Oregon, including downloadable maps and route-planning info.

Index

List of Maps

www.moon.com

DESTINATIONS | ACTIVITIES | BLOGS | MAPS | BOOKS

MOON.COM is ready to help plan your next trip! Filled with fresh trip ideas and strategies, author interviews, informative travel blogs, a detailed map library, and descriptions of all the Moon guidebooks, Moon.com is all you need to get out and explore the world—or even places in your own backyard. While at Moon.com, sign up for our monthly e-newsletter for updates on new releases, travel tips, and expert advice from our on-the-go Moon authors. As always, when you travel with Moon, expect an experience that is uncommon and truly unique.

KEEP UP WITH MOON ON FACEBOOK AND TWITTER
JOIN THE MOON PHOTO GROUP ON FLICKR